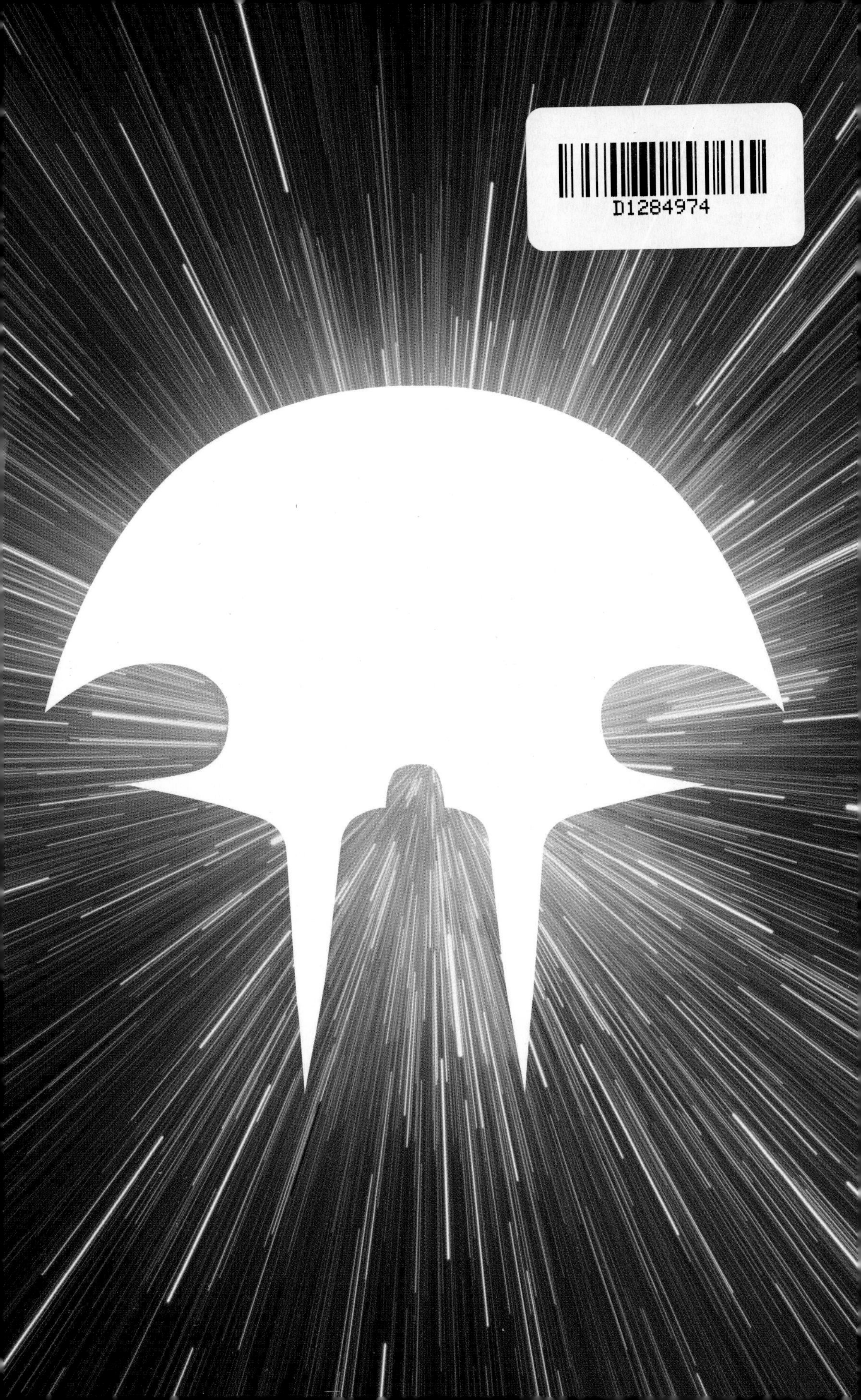

**VALIANT**®

**DAN MINTZ** Chairman  **FRED PIERCE** Publisher  **WALTER BLACK** VP Operations  **MATTHEW KLEIN** VP Sales & Marketing
**TRAVIS ESCARFULLERY** Director of Design & Production  **PETER STERN** Director of International Publishing & Merchandising
**LYSA HAWKINS, HEATHER ANTOS & DAVID WOHL**  Senior Editors  **JEFF WALKER** Production & Design Manager

# PSI-LORDS®

**WRITER**
FRED VAN LENTE

**ARTIST**
RENATO GUEDES

**LETTERER**
DAVE SHARPE

**COVERS BY**
ROD REIS
DAVID NAKAYAMA
NIC KLEIN
RAHZZAH
JULIAN TOTINO TEDESCO
ARIEL OLIVETTI
KANO

**ASSISTANT EDITOR**
DREW BAUMGARTNER

**EDITOR**
DAVID MENCHEL

**GALLERY**
RAÚL ALLÉN
JONATHAN ARTHUR ASHLEY
AL BARRIONUEVO
JUAN DOE
SCOTT FORBES
PAULINA GANUCHEAU
RENATO GUEDES
STEPHANIE HANS
STACEY LEE
TULA LOTAY
HEIDI MACDONALD
ZU ORZU
ROD REIS
DAVE SHARPE
FRED VAN LENTE

**COLLECTION COVER ART**
JONBOY MEYERS

**COLLECTION BACK COVER ART**
KANO

**COLLECTION FRONT ART**
DAVID NAKAYAMA
ROD REIS

**COLLECTION EDITOR**
IVAN COHEN

**COLLECTION DESIGNER**
STEVE BLACKWELL

Psi-Lords®. Published by Valiant Entertainment LLC. Office of Publication: 350 Seventh Avenue, New York, NY 10001. Compilation copyright © 2020 Valiant Entertainment LLC. All rights reserved. Contains materials originally published in single magazine form as Psi-Lords #1-8. Copyright © 2019 and 2020 Valiant Entertainment LLC. All rights reserved. All characters, their distinctive likeness and related indicia featured in this publication are trademarks of Valiant Entertainment LLC. The stories, characters, and incidents featured in this publication are entirely fictional. Valiant Entertainment does not read or accept unsolicited submissions of ideas, stories, or artwork. Printed in Korea. First Printing. ISBN: 9781682153529.

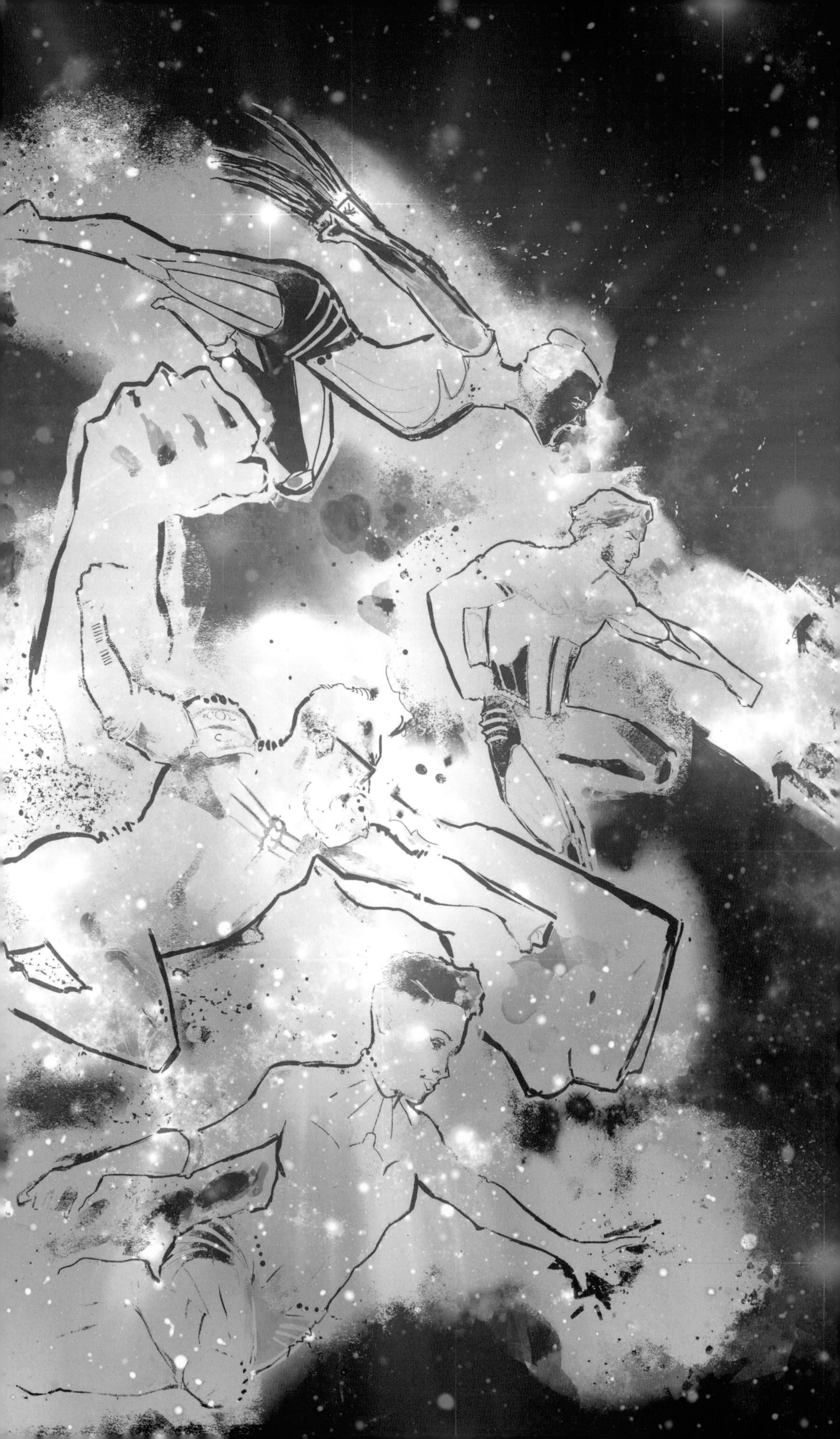

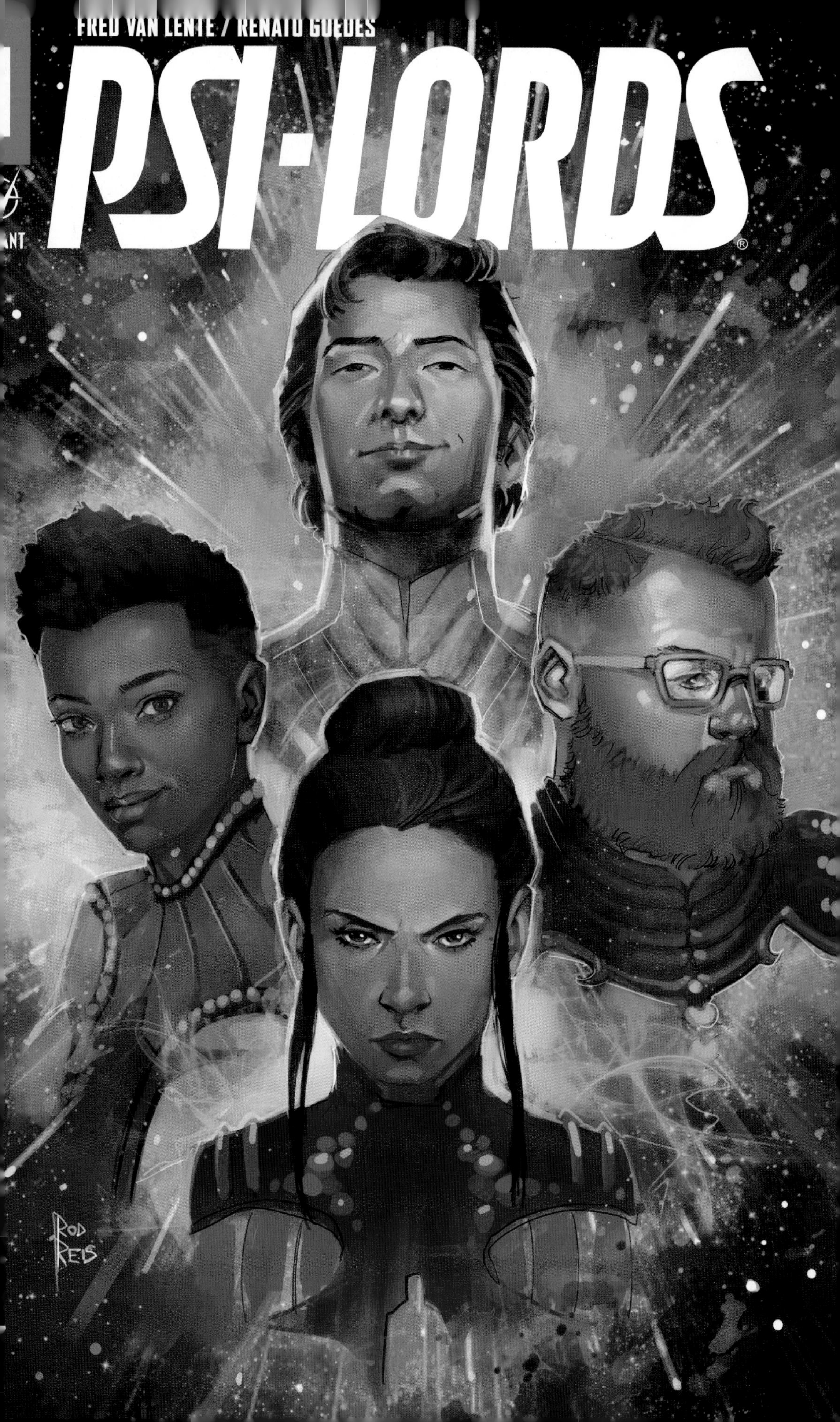

FRED VAN LENTE / RENATO GUEDES
PSI-LORDS
ROD REIS

**PSI-LORDS #**

WRITER: Fred Van Len
ARTIST: Renato Guede
LETTERER: Dave Sharp
COVER ARTIST: Rod Re
ASSISTANT EDITOR: Drew Baumgartn
EDITOR: David Mench

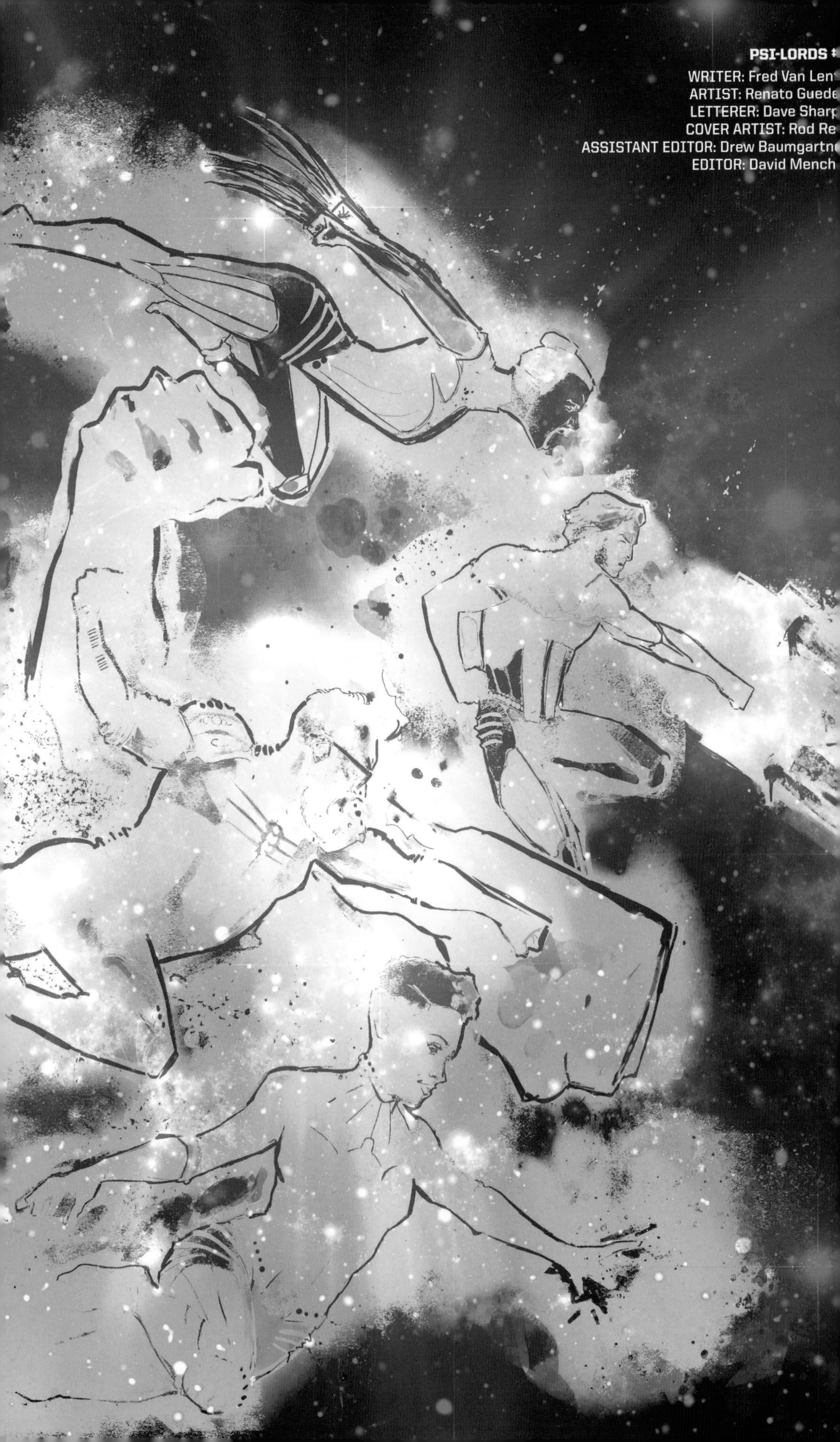

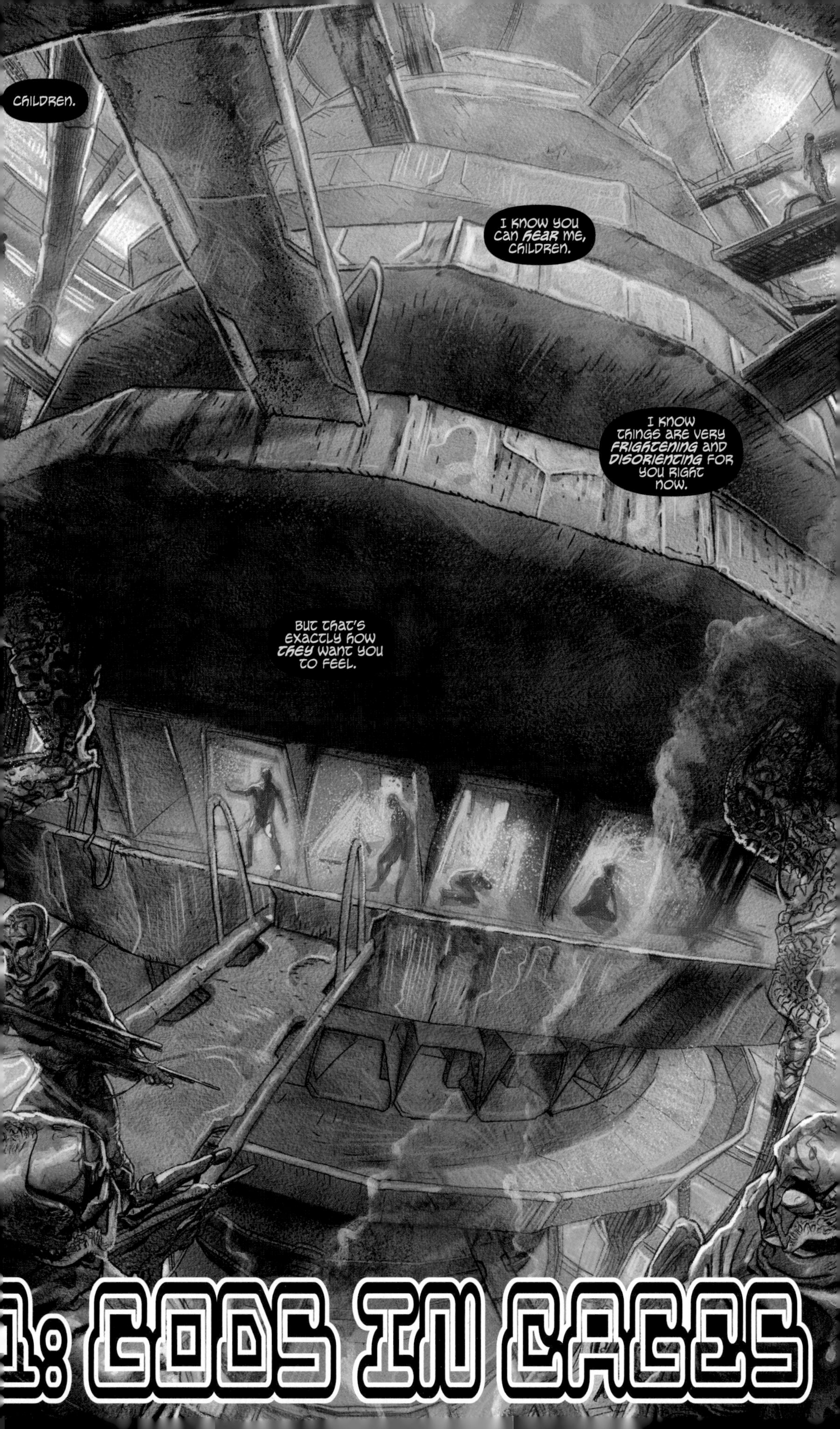
CHILDREN.
I KNOW YOU CAN HEAR ME, CHILDREN.
I KNOW THINGS ARE VERY FRIGHTENING AND DISORIENTING FOR YOU RIGHT NOW.
BUT THAT'S EXACTLY HOW THEY WANT YOU TO FEEL.
1: GODS IN CAGES

WHUDD WHAMM

KRAK

HELPLESS.

POWERLESS.

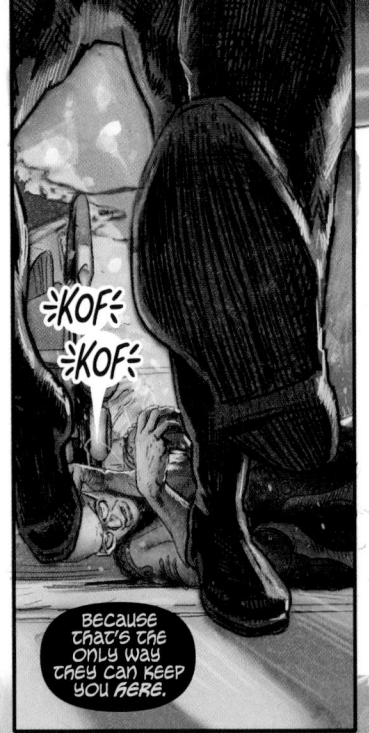

*KOF*
*KOF*

BECAUSE THAT'S THE ONLY WAY THEY CAN KEEP YOU *HERE.*

YOU'LL NEVER BREAK ME, YOU BADLY DRESSED FASCISTS!

SIT AND SPIN!

BUT I KNOW YOU.

WHO-- --PTUI!

--SAID THAT? YOU IN THE NEXT CELL? WHERE AM I? HOW'D I GET HERE?

CALL ME SCION. I'M A FRIEND.

I'M A SOLDIER. WHAT I NEED IS A *MISSION.*

AND I'LL GIVE YOU ONE, TANK. YOUR ONLY MISSION RIGHT NOW...

...IS SURVIVAL.

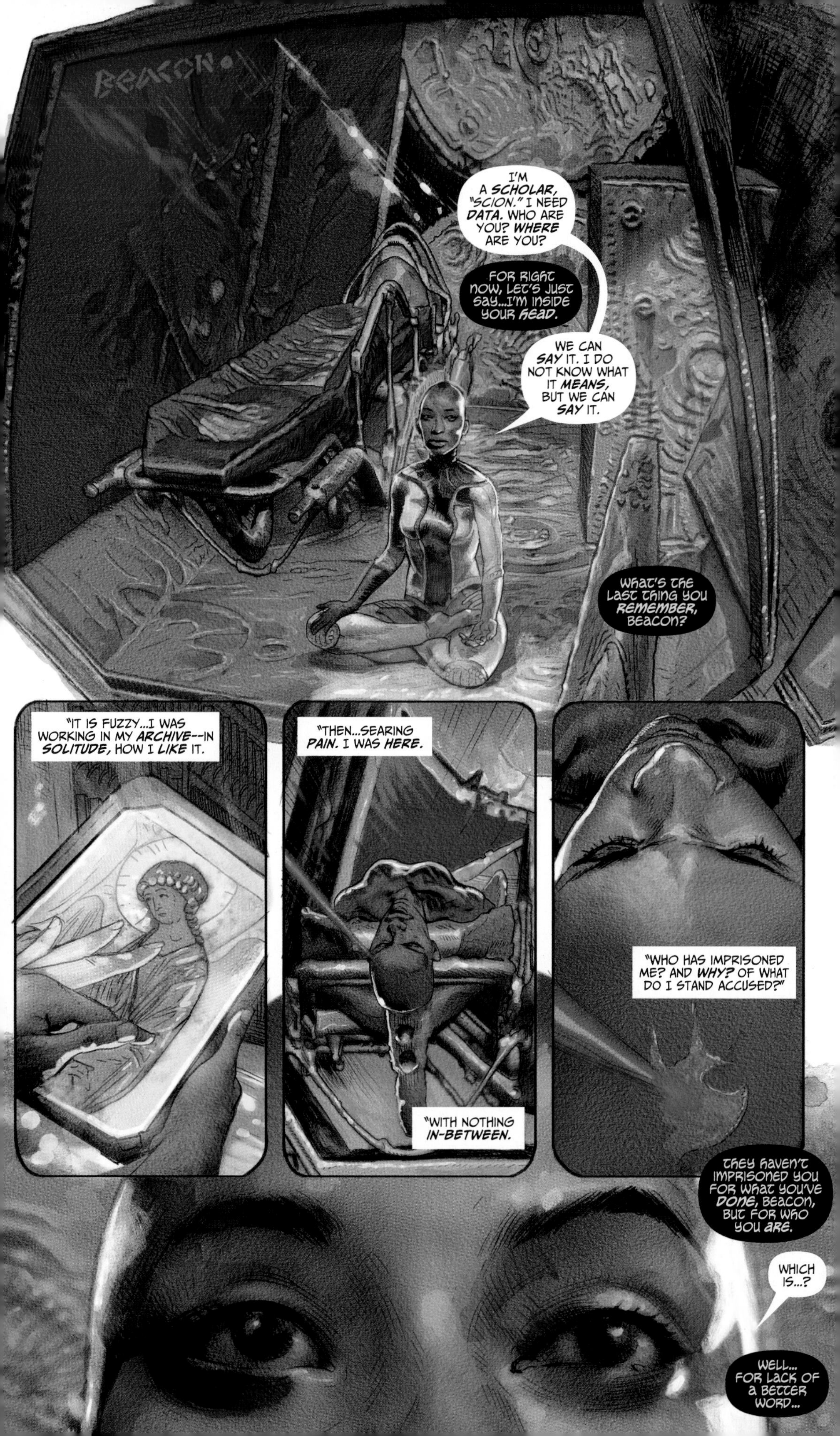
BEACON
I'M A SCHOLAR, "SCION." I NEED DATA. WHO ARE YOU? WHERE ARE YOU?
FOR RIGHT NOW, LET'S JUST SAY...I'M INSIDE YOUR HEAD.
WE CAN SAY IT. I DO NOT KNOW WHAT IT MEANS, BUT WE CAN SAY IT.
WHAT'S THE LAST THING YOU REMEMBER, BEACON?
"IT IS FUZZY...I WAS WORKING IN MY ARCHIVE--IN SOLITUDE, HOW I LIKE IT.
"THEN...SEARING PAIN. I WAS HERE.
"WITH NOTHING IN-BETWEEN.
"WHO HAS IMPRISONED ME? AND WHY? OF WHAT DO I STAND ACCUSED?"
THEY HAVEN'T IMPRISONED YOU FOR WHAT YOU'VE DONE, BEACON, BUT FOR WHO YOU ARE.
WHICH IS...?
WELL... FOR LACK OF A BETTER WORD...

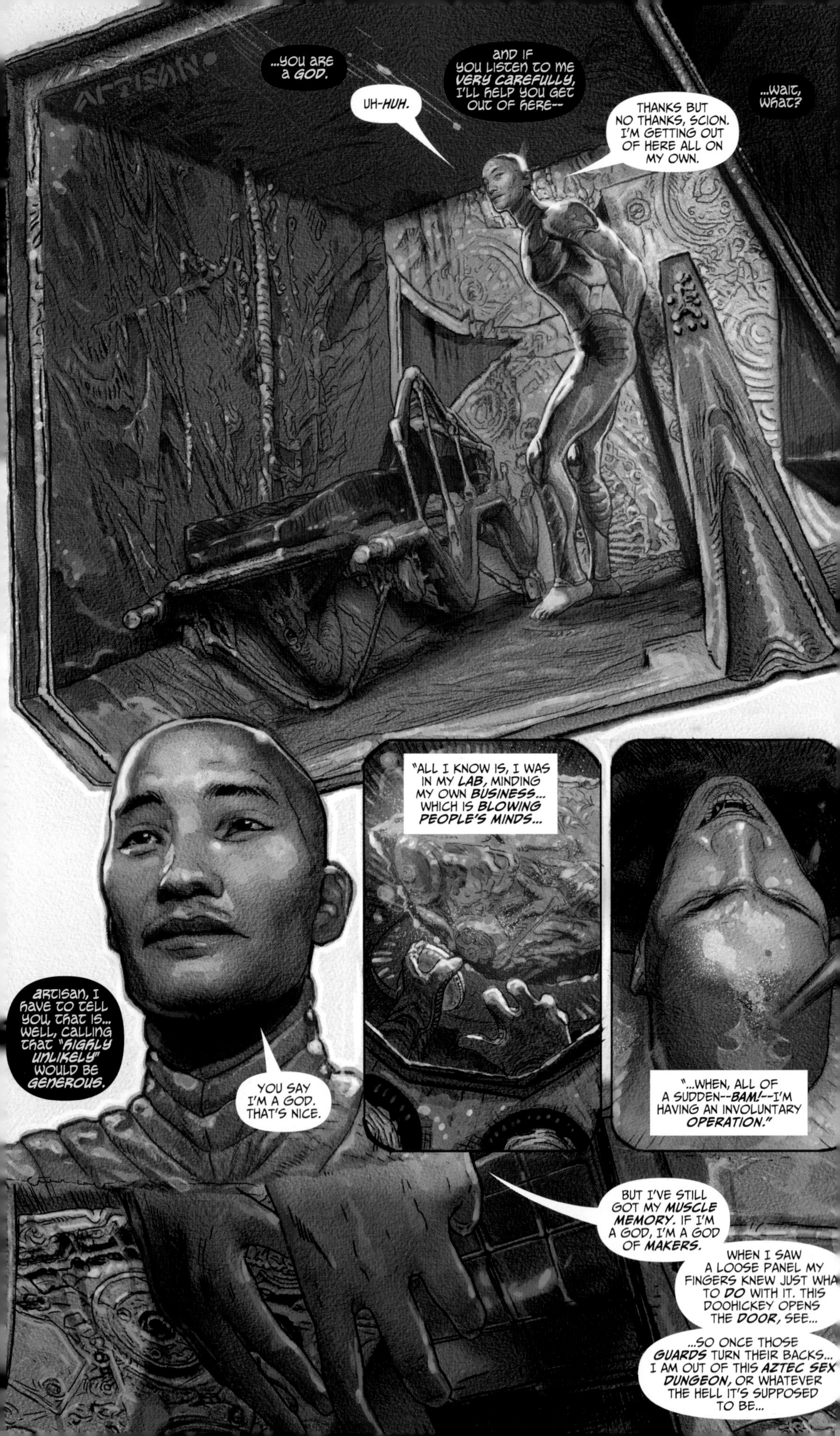

...YOU ARE A GOD.
UH-HUH.
AND IF YOU LISTEN TO ME VERY CAREFULLY, I'LL HELP YOU GET OUT OF HERE--
THANKS BUT NO THANKS, SCION. I'M GETTING OUT OF HERE ALL ON MY OWN.
...WAIT, WHAT?
ARTISAN, I HAVE TO TELL YOU, THAT IS... WELL, CALLING THAT "HIGHLY UNLIKELY" WOULD BE GENEROUS.
YOU SAY I'M A GOD. THAT'S NICE.
"ALL I KNOW IS, I WAS IN MY LAB, MINDING MY OWN BUSINESS... WHICH IS BLOWING PEOPLE'S MINDS...
"...WHEN, ALL OF A SUDDEN--BAM!--I'M HAVING AN INVOLUNTARY OPERATION."
BUT I'VE STILL GOT MY MUSCLE MEMORY. IF I'M A GOD, I'M A GOD OF MAKERS.
WHEN I SAW A LOOSE PANEL MY FINGERS KNEW JUST WHA TO DO WITH IT. THIS DOOHICKEY OPENS THE DOOR, SEE...
...SO ONCE THOSE GUARDS TURN THEIR BACKS... I AM OUT OF THIS AZTEC SEX DUNGEON, OR WHATEVER THE HELL IT'S SUPPOSED TO BE...

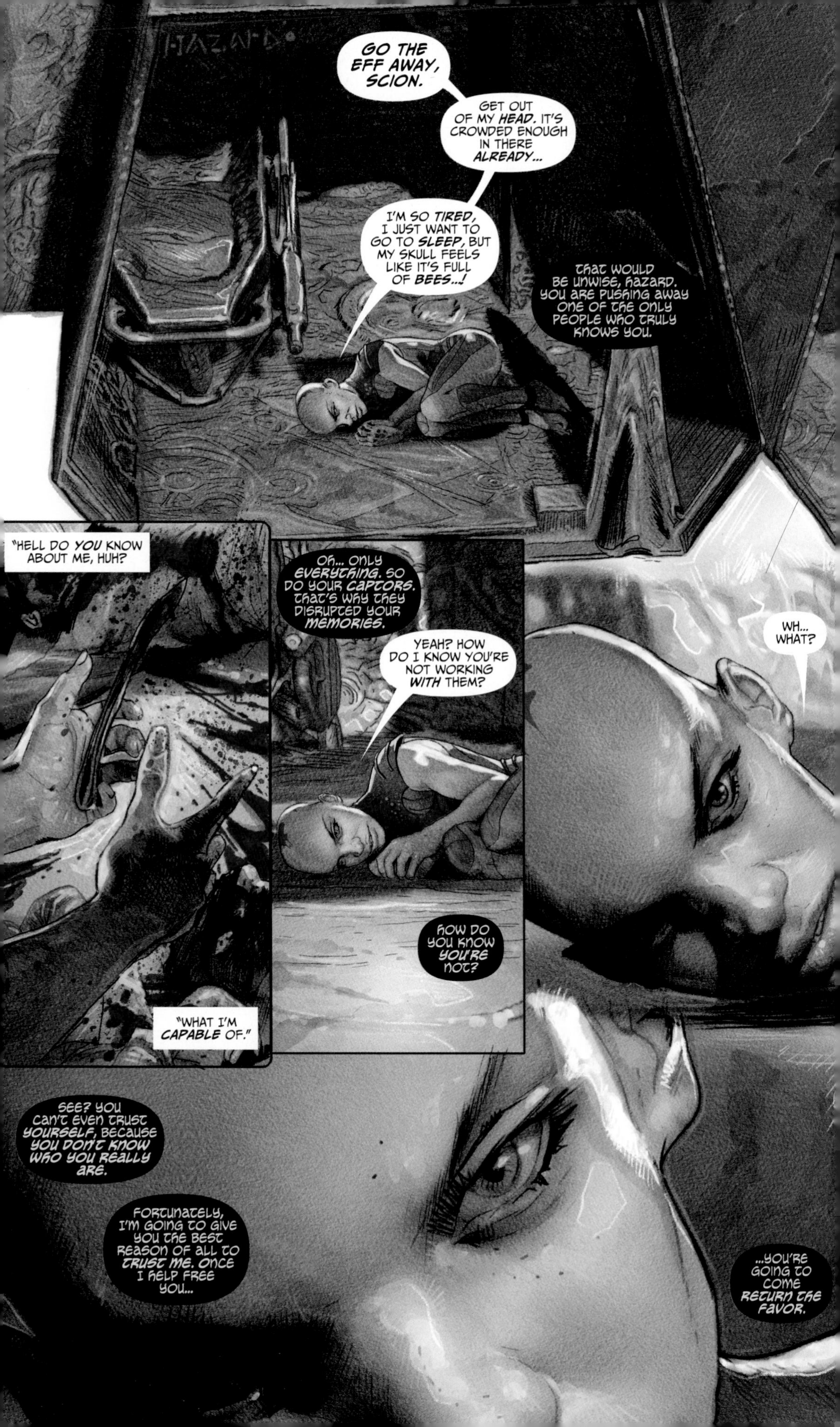

HAZARD
GO THE EFF AWAY, SCION.
GET OUT OF MY HEAD. IT'S CROWDED ENOUGH IN THERE ALREADY...
I'M SO TIRED, I JUST WANT TO GO TO SLEEP, BUT MY SKULL FEELS LIKE IT'S FULL OF BEES...!
THAT WOULD BE UNWISE, HAZARD. YOU ARE PUSHING AWAY ONE OF THE ONLY PEOPLE WHO TRULY KNOWS YOU.
"HELL DO YOU KNOW ABOUT ME, HUH?
OH... ONLY EVERYTHING. SO DO YOUR CAPTORS. THAT'S WHY THEY DISRUPTED YOUR MEMORIES.
YEAH? HOW DO I KNOW YOU'RE NOT WORKING WITH THEM?
HOW DO YOU KNOW YOU'RE NOT?
"WHAT I'M CAPABLE OF."
WH... WHAT?
SEE? YOU CAN'T EVEN TRUST YOURSELF, BECAUSE YOU DON'T KNOW WHO YOU REALLY ARE.
FORTUNATELY, I'M GOING TO GIVE YOU THE BEST REASON OF ALL TO TRUST ME. ONCE I HELP FREE YOU...
...YOU'RE GOING TO COME RETURN THE FAVOR.

BZZRRRT

ARTISAN, LISTEN TO--

HEH. GOT IT! OPEN SESAM--

SHANK

OH, CRA--

GENERALLY SPEAKING...

-AAAAAAAAAAAAAAAAHHHH!

...GODS DON'T DIE.

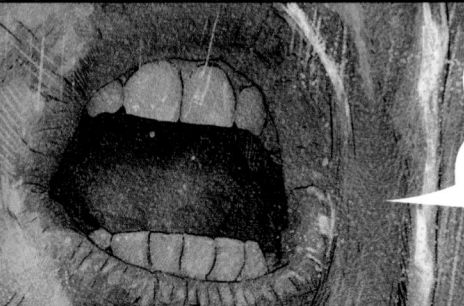

ALL RIGHT, OKAY, OKAY OKAY!

I'M A GOD I'M A GOD I'M A GOD!

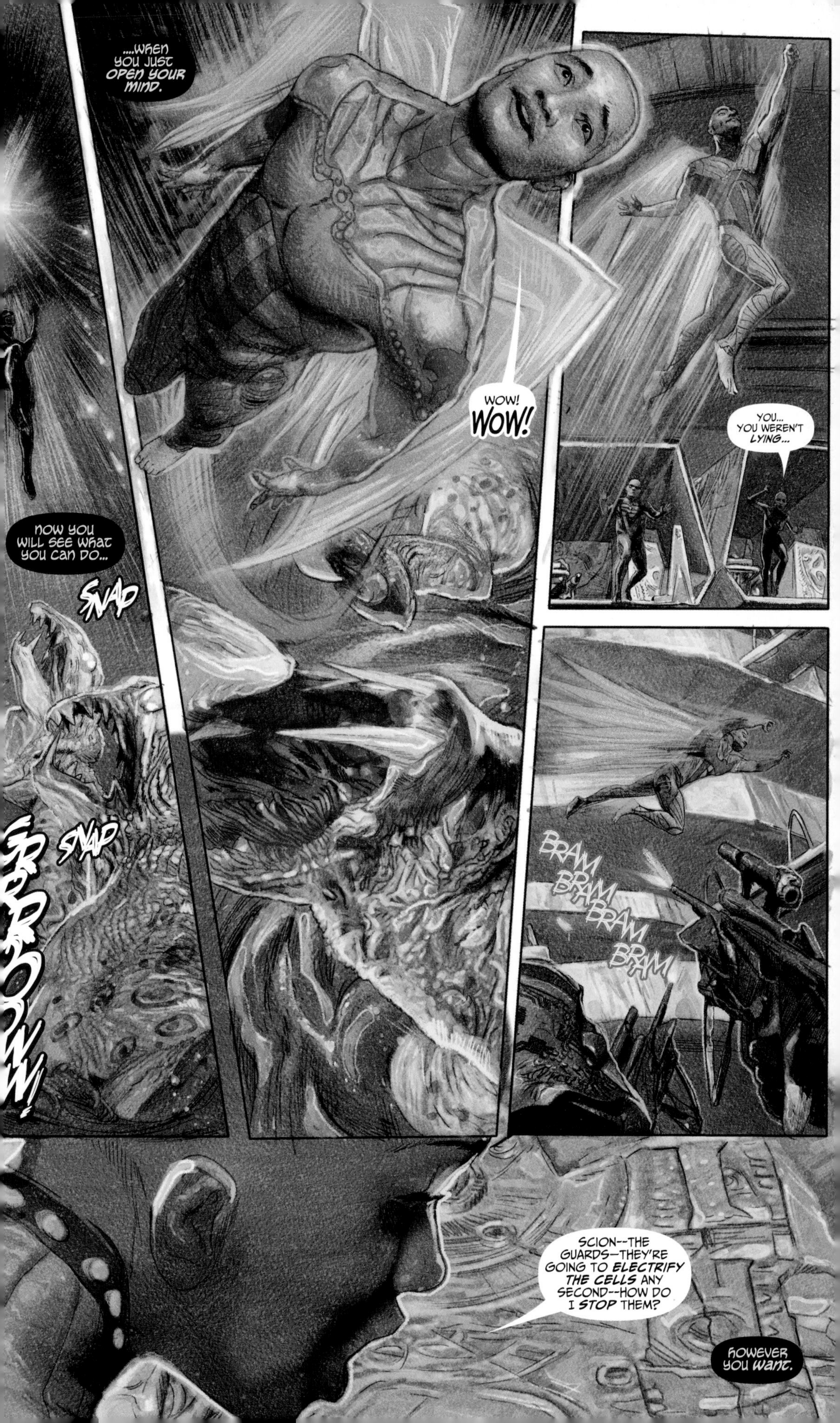
...WHEN YOU JUST OPEN YOUR MIND.
WOW! WOW!
YOU... YOU WEREN'T LYING...
NOW YOU WILL SEE WHAT YOU CAN DO...
SNAP
SNAP
GRROOWW!
BRAM BRAM BRAM BRAM BRAM
SCION--THE GUARDS--THEY'RE GOING TO ELECTRIFY THE CELLS ANY SECOND--HOW DO I STOP THEM?
HOWEVER YOU WANT.

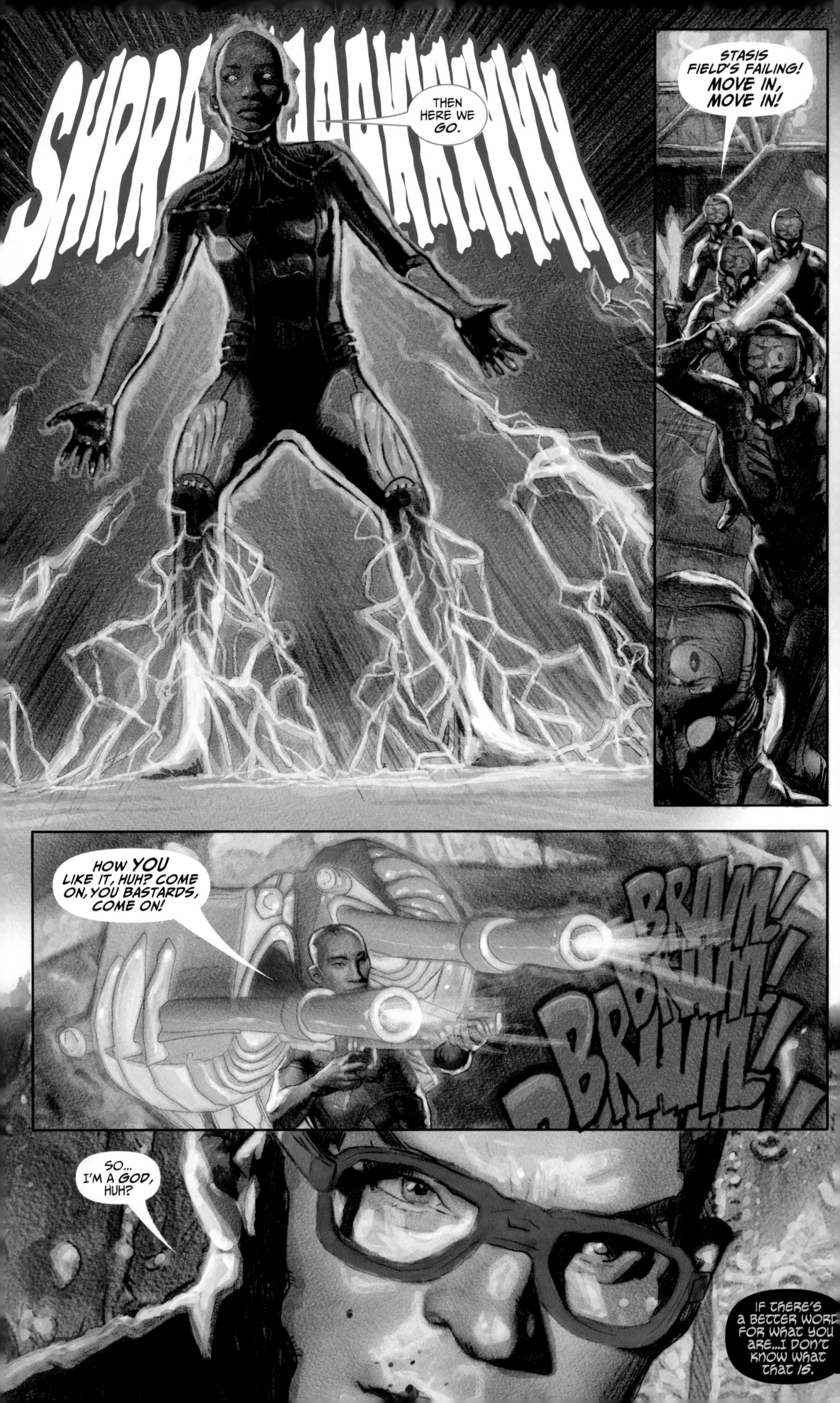
THEN HERE WE GO.
STASIS FIELD'S FAILING! MOVE IN, MOVE IN!
HOW YOU LIKE IT, HUH? COME ON, YOU BASTARDS, COME ON!
SO... I'M A GOD, HUH?
IF THERE'S A BETTER WORD FOR WHAT YOU ARE...I DON'T KNOW WHAT THAT IS.

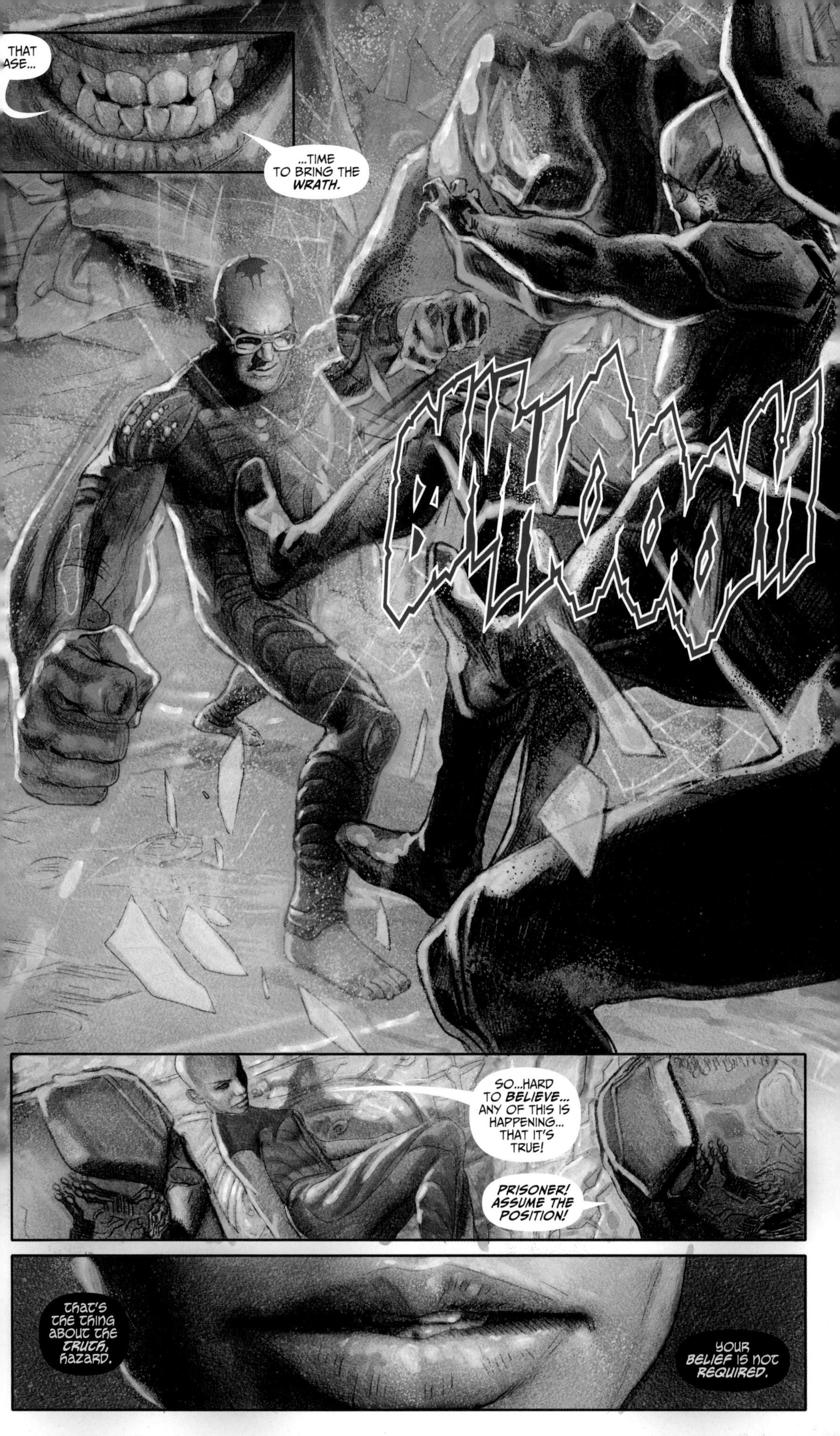
THAT
ASE...
...TIME TO BRING THE WRATH.
BHOOOM
SO...HARD TO BELIEVE... ANY OF THIS IS HAPPENING... THAT IT'S TRUE!
PRISONER! ASSUME THE POSITION!
THAT'S THE THING ABOUT THE TRUTH, HAZARD.
YOUR BELIEF IS NOT REQUIRED.

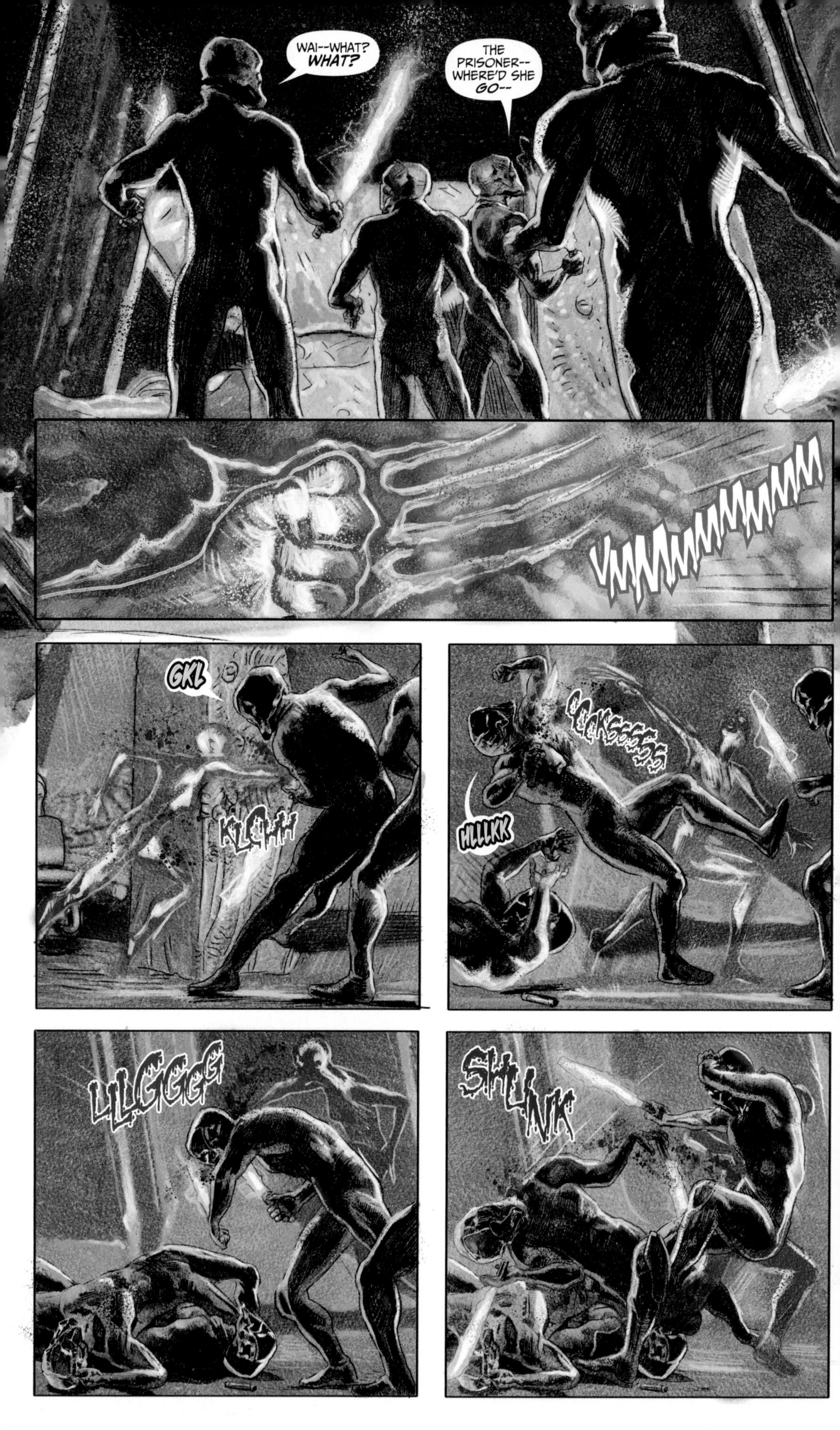
WAI--WHAT? WHAT?
THE PRISONER--WHERE'D SHE GO--
VMMMMMMMMM
GKL
KLCHH
CCKSSSSS
HLLLKK
LLLGGGG
SHUNK

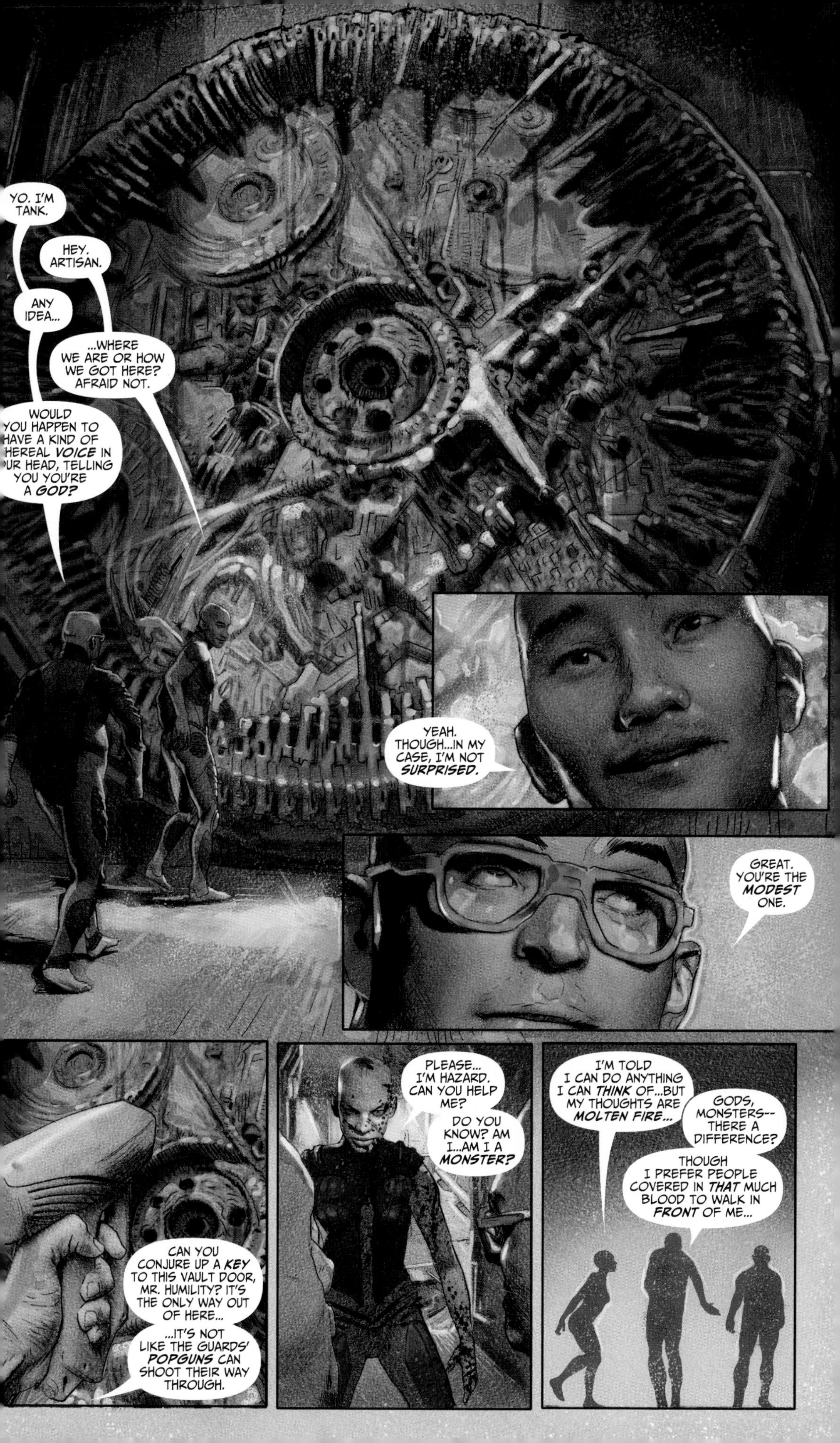
YO. I'M TANK.
HEY. ARTISAN.
ANY IDEA...
...WHERE WE ARE OR HOW WE GOT HERE? AFRAID NOT.
WOULD YOU HAPPEN TO HAVE A KIND OF HEREAL VOICE IN UR HEAD, TELLING YOU YOU'RE A GOD?
YEAH. THOUGH...IN MY CASE, I'M NOT SURPRISED.
GREAT. YOU'RE THE MODEST ONE.
CAN YOU CONJURE UP A KEY TO THIS VAULT DOOR, MR. HUMILITY? IT'S THE ONLY WAY OUT OF HERE...
...IT'S NOT LIKE THE GUARDS' POPGUNS CAN SHOOT THEIR WAY THROUGH.
PLEASE... I'M HAZARD. CAN YOU HELP ME?
DO YOU KNOW? AM I...AM I A MONSTER?
I'M TOLD I CAN DO ANYTHING I CAN THINK OF...BUT MY THOUGHTS ARE MOLTEN FIRE...
GODS, MONSTERS-- THERE A DIFFERENCE?
THOUGH I PREFER PEOPLE COVERED IN THAT MUCH BLOOD TO WALK IN FRONT OF ME...

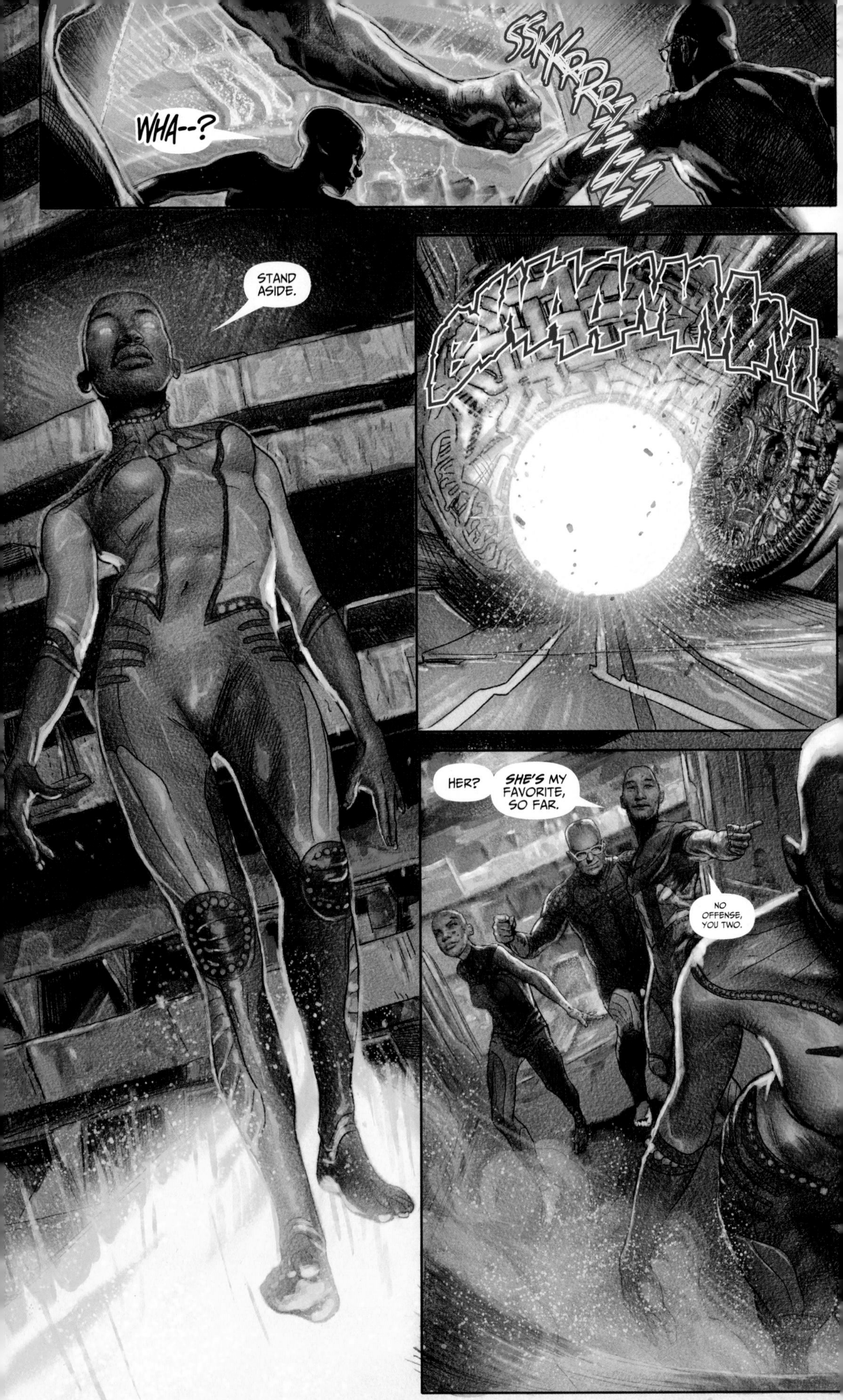
WHA--?
SSKKRRZZZZZZZ
STAND ASIDE.
HER?
SHE'S MY FAVORITE, SO FAR.
NO OFFENSE, YOU TWO.

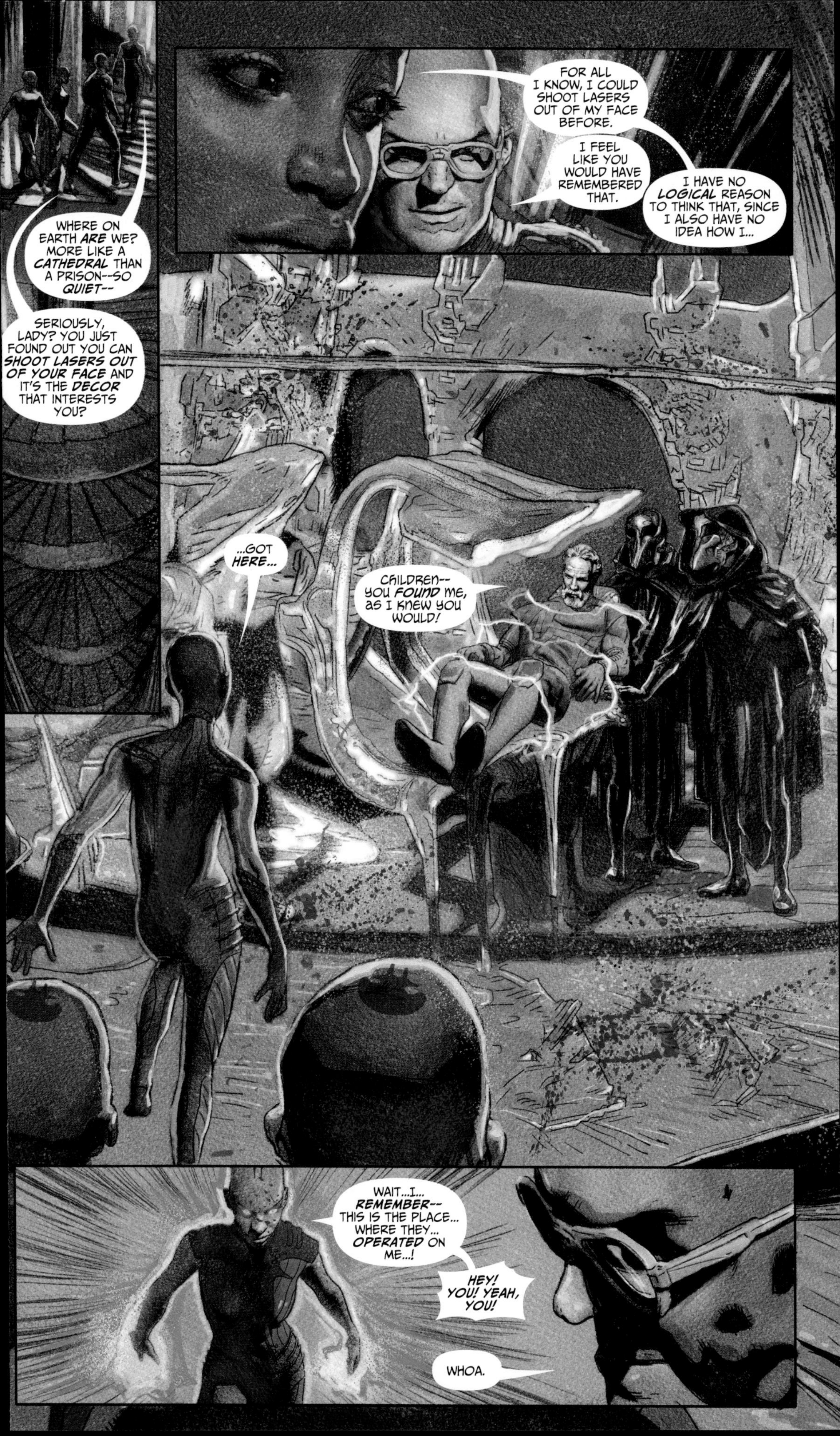
FOR ALL I KNOW, I COULD SHOOT LASERS OUT OF MY FACE BEFORE.
I FEEL LIKE YOU WOULD HAVE REMEMBERED THAT.
I HAVE NO LOGICAL REASON TO THINK THAT, SINCE I ALSO HAVE NO IDEA HOW I...
WHERE ON EARTH ARE WE? MORE LIKE A CATHEDRAL THAN A PRISON--SO QUIET--
SERIOUSLY, LADY? YOU JUST FOUND OUT YOU CAN SHOOT LASERS OUT OF YOUR FACE AND IT'S THE DECOR THAT INTERESTS YOU?
...GOT HERE...
CHILDREN-- YOU FOUND ME, AS I KNEW YOU WOULD!
WAIT...I... REMEMBER-- THIS IS THE PLACE... WHERE THEY... OPERATED ON ME...!
HEY! YOU! YEAH, YOU!
WHOA.

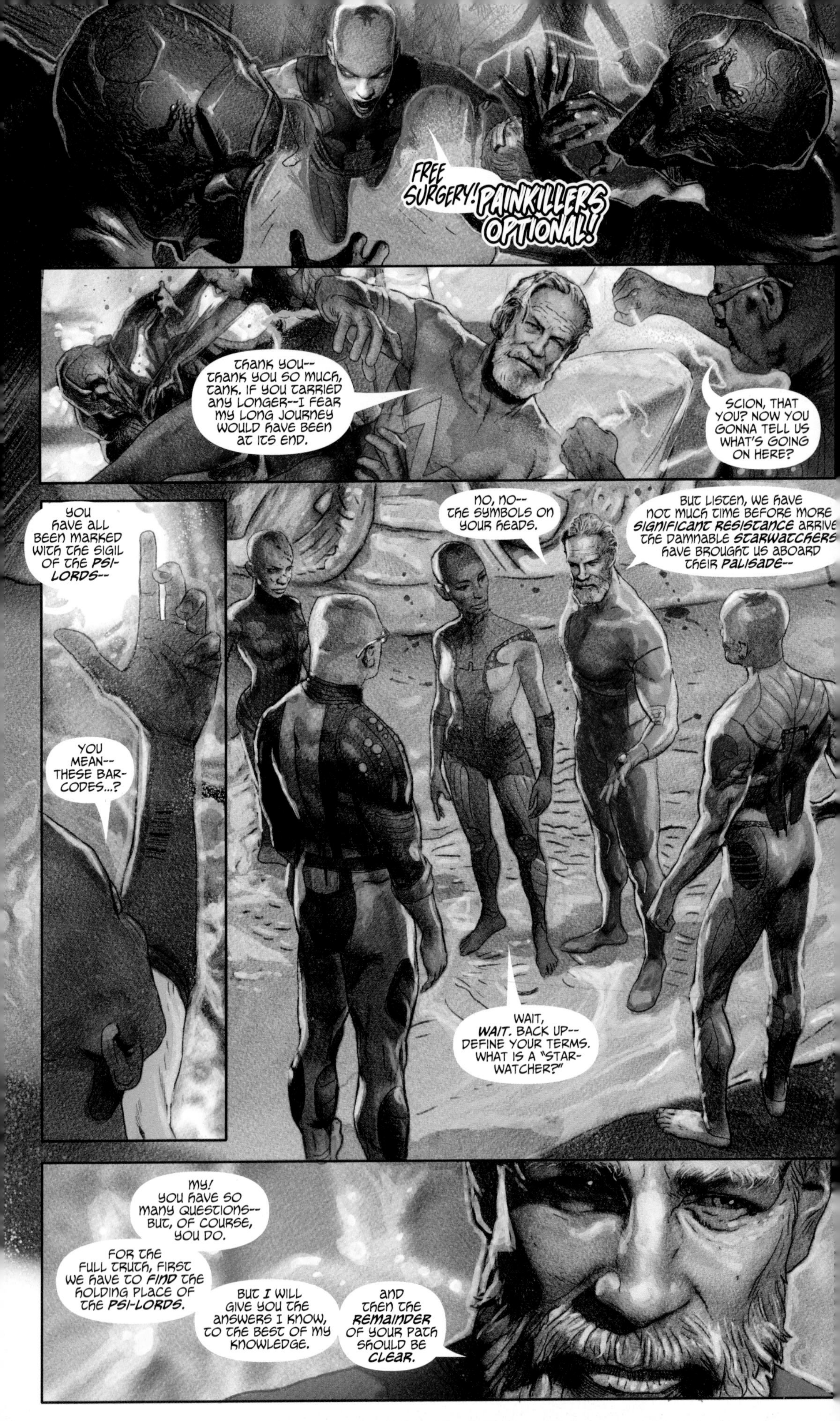
FREE SURGERY! PAINKILLERS OPTIONAL!
THANK YOU--THANK YOU SO MUCH, TANK. IF YOU TARRIED ANY LONGER--I FEAR MY LONG JOURNEY WOULD HAVE BEEN AT ITS END.
SCION, THAT YOU? NOW YOU GONNA TELL US WHAT'S GOING ON HERE?
YOU HAVE ALL BEEN MARKED WITH THE SIGIL OF THE PSI-LORDS--
YOU MEAN--THESE BAR-CODES...?
NO, NO--THE SYMBOLS ON YOUR HEADS.
BUT LISTEN, WE HAVE NOT MUCH TIME BEFORE MORE SIGNIFICANT RESISTANCE ARRIVE. THE DAMNABLE STARWATCHERS HAVE BROUGHT US ABOARD THEIR PALISADE--
WAIT, WAIT. BACK UP--DEFINE YOUR TERMS. WHAT IS A "STAR-WATCHER?"
MY! YOU HAVE SO MANY QUESTIONS--BUT, OF COURSE, YOU DO.
FOR THE FULL TRUTH, FIRST WE HAVE TO FIND THE HOLDING PLACE OF THE PSI-LORDS.
BUT I WILL GIVE YOU THE ANSWERS I KNOW, TO THE BEST OF MY KNOWLEDGE.
AND THEN THE REMAINDER OF YOUR PATH SHOULD BE CLEAR.

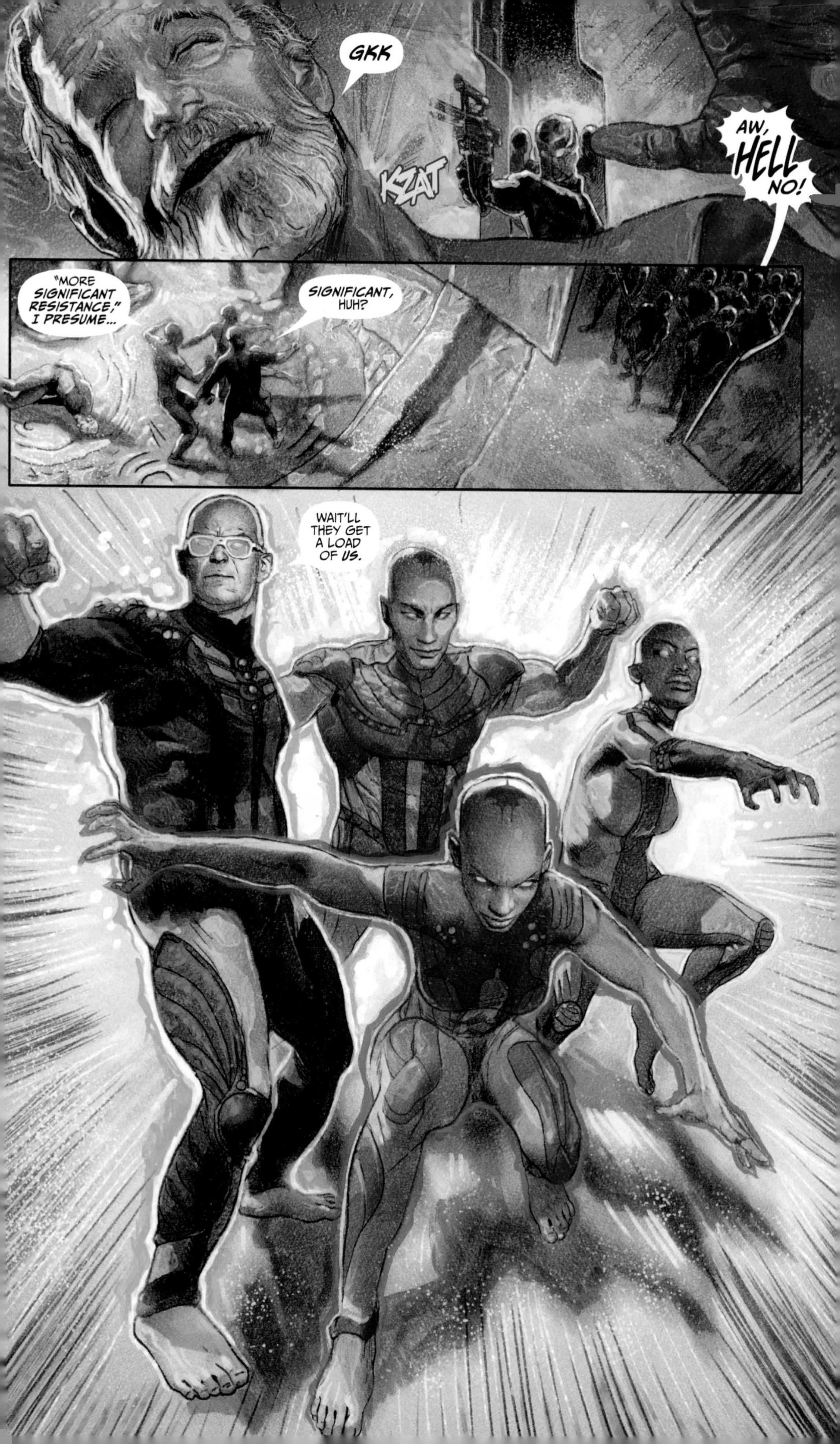
GKK
KZAT
AW, HELL NO!
"MORE SIGNIFICANT RESISTANCE," I PRESUME...
SIGNIFICANT, HUH?
WAIT'LL THEY GET A LOAD OF US.

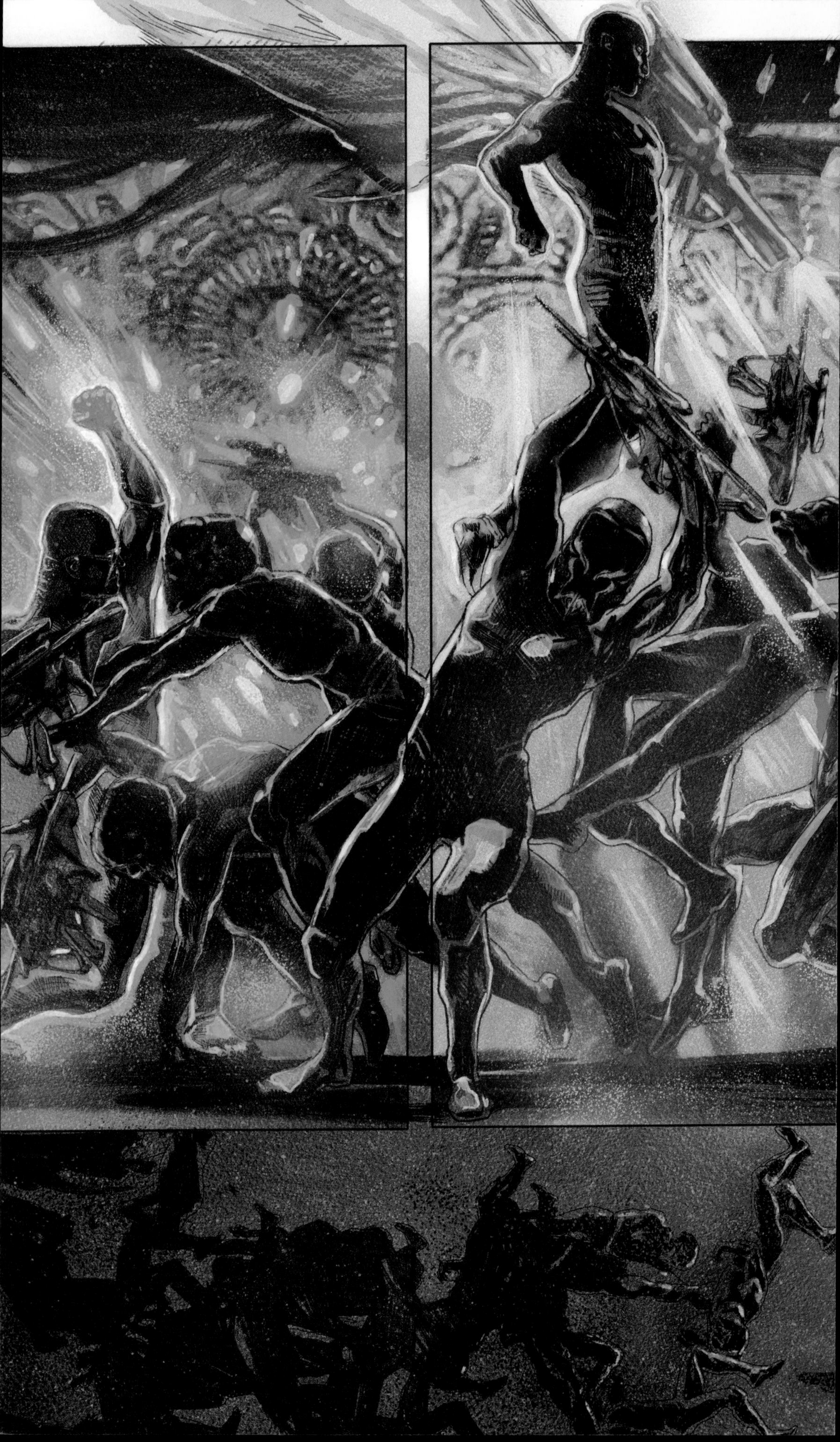

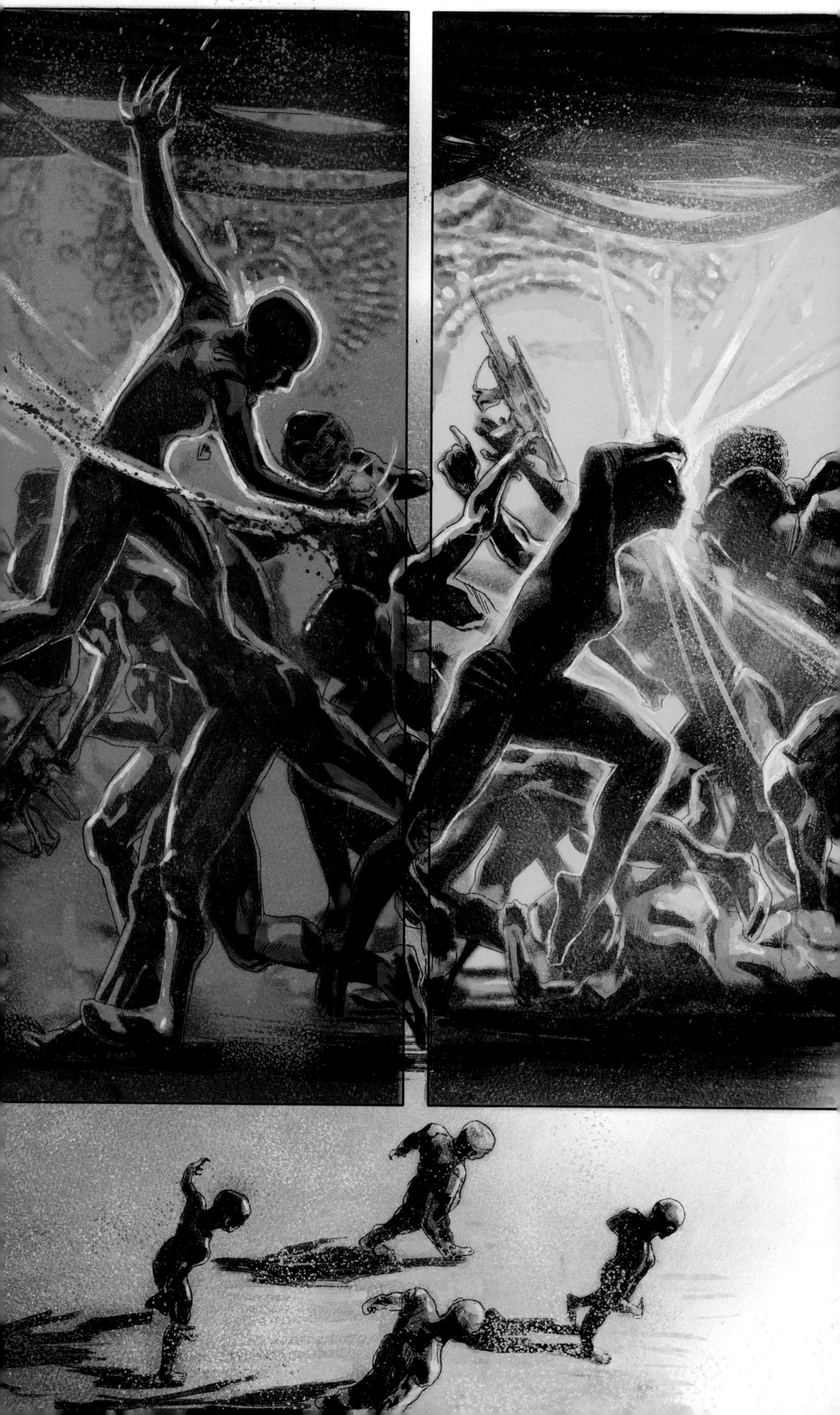

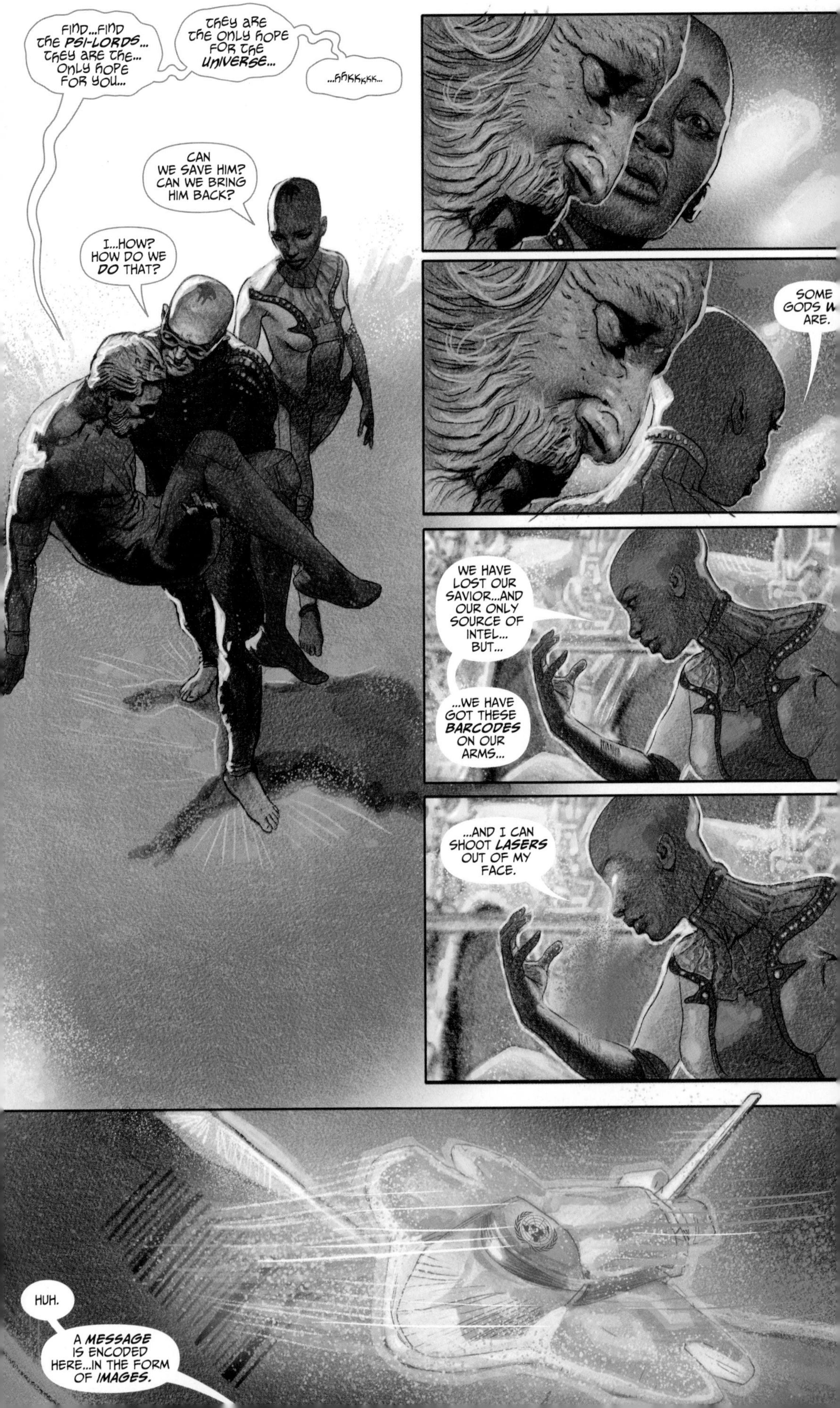

FIND...FIND THE PSI-LORDS... THEY ARE THE... ONLY HOPE FOR YOU...
THEY ARE THE ONLY HOPE FOR THE UNIVERSE...
...HHKKKKK...
CAN WE SAVE HIM? CAN WE BRING HIM BACK?
I...HOW? HOW DO WE DO THAT?
SOME GODS
ARE.
WE HAVE LOST OUR SAVIOR...AND OUR ONLY SOURCE OF INTEL... BUT...
...WE HAVE GOT THESE BARCODES ON OUR ARMS...
...AND I CAN SHOOT LASERS OUT OF MY FACE.
HUH.
A MESSAGE IS ENCODED HERE...IN THE FORM OF IMAGES.

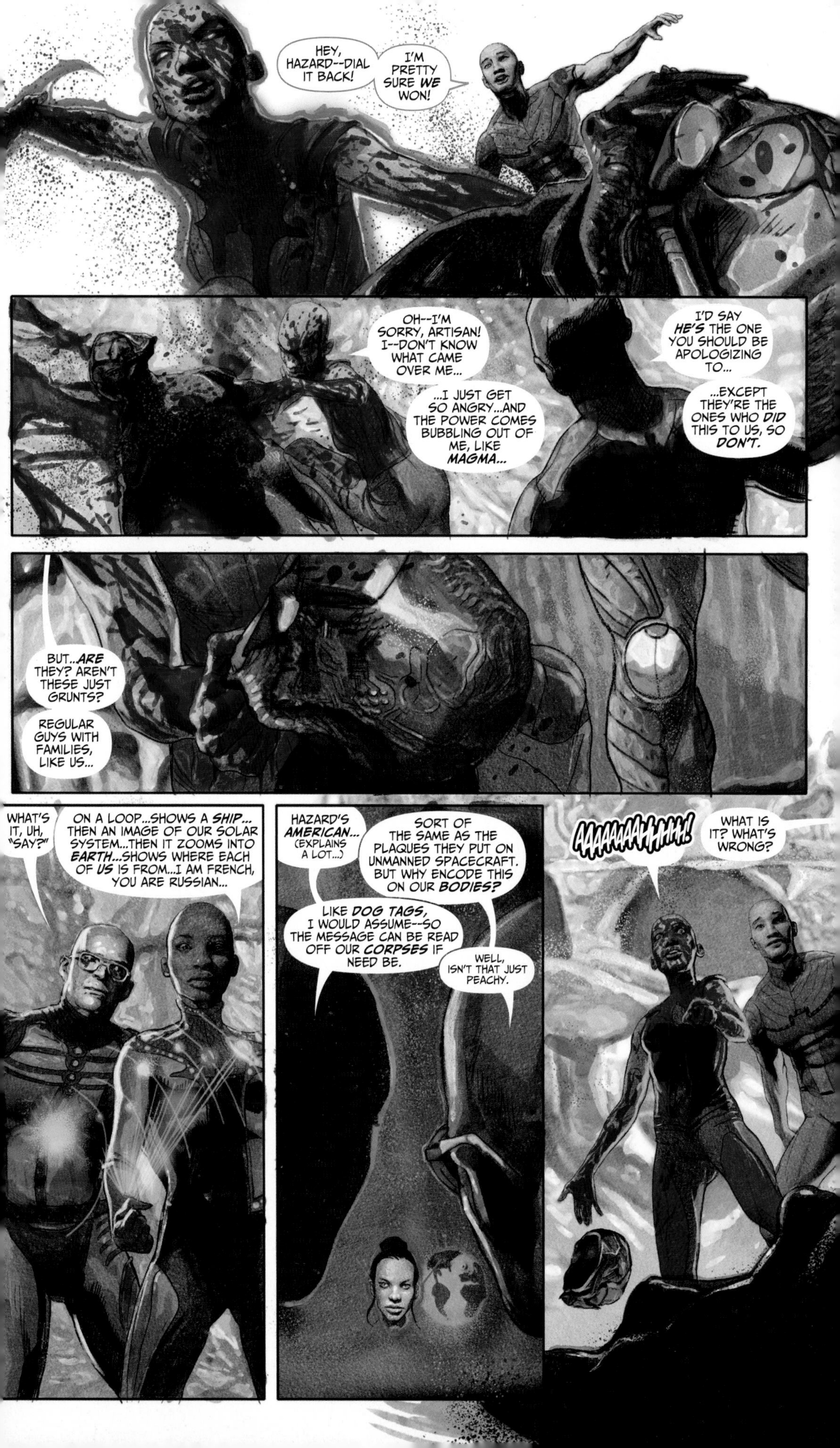
HEY, HAZARD--DIAL IT BACK!
I'M PRETTY SURE WE WON!
OH--I'M SORRY, ARTISAN! I--DON'T KNOW WHAT CAME OVER ME...
...I JUST GET SO ANGRY...AND THE POWER COMES BUBBLING OUT OF ME, LIKE MAGMA...
I'D SAY HE'S THE ONE YOU SHOULD BE APOLOGIZING TO...
...EXCEPT THEY'RE THE ONES WHO DID THIS TO US, SO DON'T.
BUT...ARE THEY? AREN'T THESE JUST GRUNTS?
REGULAR GUYS WITH FAMILIES, LIKE US...
WHAT'S IT, UH, "SAY?"
ON A LOOP...SHOWS A SHIP... THEN AN IMAGE OF OUR SOLAR SYSTEM...THEN IT ZOOMS INTO EARTH...SHOWS WHERE EACH OF US IS FROM...I AM FRENCH, YOU ARE RUSSIAN...
HAZARD'S AMERICAN... (EXPLAINS A LOT...)
SORT OF THE SAME AS THE PLAQUES THEY PUT ON UNMANNED SPACECRAFT. BUT WHY ENCODE THIS ON OUR BODIES?
LIKE DOG TAGS, I WOULD ASSUME--SO THE MESSAGE CAN BE READ OFF OUR CORPSES IF NEED BE.
WELL, ISN'T THAT JUST PEACHY.
AAAAAAAAHHHHH!
WHAT IS IT? WHAT'S WRONG?

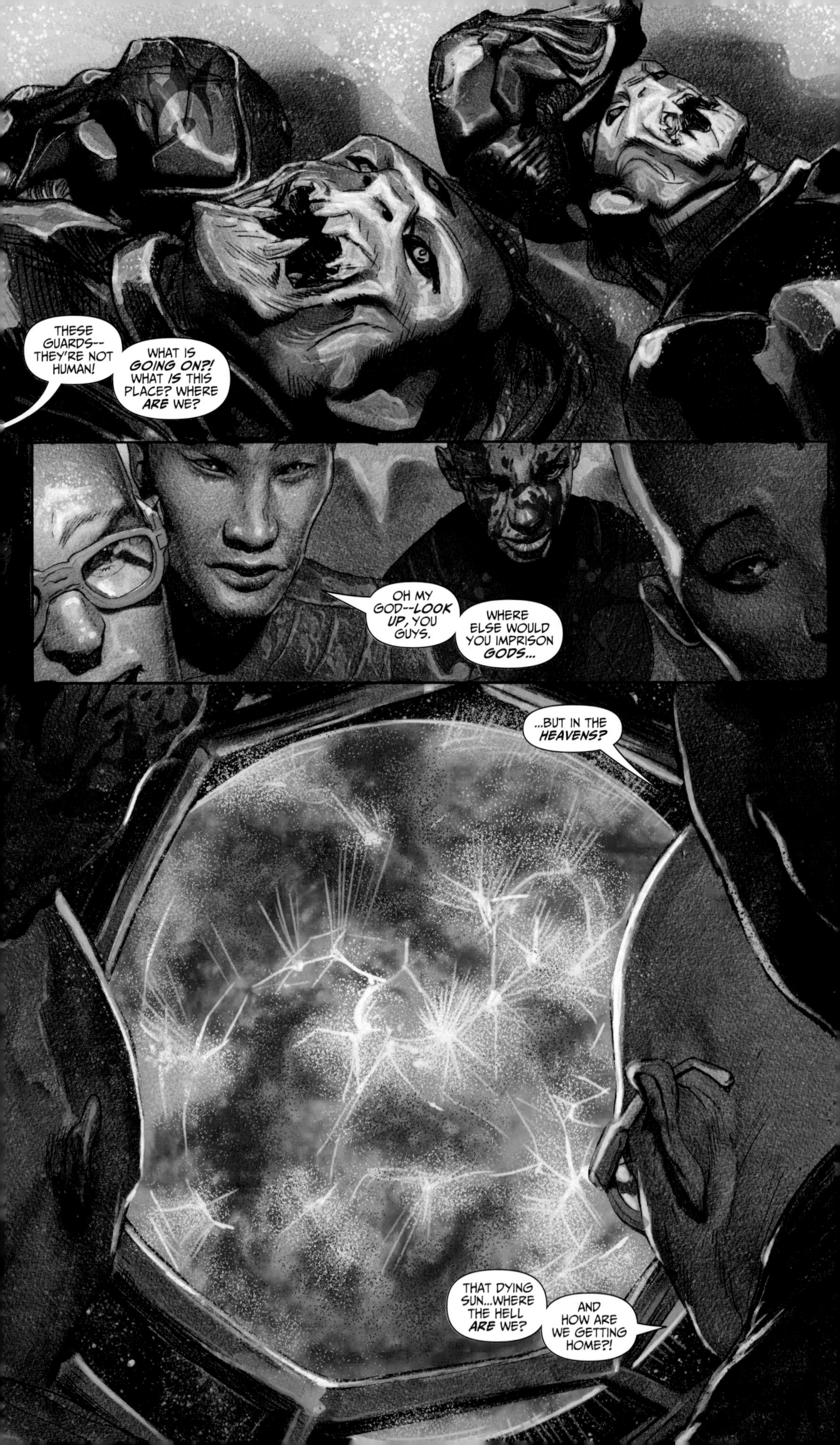
THESE GUARDS-- THEY'RE NOT HUMAN!
WHAT IS *GOING ON?!* WHAT *IS* THIS PLACE? WHERE *ARE* WE?
OH MY GOD--*LOOK UP,* YOU GUYS.
WHERE ELSE WOULD YOU IMPRISON *GODS...*
...BUT IN THE *HEAVENS?*
THAT DYING SUN...WHERE THE HELL *ARE* WE?
AND HOW ARE WE GETTING HOME?!

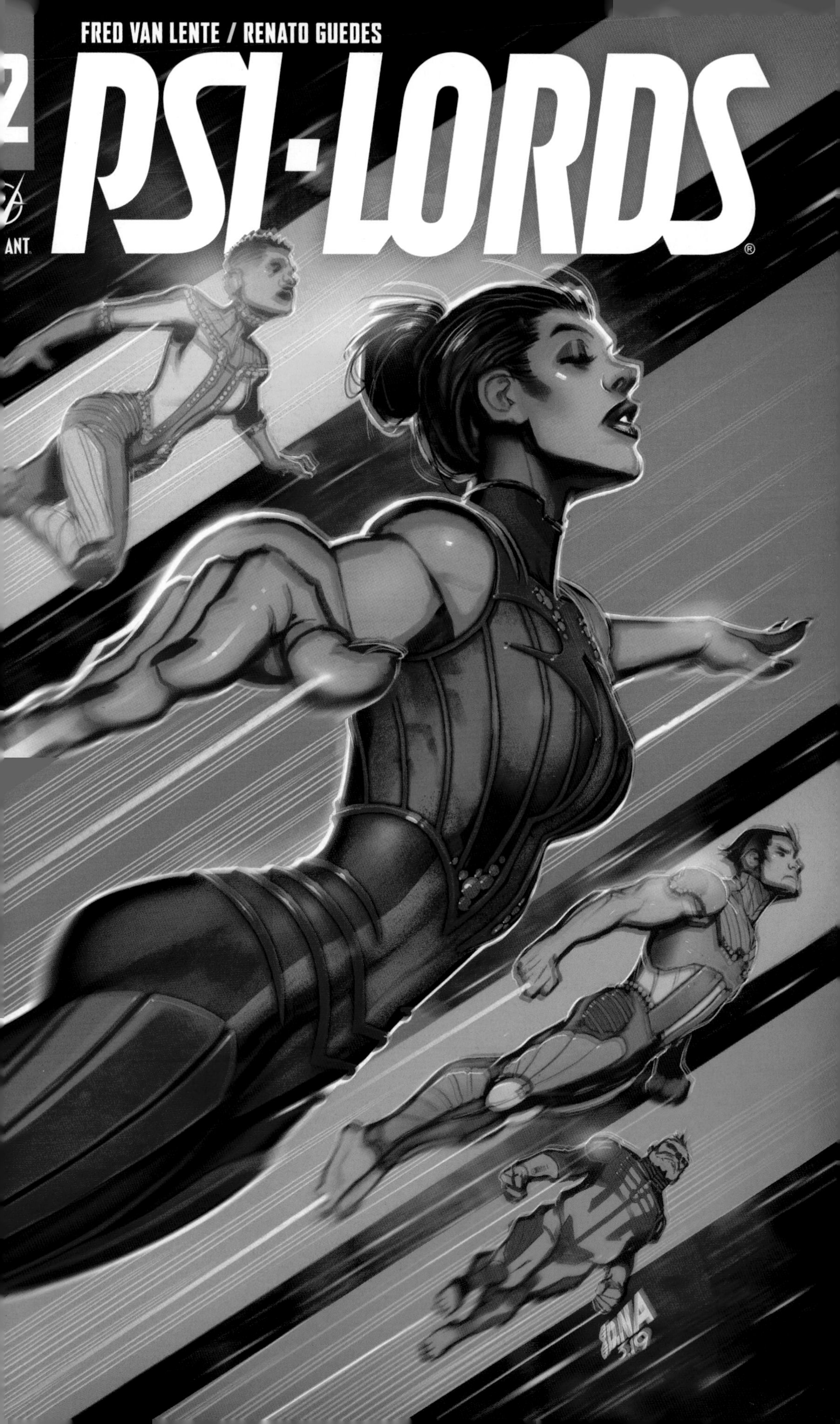
FRED VAN LENTE / RENATO GUEDES
2
PSI-LORDS®
ANT
DNA 3.19

**PSI-LORDS #**
WRITER: Fred Van Lent
ARTIST: Renato Guedes
LETTERER: Dave Sharpe
COVER ARTIST: David Nakayama
ASSISTANT EDITOR: Drew Baumgartner
EDITOR: David Menchel

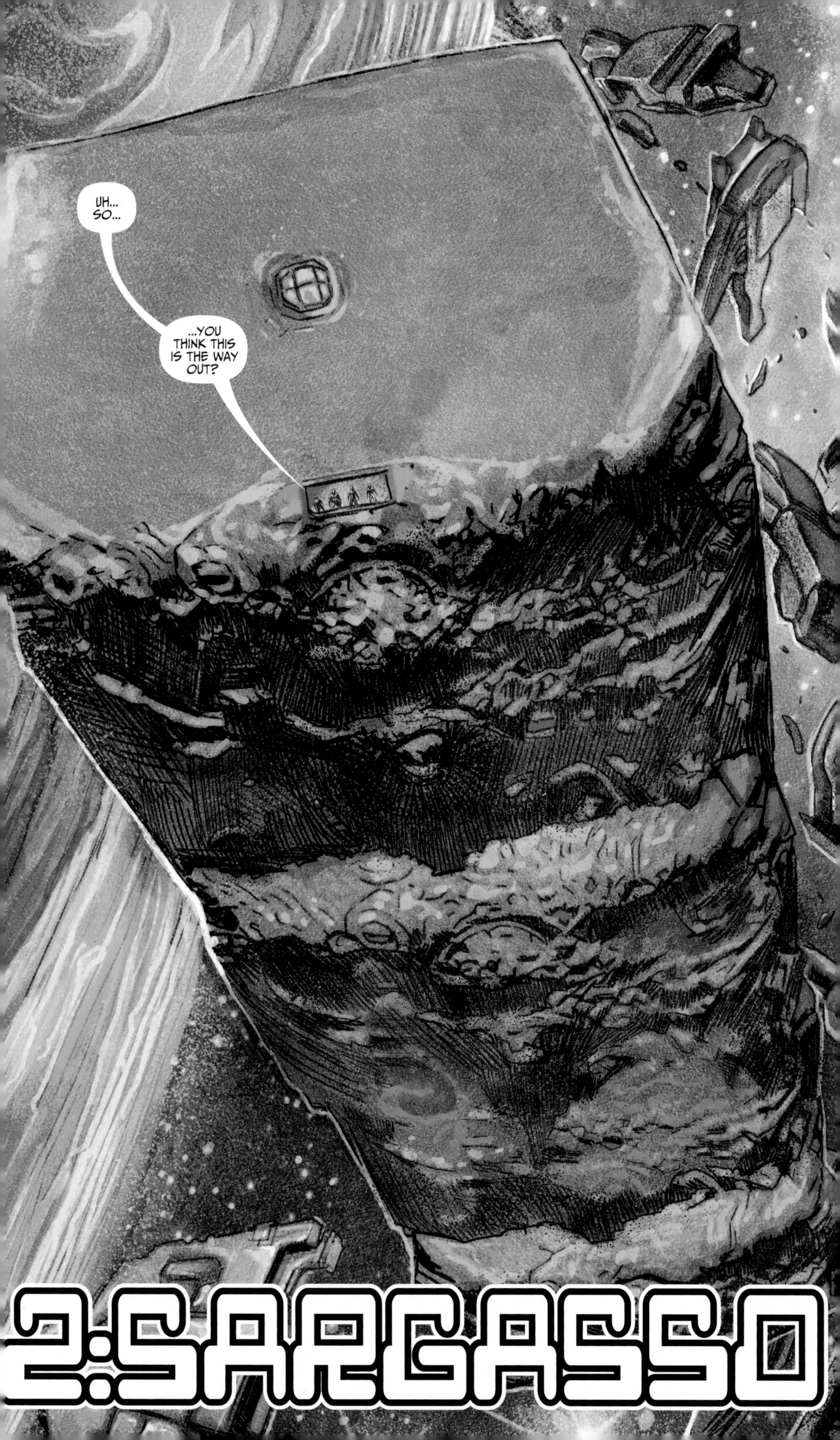
UH... SO...
...YOU THINK THIS IS THE WAY OUT?
2:SARGASSO

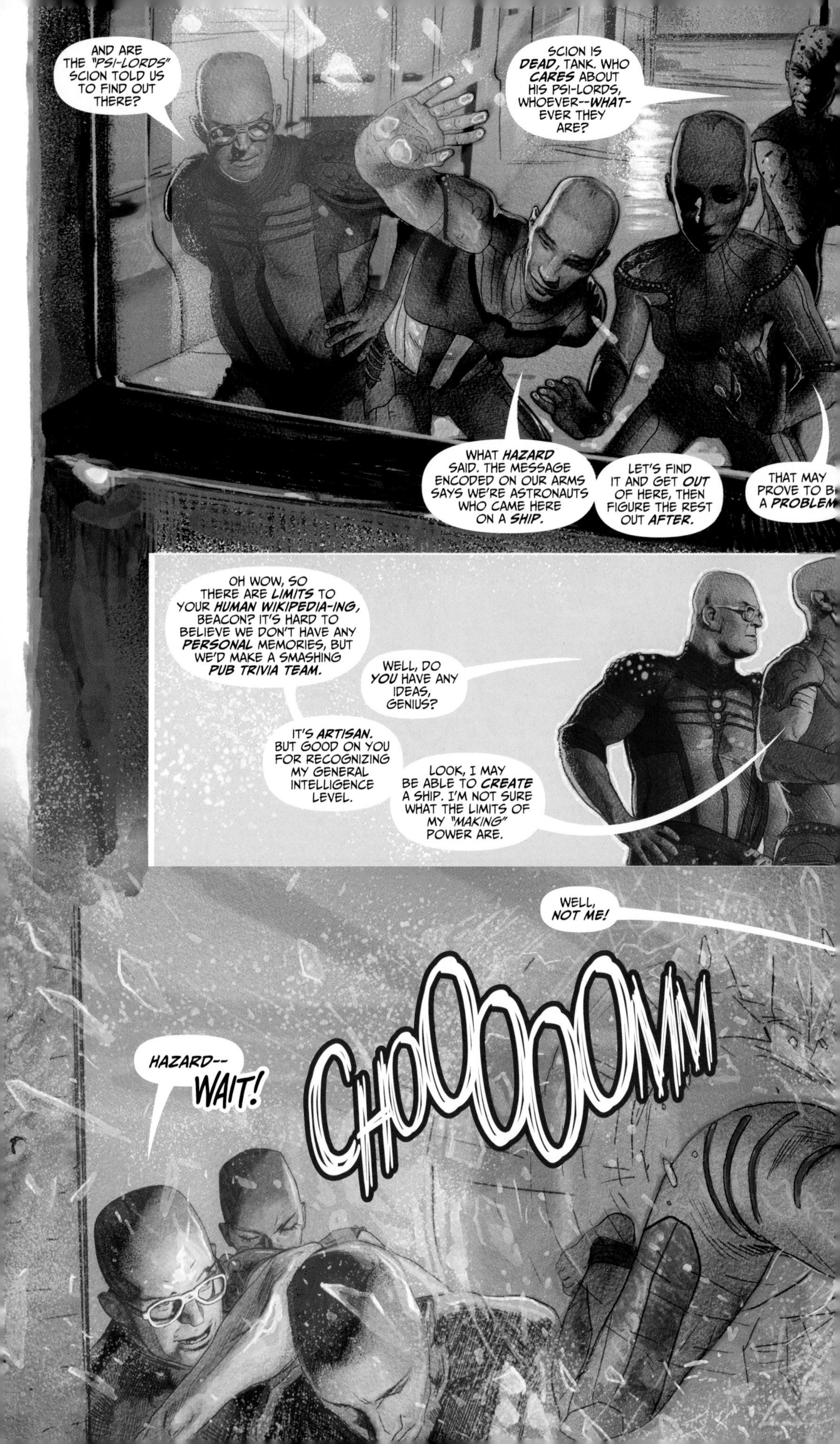

AND ARE THE "PSI-LORDS" SCION TOLD US TO FIND OUT THERE?
SCION IS DEAD, TANK. WHO CARES ABOUT HIS PSI-LORDS, WHOEVER--WHAT-EVER THEY ARE?
WHAT HAZARD SAID. THE MESSAGE ENCODED ON OUR ARMS SAYS WE'RE ASTRONAUTS WHO CAME HERE ON A SHIP.
LET'S FIND IT AND GET OUT OF HERE, THEN FIGURE THE REST OUT AFTER.
THAT MAY PROVE TO B A PROBLEM
OH WOW, SO THERE ARE LIMITS TO YOUR HUMAN WIKIPEDIA-ING, BEACON? IT'S HARD TO BELIEVE WE DON'T HAVE ANY PERSONAL MEMORIES, BUT WE'D MAKE A SMASHING PUB TRIVIA TEAM.
WELL, DO YOU HAVE ANY IDEAS, GENIUS?
IT'S ARTISAN. BUT GOOD ON YOU FOR RECOGNIZING MY GENERAL INTELLIGENCE LEVEL.
LOOK, I MAY BE ABLE TO CREATE A SHIP. I'M NOT SURE WHAT THE LIMITS OF MY "MAKING" POWER ARE.
WELL, NOT ME!
HAZARD-- WAIT!
CHOOOOOOMM

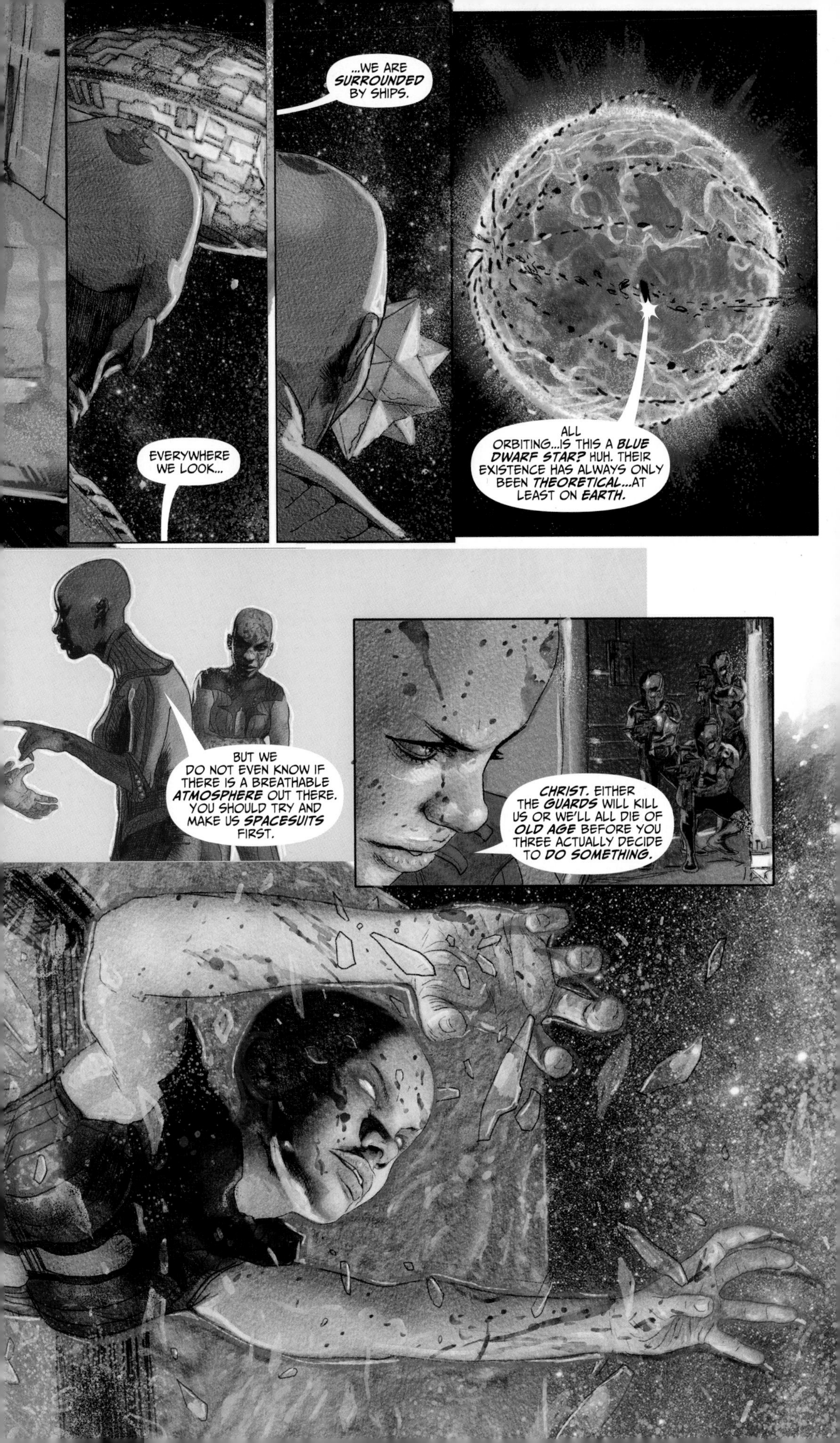
EVERYWHERE WE LOOK...
...WE ARE SURROUNDED BY SHIPS.
ALL ORBITING...IS THIS A BLUE DWARF STAR? HUH. THEIR EXISTENCE HAS ALWAYS ONLY BEEN THEORETICAL...AT LEAST ON EARTH.
BUT WE DO NOT EVEN KNOW IF THERE IS A BREATHABLE ATMOSPHERE OUT THERE. YOU SHOULD TRY AND MAKE US SPACESUITS FIRST.
CHRIST. EITHER THE GUARDS WILL KILL US OR WE'LL ALL DIE OF OLD AGE BEFORE YOU THREE ACTUALLY DECIDE TO DO SOMETHING.

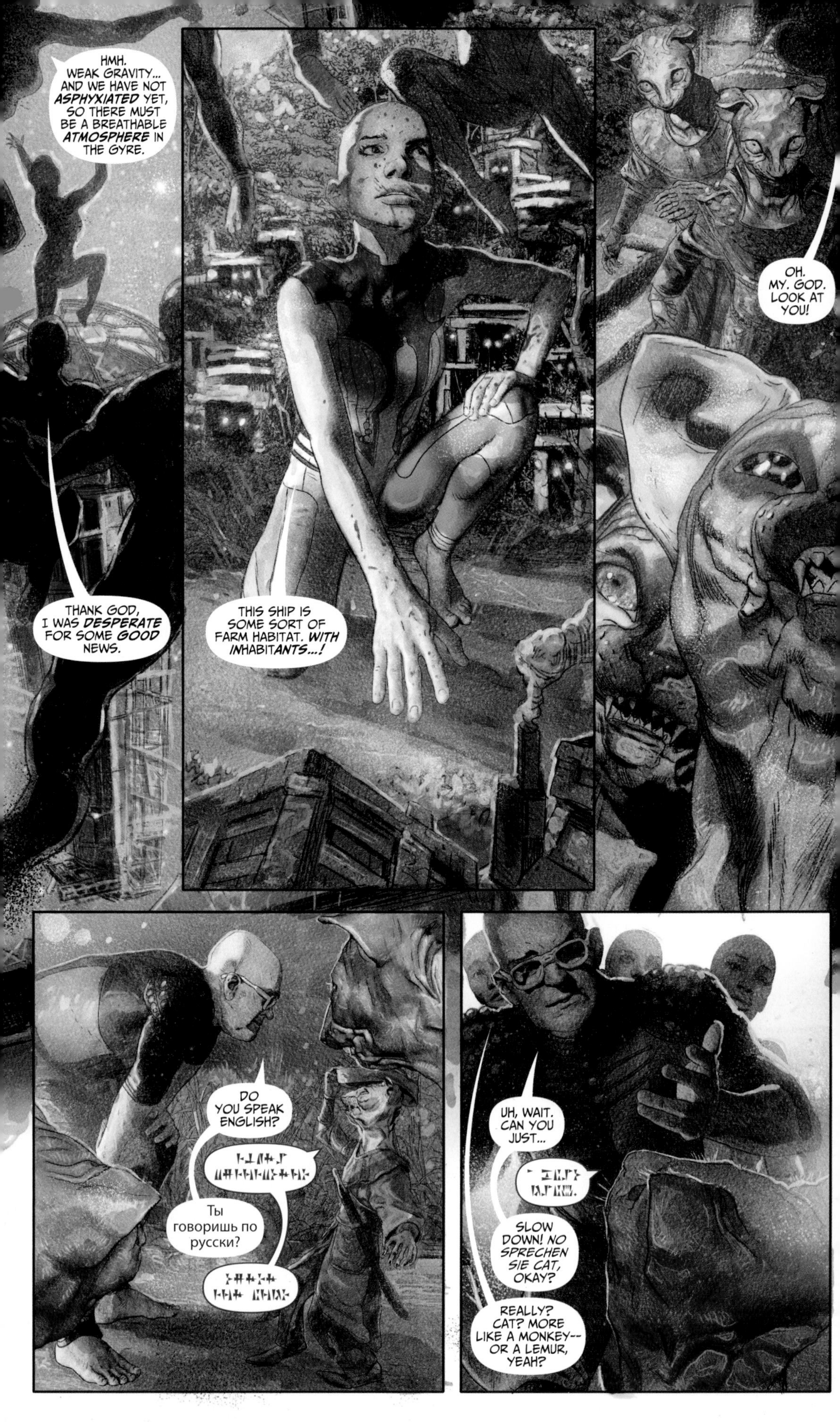
HMH. WEAK GRAVITY... AND WE HAVE NOT ASPHYXIATED YET, SO THERE MUST BE A BREATHABLE ATMOSPHERE IN THE GYRE.
THANK GOD, I WAS DESPERATE FOR SOME GOOD NEWS.
THIS SHIP IS SOME SORT OF FARM HABITAT. WITH INHABITANTS...!
OH. MY. GOD. LOOK AT YOU!
DO YOU SPEAK ENGLISH?
Ты говоришь по русски?
UH, WAIT. CAN YOU JUST...
SLOW DOWN! NO SPRECHEN SIE CAT, OKAY?
REALLY? CAT? MORE LIKE A MONKEY-- OR A LEMUR, YEAH?

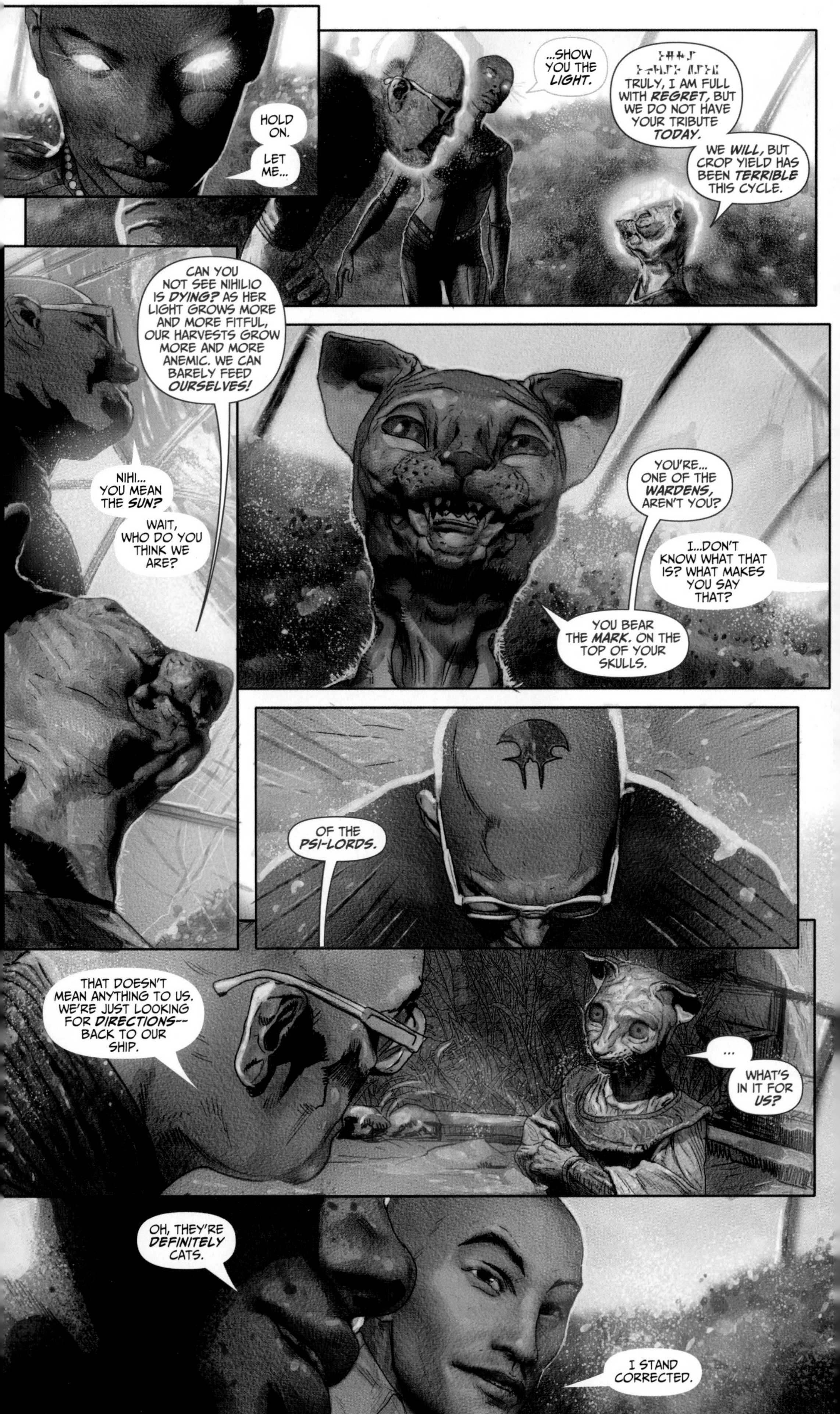
HOLD ON.
LET ME...
...SHOW YOU THE LIGHT.
TRULY, I AM FULL WITH REGRET, BUT WE DO NOT HAVE YOUR TRIBUTE TODAY.
WE WILL, BUT CROP YIELD HAS BEEN TERRIBLE THIS CYCLE.
CAN YOU NOT SEE NIHILIO IS DYING? AS HER LIGHT GROWS MORE AND MORE FITFUL, OUR HARVESTS GROW MORE AND MORE ANEMIC. WE CAN BARELY FEED OURSELVES!
NIHI... YOU MEAN THE SUN?
WAIT, WHO DO YOU THINK WE ARE?
YOU'RE... ONE OF THE WARDENS, AREN'T YOU?
I...DON'T KNOW WHAT THAT IS? WHAT MAKES YOU SAY THAT?
YOU BEAR THE MARK. ON THE TOP OF YOUR SKULLS.
OF THE PSI-LORDS.
THAT DOESN'T MEAN ANYTHING TO US. WE'RE JUST LOOKING FOR DIRECTIONS-- BACK TO OUR SHIP.
...
WHAT'S IN IT FOR US?
OH, THEY'RE DEFINITELY CATS.
I STAND CORRECTED.

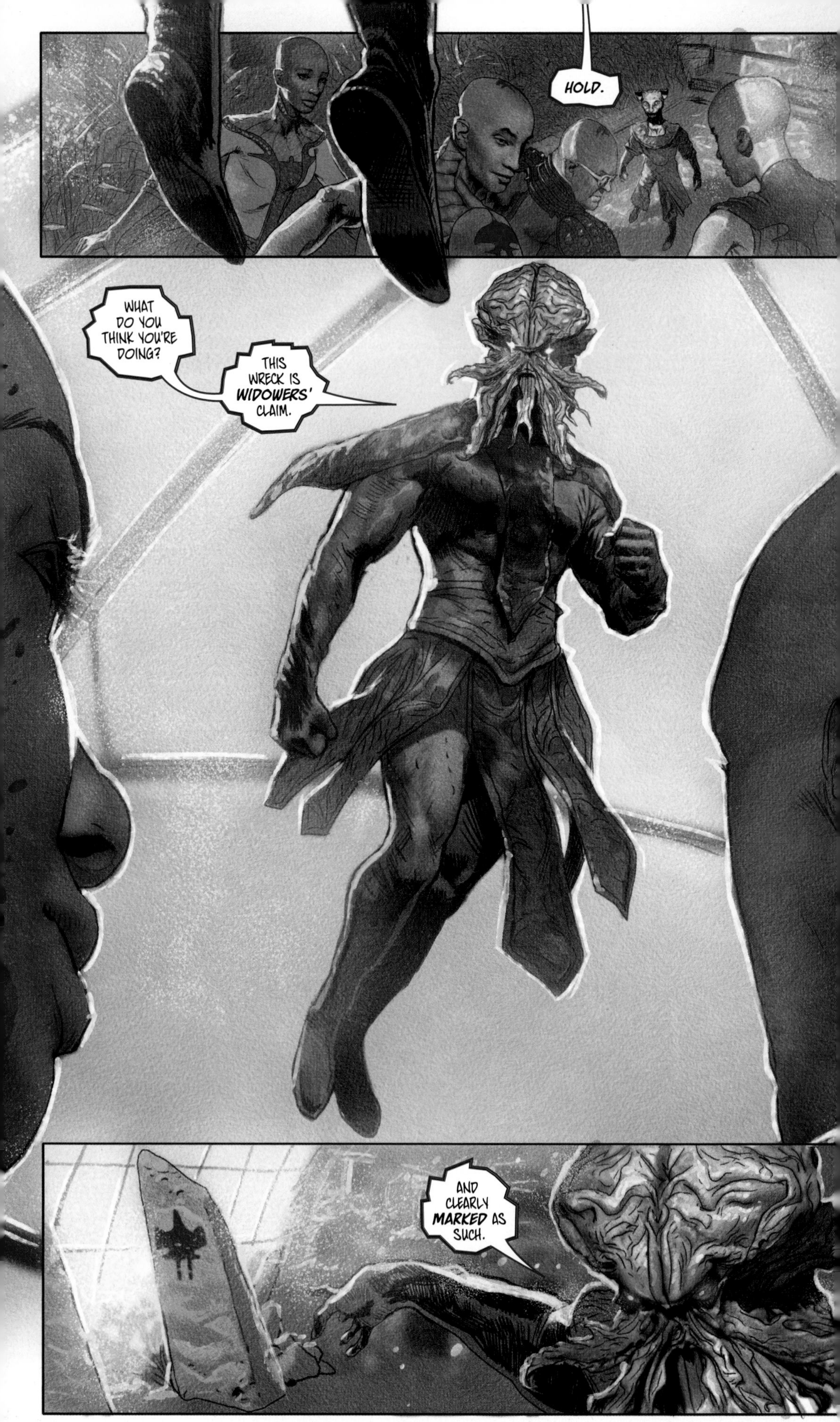
HOLD.
WHAT DO YOU THINK YOU'RE DOING?
THIS WRECK IS **WIDOWERS'** CLAIM.
AND CLEARLY **MARKED** AS SUCH.

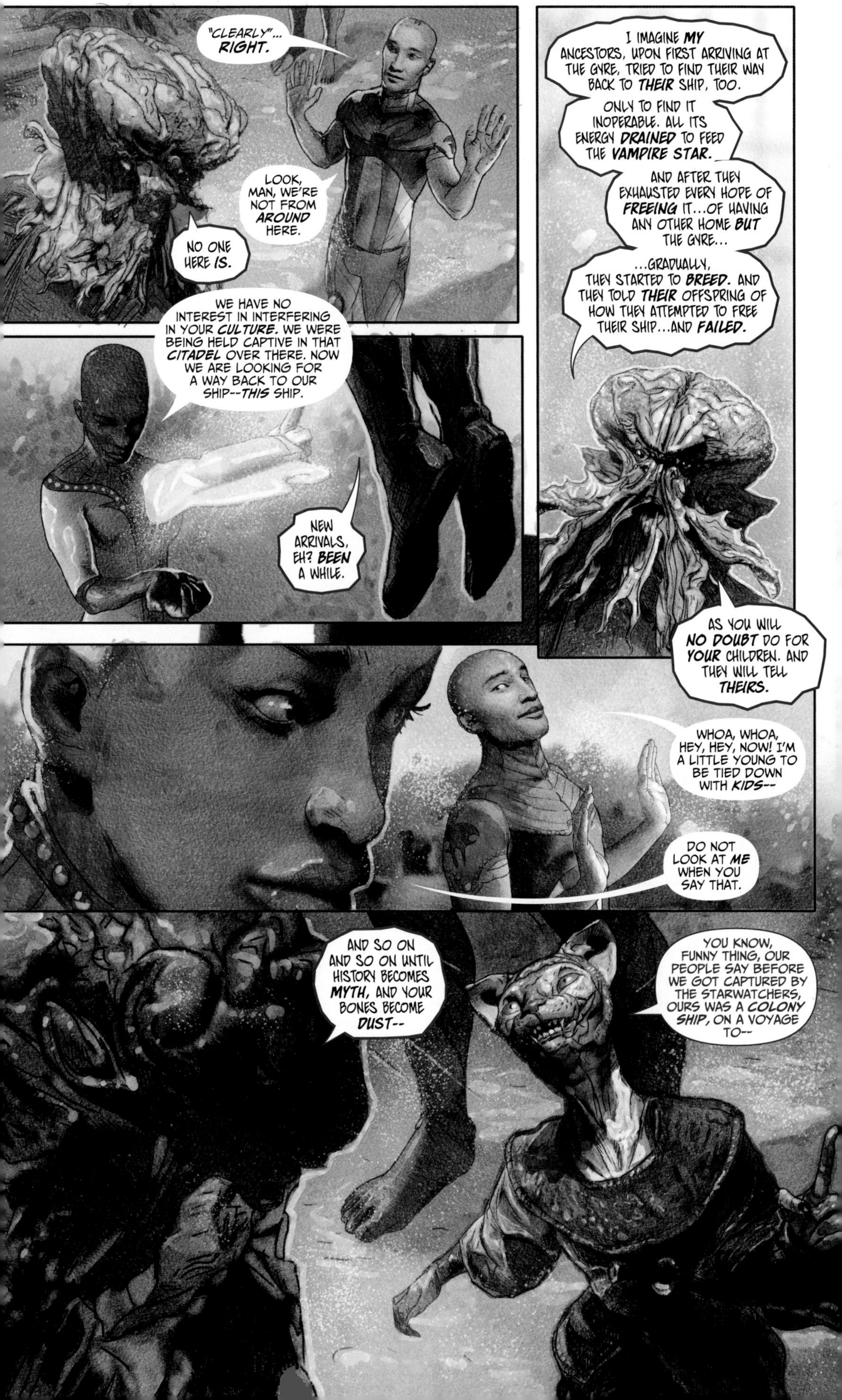
"CLEARLY"... RIGHT.
LOOK, MAN, WE'RE NOT FROM AROUND HERE.
NO ONE HERE IS.
WE HAVE NO INTEREST IN INTERFERING IN YOUR CULTURE. WE WERE BEING HELD CAPTIVE IN THAT CITADEL OVER THERE. NOW WE ARE LOOKING FOR A WAY BACK TO OUR SHIP--THIS SHIP.
NEW ARRIVALS, EH? BEEN A WHILE.
I IMAGINE MY ANCESTORS, UPON FIRST ARRIVING AT THE GYRE, TRIED TO FIND THEIR WAY BACK TO THEIR SHIP, TOO.
ONLY TO FIND IT INOPERABLE. ALL ITS ENERGY DRAINED TO FEED THE VAMPIRE STAR.
AND AFTER THEY EXHAUSTED EVERY HOPE OF FREEING IT...OF HAVING ANY OTHER HOME BUT THE GYRE...
...GRADUALLY, THEY STARTED TO BREED. AND THEY TOLD THEIR OFFSPRING OF HOW THEY ATTEMPTED TO FREE THEIR SHIP...AND FAILED.
AS YOU WILL NO DOUBT DO FOR YOUR CHILDREN. AND THEY WILL TELL THEIRS.
WHOA, WHOA, HEY, HEY, YOUNG! I'M A LITTLE YOUNG TO BE TIED DOWN WITH KIDS--
DO NOT LOOK AT ME WHEN YOU SAY THAT.
AND SO ON AND SO ON UNTIL HISTORY BECOMES MYTH, AND YOUR BONES BECOME DUST--
YOU KNOW, FUNNY THING, OUR PEOPLE SAY BEFORE WE GOT CAPTURED BY THE STARWATCHERS, OURS WAS A COLONY SHIP, ON A VOYAGE TO--

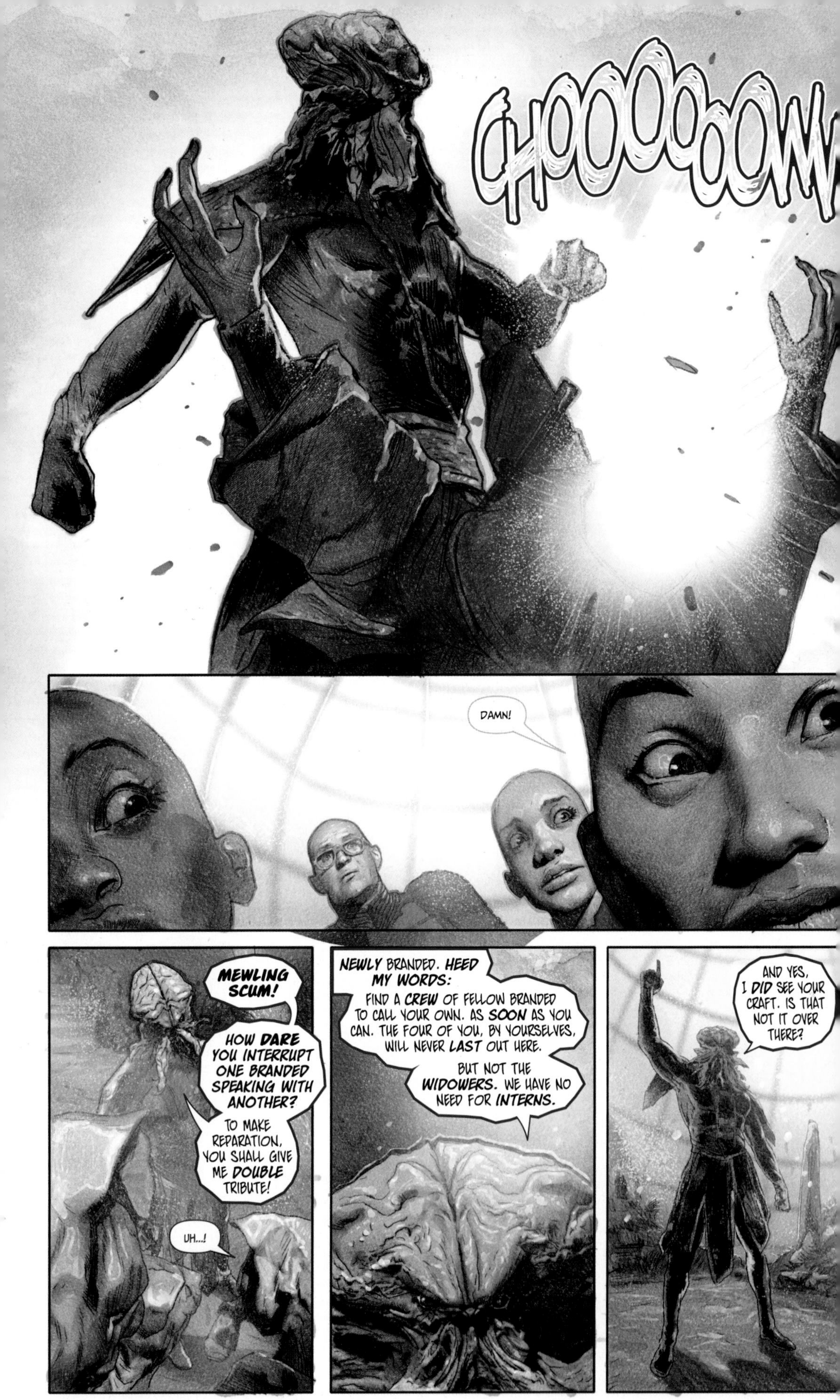
CHOOOOOOOW
DAMN!
MEWLING SCUM!
HOW DARE YOU INTERRUPT ONE BRANDED SPEAKING WITH ANOTHER?
TO MAKE REPARATION, YOU SHALL GIVE ME DOUBLE TRIBUTE!
UH...!
NEWLY BRANDED. HEED MY WORDS:
FIND A CREW OF FELLOW BRANDED TO CALL YOUR OWN. AS SOON AS YOU CAN. THE FOUR OF YOU, BY YOURSELVES, WILL NEVER LAST OUT HERE.
BUT NOT THE WIDOWERS. WE HAVE NO NEED FOR INTERNS.
AND YES, I DID SEE YOUR CRAFT. IS THAT NOT IT OVER THERE?

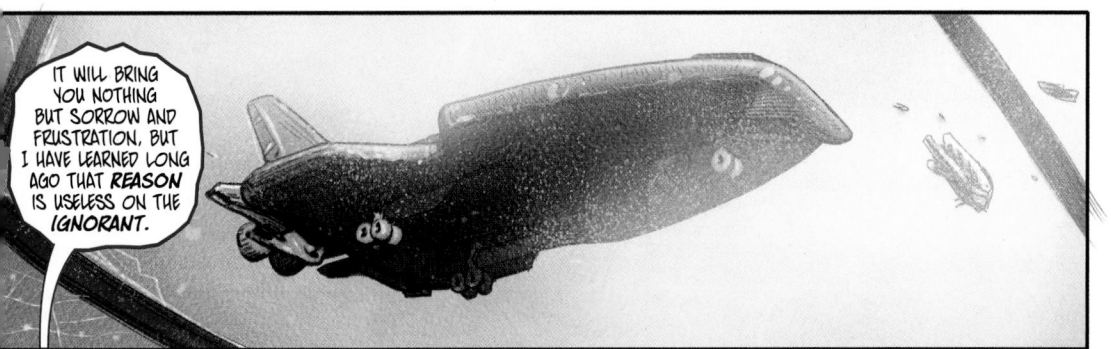

IT WILL BRING YOU NOTHING BUT SORROW AND FRUSTRATION, BUT I HAVE LEARNED LONG AGO THAT *REASON* IS USELESS ON THE *IGNORANT.*

YES--YES! MUSHROOM-HEAD IS RIGHT! THERE SHE IS! WE'RE FINALLY *GETTING SOME-WHERE--*

YOU HAVE *NONE* OF IT?!

AHHH! PLEASE! NO! MERCY!

SSHRAKK

SSHRAKK

GAAAHHH!

NO--NO NOT MY *LITTLE BROTHER!* HE'S JUST A *BOY--!*

HAZARD. *LOGICALLY...*

...WE REALLY DO NOT UNDERSTAND THE *CUSTOMS* HERE. WE HAVE NO RIGHT TO *JUDGE.* WE JUST STOPPED TO *ASK FOR DIRECTIONS.*

AND NOW WE SHOULD *WALK AWAY.*

YEAH.

YEAH.

I HEAR YOU.

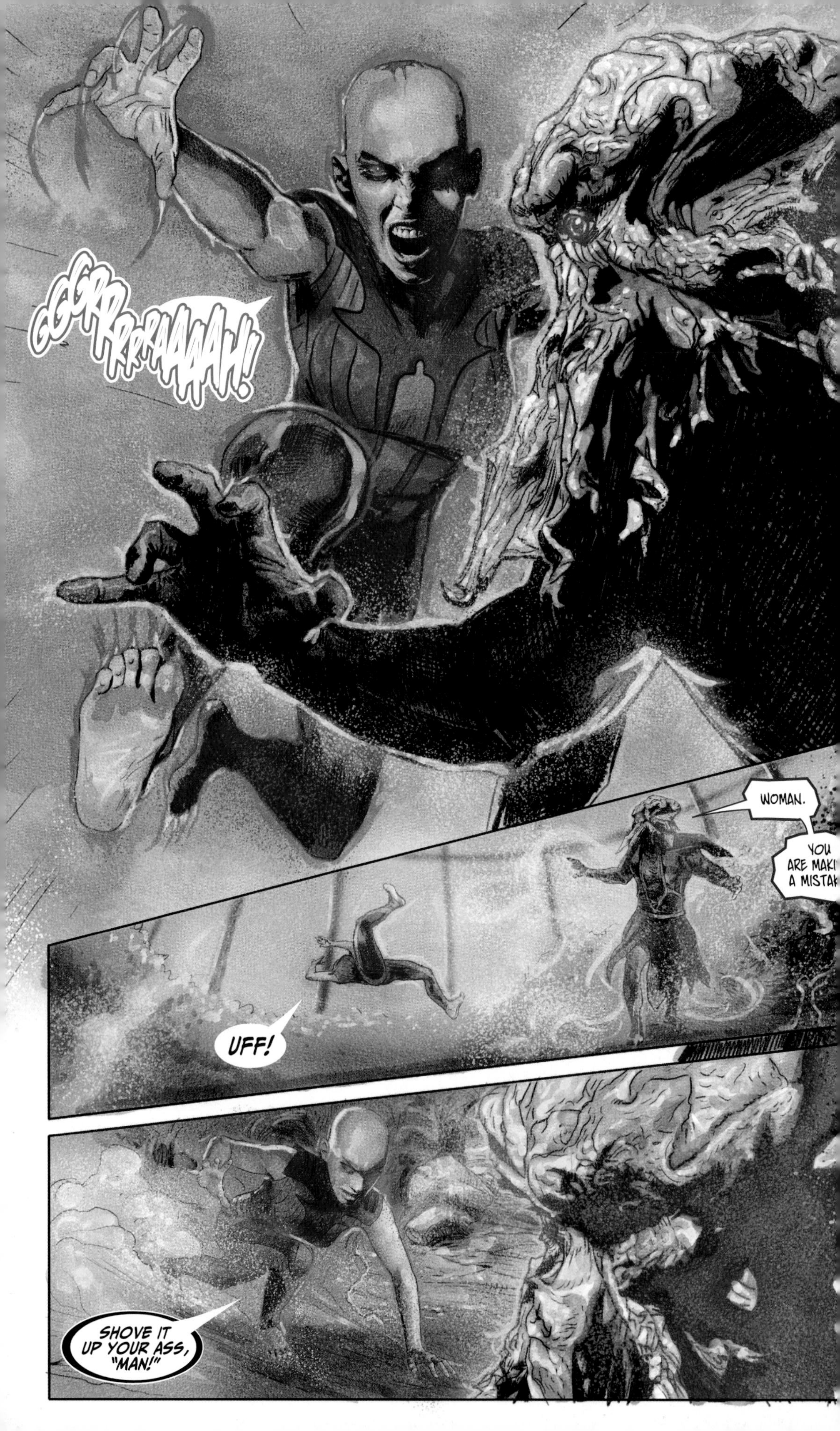
GGGRRRRRAAAAAH!
WOMAN.
YOU ARE MAKI A MISTAK
UFF!
SHOVE IT UP YOUR ASS, "MAN!"

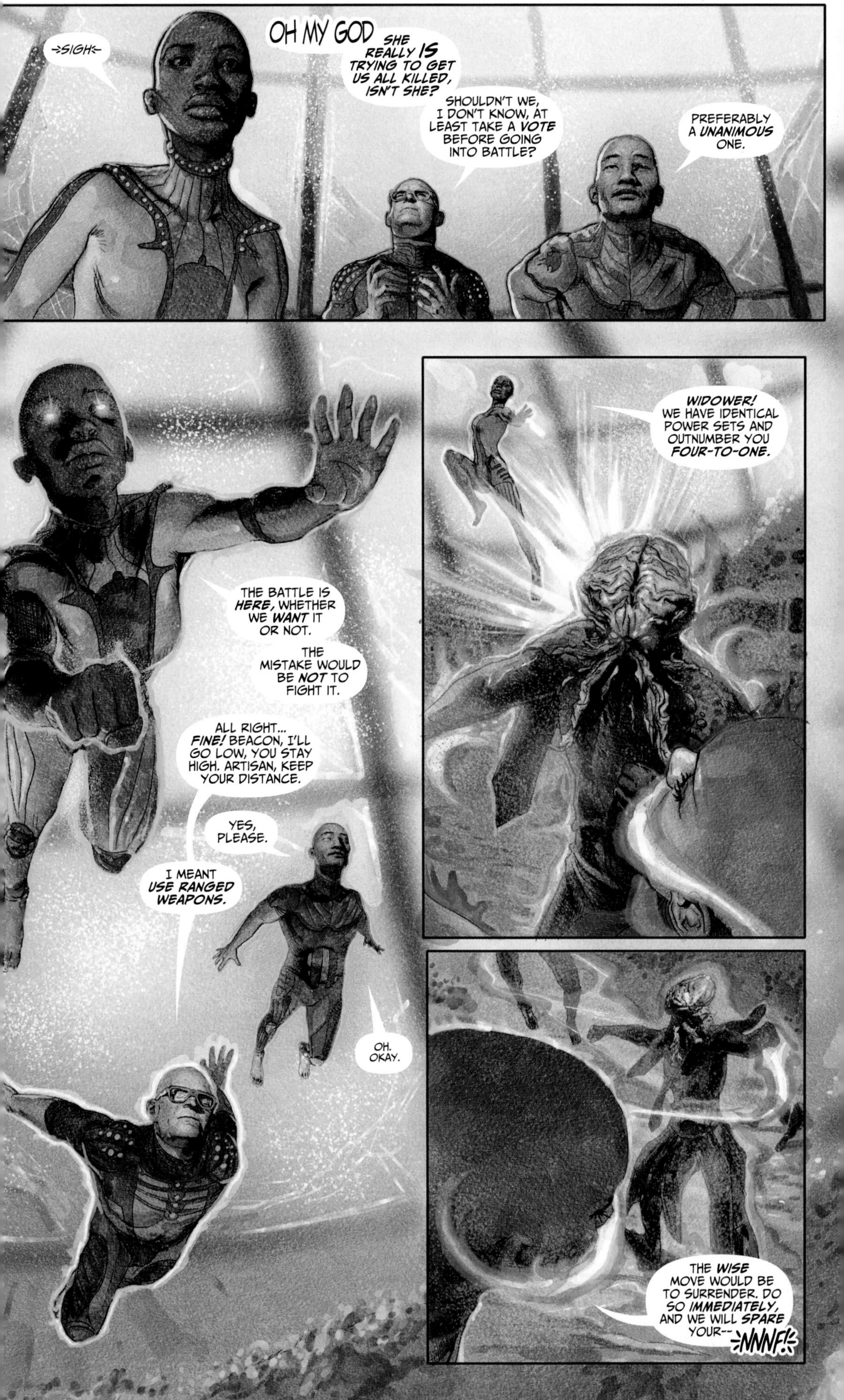

->SIGH<-
OH MY GOD
SHE REALLY IS TRYING TO GET US ALL KILLED, ISN'T SHE?
SHOULDN'T WE, I DON'T KNOW, AT LEAST TAKE A VOTE BEFORE GOING INTO BATTLE?
PREFERABLY A UNANIMOUS ONE.
THE BATTLE IS HERE, WHETHER WE WANT IT OR NOT.
THE MISTAKE WOULD BE NOT TO FIGHT IT.
ALL RIGHT... FINE! BEACON, I'LL GO LOW, YOU STAY HIGH. ARTISAN, KEEP YOUR DISTANCE.
YES, PLEASE.
I MEANT USE RANGED WEAPONS.
OH. OKAY.
WIDOWER! WE HAVE IDENTICAL POWER SETS AND OUTNUMBER YOU FOUR-TO-ONE.
THE WISE MOVE WOULD BE TO SURRENDER. DO SO IMMEDIATELY, AND WE WILL SPARE YOUR--
NNNF!

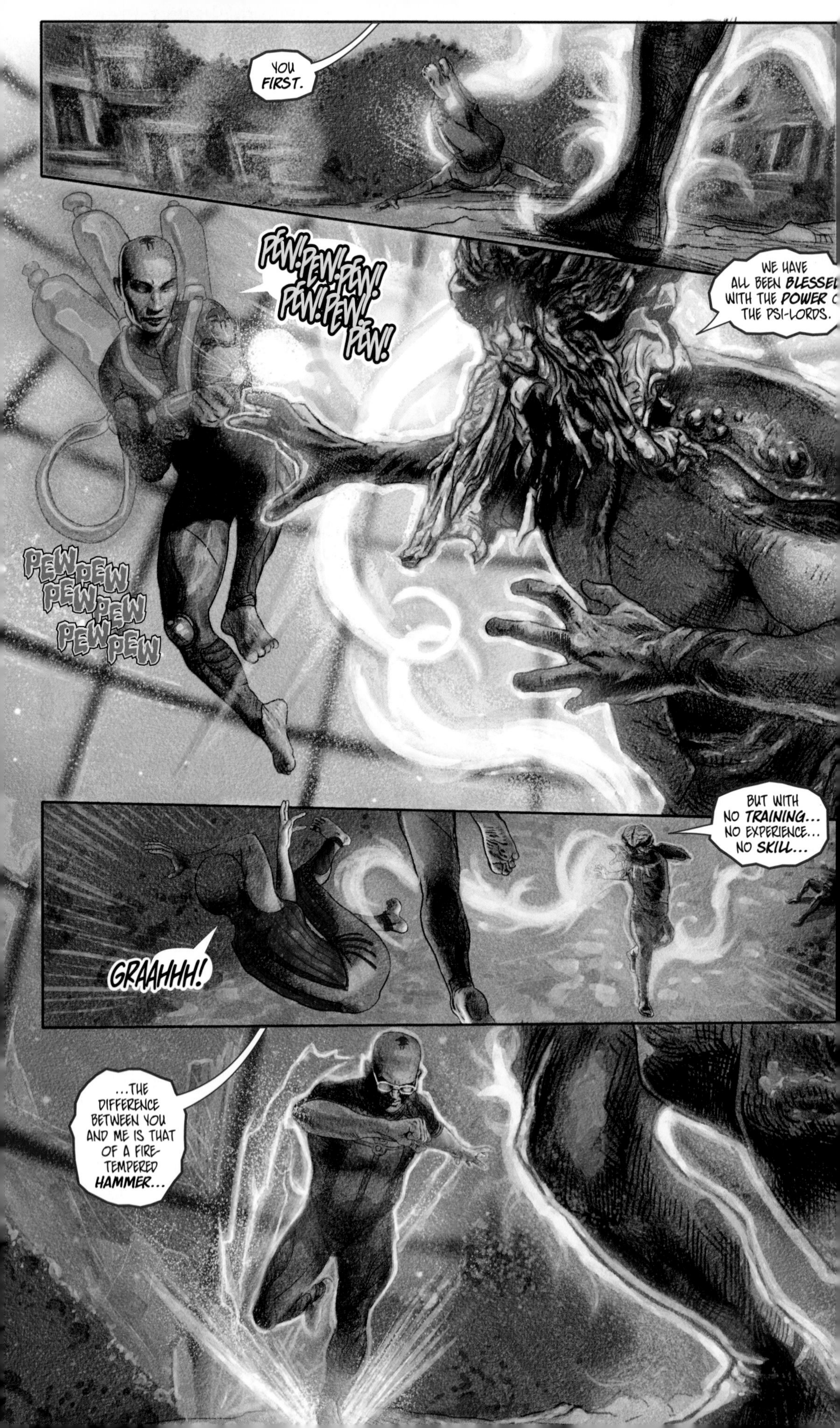
YOU FIRST.
PEW! PEW! PEW! PEW! PEW! PEW!
PEW PEW PEW PEW PEW PEW
WE HAVE ALL BEEN BLESSED WITH THE POWER OF THE PSI-LORDS.
BUT WITH NO TRAINING... NO EXPERIENCE... NO SKILL...
GRAAHHH!
...THE DIFFERENCE BETWEEN YOU AND ME IS THAT OF A FIRE-TEMPERED HAMMER...

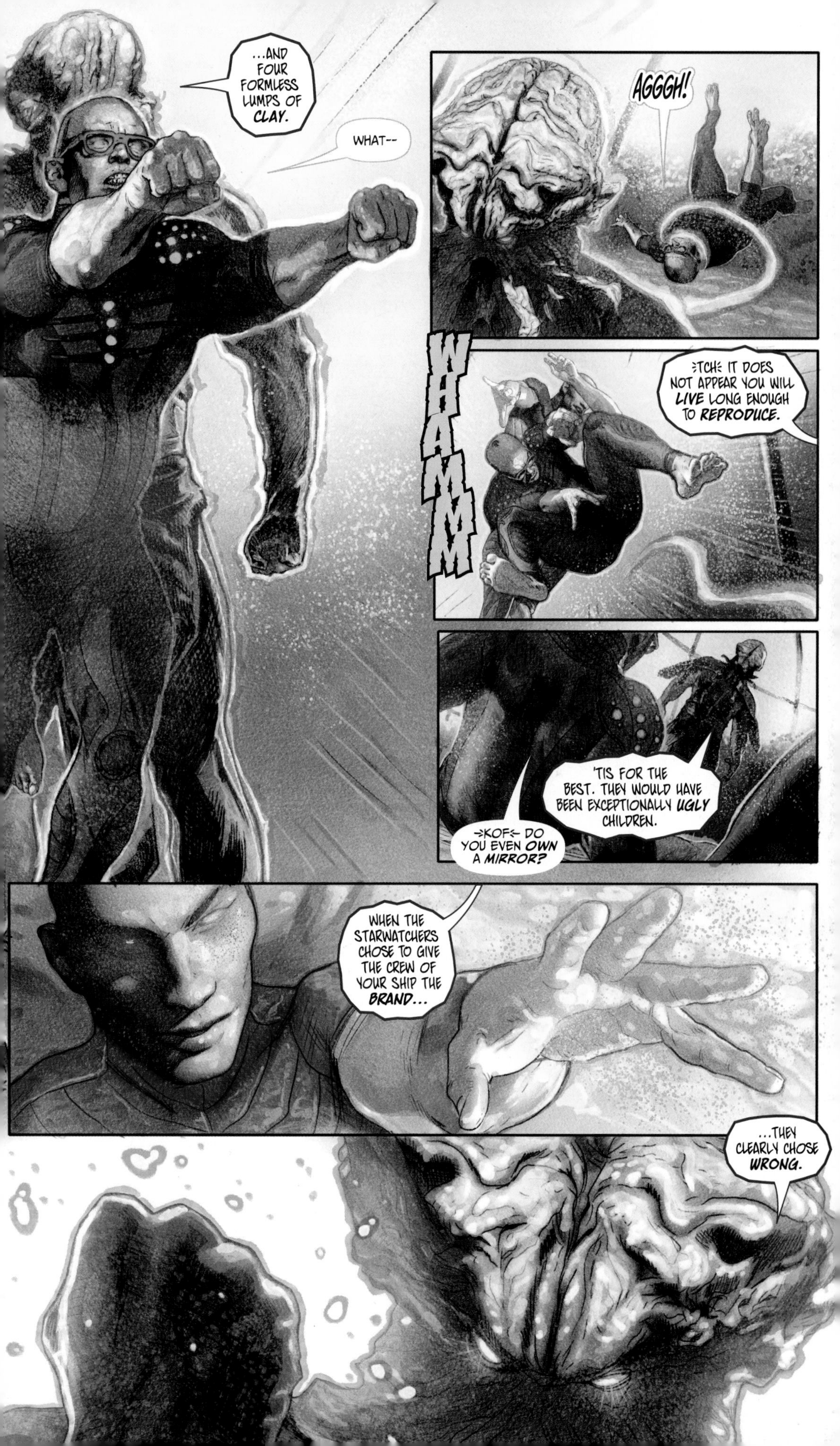
...AND FOUR FORMLESS LUMPS OF CLAY.
WHAT--
AGGGH!
WHAMMM
=TCH= IT DOES NOT APPEAR YOU WILL LIVE LONG ENOUGH TO REPRODUCE.
'TIS FOR THE BEST. THEY WOULD HAVE BEEN EXCEPTIONALLY UGLY CHILDREN.
=KOF= DO YOU EVEN OWN A MIRROR?
WHEN THE STARWATCHERS CHOSE TO GIVE THE CREW OF YOUR SHIP THE BRAND...
...THEY CLEARLY CHOSE WRONG.

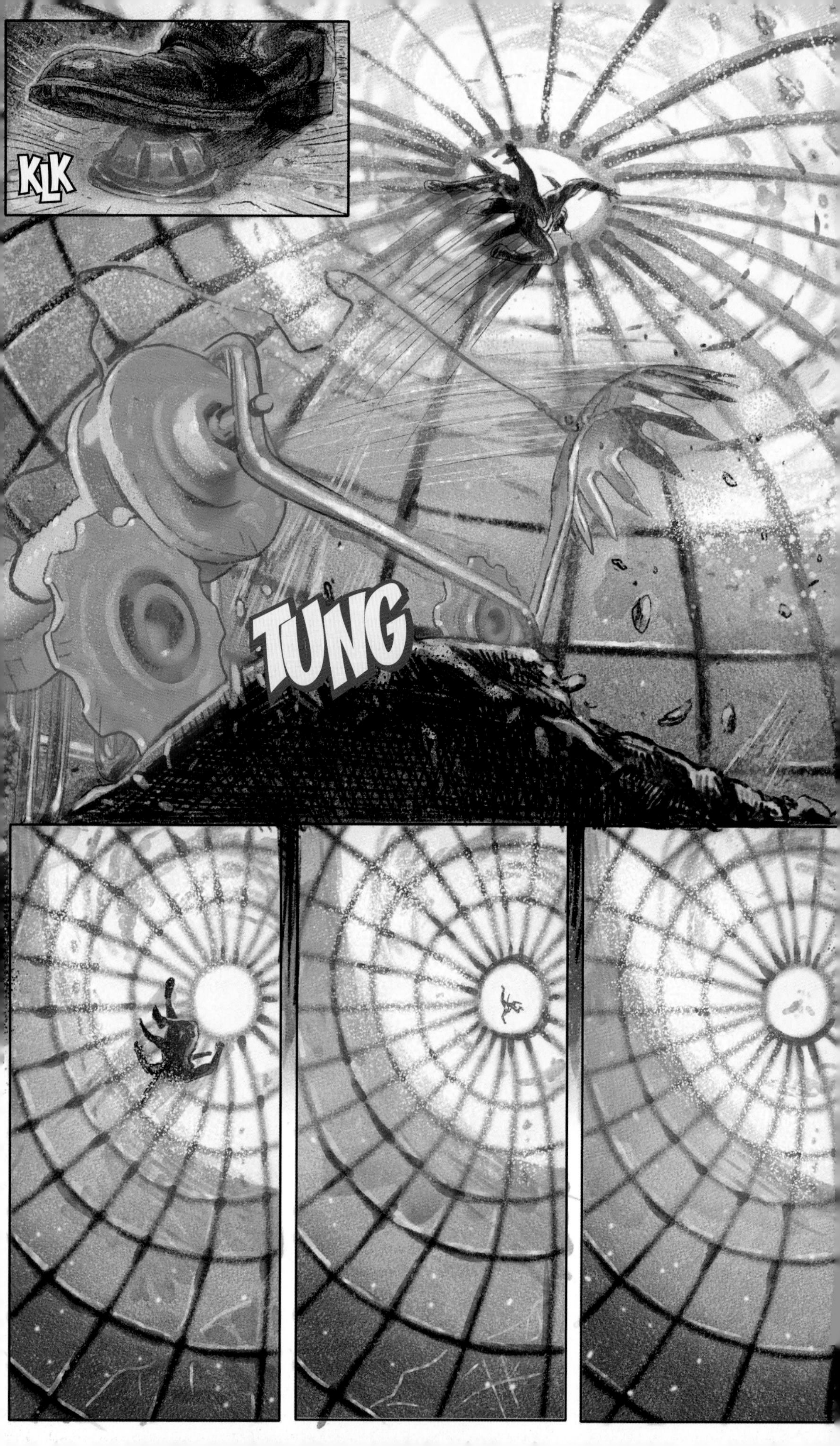
KLK
TUNG

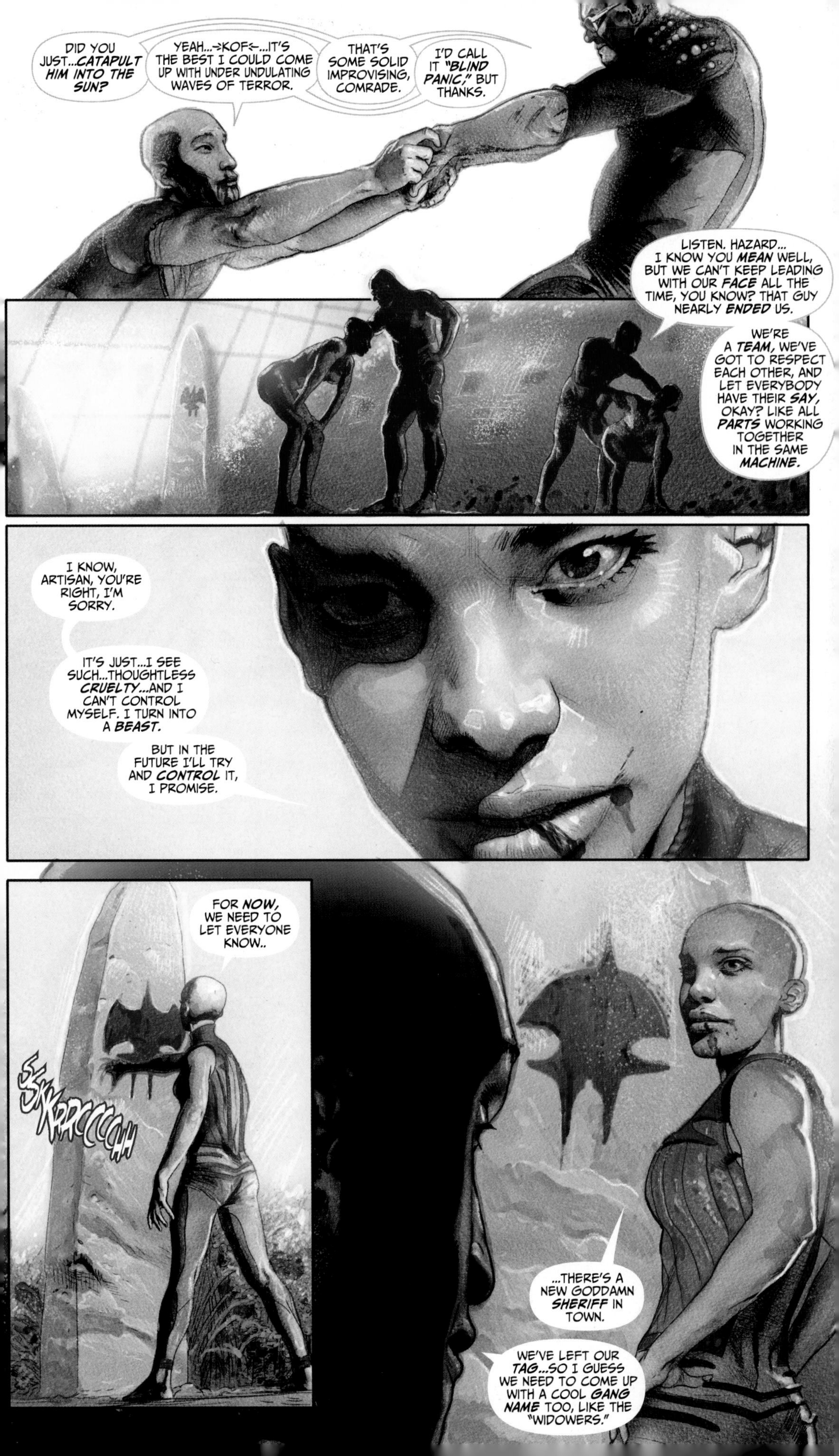

DID YOU JUST...CATAPULT HIM INTO THE SUN?
YEAH...>KOF<...IT'S THE BEST I COULD COME UP WITH UNDER UNDULATING WAVES OF TERROR.
THAT'S SOME SOLID IMPROVISING, COMRADE.
I'D CALL IT "BLIND PANIC," BUT THANKS.
LISTEN. HAZARD... I KNOW YOU MEAN WELL, BUT WE CAN'T KEEP LEADING WITH OUR FACE ALL THE TIME, YOU KNOW? THAT GUY NEARLY ENDED US.
WE'RE A TEAM, WE'VE GOT TO RESPECT EACH OTHER, AND LET EVERYBODY HAVE THEIR SAY, OKAY? LIKE ALL PARTS WORKING TOGETHER IN THE SAME MACHINE.
I KNOW, ARTISAN, YOU'RE RIGHT, I'M SORRY.
IT'S JUST...I SEE SUCH...THOUGHTLESS CRUELTY...AND I CAN'T CONTROL MYSELF. I TURN INTO A BEAST.
BUT IN THE FUTURE I'LL TRY AND CONTROL IT, I PROMISE.
FOR NOW, WE NEED TO LET EVERYONE KNOW..
SSSKRRCCCCHH
...THERE'S A NEW GODDAMN SHERIFF IN TOWN.
WE'VE LEFT OUR TAG...SO I GUESS WE NEED TO COME UP WITH A COOL GANG NAME TOO, LIKE THE "WIDOWERS."

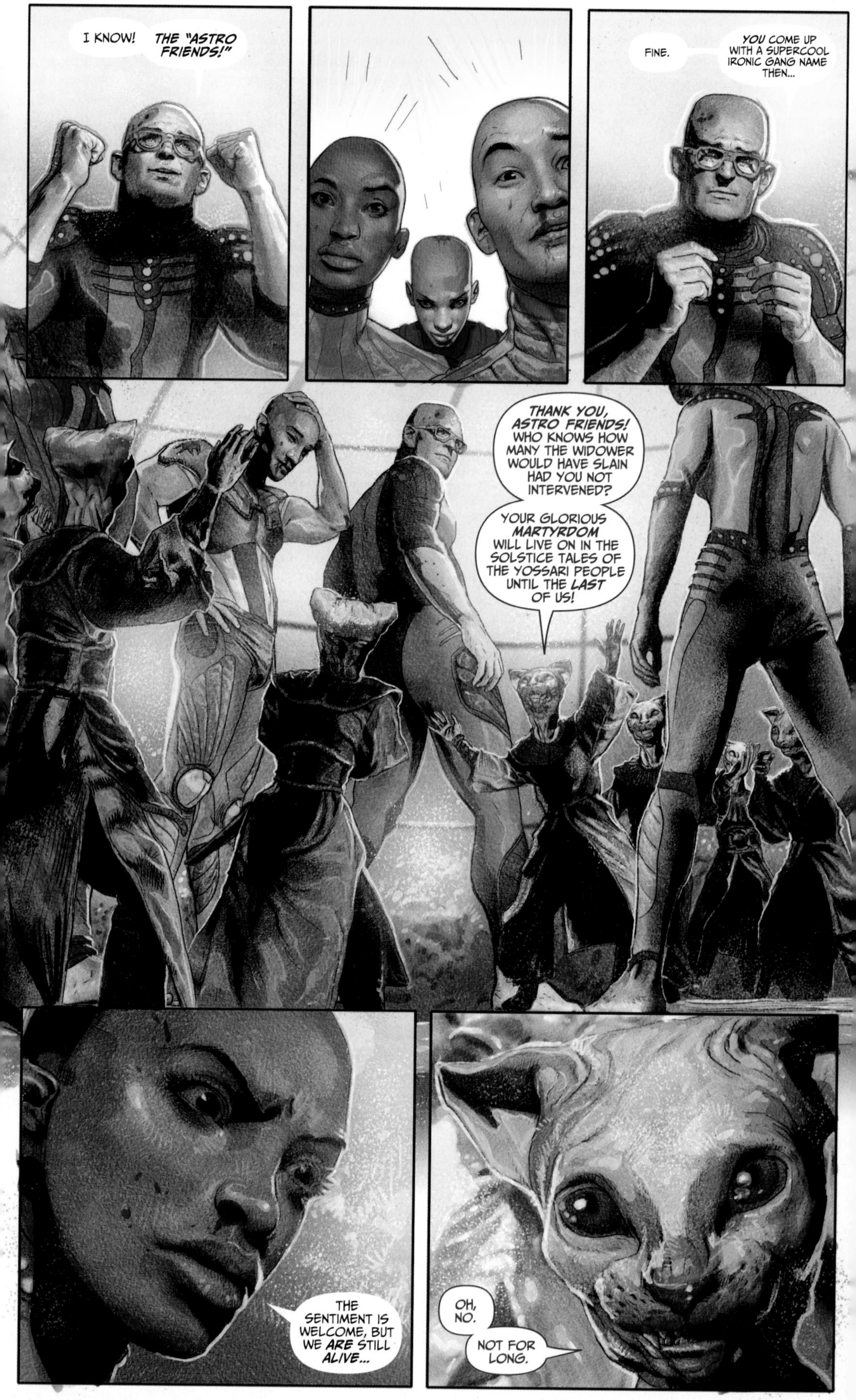
I KNOW!
THE "ASTRO FRIENDS!"
FINE.
YOU COME UP WITH A SUPERCOOL IRONIC GANG NAME THEN...
THANK YOU, ASTRO FRIENDS! WHO KNOWS HOW MANY THE WIDOWER WOULD HAVE SLAIN HAD YOU NOT INTERVENED?
YOUR GLORIOUS MARTYRDOM WILL LIVE ON IN THE SOLSTICE TALES OF THE YOSSARI PEOPLE UNTIL THE LAST OF US!
THE SENTIMENT IS WELCOME, BUT WE ARE STILL ALIVE...
OH, NO.
NOT FOR LONG.

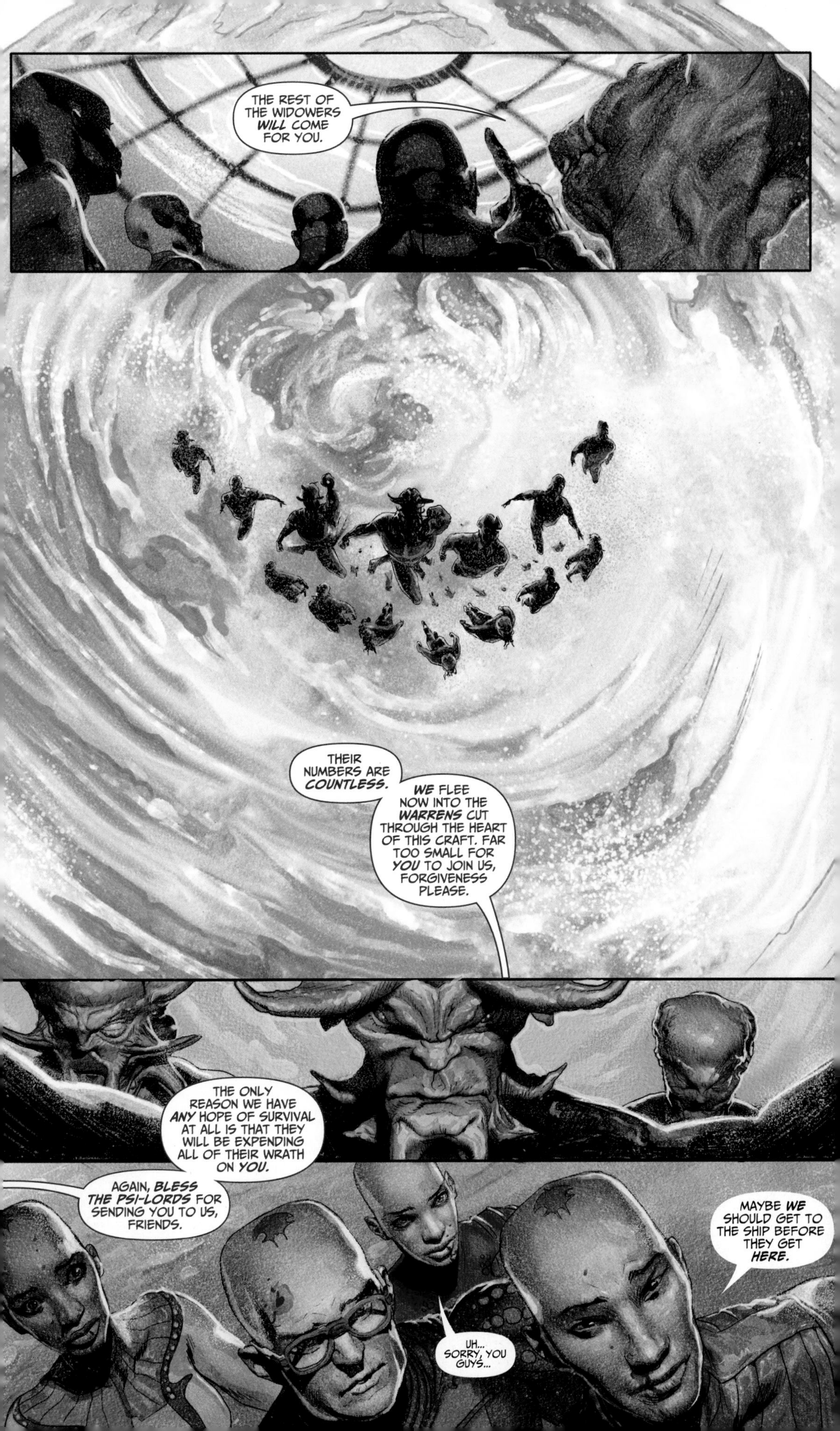
THE REST OF THE WIDOWERS WILL COME FOR YOU.
THEIR NUMBERS ARE COUNTLESS.
WE FLEE NOW INTO THE WARRENS CUT THROUGH THE HEART OF THIS CRAFT. FAR TOO SMALL FOR YOU TO JOIN US, FORGIVENESS PLEASE.
THE ONLY REASON WE HAVE ANY HOPE OF SURVIVAL AT ALL IS THAT THEY WILL BE EXPENDING ALL OF THEIR WRATH ON YOU.
AGAIN, BLESS THE PSI-LORDS FOR SENDING YOU TO US, FRIENDS.
UH... SORRY, YOU GUYS...
MAYBE WE SHOULD GET TO THE SHIP BEFORE THEY GET HERE.

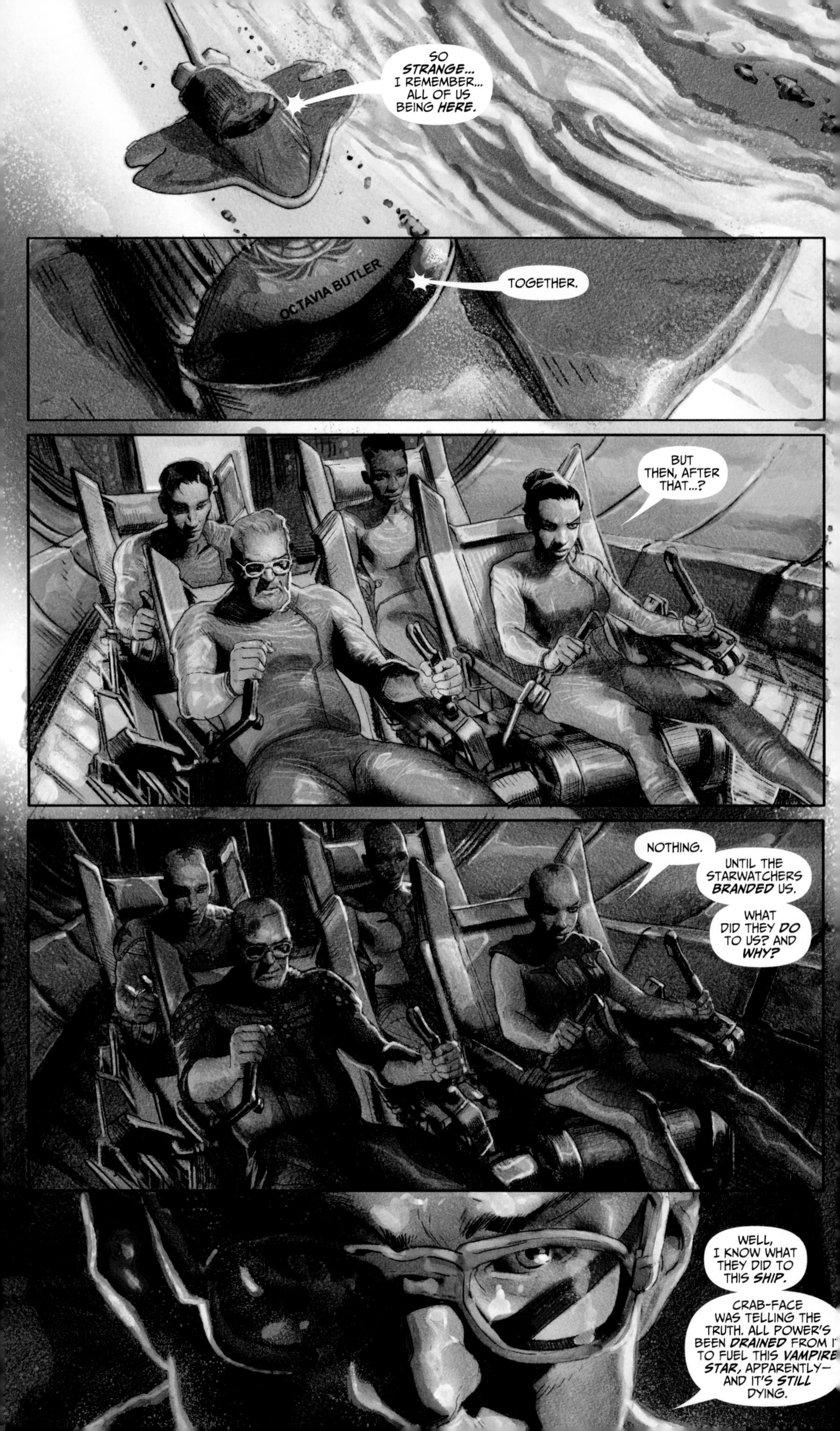
SO STRANGE... I REMEMBER... ALL OF US BEING HERE.
OCTAVIA BUTLER
TOGETHER.
BUT THEN, AFTER THAT...?
NOTHING.
UNTIL THE STARWATCHERS BRANDED US.
WHAT DID THEY DO TO US? AND WHY?
WELL, I KNOW WHAT THEY DID TO THIS SHIP.
CRAB-FACE WAS TELLING THE TRUTH. ALL POWER'S BEEN DRAINED FROM IT TO FUEL THIS VAMPIRE STAR, APPARENTLY— AND IT'S STILL DYING.

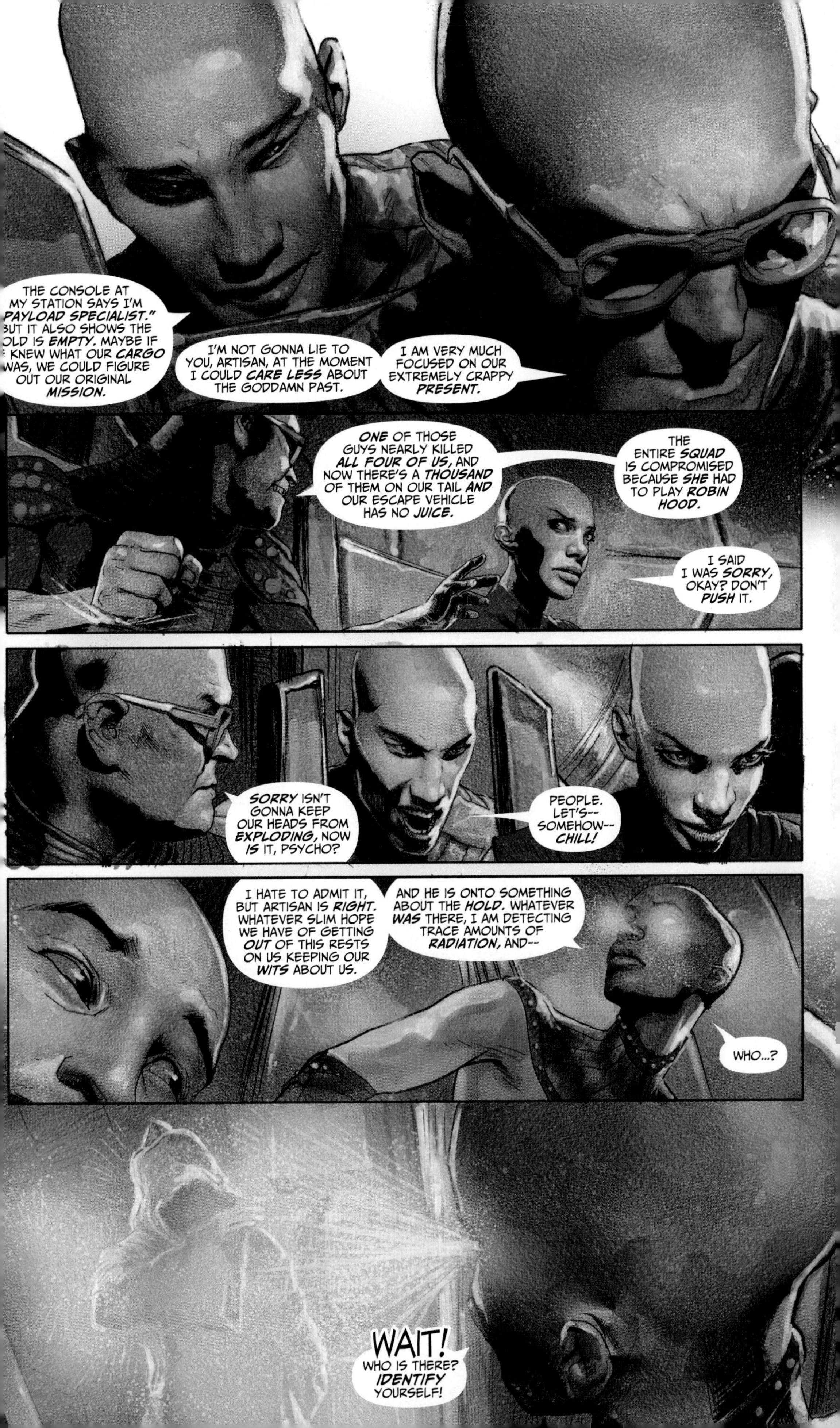
THE CONSOLE AT MY STATION SAYS I'M "PAYLOAD SPECIALIST." BUT IT ALSO SHOWS THE HOLD IS EMPTY. MAYBE IF I KNEW WHAT OUR CARGO WAS, WE COULD FIGURE OUT OUR ORIGINAL MISSION.
I'M NOT GONNA LIE TO YOU, ARTISAN, AT THE MOMENT I COULD CARE LESS ABOUT THE GODDAMN PAST.
I AM VERY MUCH FOCUSED ON OUR EXTREMELY CRAPPY PRESENT.
ONE OF THOSE GUYS NEARLY KILLED ALL FOUR OF US, AND NOW THERE'S A THOUSAND OF THEM ON OUR TAIL AND OUR ESCAPE VEHICLE HAS NO JUICE.
THE ENTIRE SQUAD IS COMPROMISED BECAUSE SHE HAD TO PLAY ROBIN HOOD.
I SAID I WAS SORRY, OKAY? DON'T PUSH IT.
SORRY ISN'T GONNA KEEP OUR HEADS FROM EXPLODING, NOW IS IT, PSYCHO?
PEOPLE. LET'S-- SOMEHOW-- CHILL!
I HATE TO ADMIT IT, BUT ARTISAN IS RIGHT. WHATEVER SLIM HOPE WE HAVE OF GETTING OUT OF THIS RESTS ON US KEEPING OUR WITS ABOUT US.
AND HE IS ONTO SOMETHING ABOUT THE HOLD. WHATEVER WAS THERE, I AM DETECTING TRACE AMOUNTS OF RADIATION, AND--
WHO...?
WAIT! WHO IS THERE? IDENTIFY YOURSELF!

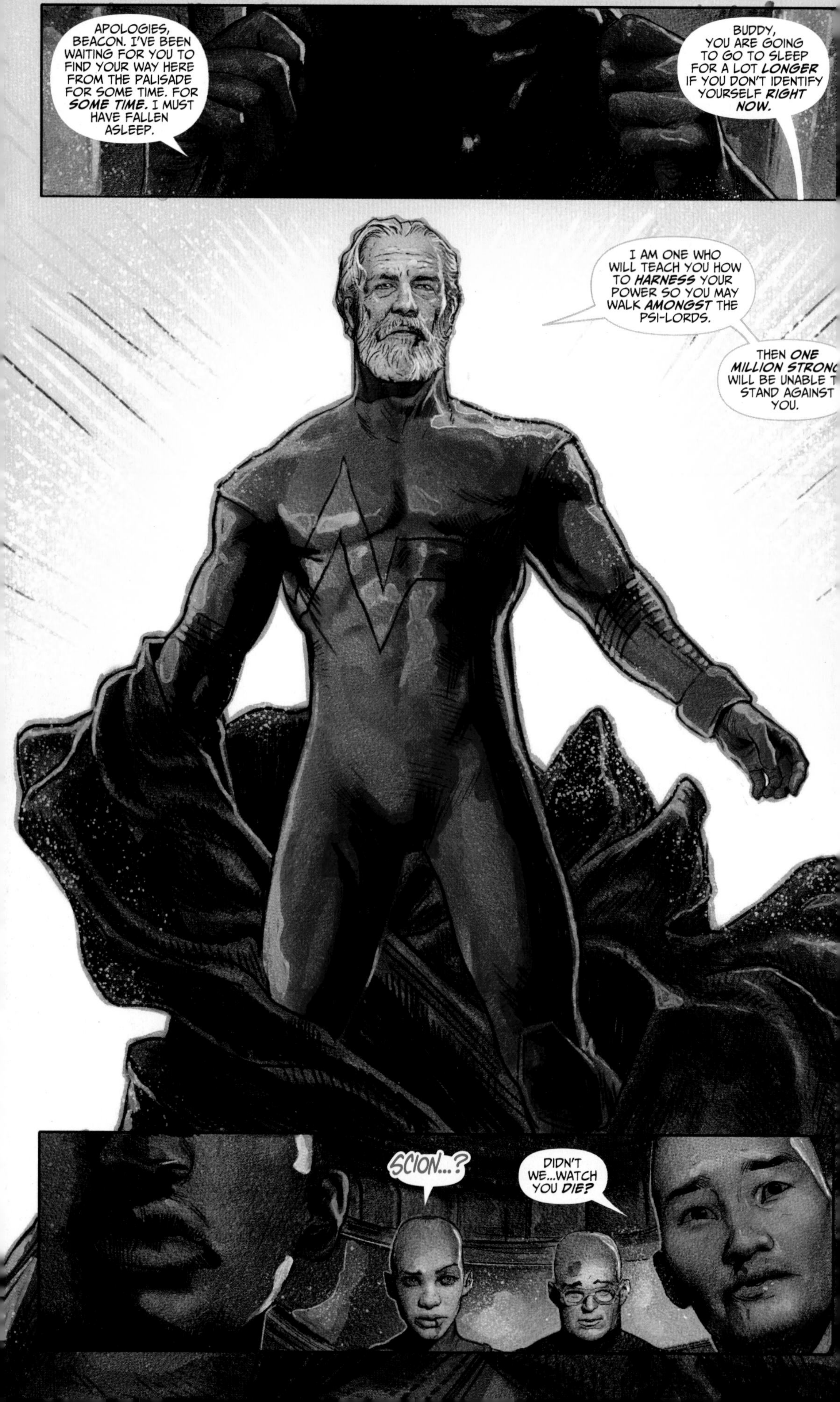
APOLOGIES, BEACON. I'VE BEEN WAITING FOR YOU TO FIND YOUR WAY HERE FROM THE PALISADE FOR SOME TIME. FOR *SOME TIME.* I MUST HAVE FALLEN ASLEEP.
BUDDY, YOU ARE GOING TO GO TO SLEEP FOR A LOT *LONGER* IF YOU DON'T IDENTIFY YOURSELF *RIGHT NOW.*
I AM ONE WHO WILL TEACH YOU HOW TO *HARNESS* YOUR POWER SO YOU MAY WALK *AMONGST* THE PSI-LORDS.
THEN *ONE MILLION STRONG* WILL BE UNABLE TO STAND AGAINST YOU.
SCION...?
DIDN'T WE...WATCH YOU *DIE?*

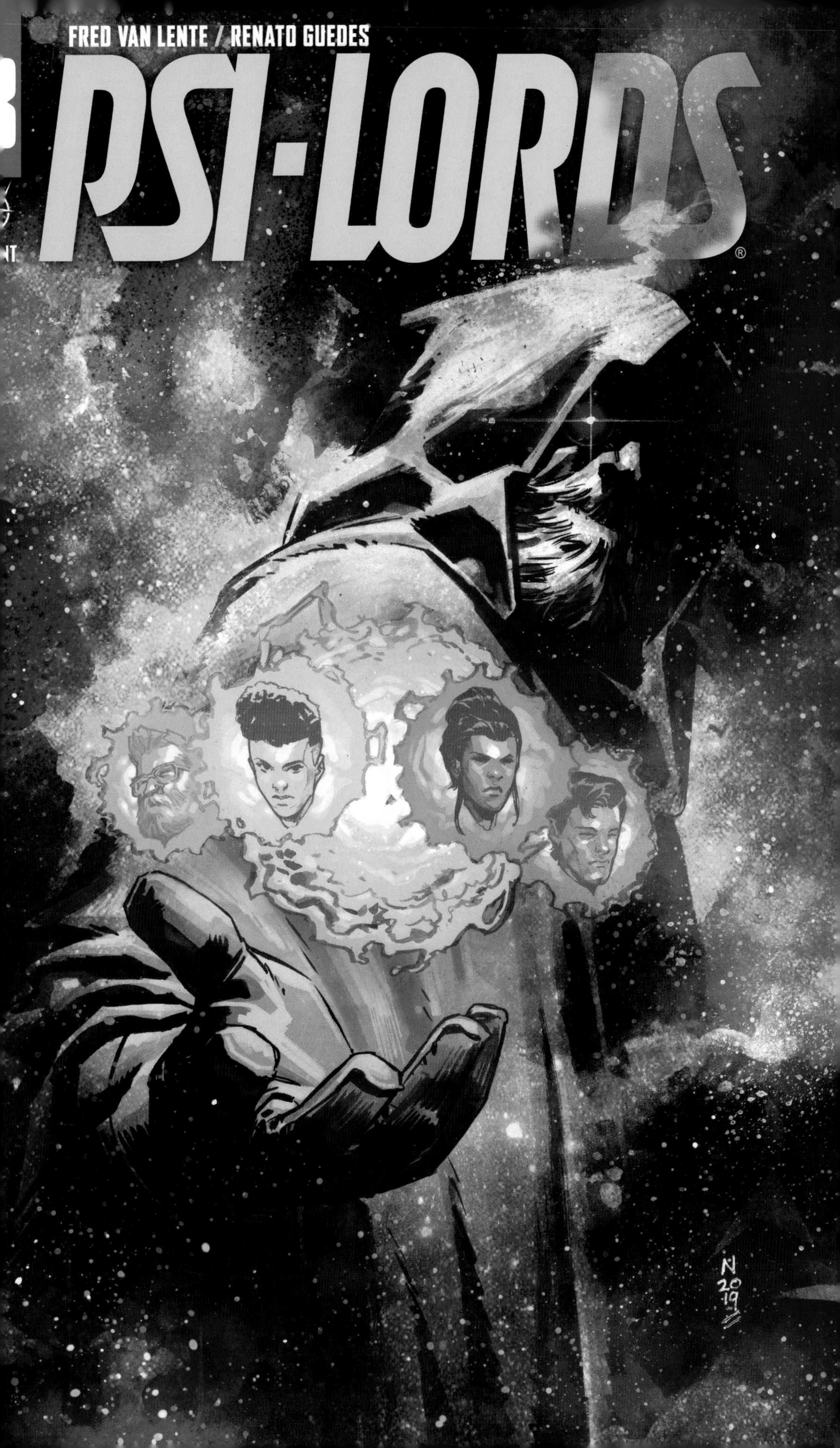
FRED VAN LENTE / RENATO GUEDES
PSI-LORDS®

**PSI-LORDS**
WRITER: Fred Van Len
ARTIST: Renato Gued
LETTERER: Dave Shar
COVER ARTIST: Nic Kl
ASSISTANT EDITOR: Drew Baumgartn
EDITOR: David Menc

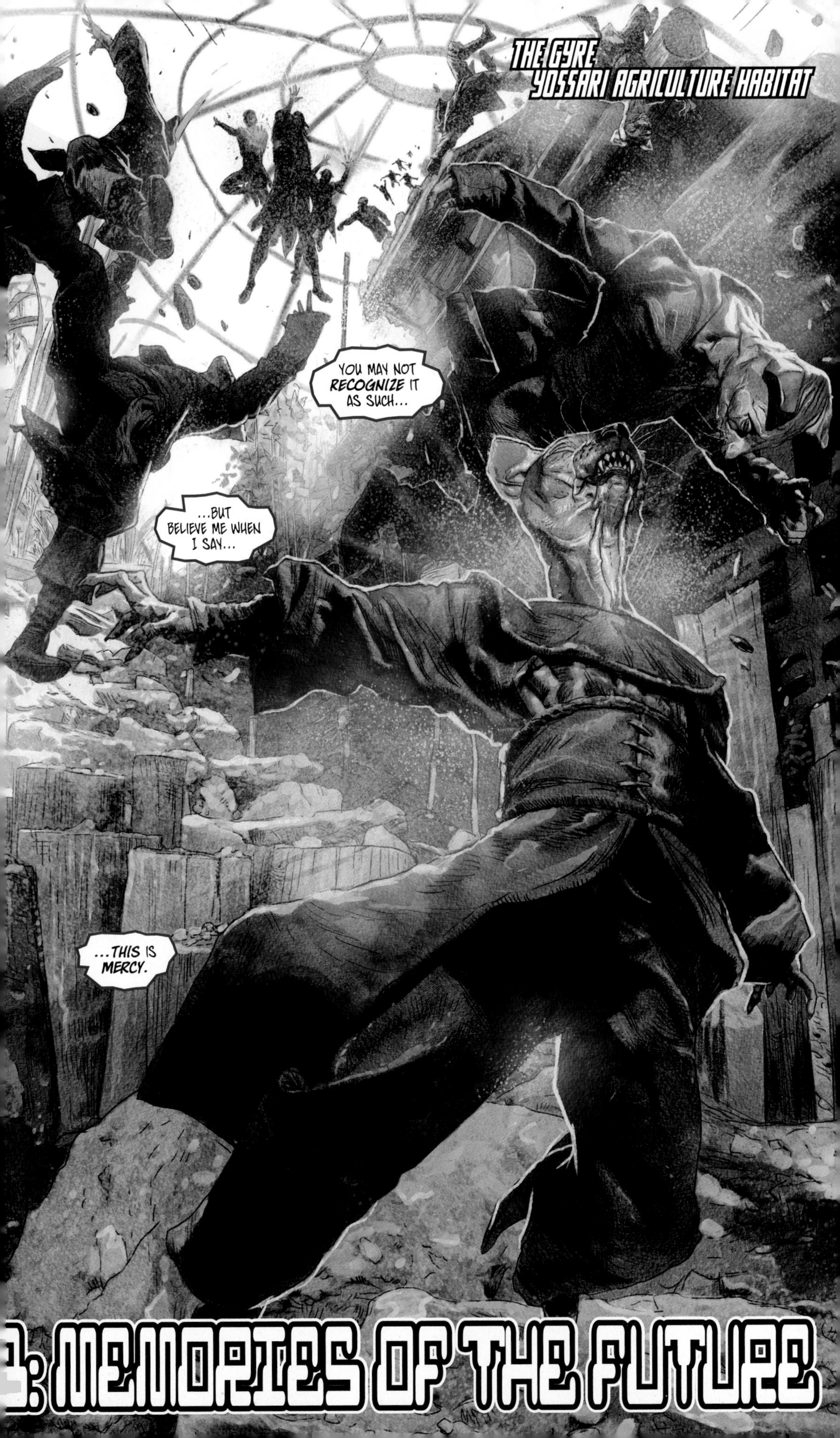
THE GYRE
YOSSARI AGRICULTURE HABITAT
YOU MAY NOT RECOGNIZE IT AS SUCH...
...BUT BELIEVE ME WHEN I SAY...
...THIS IS MERCY.
1: MEMORIES OF THE FUTURE

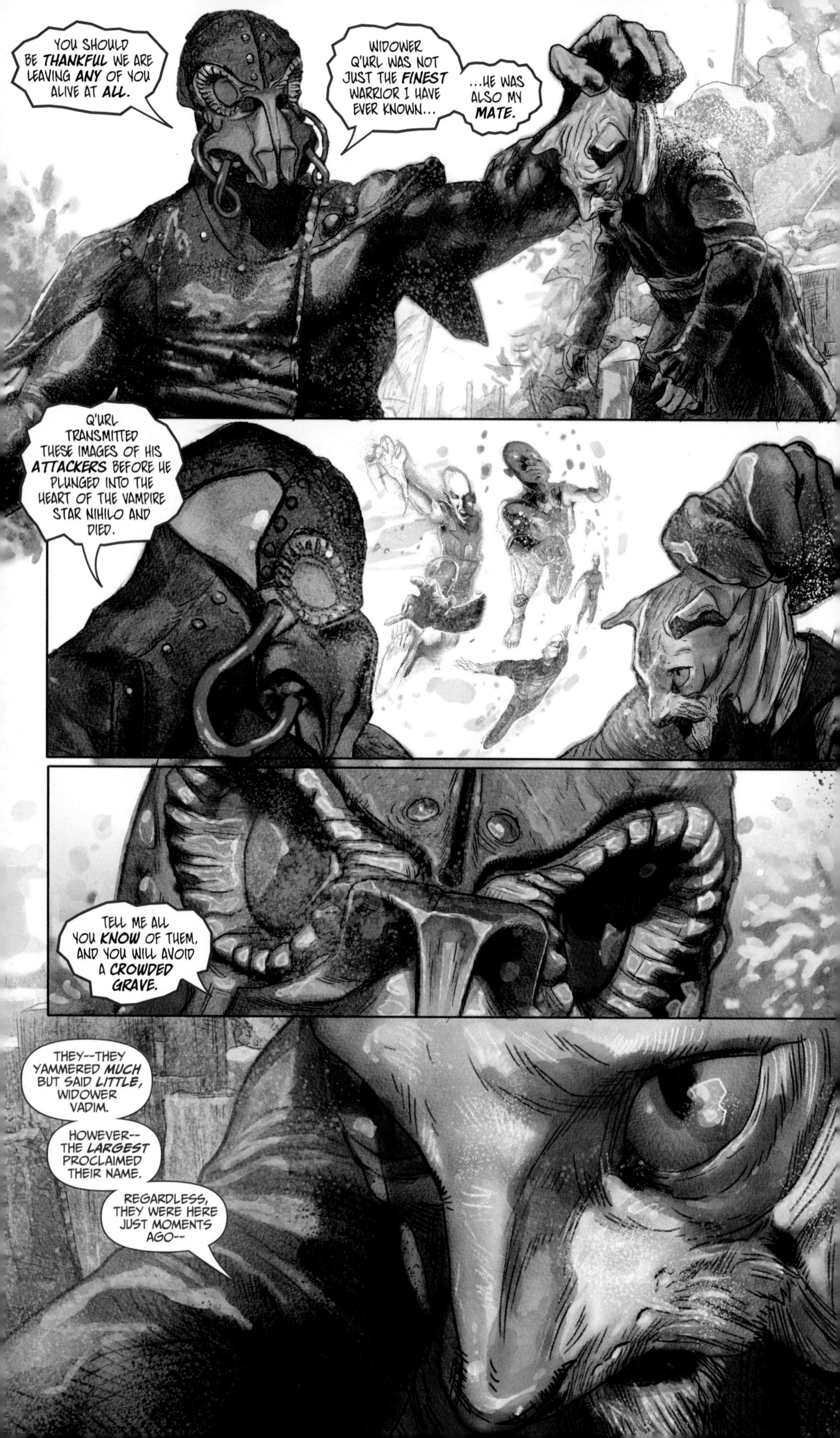
YOU SHOULD BE **THANKFUL** WE ARE LEAVING **ANY** OF YOU ALIVE AT **ALL.**
WIDOWER Q'URL WAS NOT JUST THE **FINEST** WARRIOR I HAVE EVER KNOWN...
...HE WAS ALSO MY **MATE.**
Q'URL TRANSMITTED THESE IMAGES OF HIS **ATTACKERS** BEFORE HE PLUNGED INTO THE HEART OF THE VAMPIRE STAR NIHILO AND DIED.
TELL ME ALL YOU **KNOW** OF THEM, AND YOU WILL AVOID A **CROWDED GRAVE.**
THEY--THEY YAMMERED *MUCH* BUT SAID *LITTLE,* WIDOWER VADIM.
HOWEVER-- THE *LARGEST* PROCLAIMED THEIR NAME.
REGARDLESS, THEY WERE HERE JUST MOMENTS AGO--

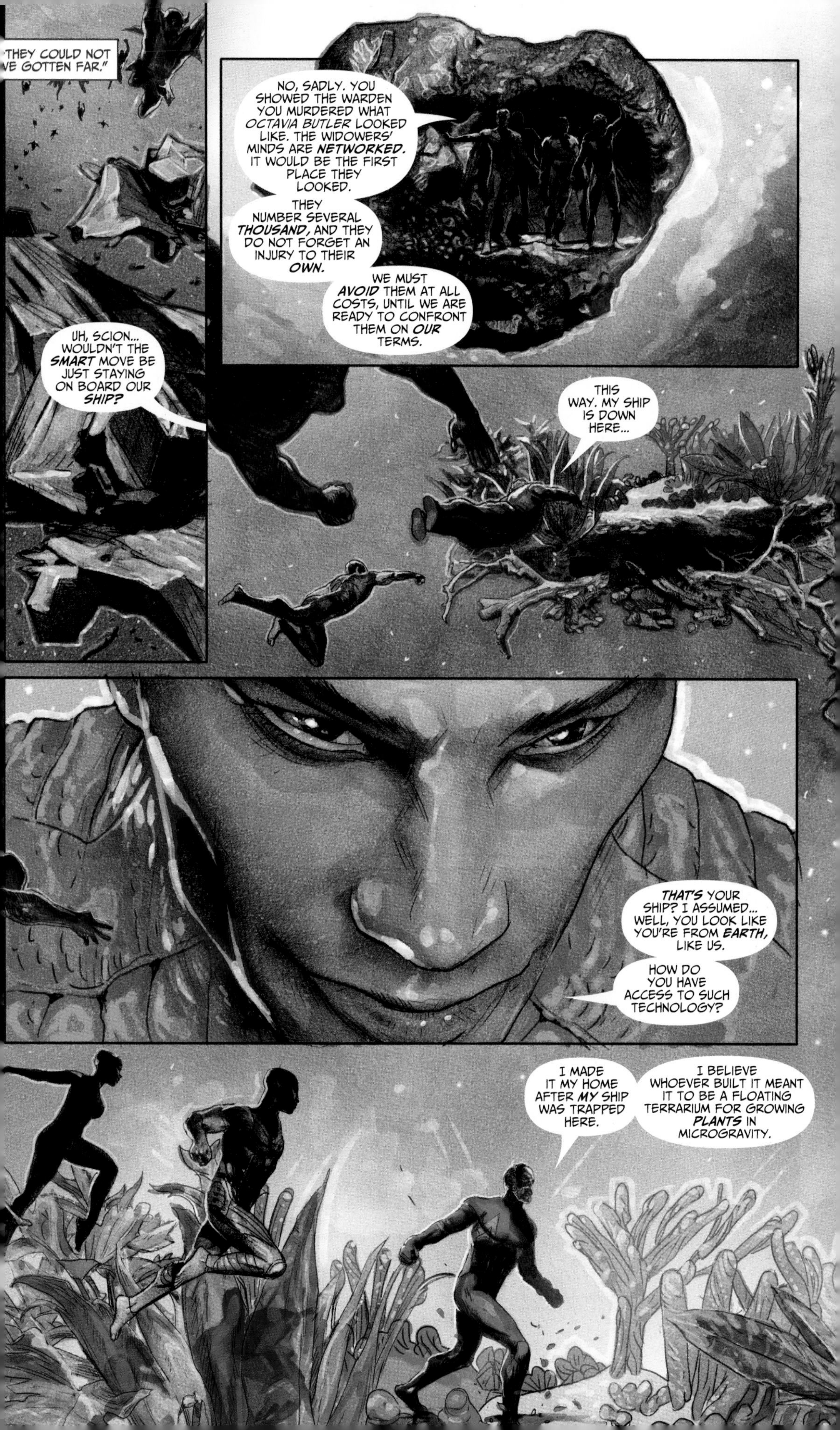
"THEY COULD NOT VE GOTTEN FAR."
NO, SADLY. YOU SHOWED THE WARDEN YOU MURDERED WHAT *OCTAVIA BUTLER* LOOKED LIKE. THE WIDOWERS' MINDS ARE ***NETWORKED.*** IT WOULD BE THE FIRST PLACE THEY LOOKED.
THEY NUMBER SEVERAL ***THOUSAND,*** AND THEY DO NOT FORGET AN INJURY TO THEIR ***OWN.***
WE MUST ***AVOID*** THEM AT ALL COSTS, UNTIL WE ARE READY TO CONFRONT THEM ON ***OUR*** TERMS.
UH, SCION... WOULDN'T THE ***SMART*** MOVE BE JUST STAYING ON BOARD OUR ***SHIP?***
THIS WAY. MY SHIP IS DOWN HERE...
***THAT'S*** YOUR SHIP? I ASSUMED... WELL, YOU LOOK LIKE YOU'RE FROM ***EARTH,*** LIKE US.
HOW DO YOU HAVE ACCESS TO SUCH TECHNOLOGY?
I MADE IT MY HOME AFTER ***MY*** SHIP WAS TRAPPED HERE.
I BELIEVE WHOEVER BUILT IT MEANT IT TO BE A FLOATING TERRARIUM FOR GROWING ***PLANTS*** IN MICROGRAVITY.

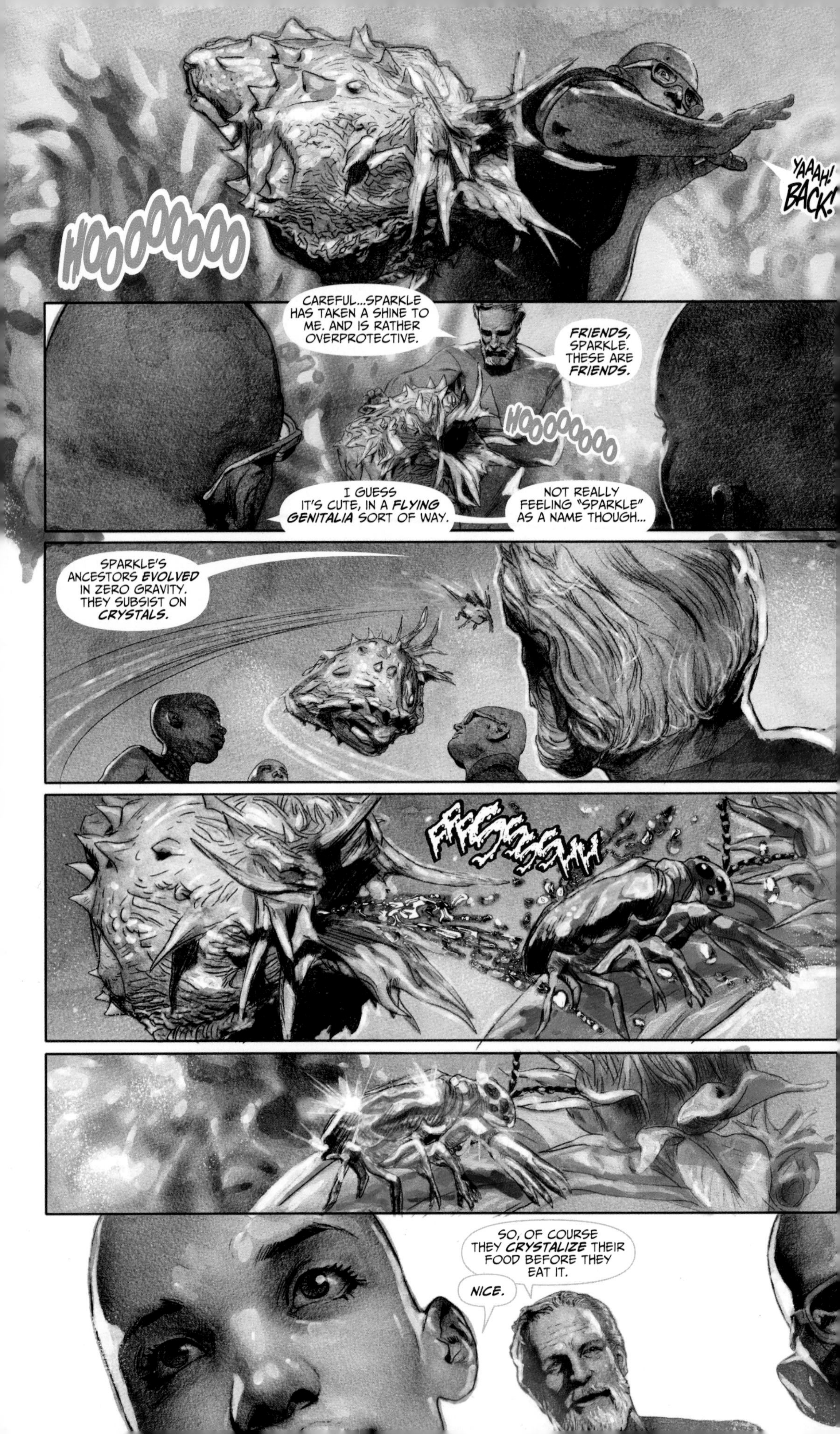
YAAAH! BACK!
HOOOOOOOOO
CAREFUL...SPARKLE HAS TAKEN A SHINE TO ME. AND IS RATHER OVERPROTECTIVE.
FRIENDS, SPARKLE. THESE ARE FRIENDS.
HOOOOOOOOO
I GUESS IT'S CUTE, IN A FLYING GENITALIA SORT OF WAY.
NOT REALLY FEELING "SPARKLE" AS A NAME THOUGH...
SPARKLE'S ANCESTORS EVOLVED IN ZERO GRAVITY. THEY SUBSIST ON CRYSTALS.
FFFSSSSHH
SO, OF COURSE THEY CRYSTALIZE THEIR FOOD BEFORE THEY EAT IT.
NICE.

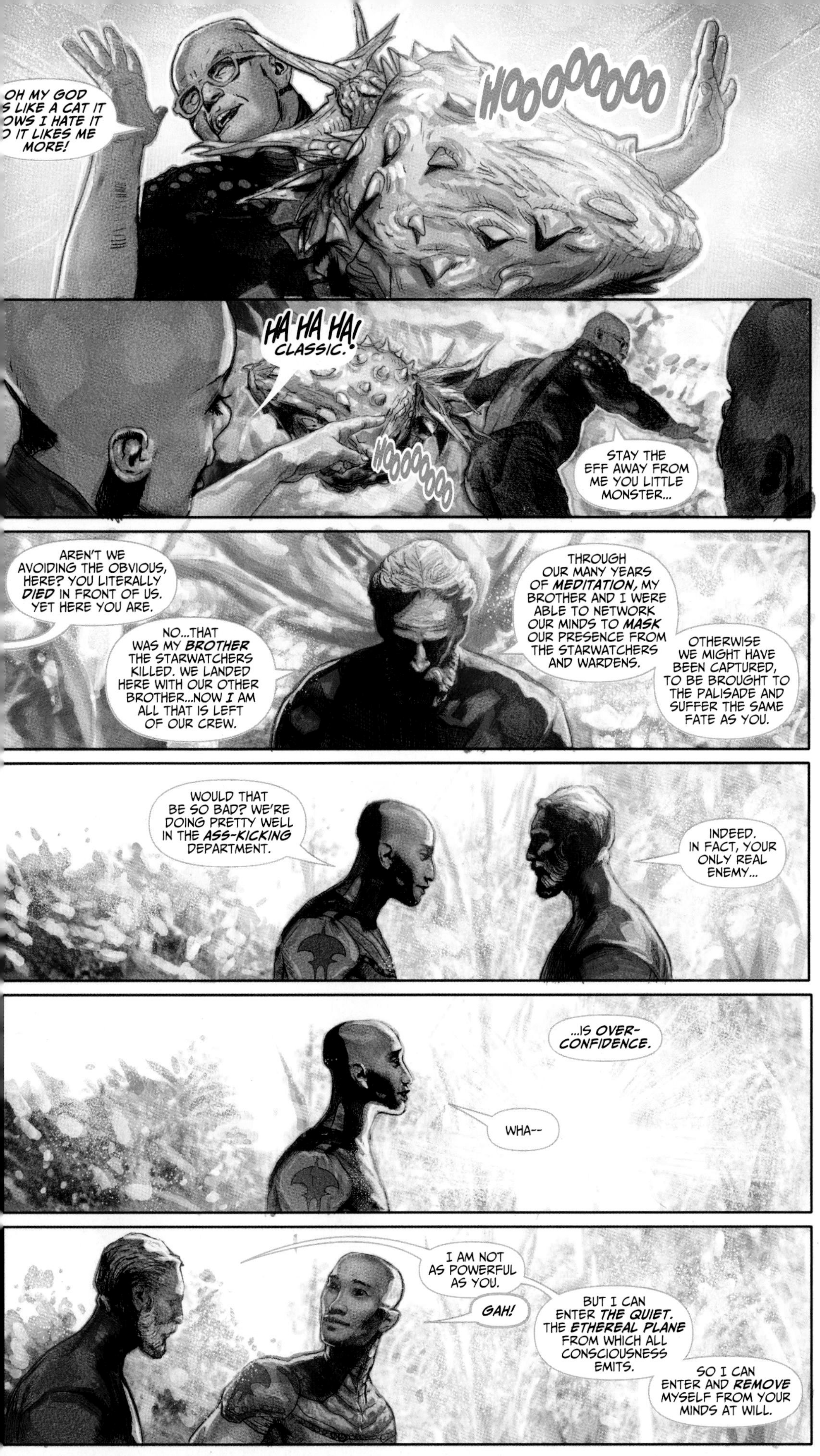
OH MY GOD
S LIKE A CAT IT
OWS I HATE IT
O IT LIKES ME
MORE!
HOOOOOOOOO
HA HA HA! CLASSIC.
HOOOOOOOO
STAY THE EFF AWAY FROM ME YOU LITTLE MONSTER...
AREN'T WE AVOIDING THE OBVIOUS, HERE? YOU LITERALLY DIED IN FRONT OF US. YET HERE YOU ARE.
NO...THAT WAS MY BROTHER THE STARWATCHERS KILLED. WE LANDED HERE WITH OUR OTHER BROTHER...NOW I AM ALL THAT IS LEFT OF OUR CREW.
THROUGH OUR MANY YEARS OF MEDITATION, MY BROTHER AND I WERE ABLE TO NETWORK OUR MINDS TO MASK OUR PRESENCE FROM THE STARWATCHERS AND WARDENS.
OTHERWISE WE MIGHT HAVE BEEN CAPTURED, TO BE BROUGHT TO THE PALISADE AND SUFFER THE SAME FATE AS YOU.
WOULD THAT BE SO BAD? WE'RE DOING PRETTY WELL IN THE ASS-KICKING DEPARTMENT.
INDEED. IN FACT, YOUR ONLY REAL ENEMY...
...IS OVER-CONFIDENCE.
WHA--
I AM NOT AS POWERFUL AS YOU.
GAH!
BUT I CAN ENTER THE QUIET. THE ETHEREAL PLANE FROM WHICH ALL CONSCIOUSNESS EMITS.
SO I CAN ENTER AND REMOVE MYSELF FROM YOUR MINDS AT WILL.

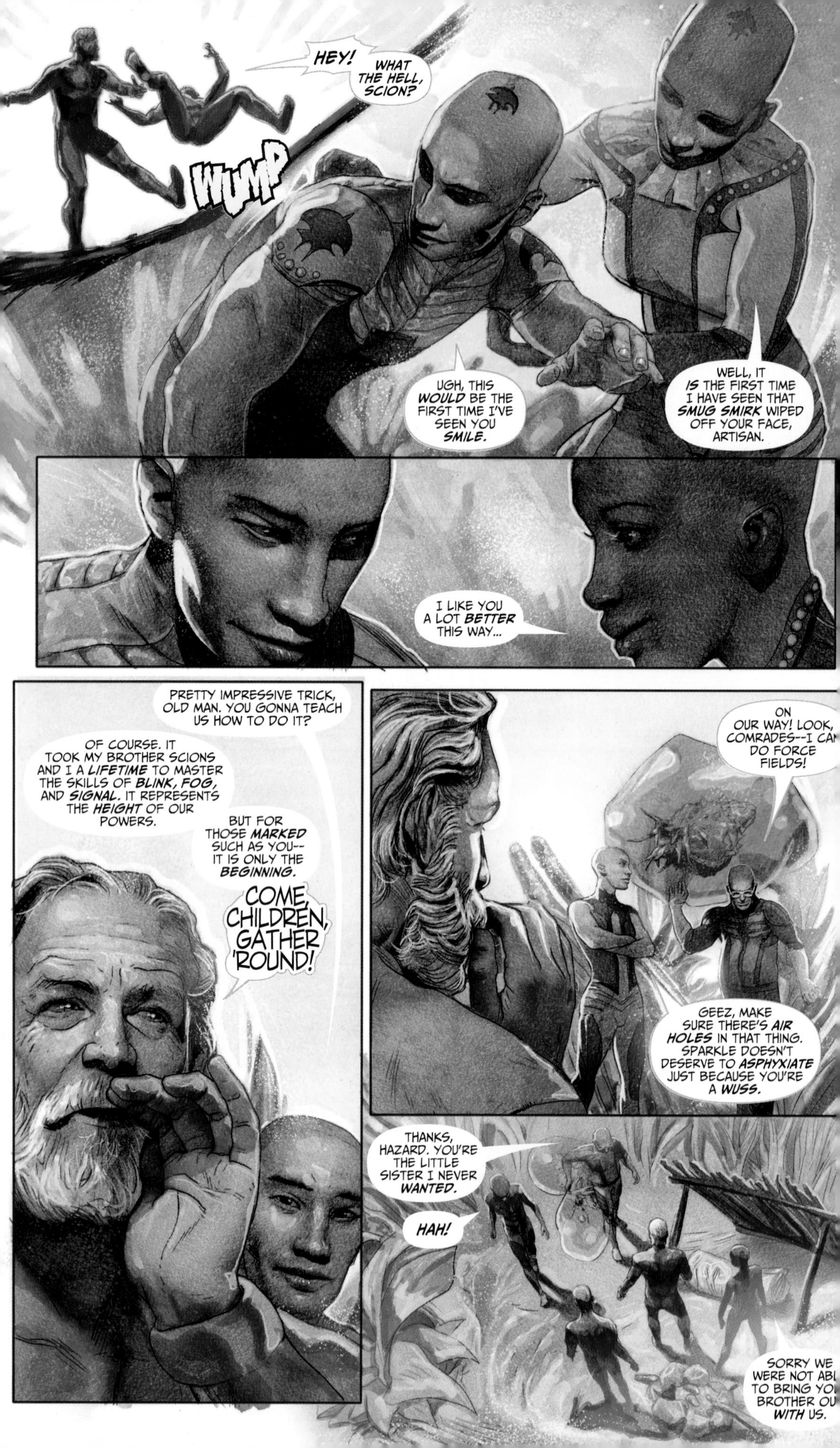

HEY!
WHAT THE HELL, SCION?
WUMP
UGH, THIS WOULD BE THE FIRST TIME I'VE SEEN YOU SMILE.
WELL, IT IS THE FIRST TIME I HAVE SEEN THAT SMUG SMIRK WIPED OFF YOUR FACE, ARTISAN.
I LIKE YOU A LOT BETTER THIS WAY...
PRETTY IMPRESSIVE TRICK, OLD MAN. YOU GONNA TEACH US HOW TO DO IT?
OF COURSE. IT TOOK MY BROTHER SCIONS AND I A LIFETIME TO MASTER THE SKILLS OF BLINK, FOG, AND SIGNAL. IT REPRESENTS THE HEIGHT OF OUR POWERS.
BUT FOR THOSE MARKED SUCH AS YOU-- IT IS ONLY THE BEGINNING.
COME, CHILDREN, GATHER 'ROUND!
ON OUR WAY! LOOK, COMRADES--I CA
DO FORCE FIELDS!
GEEZ, MAKE SURE THERE'S AIR HOLES IN THAT THING. SPARKLE DOESN'T DESERVE TO ASPHYXIATE JUST BECAUSE YOU'RE A WUSS.
THANKS, HAZARD. YOU'RE THE LITTLE SISTER I NEVER WANTED.
HAH!
SORRY WE WERE NOT ABL
TO BRING YO
BROTHER OU
WITH US.

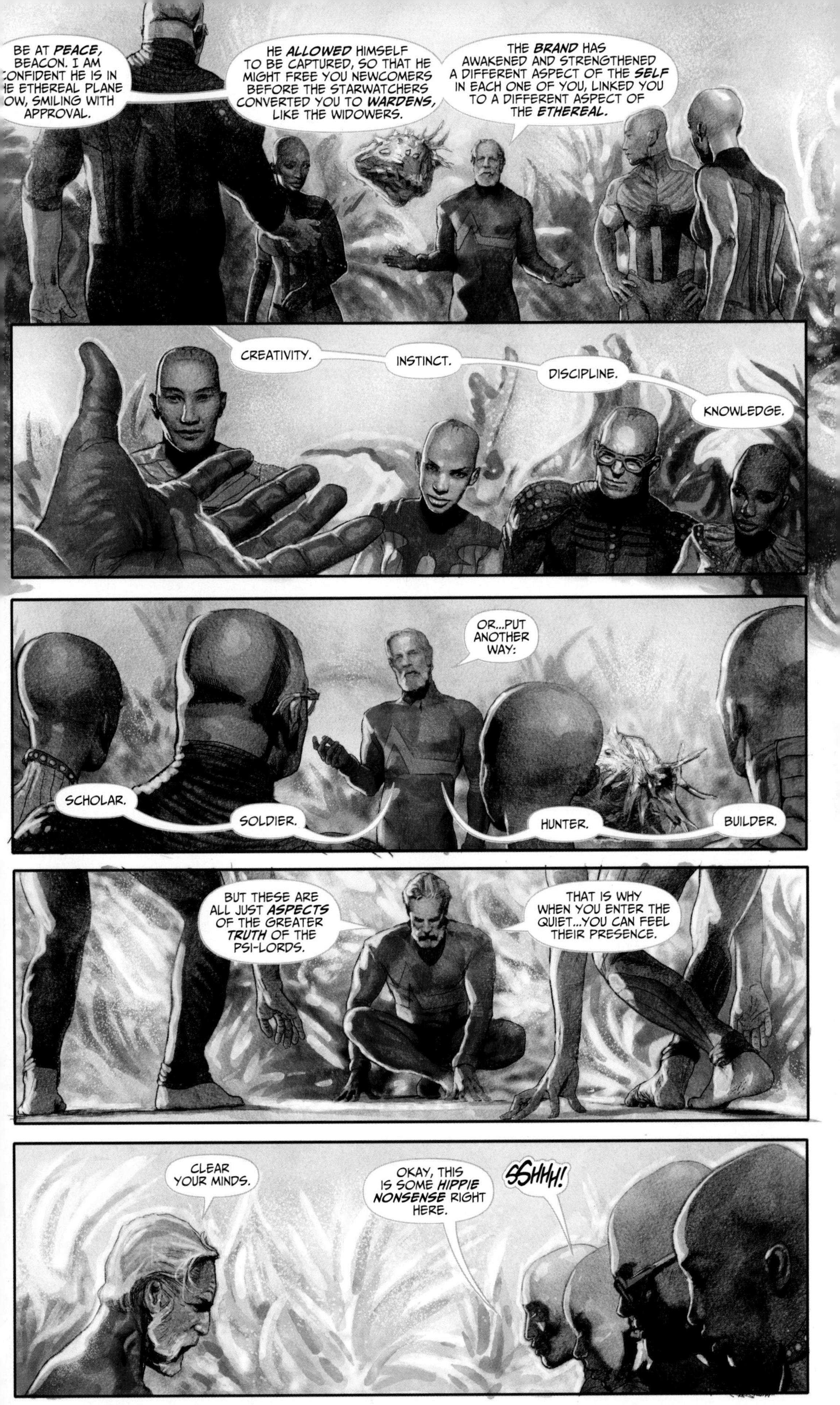
BE AT PEACE, BEACON. I AM CONFIDENT HE IS IN THE ETHEREAL PLANE NOW, SMILING WITH APPROVAL.
HE ALLOWED HIMSELF TO BE CAPTURED, SO THAT HE MIGHT FREE YOU NEWCOMERS BEFORE THE STARWATCHERS CONVERTED YOU TO WARDENS, LIKE THE WIDOWERS.
THE BRAND HAS AWAKENED AND STRENGTHENED A DIFFERENT ASPECT OF THE SELF IN EACH ONE OF YOU, LINKED YOU TO A DIFFERENT ASPECT OF THE ETHEREAL.
CREATIVITY.
INSTINCT.
DISCIPLINE.
KNOWLEDGE.
OR...PUT ANOTHER WAY:
SCHOLAR.
SOLDIER.
HUNTER.
BUILDER.
BUT THESE ARE ALL JUST ASPECTS OF THE GREATER TRUTH OF THE PSI-LORDS.
THAT IS WHY WHEN YOU ENTER THE QUIET...YOU CAN FEEL THEIR PRESENCE.
CLEAR YOUR MINDS.
OKAY, THIS IS SOME HIPPIE NONSENSE RIGHT HERE.
SSHHH!

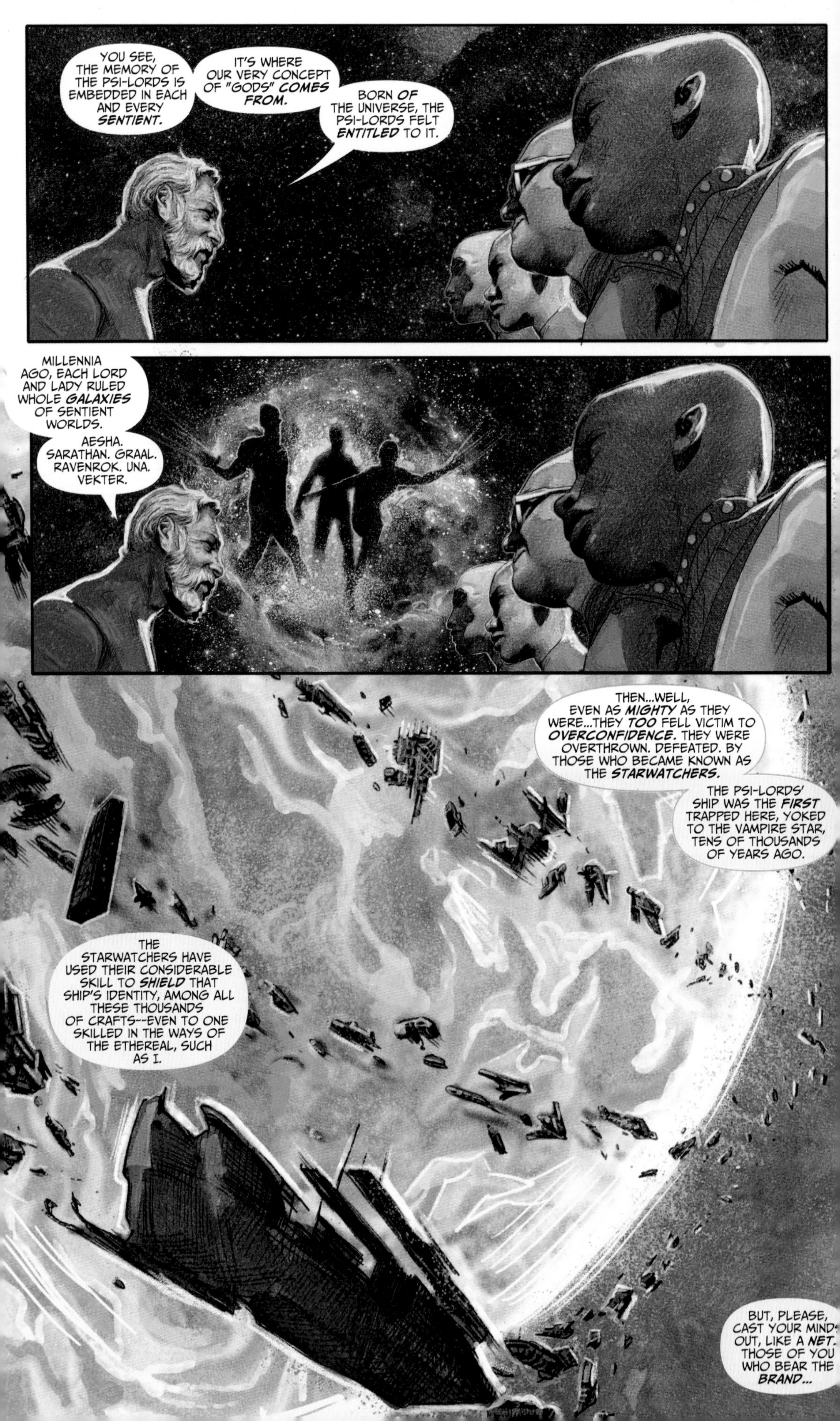

YOU SEE, THE MEMORY OF THE PSI-LORDS IS EMBEDDED IN EACH AND EVERY SENTIENT.
IT'S WHERE OUR VERY CONCEPT OF "GODS" COMES FROM.
BORN OF THE UNIVERSE, THE PSI-LORDS FELT ENTITLED TO IT.
MILLENNIA AGO, EACH LORD AND LADY RULED WHOLE GALAXIES OF SENTIENT WORLDS.
AESHA. SARATHAN. GRAAL. RAVENROK. UNA. VEKTER.
THEN...WELL, EVEN AS MIGHTY AS THEY WERE...THEY TOO FELL VICTIM TO OVERCONFIDENCE. THEY WERE OVERTHROWN. DEFEATED. BY THOSE WHO BECAME KNOWN AS THE STARWATCHERS.
THE PSI-LORDS' SHIP WAS THE FIRST TRAPPED HERE, YOKED TO THE VAMPIRE STAR, TENS OF THOUSANDS OF YEARS AGO.
THE STARWATCHERS HAVE USED THEIR CONSIDERABLE SKILL TO SHIELD THAT SHIP'S IDENTITY, AMONG ALL THESE THOUSANDS OF CRAFTS--EVEN TO ONE SKILLED IN THE WAYS OF THE ETHEREAL, SUCH AS I.
BUT, PLEASE, CAST YOUR MIND OUT, LIKE A NET. THOSE OF YOU WHO BEAR THE BRAND...

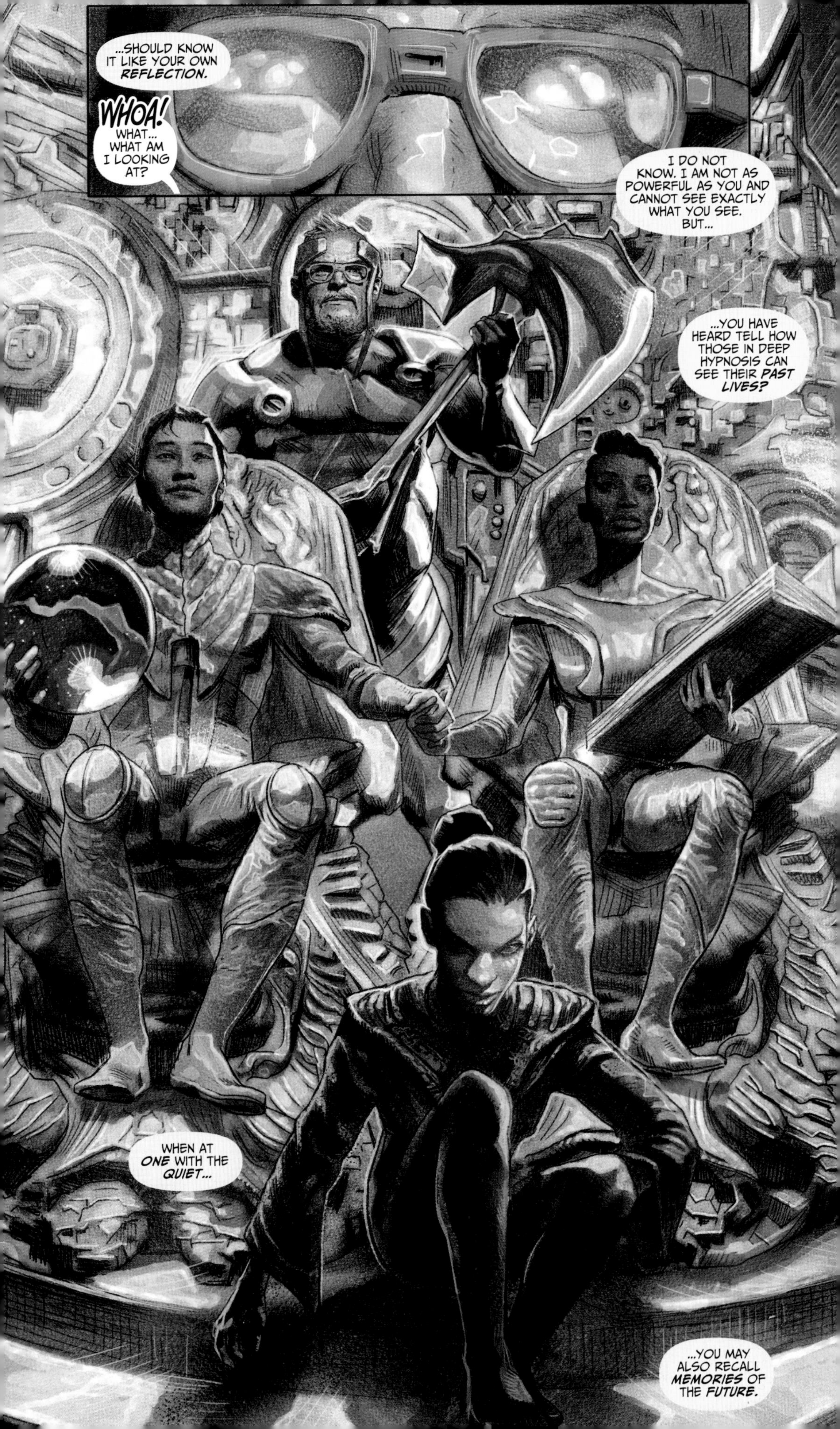
...SHOULD KNOW IT LIKE YOUR OWN *REFLECTION*.
WHOA! WHAT... WHAT AM I LOOKING AT?
I DO NOT KNOW. I AM NOT AS POWERFUL AS YOU AND CANNOT SEE EXACTLY WHAT YOU SEE. BUT...
...YOU HAVE HEARD TELL HOW THOSE IN DEEP HYPNOSIS CAN SEE THEIR *PAST LIVES?*
WHEN AT *ONE* WITH THE *QUIET*...
...YOU MAY ALSO RECALL *MEMORIES* OF THE *FUTURE*.

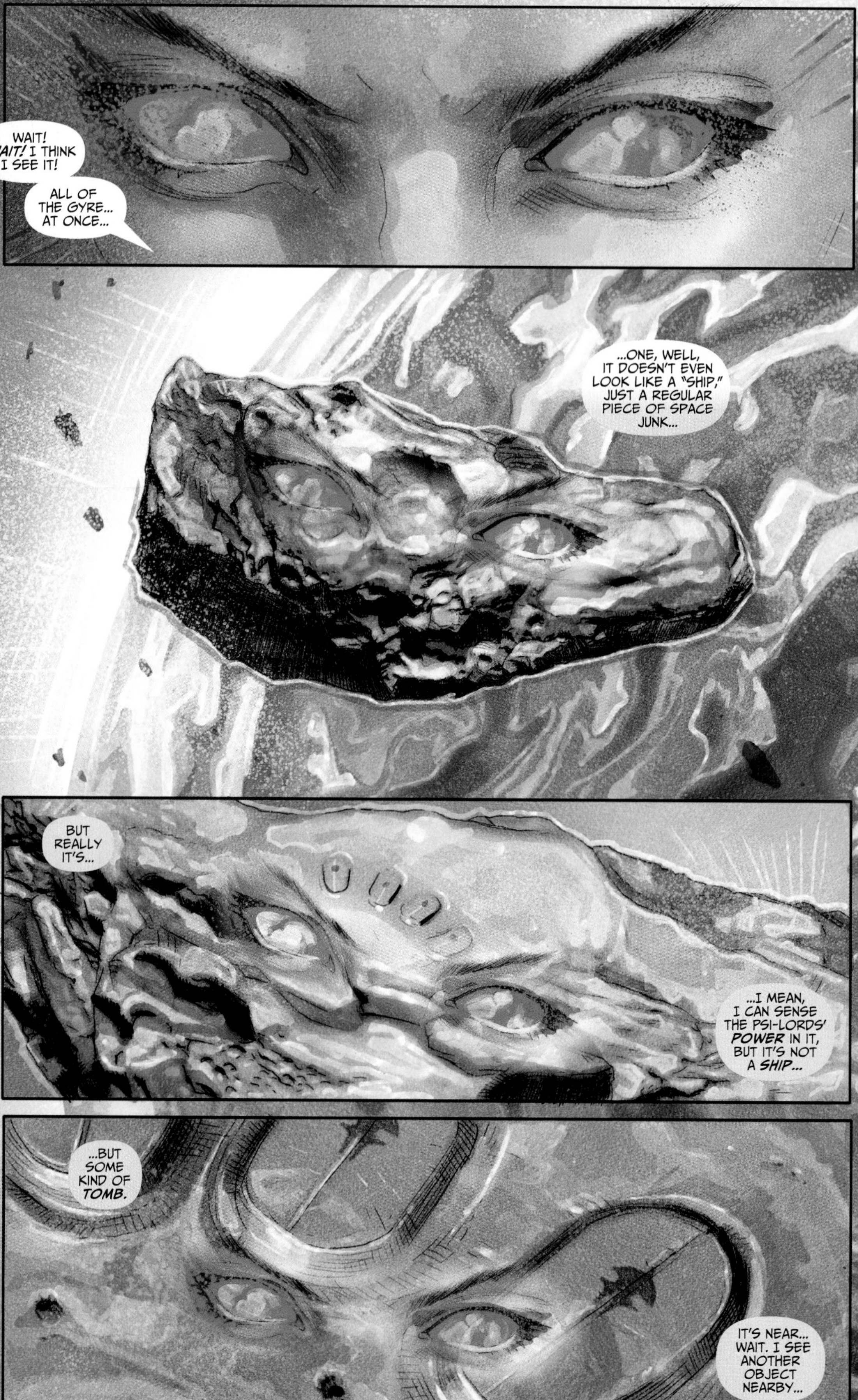
WAIT! WAIT! I THINK I SEE IT!
ALL OF THE GYRE... AT ONCE...
...ONE, WELL, IT DOESN'T EVEN LOOK LIKE A "SHIP," JUST A REGULAR PIECE OF SPACE JUNK...
BUT REALLY IT'S...
...I MEAN, I CAN SENSE THE PSI-LORDS' POWER IN IT, BUT IT'S NOT A SHIP...
...BUT SOME KIND OF TOMB.
IT'S NEAR... WAIT. I SEE ANOTHER OBJECT NEARBY...

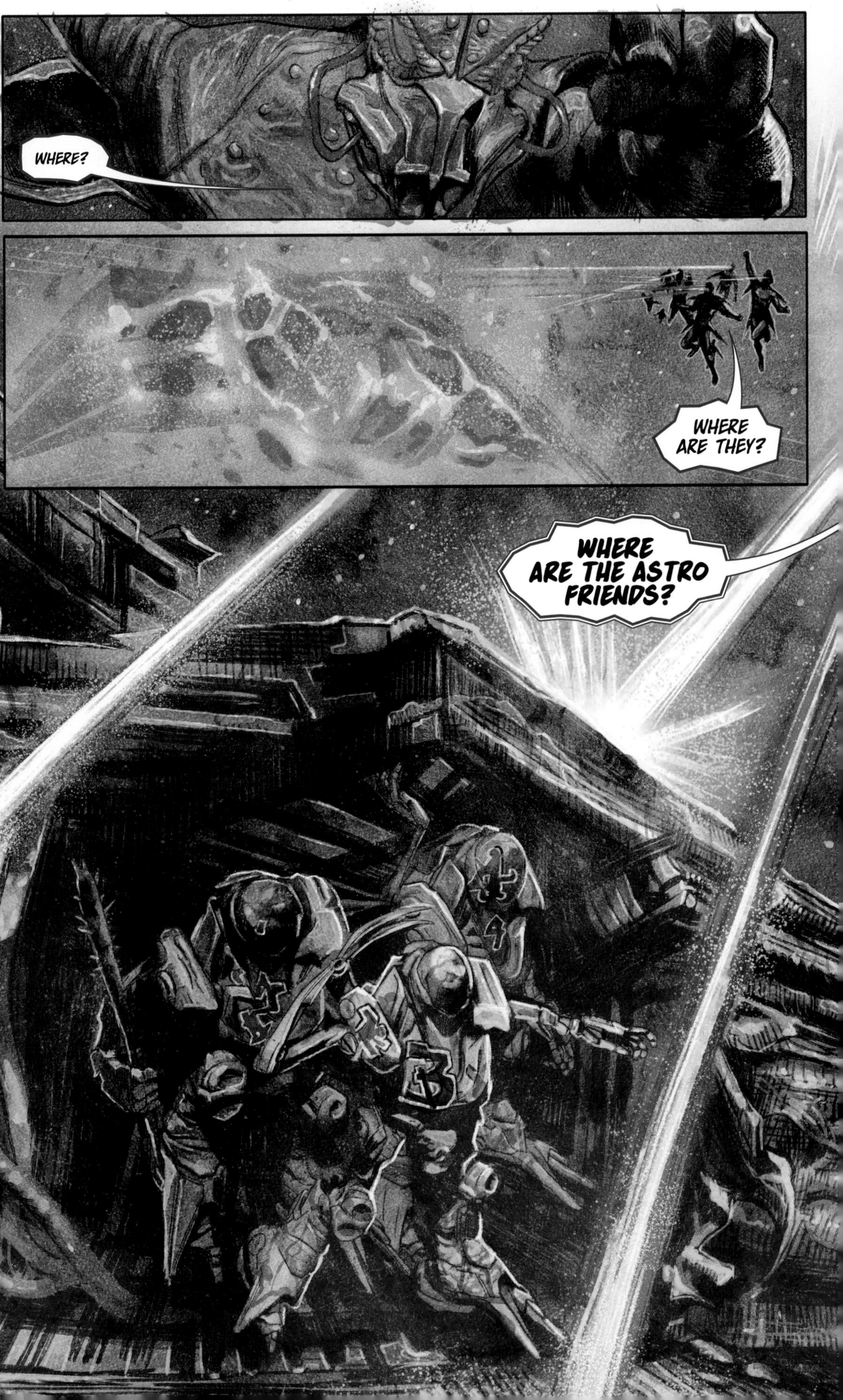
WHERE?
WHERE ARE THEY?
WHERE ARE THE ASTRO FRIENDS?

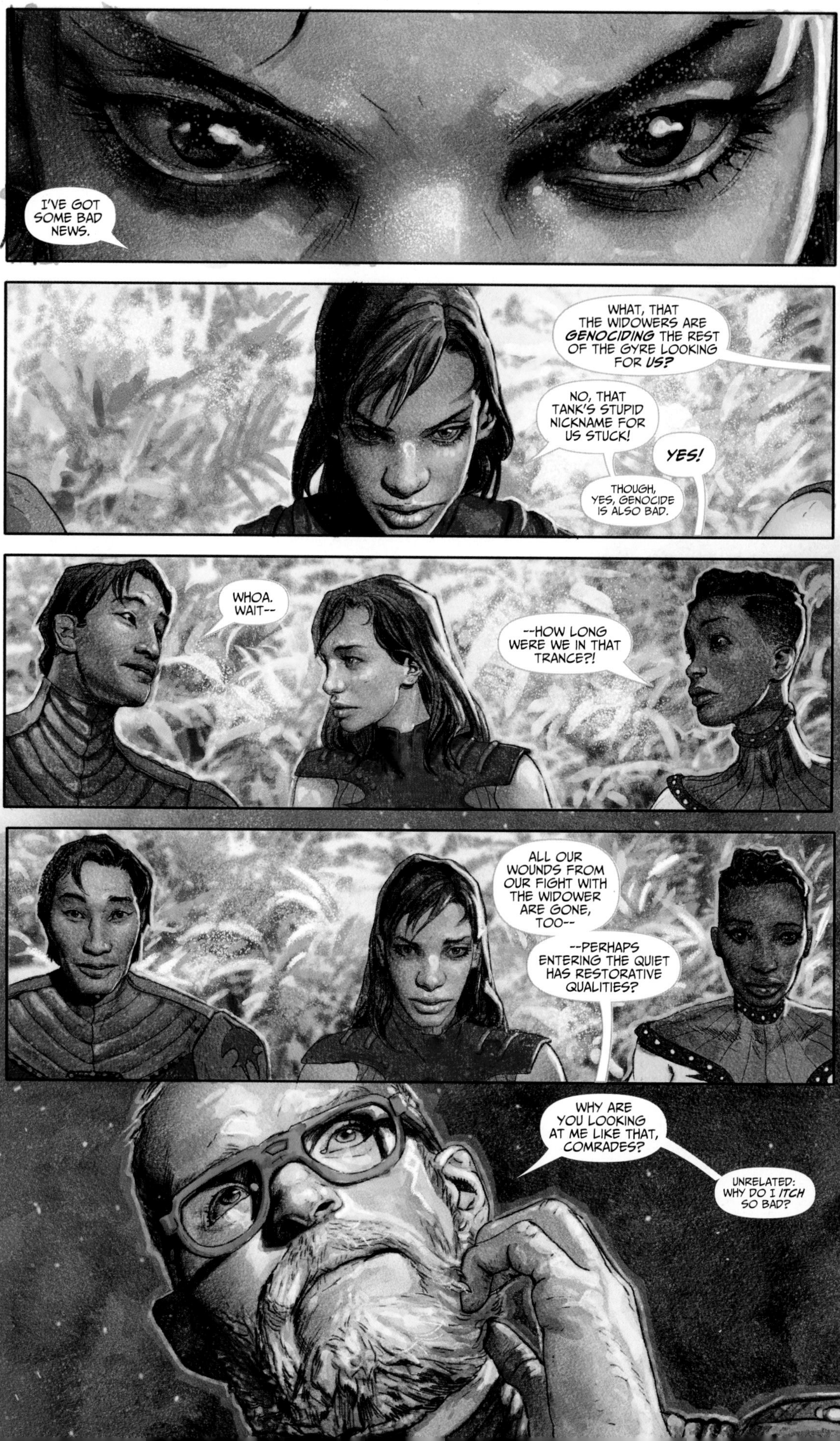
I'VE GOT SOME BAD NEWS.
WHAT, THAT THE WIDOWERS ARE GENOCIDING THE REST OF THE GYRE LOOKING FOR US?
NO, THAT TANK'S STUPID NICKNAME FOR US STUCK!
YES!
THOUGH, YES, GENOCIDE IS ALSO BAD.
WHOA. WAIT--
--HOW LONG WERE WE IN THAT TRANCE?!
ALL OUR WOUNDS FROM OUR FIGHT WITH THE WIDOWER ARE GONE, TOO--
--PERHAPS ENTERING THE QUIET HAS RESTORATIVE QUALITIES?
WHY ARE YOU LOOKING AT ME LIKE THAT, COMRADES?
UNRELATED: WHY DO I ITCH SO BAD?

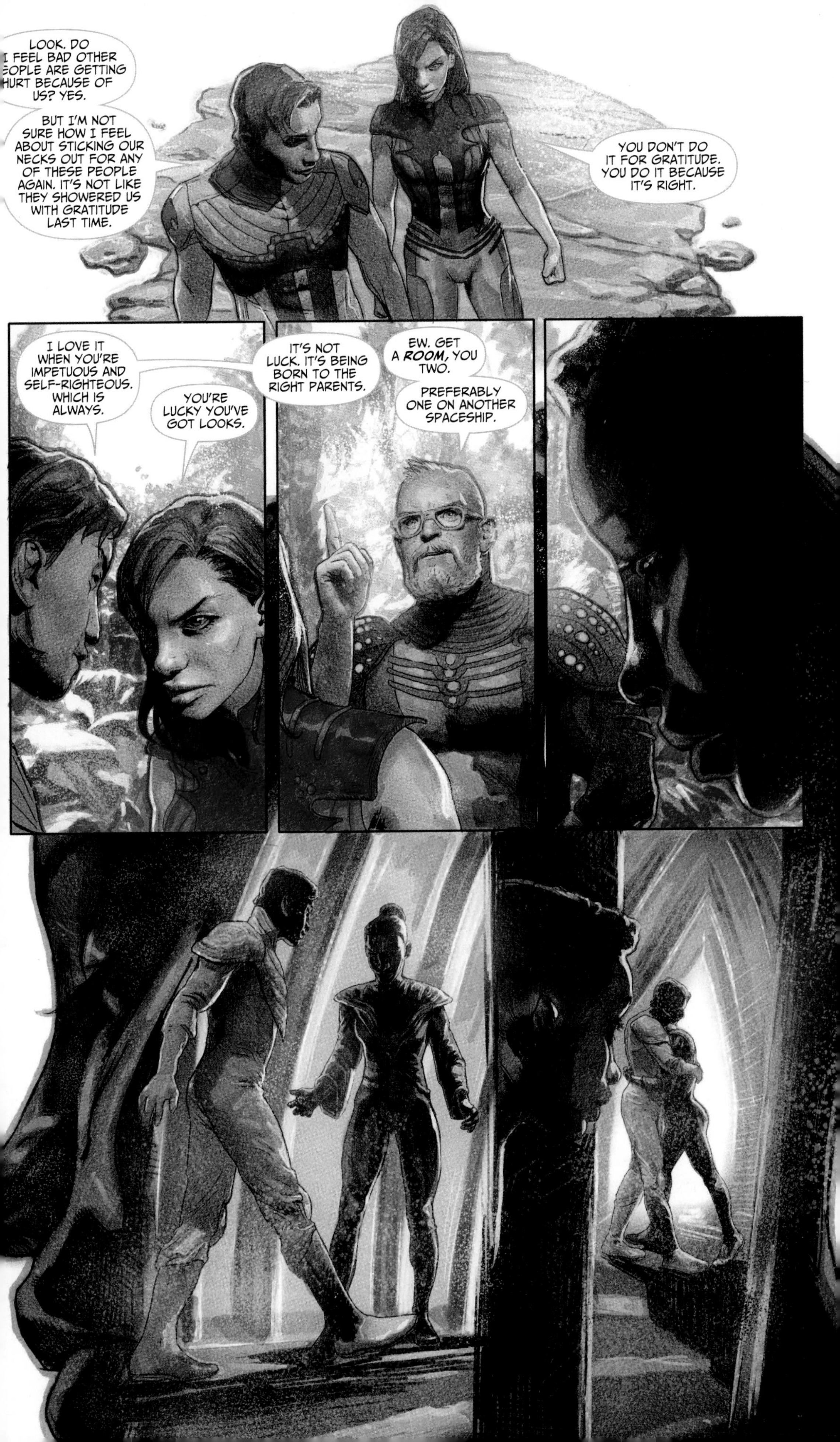
LOOK. DO I FEEL BAD OTHER PEOPLE ARE GETTING HURT BECAUSE OF US? YES.
BUT I'M NOT SURE HOW I FEEL ABOUT STICKING OUR NECKS OUT FOR ANY OF THESE PEOPLE AGAIN. IT'S NOT LIKE THEY SHOWERED US WITH GRATITUDE LAST TIME.
YOU DON'T DO IT FOR GRATITUDE. YOU DO IT BECAUSE IT'S RIGHT.
I LOVE IT WHEN YOU'RE IMPETUOUS AND SELF-RIGHTEOUS. WHICH IS ALWAYS.
YOU'RE LUCKY YOU'VE GOT LOOKS.
IT'S NOT LUCK. IT'S BEING BORN TO THE RIGHT PARENTS.
EW. GET A ROOM, YOU TWO.
PREFERABLY ONE ON ANOTHER SPACESHIP.

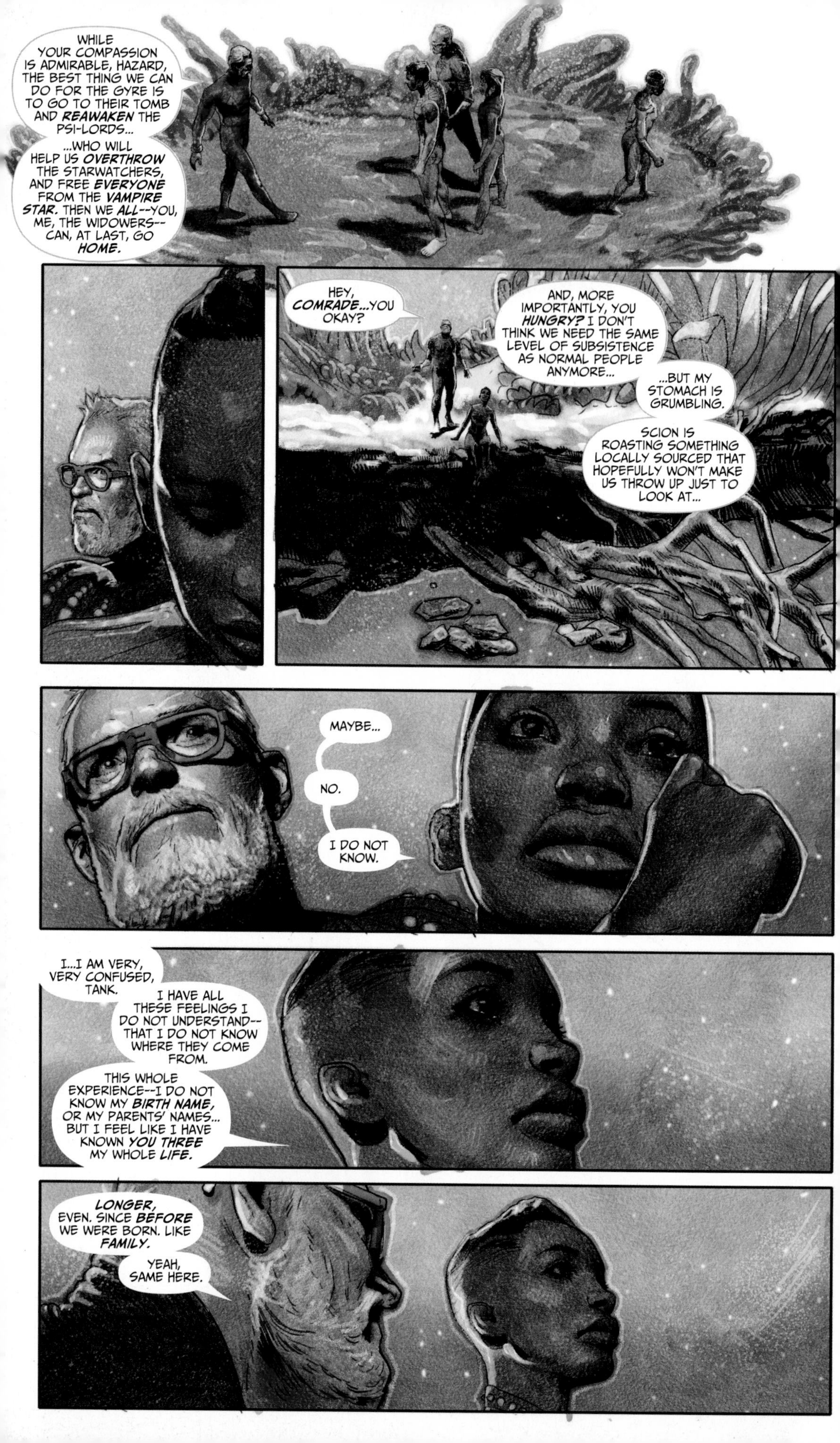
WHILE YOUR COMPASSION IS ADMIRABLE, HAZARD, THE BEST THING WE CAN DO FOR THE GYRE IS TO GO TO THEIR TOMB AND REAWAKEN THE PSI-LORDS...
...WHO WILL HELP US OVERTHROW THE STARWATCHERS, AND FREE EVERYONE FROM THE VAMPIRE STAR. THEN WE ALL--YOU, ME, THE WIDOWERS--CAN, AT LAST, GO HOME.
HEY, COMRADE...YOU OKAY?
AND, MORE IMPORTANTLY, YOU HUNGRY? I DON'T THINK WE NEED THE SAME LEVEL OF SUBSISTENCE AS NORMAL PEOPLE ANYMORE...
...BUT MY STOMACH IS GRUMBLING.
SCION IS ROASTING SOMETHING LOCALLY SOURCED THAT HOPEFULLY WON'T MAKE US THROW UP JUST TO LOOK AT...
MAYBE...
NO.
I DO NOT KNOW.
I...I AM VERY, VERY CONFUSED, TANK.
I HAVE ALL THESE FEELINGS I DO NOT UNDERSTAND--THAT I DO NOT KNOW WHERE THEY COME FROM.
THIS WHOLE EXPERIENCE--I DO NOT KNOW MY BIRTH NAME, OR MY PARENTS' NAMES... BUT I FEEL LIKE I HAVE KNOWN YOU THREE MY WHOLE LIFE.
LONGER, EVEN. SINCE BEFORE WE WERE BORN. LIKE FAMILY.
YEAH, SAME HERE.

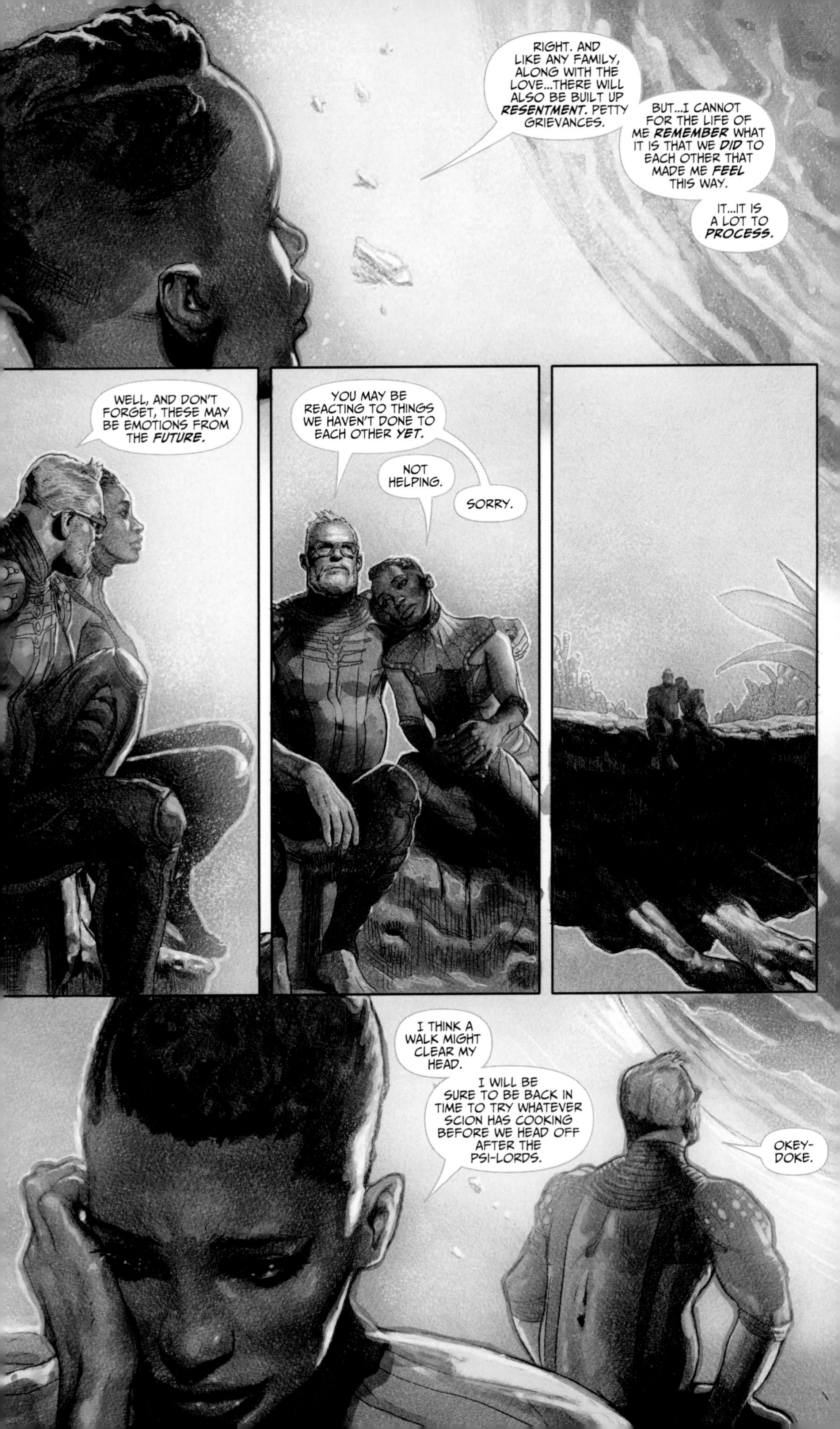
RIGHT. AND LIKE ANY FAMILY, ALONG WITH THE LOVE...THERE WILL ALSO BE BUILT UP RESENTMENT. PETTY GRIEVANCES.
BUT...I CANNOT FOR THE LIFE OF ME REMEMBER WHAT IT IS THAT WE DID TO EACH OTHER THAT MADE ME FEEL THIS WAY.
IT...IT IS A LOT TO PROCESS.
WELL, AND DON'T FORGET, THESE MAY BE EMOTIONS FROM THE FUTURE.
YOU MAY BE REACTING TO THINGS WE HAVEN'T DONE TO EACH OTHER YET.
NOT HELPING.
SORRY.
I THINK A WALK MIGHT CLEAR MY HEAD.
I WILL BE SURE TO BE BACK IN TIME TO TRY WHATEVER SCION HAS COOKING BEFORE WE HEAD OFF AFTER THE PSI-LORDS.
OKEY-DOKE.

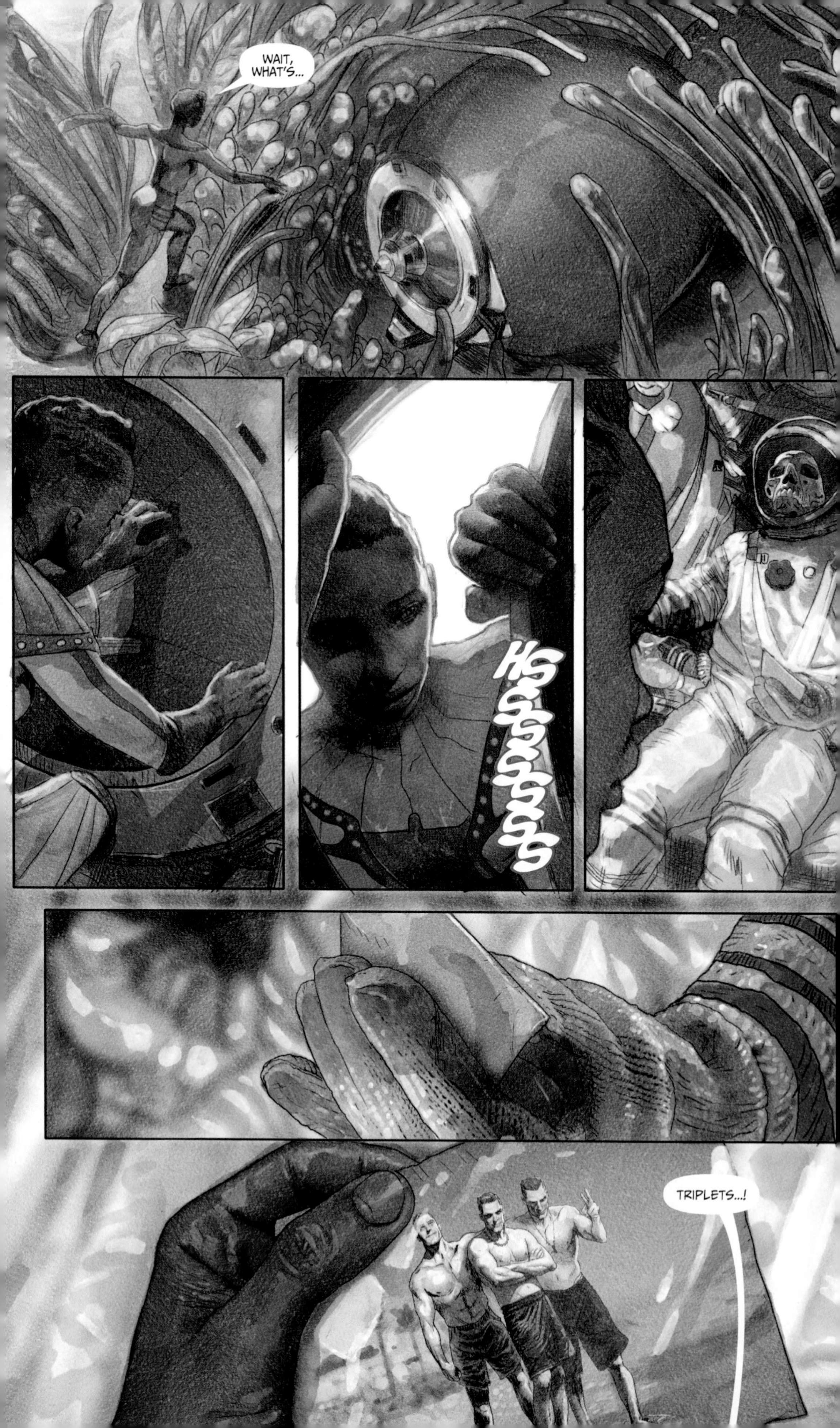
WAIT, WHAT'S...
HSSSSSSSSS
TRIPLETS...!

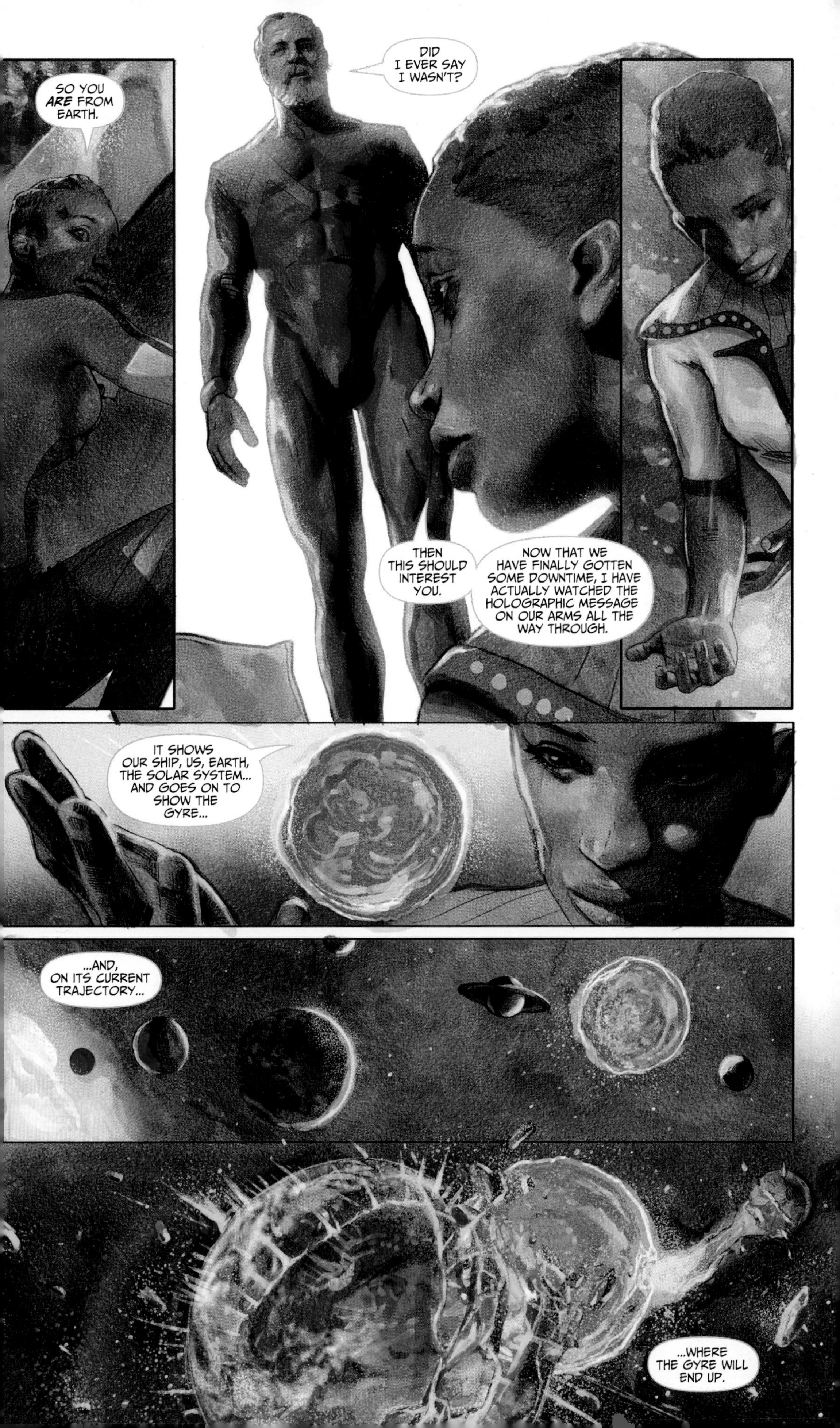
SO YOU ARE FROM EARTH.
DID I EVER SAY I WASN'T?
THEN THIS SHOULD INTEREST YOU.
NOW THAT WE HAVE FINALLY GOTTEN SOME DOWNTIME, I HAVE ACTUALLY WATCHED THE HOLOGRAPHIC MESSAGE ON OUR ARMS ALL THE WAY THROUGH.
IT SHOWS OUR SHIP, US, EARTH, THE SOLAR SYSTEM... AND GOES ON TO SHOW THE GYRE...
...AND, ON ITS CURRENT TRAJECTORY...
...WHERE THE GYRE WILL END UP.

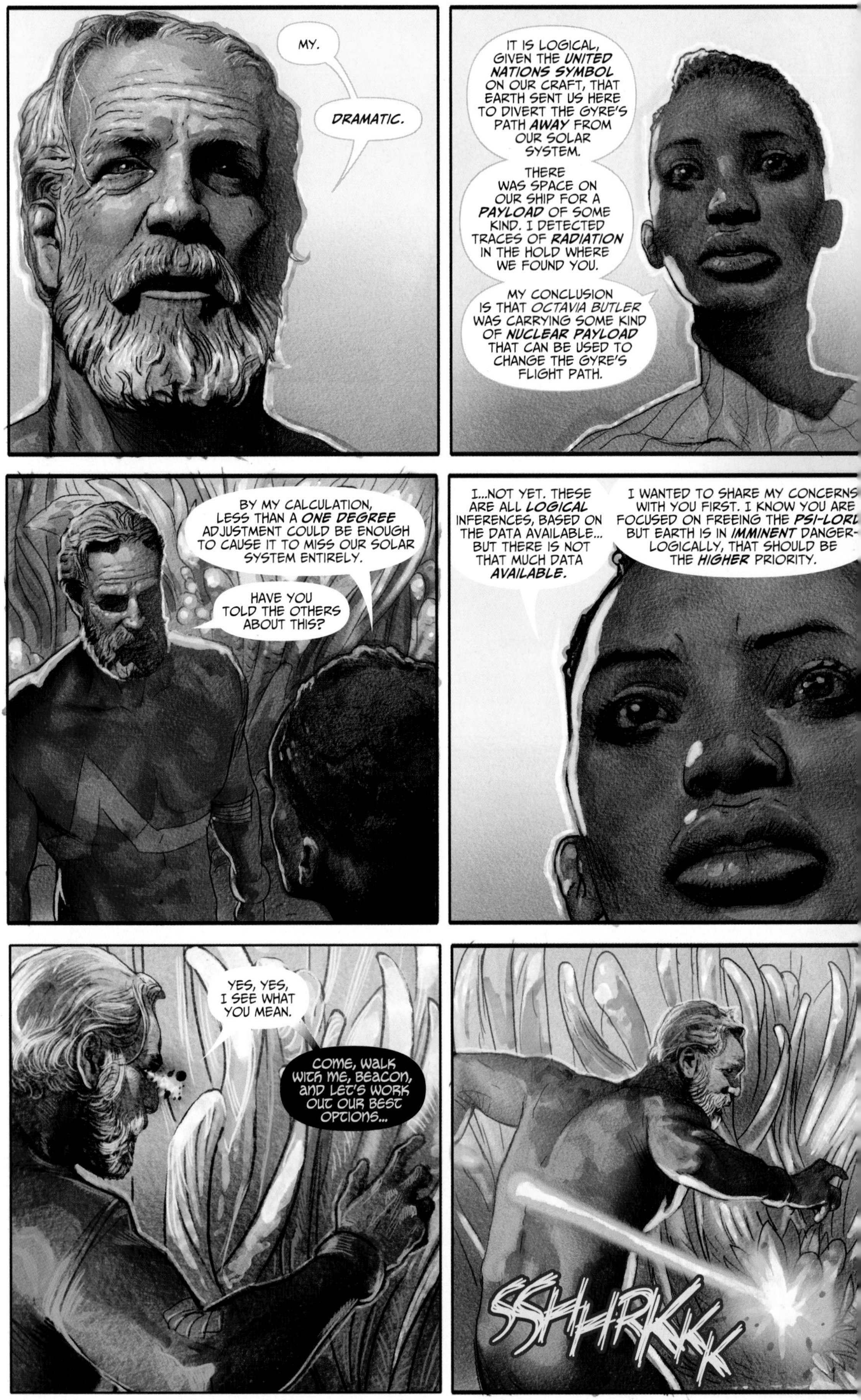
MY.
DRAMATIC.
IT IS LOGICAL, GIVEN THE UNITED NATIONS SYMBOL ON OUR CRAFT, THAT EARTH SENT US HERE TO DIVERT THE GYRE'S PATH AWAY FROM OUR SOLAR SYSTEM.
THERE WAS SPACE ON OUR SHIP FOR A PAYLOAD OF SOME KIND. I DETECTED TRACES OF RADIATION IN THE HOLD WHERE WE FOUND YOU.
MY CONCLUSION IS THAT OCTAVIA BUTLER WAS CARRYING SOME KIND OF NUCLEAR PAYLOAD THAT CAN BE USED TO CHANGE THE GYRE'S FLIGHT PATH.
BY MY CALCULATION, LESS THAN A ONE DEGREE ADJUSTMENT COULD BE ENOUGH TO CAUSE IT TO MISS OUR SOLAR SYSTEM ENTIRELY.
HAVE YOU TOLD THE OTHERS ABOUT THIS?
I...NOT YET. THESE ARE ALL LOGICAL INFERENCES, BASED ON THE DATA AVAILABLE... BUT THERE IS NOT THAT MUCH DATA AVAILABLE.
I WANTED TO SHARE MY CONCERNS WITH YOU FIRST. I KNOW YOU ARE FOCUSED ON FREEING THE PSI-LORD BUT EARTH IS IN IMMINENT DANGER-- LOGICALLY, THAT SHOULD BE THE HIGHER PRIORITY.
YES, YES, I SEE WHAT YOU MEAN.
COME, WALK WITH ME, BEACON, AND LET'S WORK OUT OUR BEST OPTIONS...
SSHHRKKKK

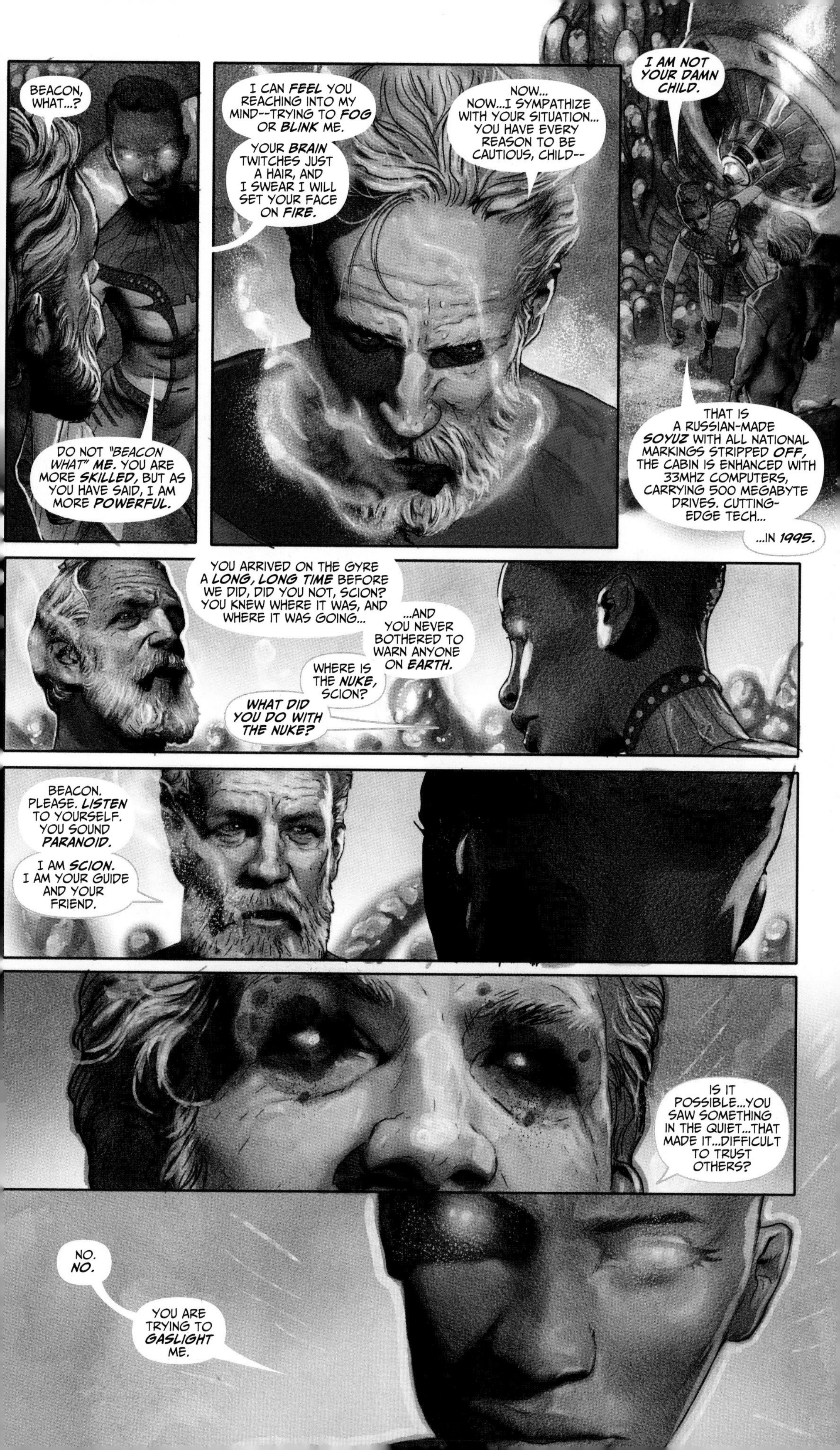
BEACON, WHAT...?
DO NOT "BEACON WHAT" ME. YOU ARE MORE SKILLED, BUT AS YOU HAVE SAID, I AM MORE POWERFUL.
I CAN FEEL YOU REACHING INTO MY MIND--TRYING TO FOG OR BLINK ME.
YOUR BRAIN TWITCHES JUST A HAIR, AND I SWEAR I WILL SET YOUR FACE ON FIRE.
NOW... NOW...I SYMPATHIZE WITH YOUR SITUATION... YOU HAVE EVERY REASON TO BE CAUTIOUS, CHILD--
I AM NOT YOUR DAMN CHILD.
THAT IS A RUSSIAN-MADE SOYUZ WITH ALL NATIONAL MARKINGS STRIPPED OFF, THE CABIN IS ENHANCED WITH 33MHZ COMPUTERS, CARRYING 500 MEGABYTE DRIVES. CUTTING-EDGE TECH...
...IN 1995.
YOU ARRIVED ON THE GYRE A LONG, LONG TIME BEFORE WE DID, DID YOU NOT, SCION? YOU KNEW WHERE IT WAS, AND WHERE IT WAS GOING...
...AND YOU NEVER BOTHERED TO WARN ANYONE ON EARTH.
WHERE IS THE NUKE, SCION?
WHAT DID YOU DO WITH THE NUKE?
BEACON. PLEASE. LISTEN TO YOURSELF. YOU SOUND PARANOID.
I AM SCION. I AM YOUR GUIDE AND YOUR FRIEND.
IS IT POSSIBLE...YOU SAW SOMETHING IN THE QUIET...THAT MADE IT...DIFFICULT TO TRUST OTHERS?
NO. NO.
YOU ARE TRYING TO GASLIGHT ME.

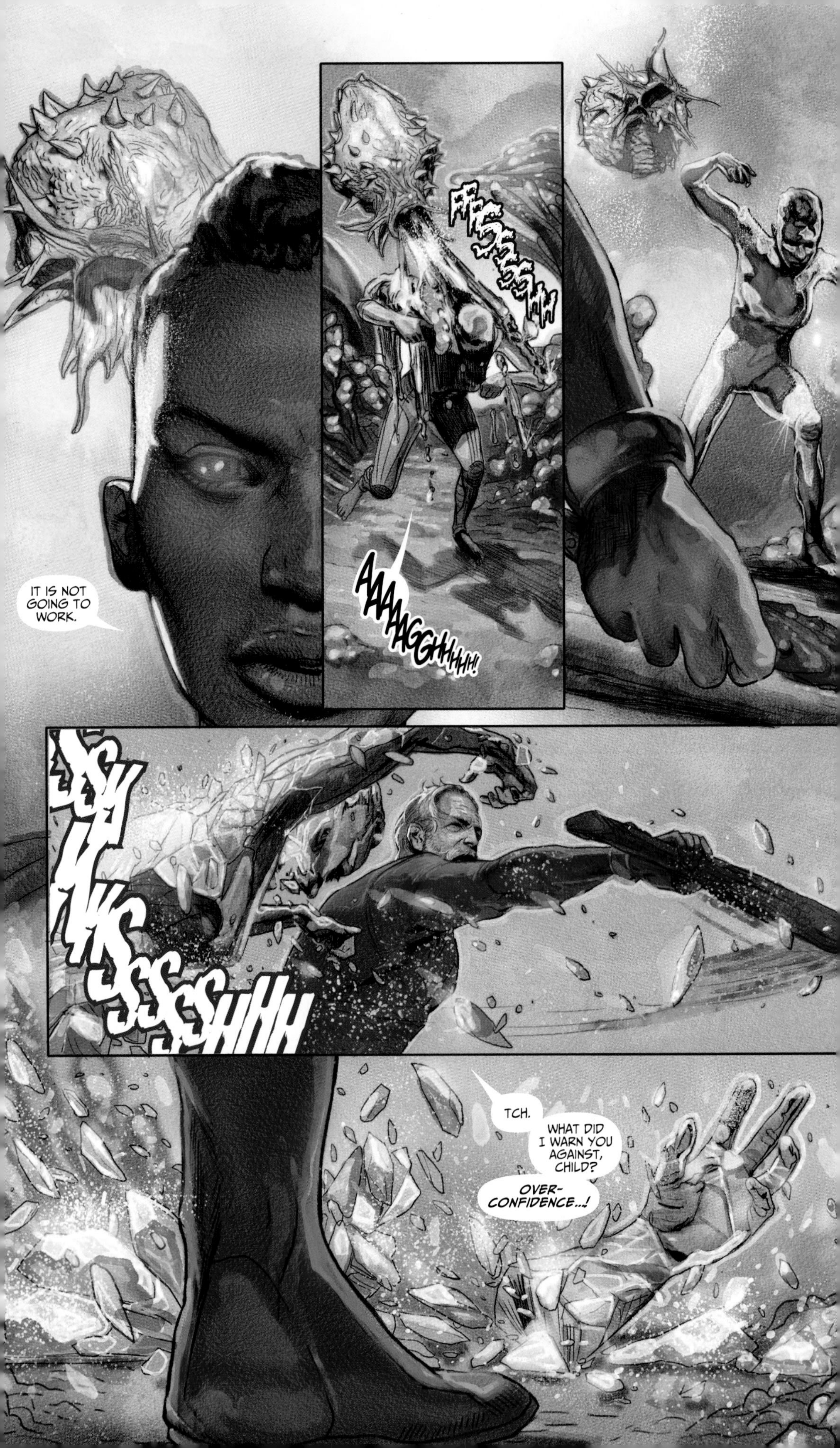

IT IS NOT GOING TO WORK.
FFSSSSSHHH
AAAAAGGHHHHH!
SSKKSSSSHHH
TCH.
WHAT DID I WARN YOU AGAINST, CHILD?
OVER-CONFIDENCE...!

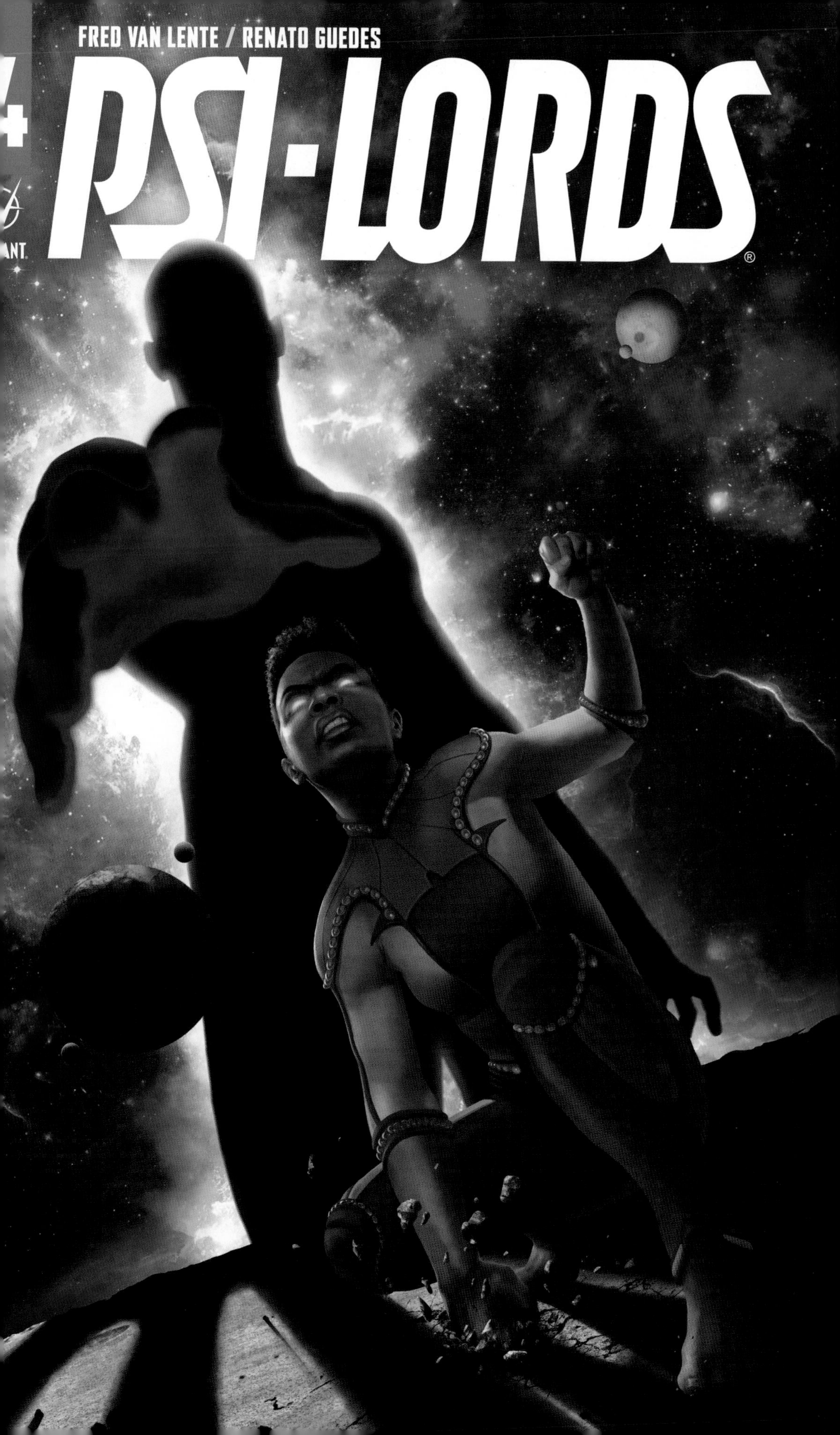

FRED VAN LENTE / RENATO GUEDES
PSI-LORDS

**PSI-LORDS #**
WRITER: Fred Van Len
ARTIST: Renato Guede
LETTERER: Dave Sharp
COVER ARTIST: Rahzza
ASSISTANT EDITOR: Drew Baumgartn
EDITOR: David Mench

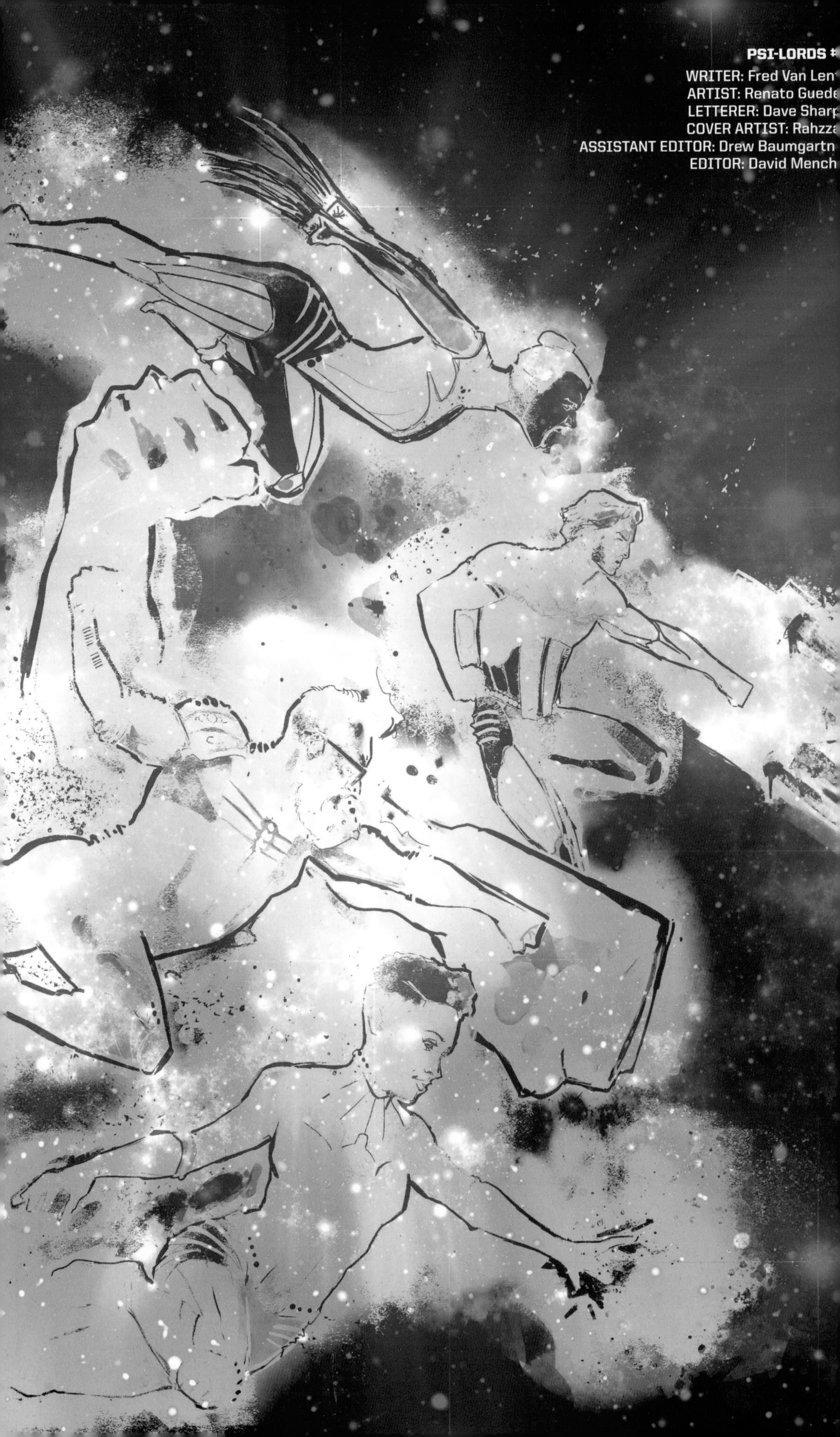

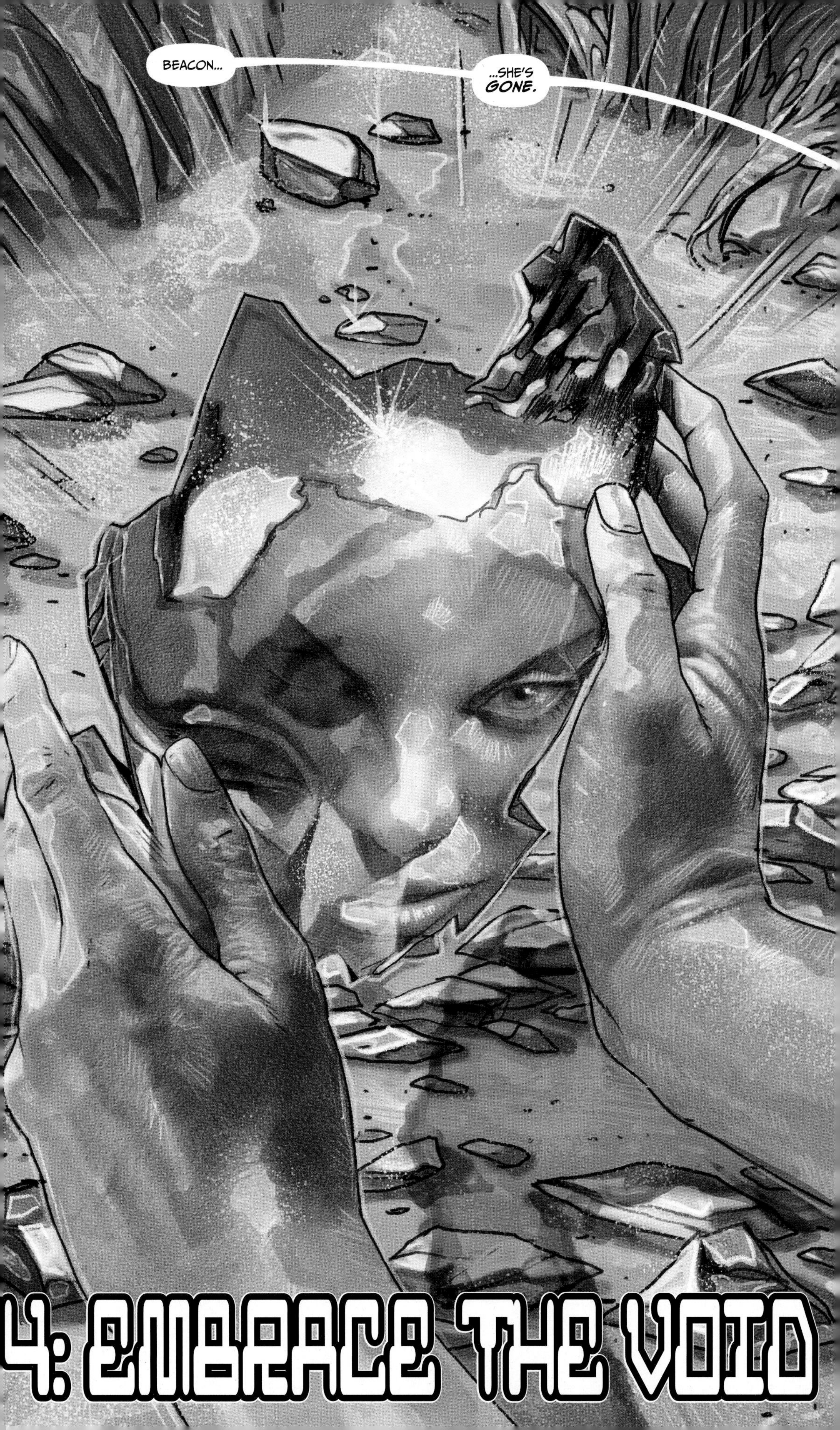
BEACON...
...SHE'S GONE.
4: EMBRACE THE VOID

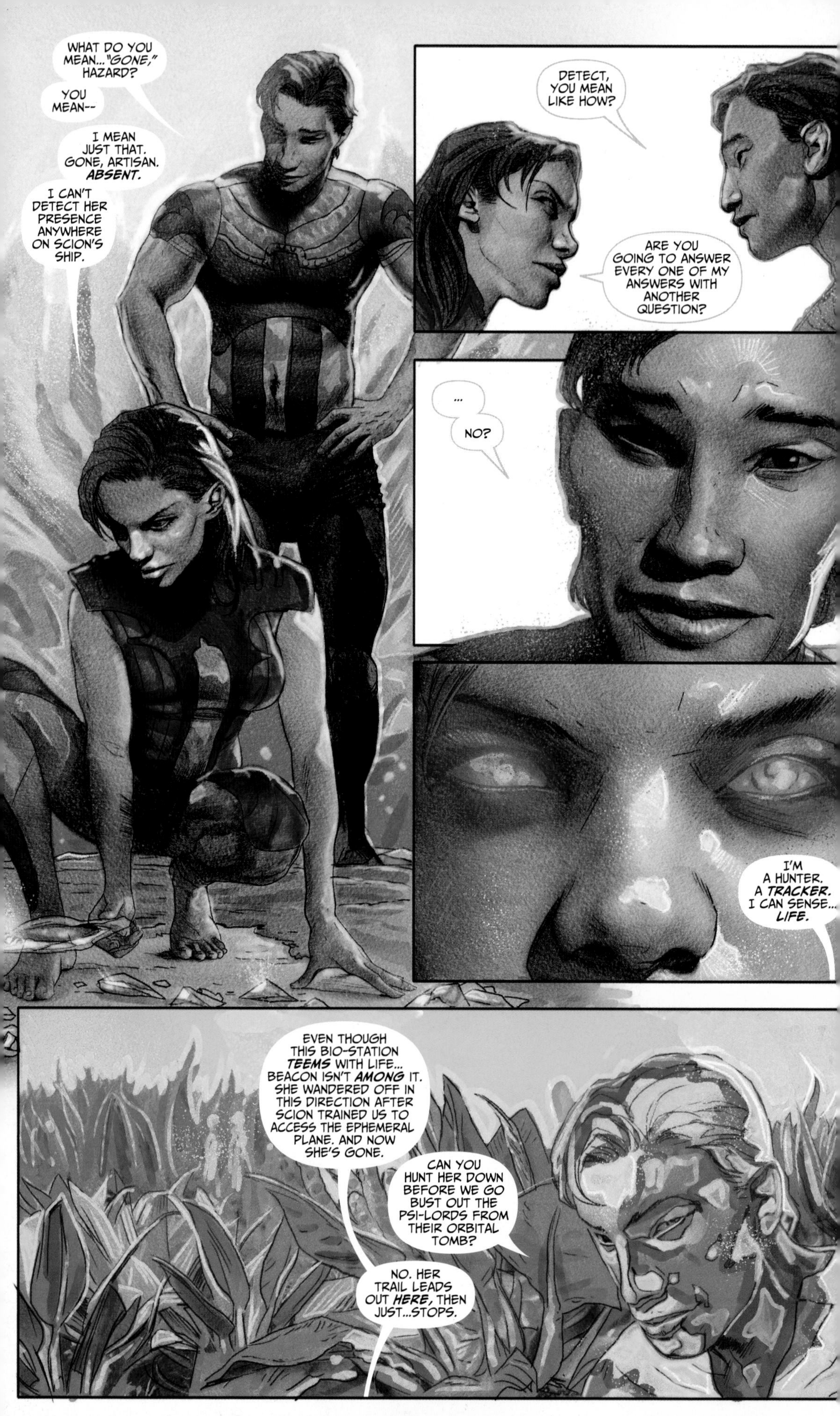
WHAT DO YOU MEAN..."GONE," HAZARD?
YOU MEAN--
I MEAN JUST THAT. GONE, ARTISAN. ABSENT.
I CAN'T DETECT HER PRESENCE ANYWHERE ON SCION'S SHIP.
DETECT, YOU MEAN LIKE HOW?
ARE YOU GOING TO ANSWER EVERY ONE OF MY ANSWERS WITH ANOTHER QUESTION?
...
NO?
I'M A HUNTER. A TRACKER. I CAN SENSE... LIFE.
EVEN THOUGH THIS BIO-STATION TEEMS WITH LIFE... BEACON ISN'T AMONG IT. SHE WANDERED OFF IN THIS DIRECTION AFTER SCION TRAINED US TO ACCESS THE EPHEMERAL PLANE. AND NOW SHE'S GONE.
CAN YOU HUNT HER DOWN BEFORE WE GO BUST OUT THE PSI-LORDS FROM THEIR ORBITAL TOMB?
NO. HER TRAIL LEADS OUT HERE, THEN JUST...STOPS.

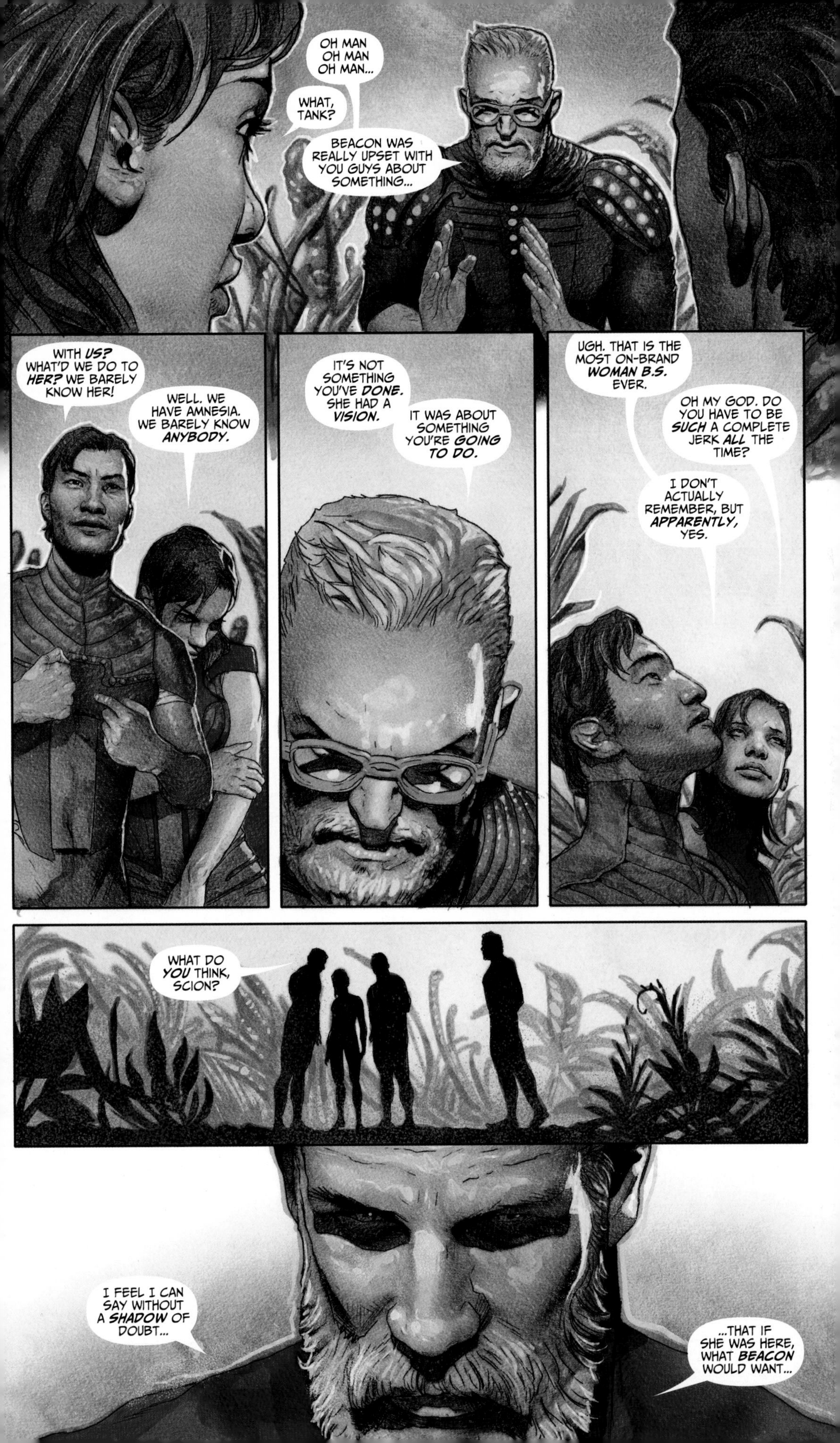
OH MAN
OH MAN
OH MAN...
WHAT, TANK?
BEACON WAS REALLY UPSET WITH YOU GUYS ABOUT SOMETHING...
WITH US? WHAT'D WE DO TO HER? WE BARELY KNOW HER!
WELL. WE HAVE AMNESIA. WE BARELY KNOW ANYBODY.
IT'S NOT SOMETHING YOU'VE DONE. SHE HAD A VISION.
IT WAS ABOUT SOMETHING YOU'RE GOING TO DO.
UGH. THAT IS THE MOST ON-BRAND WOMAN B.S. EVER.
OH MY GOD. DO YOU HAVE TO BE SUCH A COMPLETE JERK ALL THE TIME?
I DON'T ACTUALLY REMEMBER, BUT APPARENTLY, YES.
WHAT DO YOU THINK, SCION?
I FEEL I CAN SAY WITHOUT A SHADOW OF DOUBT...
...THAT IF SHE WAS HERE, WHAT BEACON WOULD WANT...

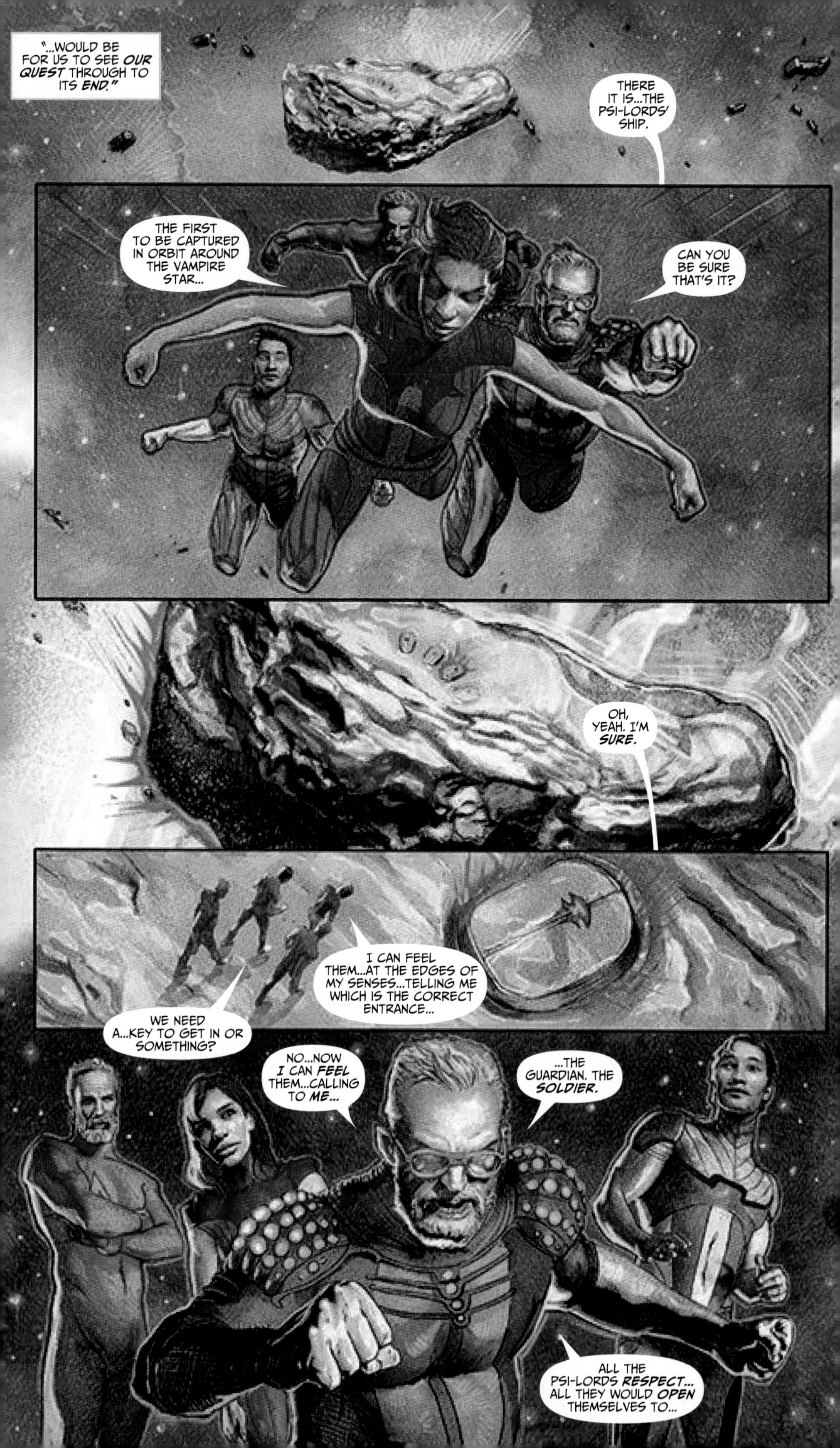
"...WOULD BE FOR US TO SEE OUR QUEST THROUGH TO ITS END."
THERE IT IS...THE PSI-LORDS' SHIP.
THE FIRST TO BE CAPTURED IN ORBIT AROUND THE VAMPIRE STAR...
CAN YOU BE SURE THAT'S IT?
OH, YEAH. I'M SURE.
I CAN FEEL THEM...AT THE EDGES OF MY SENSES...TELLING ME WHICH IS THE CORRECT ENTRANCE...
WE NEED A...KEY TO GET IN OR SOMETHING?
NO...NOW I CAN FEEL THEM...CALLING TO ME...
...THE GUARDIAN. THE SOLDIER.
ALL THE PSI-LORDS RESPECT... ALL THEY WOULD OPEN THEMSELVES TO...

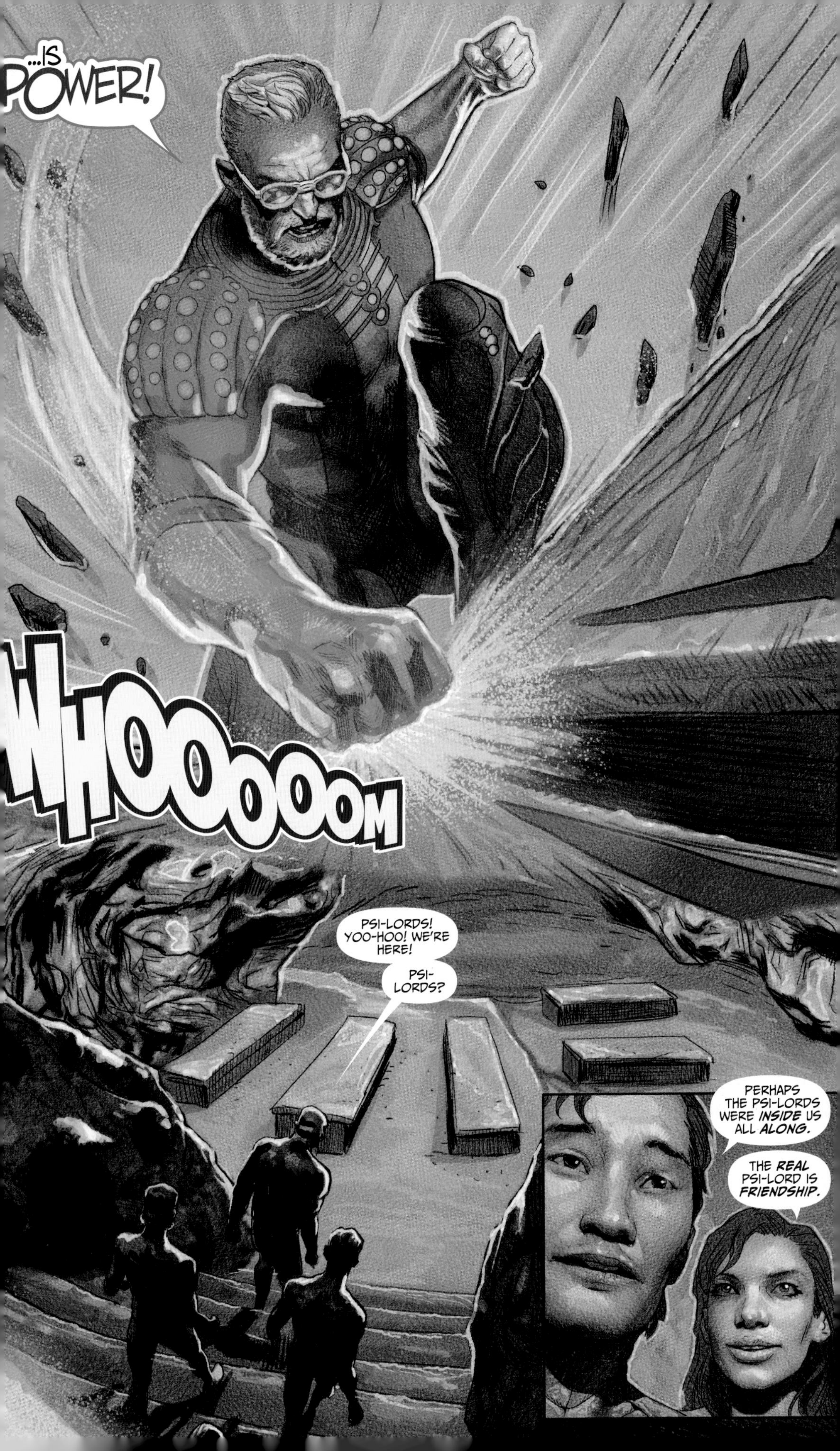
...IS POWER!
WHOOOOOOM
PSI-LORDS! YOO-HOO! WE'RE HERE!
PSI-LORDS?
PERHAPS THE PSI-LORDS WERE *INSIDE* US ALL *ALONG*.
THE *REAL* PSI-LORD IS *FRIENDSHIP*.

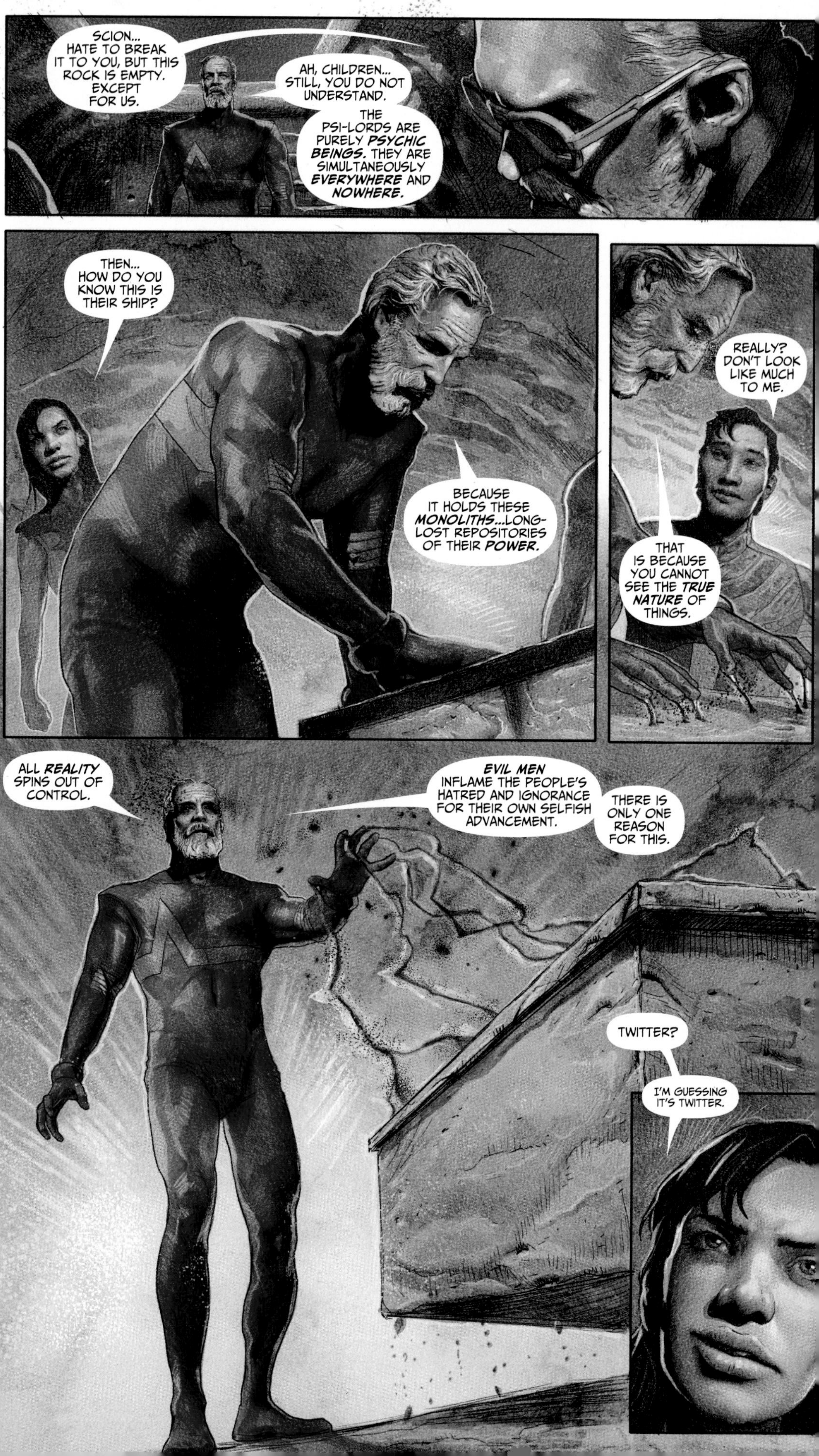
SCION... HATE TO BREAK IT TO YOU, BUT THIS ROCK IS EMPTY. EXCEPT FOR US.
AH, CHILDREN... STILL, YOU DO NOT UNDERSTAND.
THE PSI-LORDS ARE PURELY PSYCHIC BEINGS. THEY ARE SIMULTANEOUSLY EVERYWHERE AND NOWHERE.
THEN... HOW DO YOU KNOW THIS IS THEIR SHIP?
BECAUSE IT HOLDS THESE MONOLITHS...LONG-LOST REPOSITORIES OF THEIR POWER.
REALLY? DON'T LOOK LIKE MUCH TO ME.
THAT IS BECAUSE YOU CANNOT SEE THE TRUE NATURE OF THINGS.
ALL REALITY SPINS OUT OF CONTROL.
EVIL MEN INFLAME THE PEOPLE'S HATRED AND IGNORANCE FOR THEIR OWN SELFISH ADVANCEMENT.
THERE IS ONLY ONE REASON FOR THIS.
TWITTER?
I'M GUESSING IT'S TWITTER.

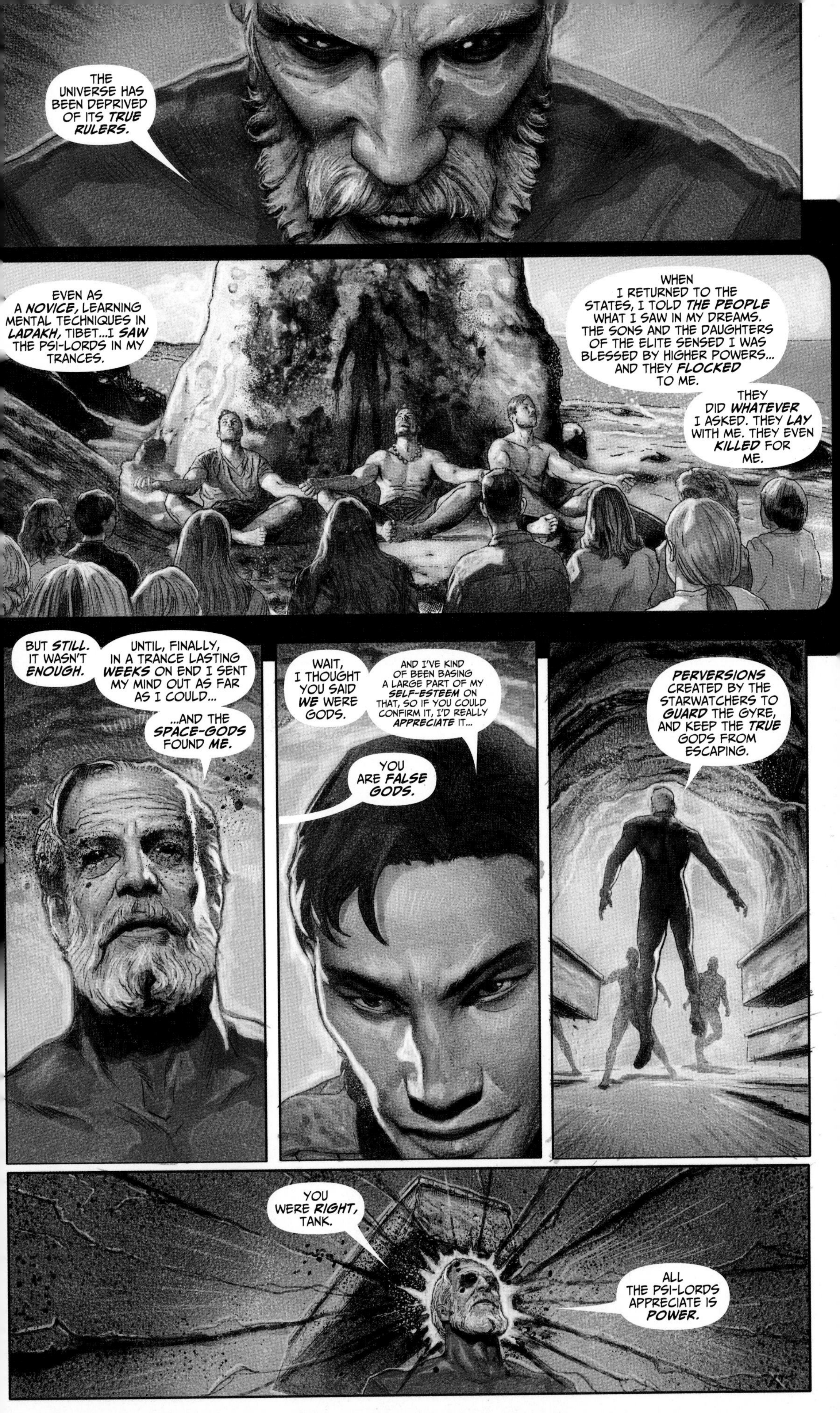
THE UNIVERSE HAS BEEN DEPRIVED OF ITS TRUE RULERS.
EVEN AS A NOVICE, LEARNING MENTAL TECHNIQUES IN LADAKH, TIBET...I SAW THE PSI-LORDS IN MY TRANCES.
WHEN I RETURNED TO THE STATES, I TOLD THE PEOPLE WHAT I SAW IN MY DREAMS. THE SONS AND THE DAUGHTERS OF THE ELITE SENSED I WAS BLESSED BY HIGHER POWERS... AND THEY FLOCKED TO ME.
THEY DID WHATEVER I ASKED. THEY LAY WITH ME. THEY EVEN KILLED FOR ME.
BUT STILL. IT WASN'T ENOUGH.
UNTIL, FINALLY, IN A TRANCE LASTING WEEKS ON END I SENT MY MIND OUT AS FAR AS I COULD...
...AND THE SPACE-GODS FOUND ME.
WAIT, I THOUGHT YOU SAID WE WERE GODS.
AND I'VE KIND OF BEEN BASING A LARGE PART OF MY SELF-ESTEEM ON THAT, SO IF YOU COULD CONFIRM IT, I'D REALLY APPRECIATE IT...
YOU ARE FALSE GODS.
PERVERSIONS CREATED BY THE STARWATCHERS TO GUARD THE GYRE, AND KEEP THE TRUE GODS FROM ESCAPING.
YOU WERE RIGHT, TANK.
ALL THE PSI-LORDS APPRECIATE IS POWER.

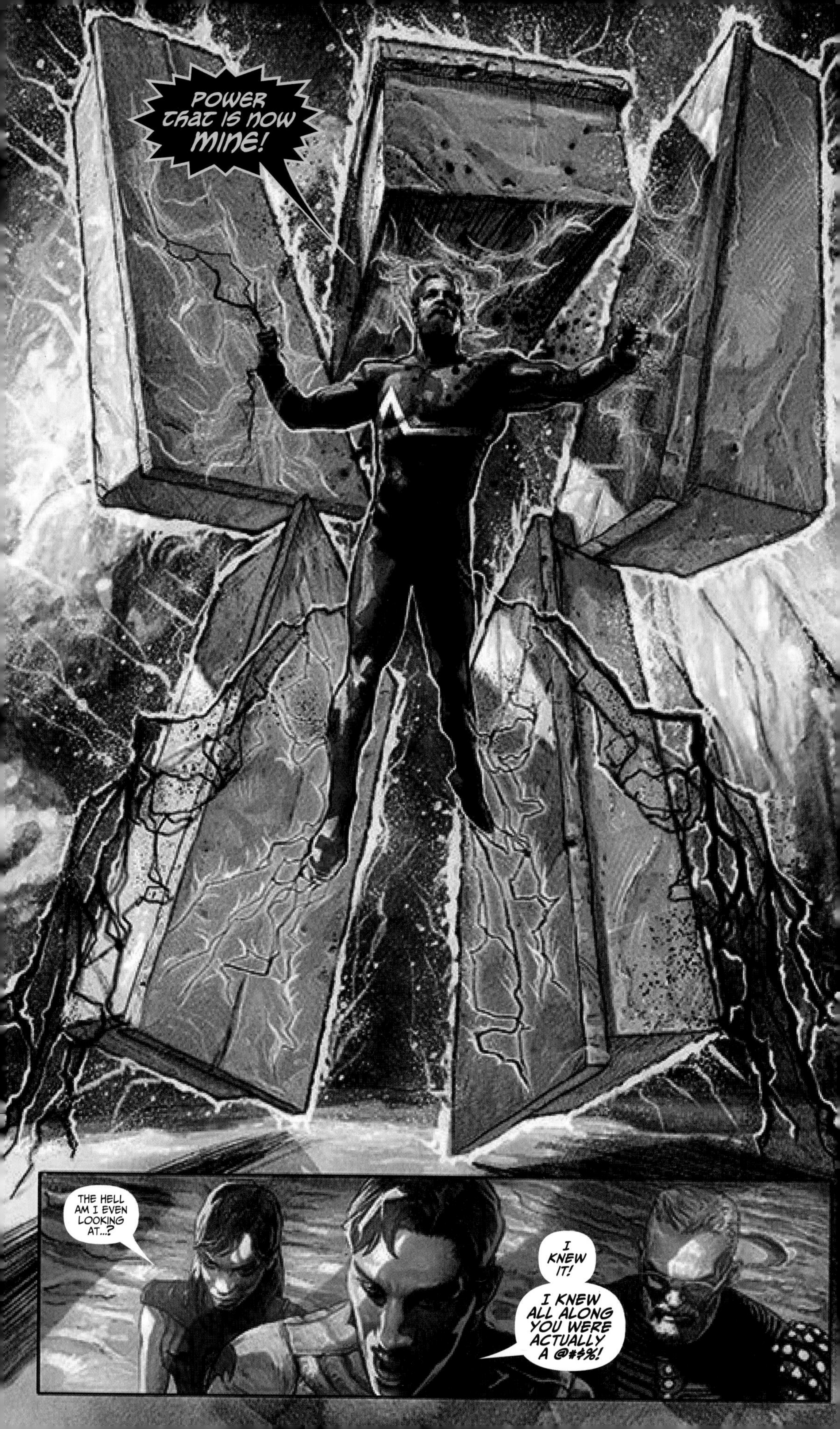
POWER THAT IS NOW MINE!
THE HELL AM I EVEN LOOKING AT...?
I KNEW IT!
I KNEW ALL ALONG YOU WERE ACTUALLY A @#$%!

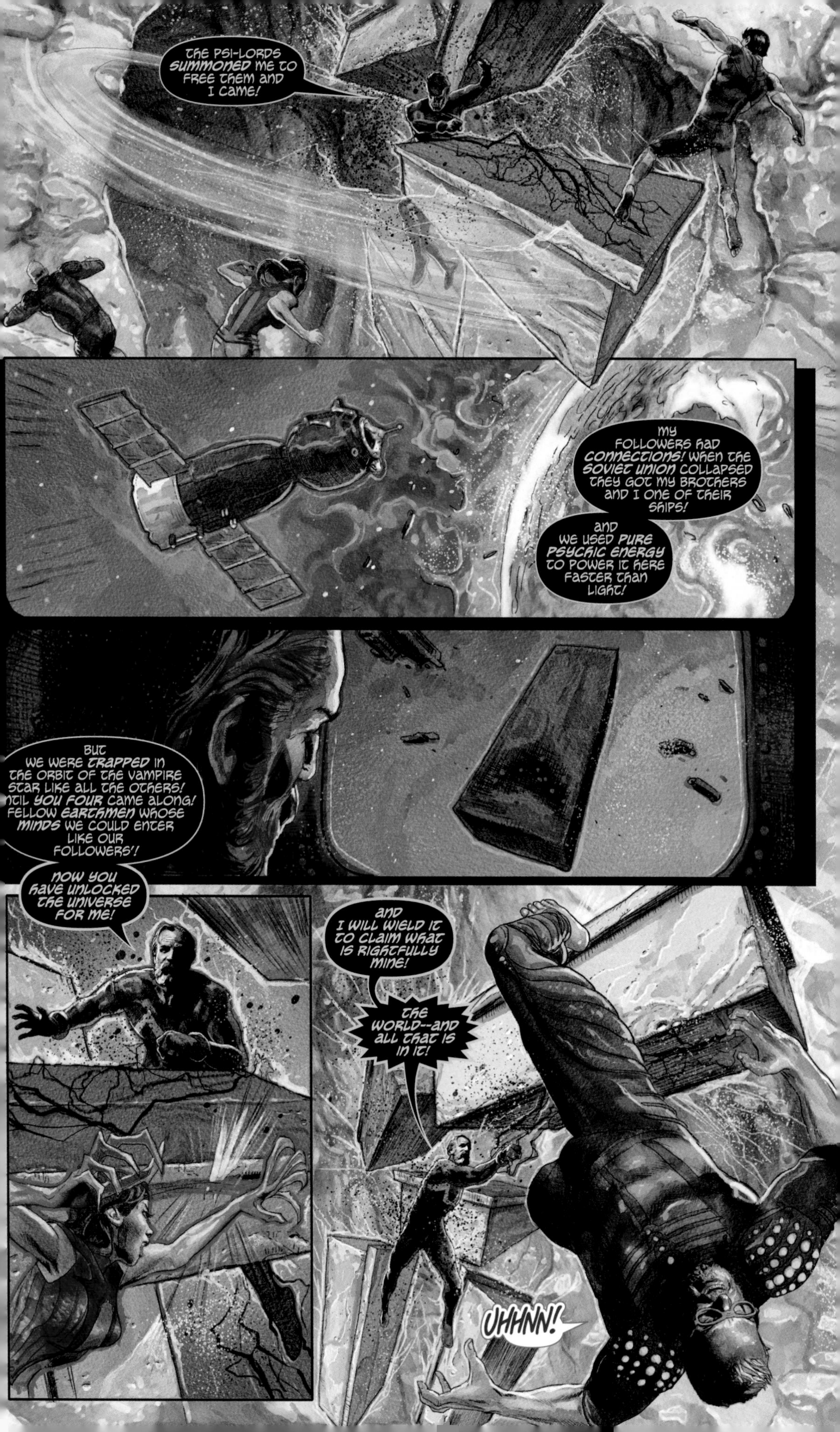
THE PSI-LORDS SUMMONED ME TO FREE THEM AND I CAME!
MY FOLLOWERS HAD CONNECTIONS! WHEN THE SOVIET UNION COLLAPSED THEY GOT MY BROTHERS AND I ONE OF THEIR SHIPS!
AND WE USED PURE PSYCHIC ENERGY TO POWER IT HERE FASTER THAN LIGHT!
BUT WE WERE TRAPPED IN THE ORBIT OF THE VAMPIRE STAR LIKE ALL THE OTHERS! NTIL YOU FOUR CAME ALONG! FELLOW EARTHMEN WHOSE MINDS WE COULD ENTER LIKE OUR FOLLOWERS'!
NOW YOU HAVE UNLOCKED THE UNIVERSE FOR ME!
AND I WILL WIELD IT TO CLAIM WHAT IS RIGHTFULLY MINE!
THE WORLD--AND ALL THAT IS IN IT!
UHHNN!

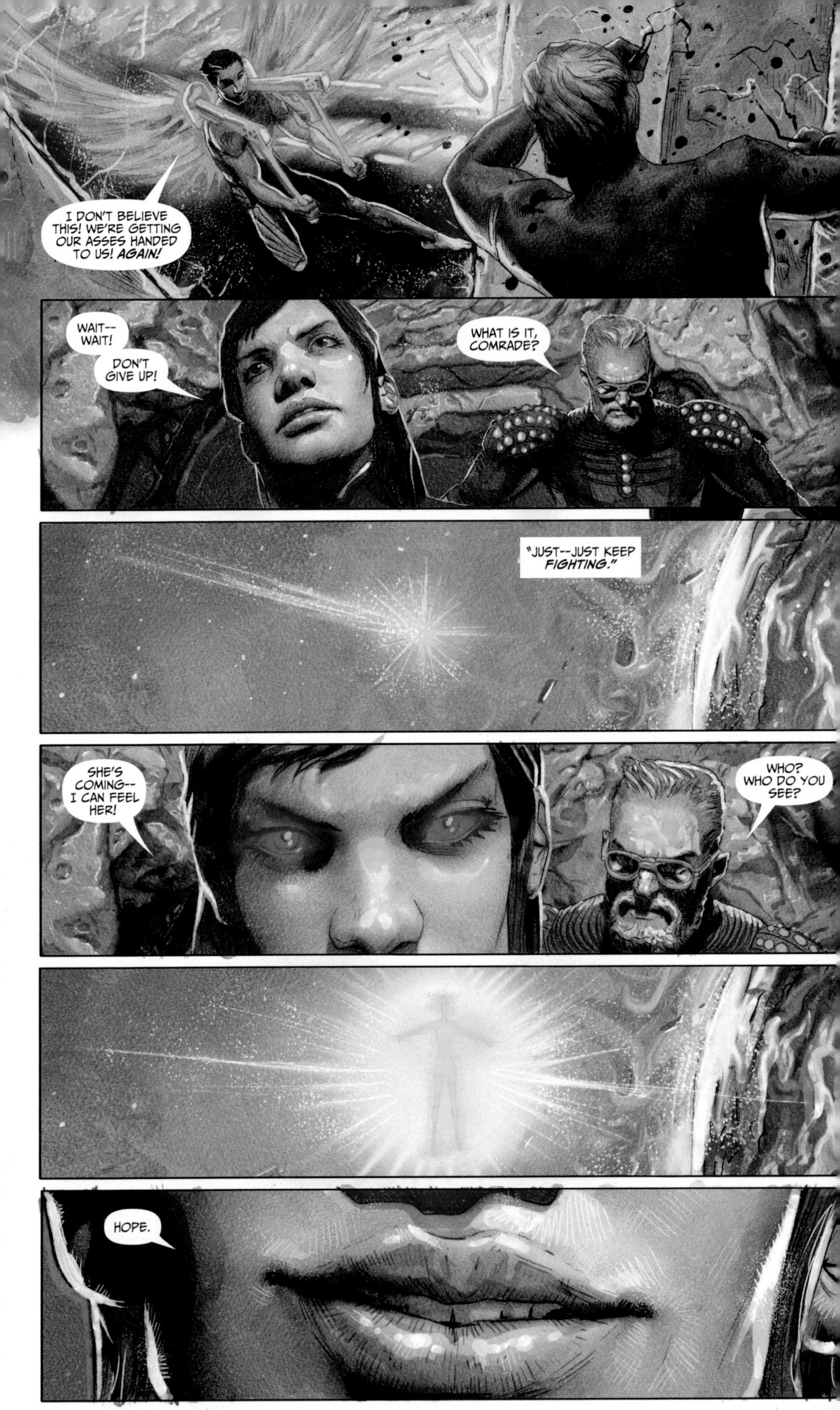
I DON'T BELIEVE THIS! WE'RE GETTING OUR ASSES HANDED TO US! AGAIN!
WAIT-- WAIT!
DON'T GIVE UP!
WHAT IS IT, COMRADE?
"JUST--JUST KEEP FIGHTING."
SHE'S COMING-- I CAN FEEL HER!
WHO? WHO DO YOU SEE?
HOPE.

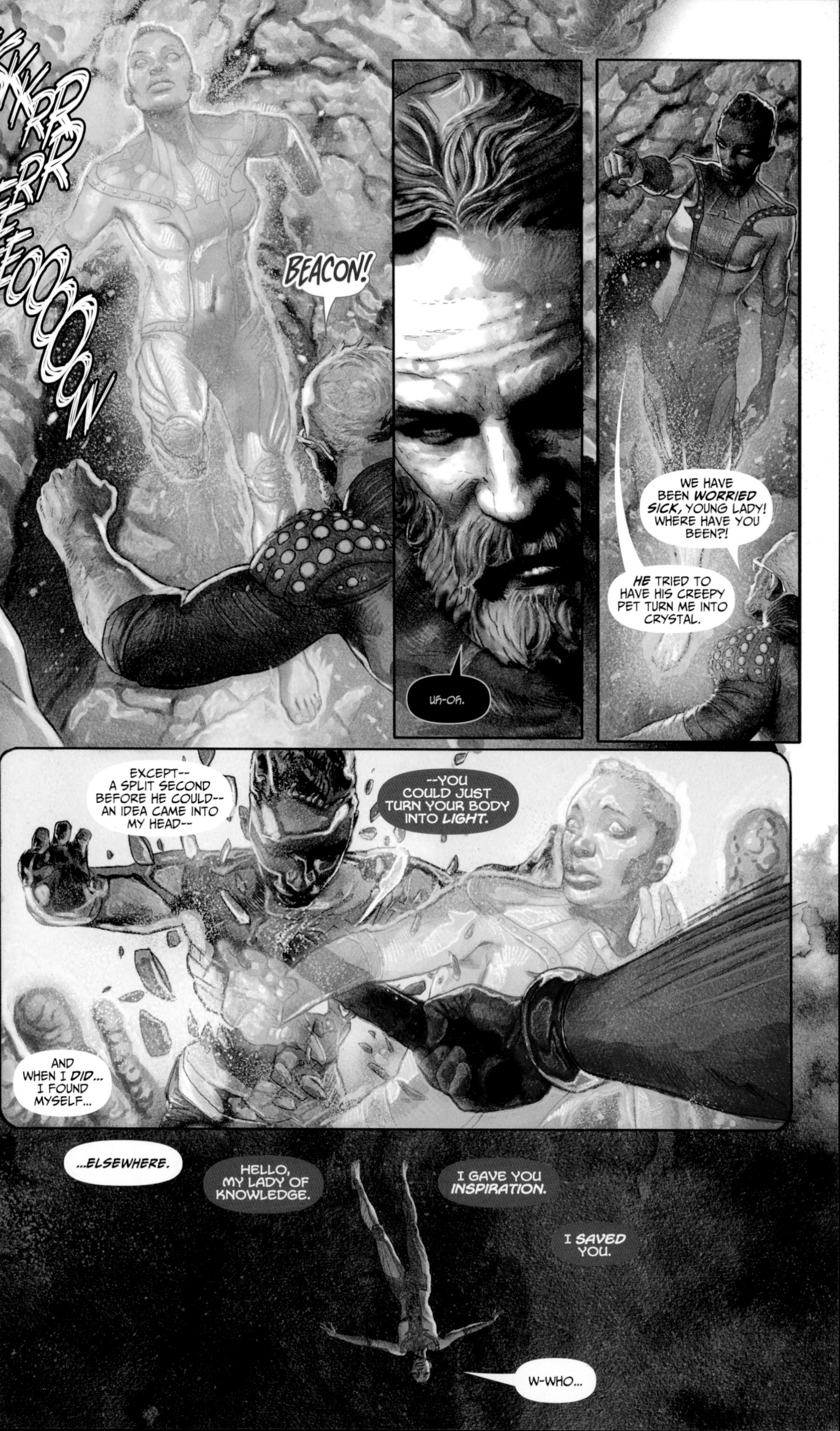

KKKRR
RRRR
FFEOOOOOW
BEACON!
UH-OH.
WE HAVE BEEN WORRIED SICK, YOUNG LADY! WHERE HAVE YOU BEEN?!
HE TRIED TO HAVE HIS CREEPY PET TURN ME INTO CRYSTAL.
EXCEPT-- A SPLIT SECOND BEFORE HE COULD-- AN IDEA CAME INTO MY HEAD--
--YOU COULD JUST TURN YOUR BODY INTO LIGHT.
AND WHEN I DID... I FOUND MYSELF...
...ELSEWHERE.
HELLO, MY LADY OF KNOWLEDGE.
I GAVE YOU INSPIRATION.
I SAVED YOU.
W-WHO...

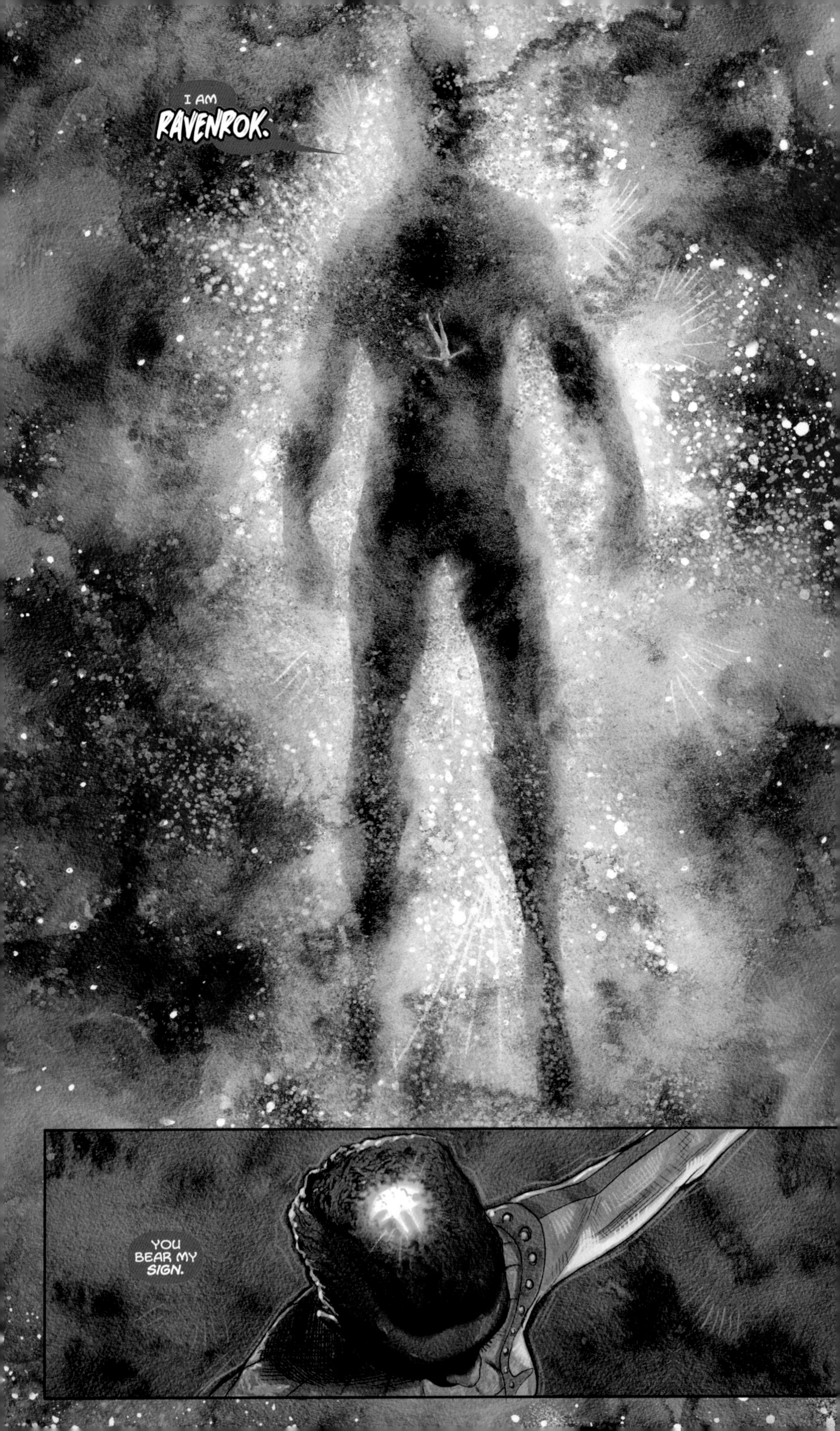
I AM RAVENROK.
YOU BEAR MY SIGN.

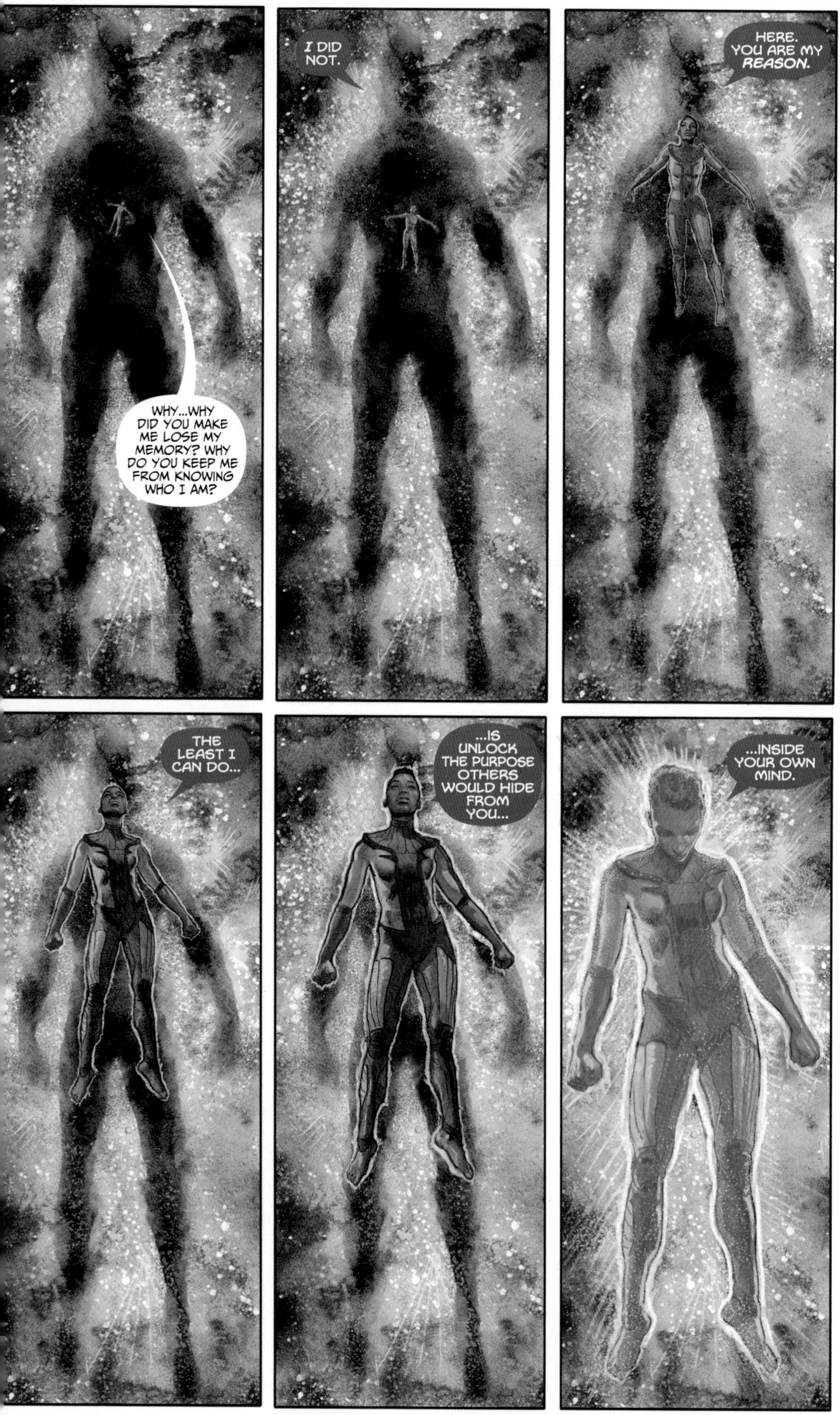
WHY...WHY DID YOU MAKE ME LOSE MY MEMORY? WHY DO YOU KEEP ME FROM KNOWING WHO I AM?
I DID NOT.
HERE. YOU ARE MY *REASON.*
THE LEAST I CAN DO...
...IS UNLOCK THE PURPOSE OTHERS WOULD HIDE FROM YOU...
...INSIDE YOUR OWN MIND.

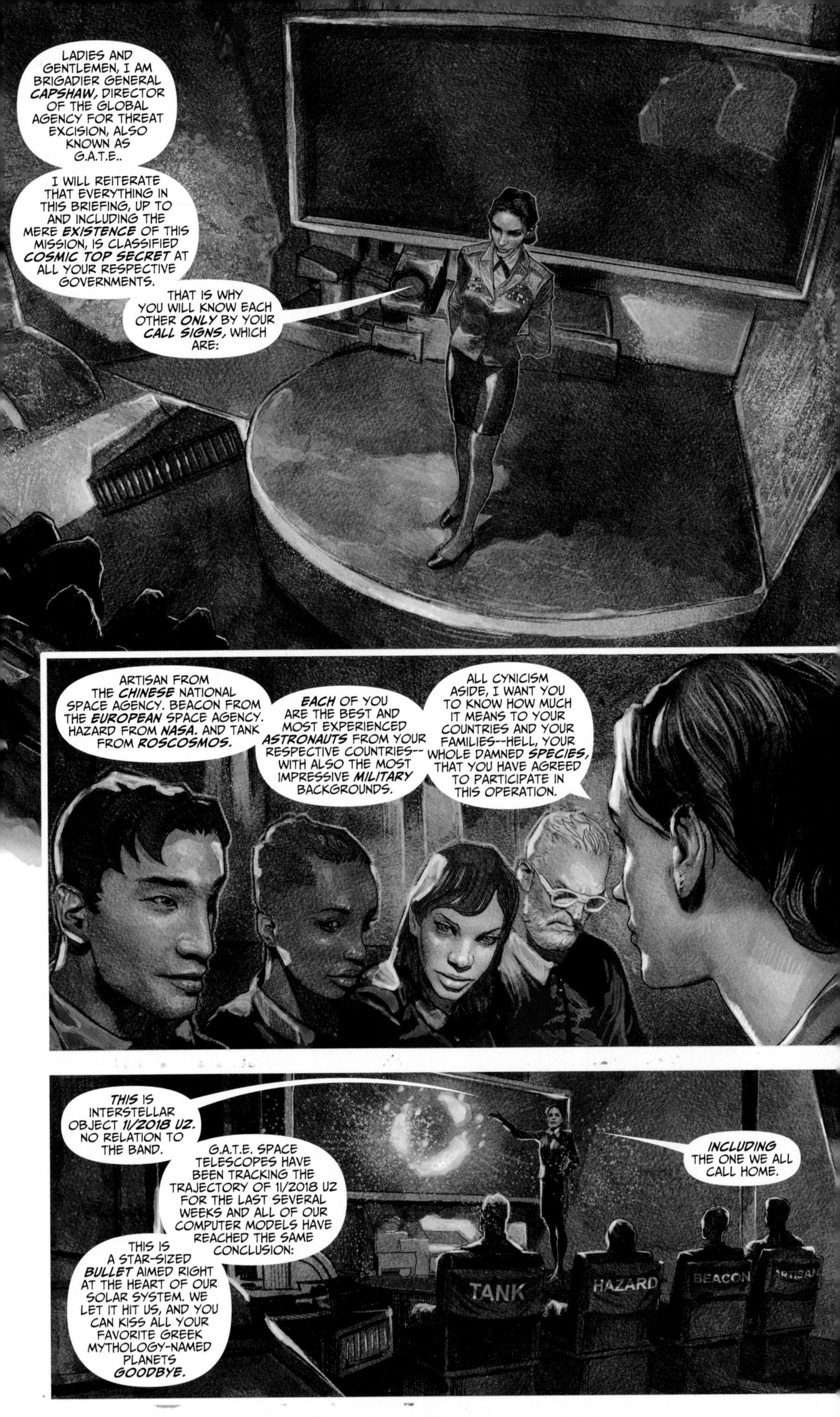
LADIES AND GENTLEMEN, I AM BRIGADIER GENERAL CAPSHAW, DIRECTOR OF THE GLOBAL AGENCY FOR THREAT EXCISION, ALSO KNOWN AS G.A.T.E..
I WILL REITERATE THAT EVERYTHING IN THIS BRIEFING, UP TO AND INCLUDING THE MERE EXISTENCE OF THIS MISSION, IS CLASSIFIED COSMIC TOP SECRET AT ALL YOUR RESPECTIVE GOVERNMENTS.
THAT IS WHY YOU WILL KNOW EACH OTHER ONLY BY YOUR CALL SIGNS, WHICH ARE:
ARTISAN FROM THE CHINESE NATIONAL SPACE AGENCY. BEACON FROM THE EUROPEAN SPACE AGENCY. HAZARD FROM NASA. AND TANK FROM ROSCOSMOS.
EACH OF YOU ARE THE BEST AND MOST EXPERIENCED ASTRONAUTS FROM YOUR RESPECTIVE COUNTRIES-- WITH ALSO THE MOST IMPRESSIVE MILITARY BACKGROUNDS.
ALL CYNICISM ASIDE, I WANT YOU TO KNOW HOW MUCH IT MEANS TO YOUR COUNTRIES AND YOUR FAMILIES--HELL, YOUR WHOLE DAMNED SPECIES, THAT YOU HAVE AGREED TO PARTICIPATE IN THIS OPERATION.
THIS IS INTERSTELLAR OBJECT 1I/2018 U2. NO RELATION TO THE BAND.
G.A.T.E. SPACE TELESCOPES HAVE BEEN TRACKING THE TRAJECTORY OF 1I/2018 U2 FOR THE LAST SEVERAL WEEKS AND ALL OF OUR COMPUTER MODELS HAVE REACHED THE SAME CONCLUSION:
THIS IS A STAR-SIZED BULLET AIMED RIGHT AT THE HEART OF OUR SOLAR SYSTEM. WE LET IT HIT US, AND YOU CAN KISS ALL YOUR FAVORITE GREEK MYTHOLOGY-NAMED PLANETS GOODBYE.
INCLUDING THE ONE WE ALL CALL HOME.
TANK
HAZARD
BEACON
ARTISAN

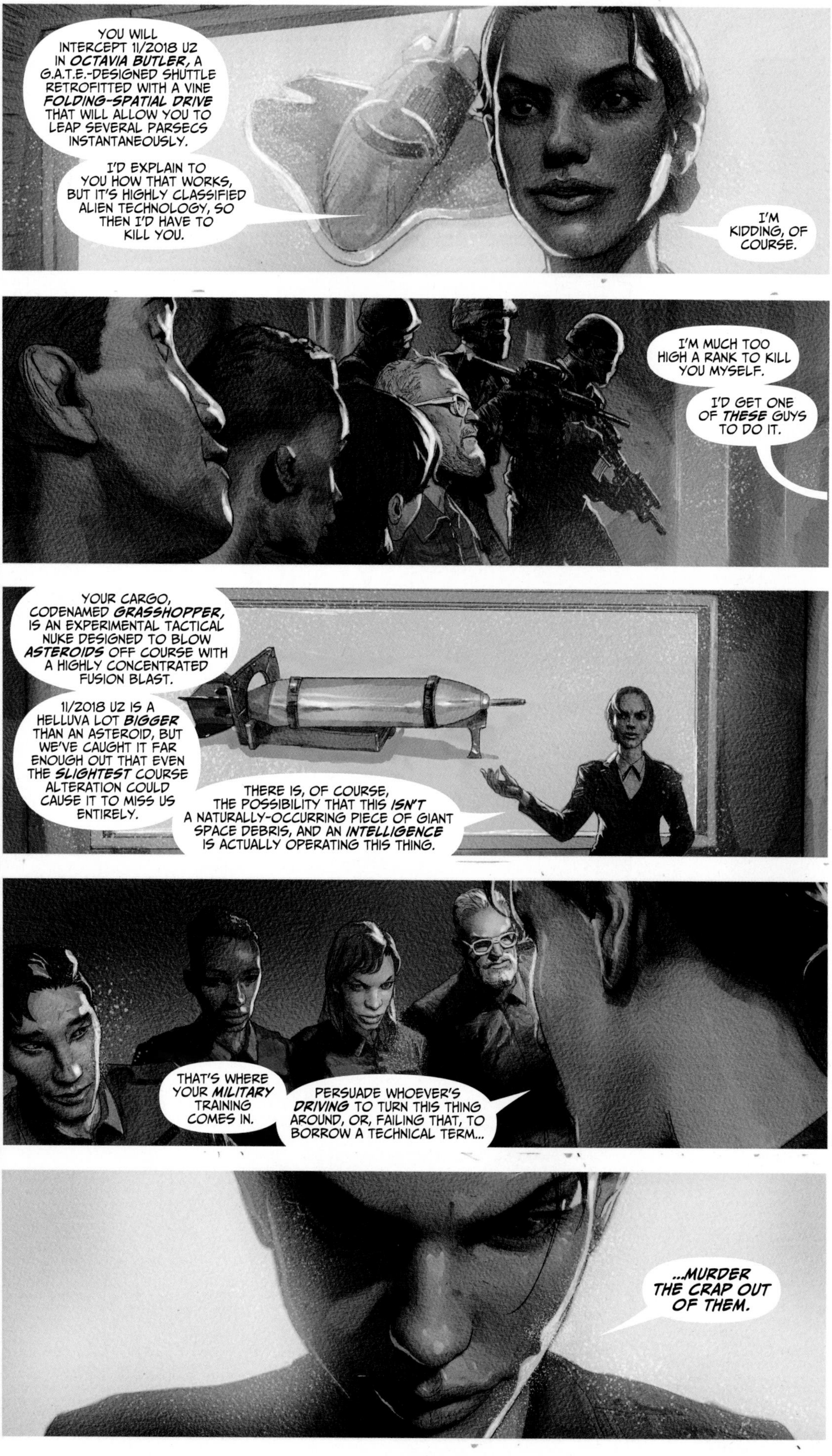
YOU WILL INTERCEPT 11/2018 U2 IN OCTAVIA BUTLER, A G.A.T.E.-DESIGNED SHUTTLE RETROFITTED WITH A VINE FOLDING-SPATIAL DRIVE THAT WILL ALLOW YOU TO LEAP SEVERAL PARSECS INSTANTANEOUSLY.
I'D EXPLAIN TO YOU HOW THAT WORKS, BUT IT'S HIGHLY CLASSIFIED ALIEN TECHNOLOGY, SO THEN I'D HAVE TO KILL YOU.
I'M KIDDING, OF COURSE.
I'M MUCH TOO HIGH A RANK TO KILL YOU MYSELF.
I'D GET ONE OF THESE GUYS TO DO IT.
YOUR CARGO, CODENAMED GRASSHOPPER, IS AN EXPERIMENTAL TACTICAL NUKE DESIGNED TO BLOW ASTEROIDS OFF COURSE WITH A HIGHLY CONCENTRATED FUSION BLAST.
11/2018 U2 IS A HELLUVA LOT BIGGER THAN AN ASTEROID, BUT WE'VE CAUGHT IT FAR ENOUGH OUT THAT EVEN THE SLIGHTEST COURSE ALTERATION COULD CAUSE IT TO MISS US ENTIRELY.
THERE IS, OF COURSE, THE POSSIBILITY THAT THIS ISN'T A NATURALLY-OCCURRING PIECE OF GIANT SPACE DEBRIS, AND AN INTELLIGENCE IS ACTUALLY OPERATING THIS THING.
THAT'S WHERE YOUR MILITARY TRAINING COMES IN.
PERSUADE WHOEVER'S DRIVING TO TURN THIS THING AROUND, OR, FAILING THAT, TO BORROW A TECHNICAL TERM...
...MURDER THE CRAP OUT OF THEM.

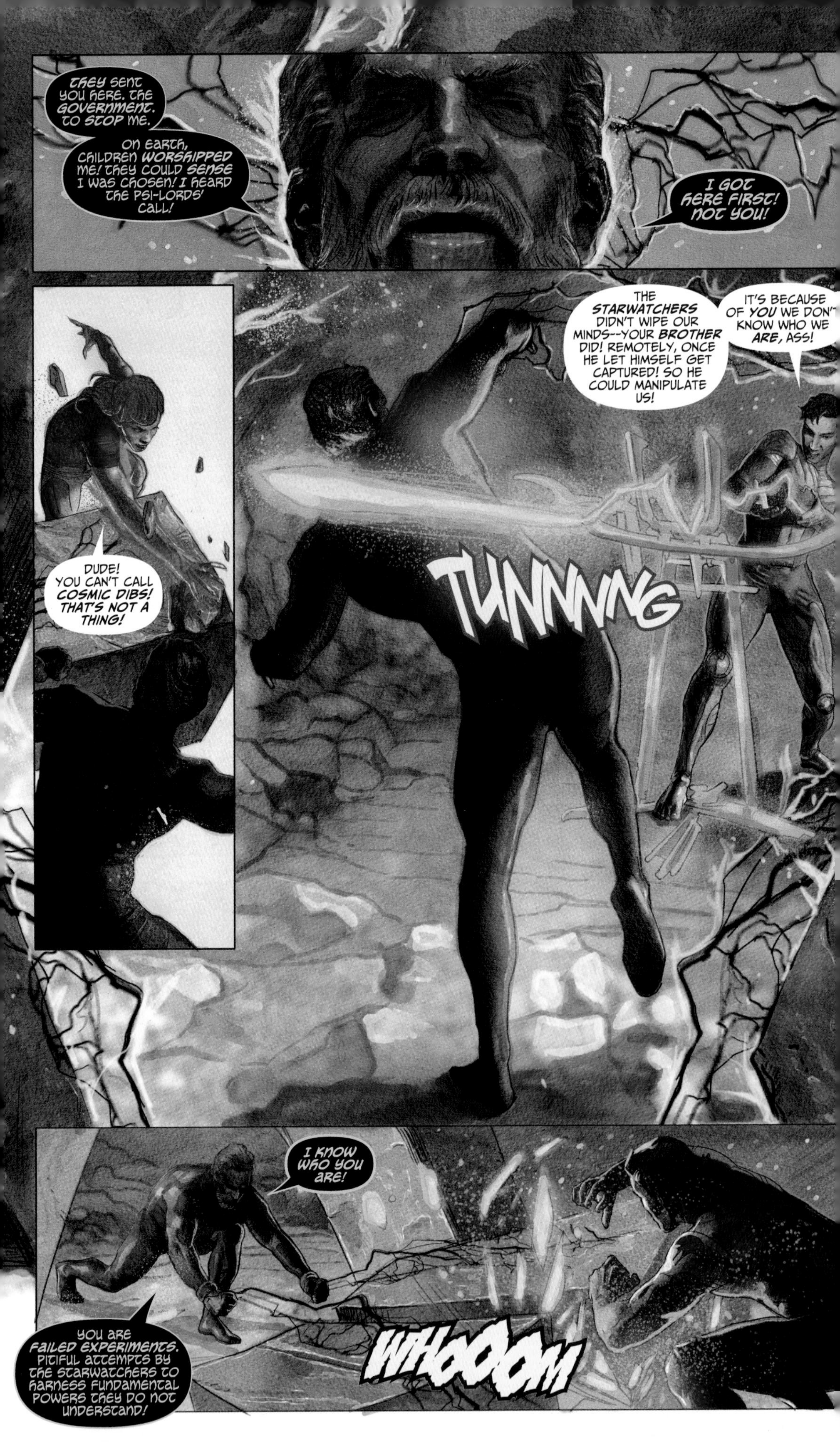

THEY SENT YOU HERE. THE GOVERNMENT. TO STOP ME.
ON EARTH, CHILDREN WORSHIPPED ME! THEY COULD SENSE I WAS CHOSEN! I HEARD THE PSI-LORDS' CALL!
I GOT HERE FIRST! NOT YOU!
DUDE! YOU CAN'T CALL COSMIC DIBS! THAT'S NOT A THING!
THE STARWATCHERS DIDN'T WIPE OUR MINDS--YOUR BROTHER DID! REMOTELY, ONCE HE LET HIMSELF GET CAPTURED! SO HE COULD MANIPULATE US!
IT'S BECAUSE OF YOU WE DON'T KNOW WHO WE ARE, ASS!
TUNNNNG
I KNOW WHO YOU ARE!
YOU ARE FAILED EXPERIMENTS. PITIFUL ATTEMPTS BY THE STARWATCHERS TO HARNESS FUNDAMENTAL POWERS THEY DO NOT UNDERSTAND!
WHOOOM

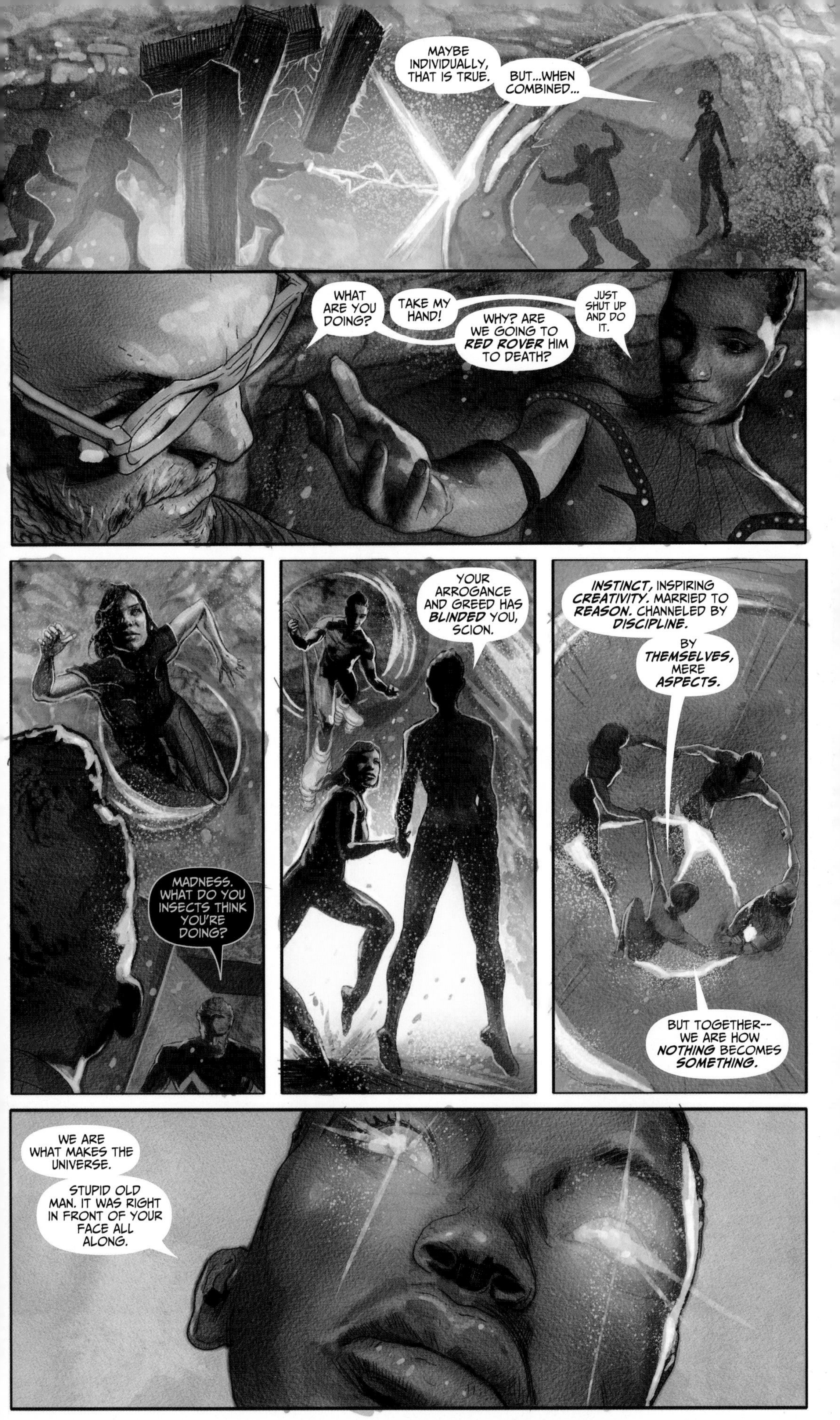
MAYBE INDIVIDUALLY, THAT IS TRUE.
BUT...WHEN COMBINED...
WHAT ARE YOU DOING?
TAKE MY HAND!
WHY? ARE WE GOING TO RED ROVER HIM TO DEATH?
JUST SHUT UP AND DO IT.
MADNESS. WHAT DO YOU INSECTS THINK YOU'RE DOING?
YOUR ARROGANCE AND GREED HAS BLINDED YOU, SCION.
INSTINCT, INSPIRING CREATIVITY. MARRIED TO REASON. CHANNELED BY DISCIPLINE.
BY THEMSELVES, MERE ASPECTS.
BUT TOGETHER-- WE ARE HOW NOTHING BECOMES SOMETHING.
WE ARE WHAT MAKES THE UNIVERSE.
STUPID OLD MAN. IT WAS RIGHT IN FRONT OF YOUR FACE ALL ALONG.

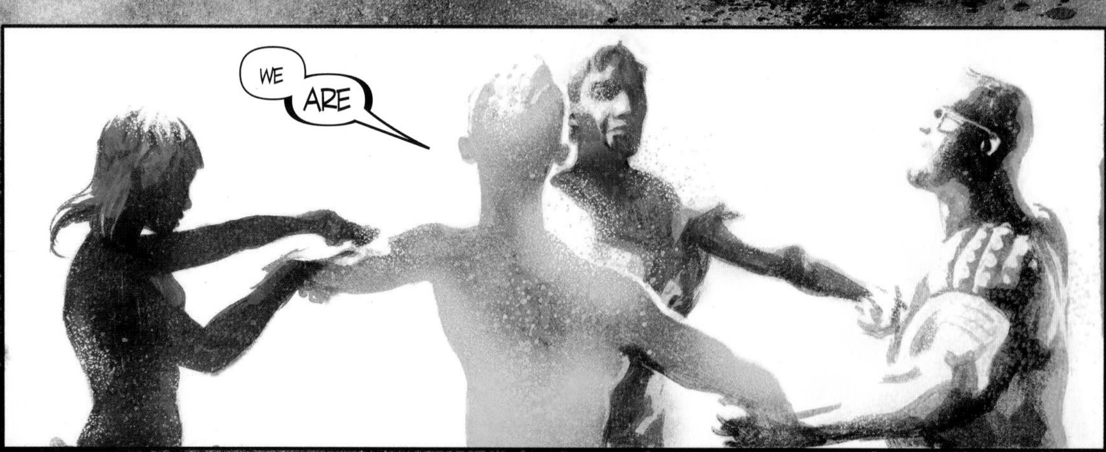
WE
ARE

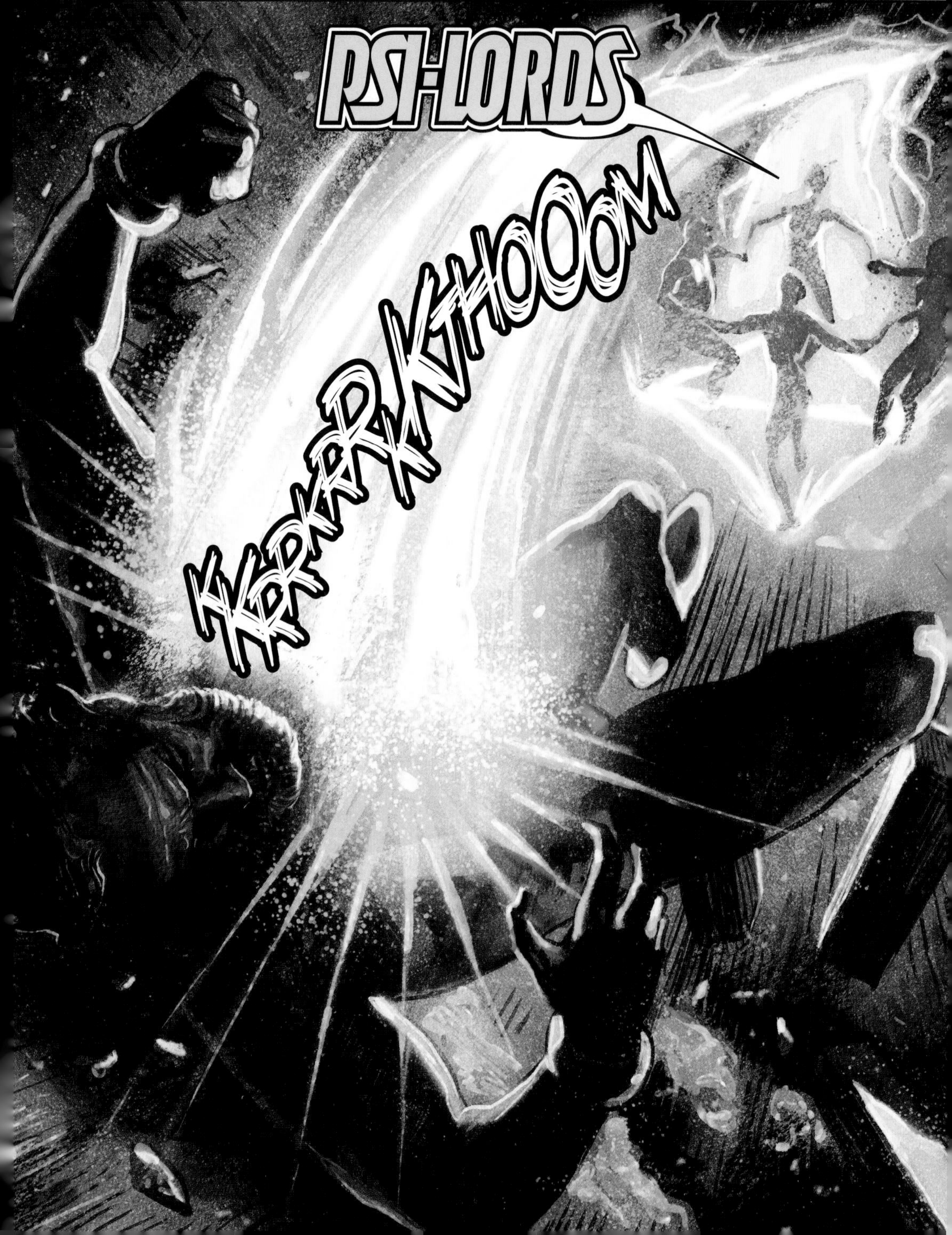
PSI-LORDS
KKRKRRKKTHOOOM

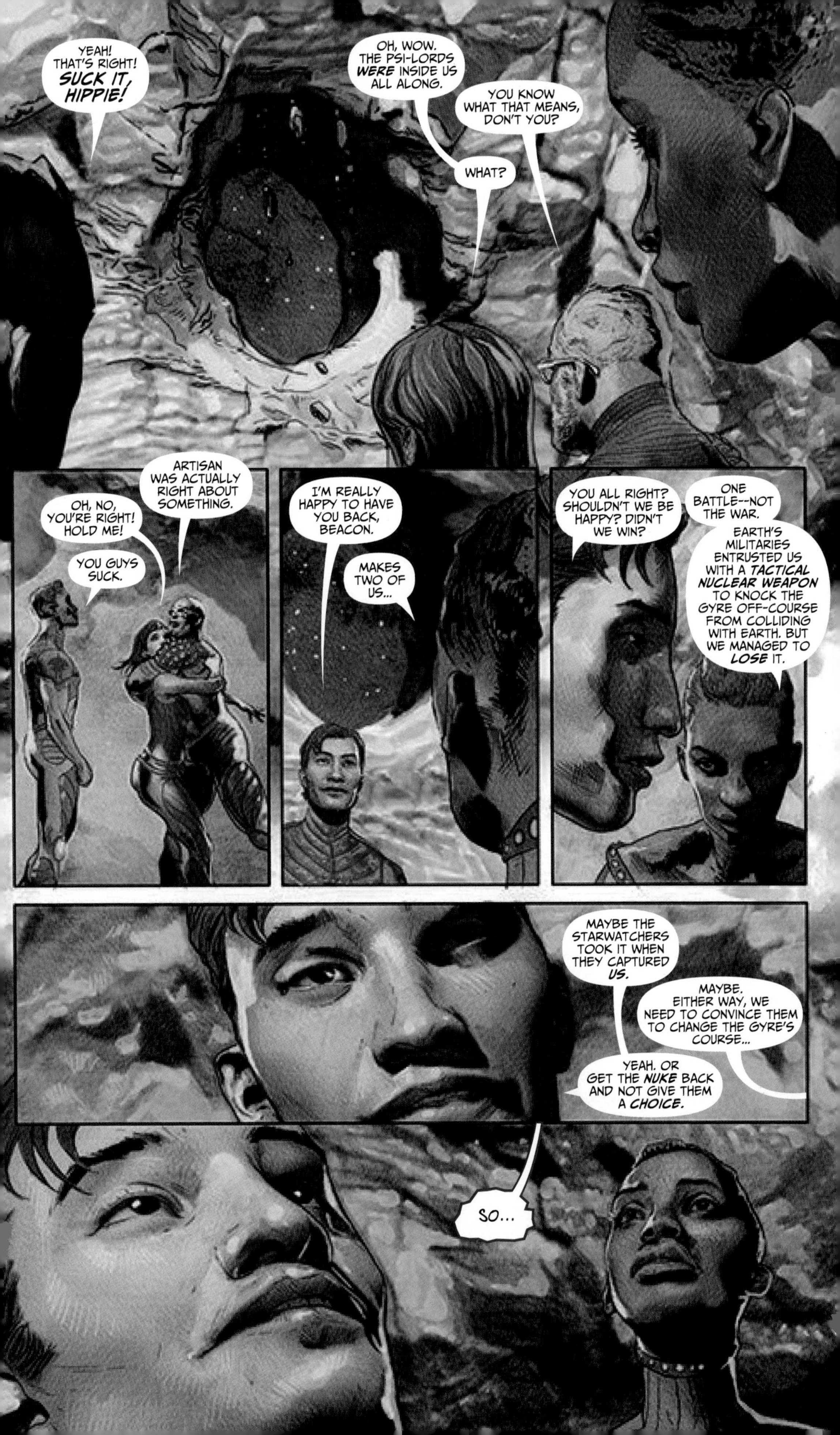
YEAH! THAT'S RIGHT! SUCK IT, HIPPIE!
OH, WOW. THE PSI-LORDS WERE INSIDE US ALL ALONG.
YOU KNOW WHAT THAT MEANS, DON'T YOU?
WHAT?
ARTISAN WAS ACTUALLY RIGHT ABOUT SOMETHING.
OH, NO, YOU'RE RIGHT! HOLD ME!
YOU GUYS SUCK.
I'M REALLY HAPPY TO HAVE YOU BACK, BEACON.
MAKES TWO OF US...
YOU ALL RIGHT? SHOULDN'T WE BE HAPPY? DIDN'T WE WIN?
ONE BATTLE--NOT THE WAR.
EARTH'S MILITARIES ENTRUSTED US WITH A TACTICAL NUCLEAR WEAPON TO KNOCK THE GYRE OFF-COURSE FROM COLLIDING WITH EARTH. BUT WE MANAGED TO LOSE IT.
MAYBE THE STARWATCHERS TOOK IT WHEN THEY CAPTURED US.
MAYBE. EITHER WAY, WE NEED TO CONVINCE THEM TO CHANGE THE GYRE'S COURSE...
YEAH. OR GET THE NUKE BACK AND NOT GIVE THEM A CHOICE.
SO...

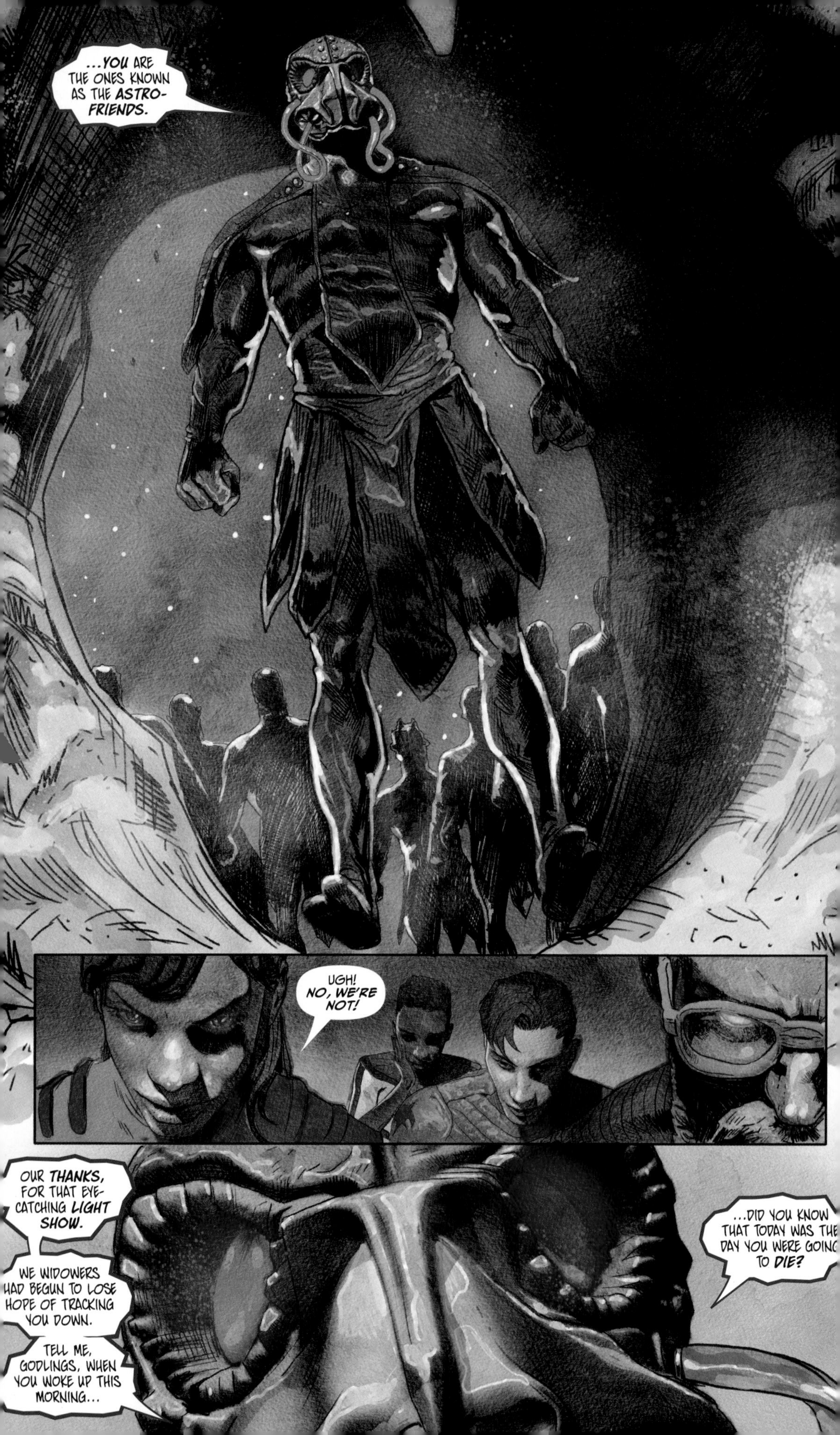
...YOU ARE THE ONES KNOWN AS THE ASTRO-FRIENDS.
UGH! NO, WE'RE NOT!
OUR THANKS, FOR THAT EYE-CATCHING LIGHT SHOW.
WE WIDOWERS HAD BEGUN TO LOSE HOPE OF TRACKING YOU DOWN.
TELL ME, GODLINGS, WHEN YOU WOKE UP THIS MORNING...
...DID YOU KNOW THAT TODAY WAS THE DAY YOU WERE GOING TO DIE?

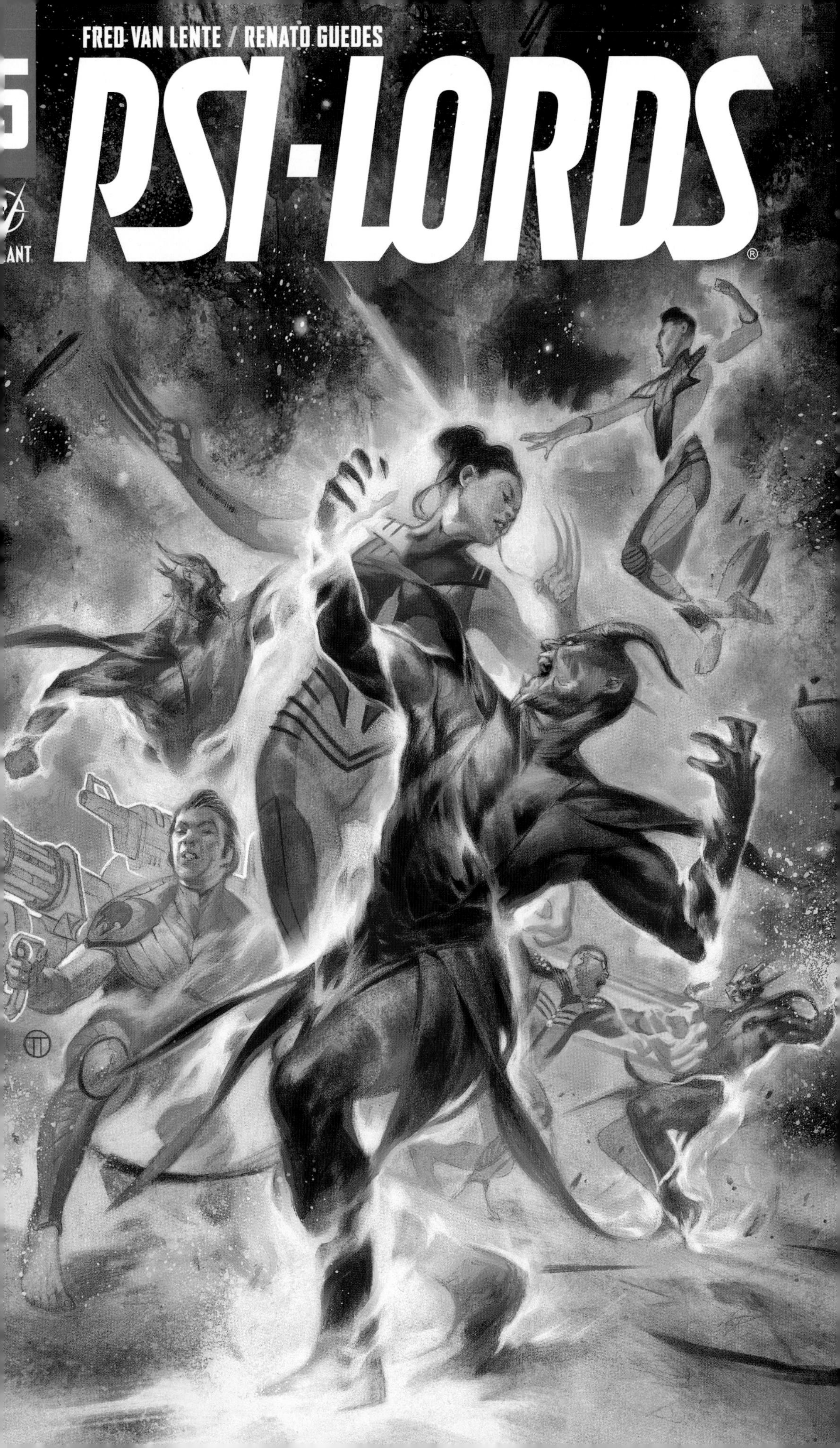
FRED VAN LENTE / RENATO GUEDES
PSI-LORDS
5

**PSI-LORDS #**

WRITER: Fred Van Len
ARTIST: Renato Guede
LETTERER: Dave Sharp
COVER ARTIST: Julian Totino Tedesc
ASSISTANT EDITOR: Drew Baumgartn
EDITOR: David Mench

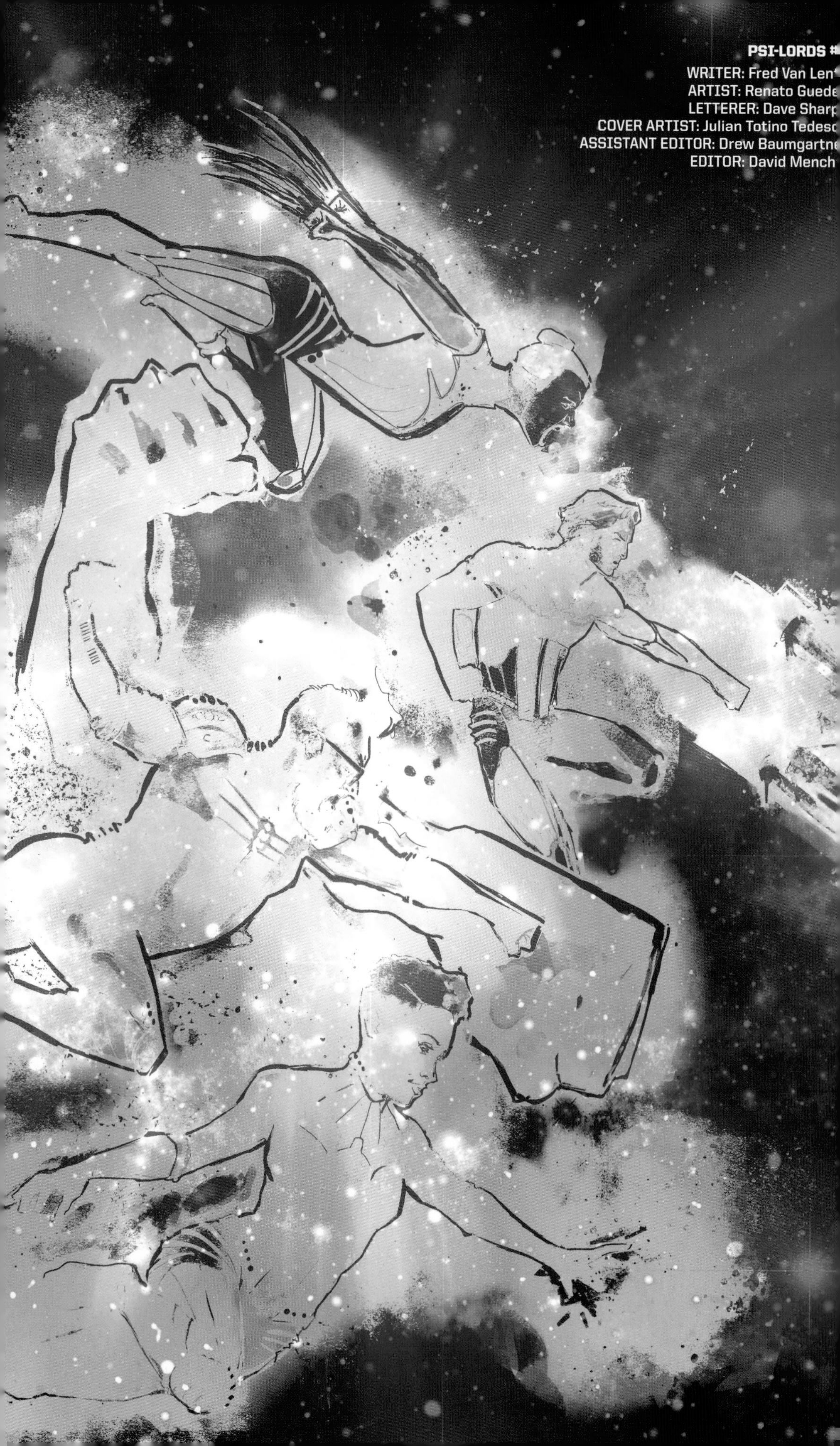

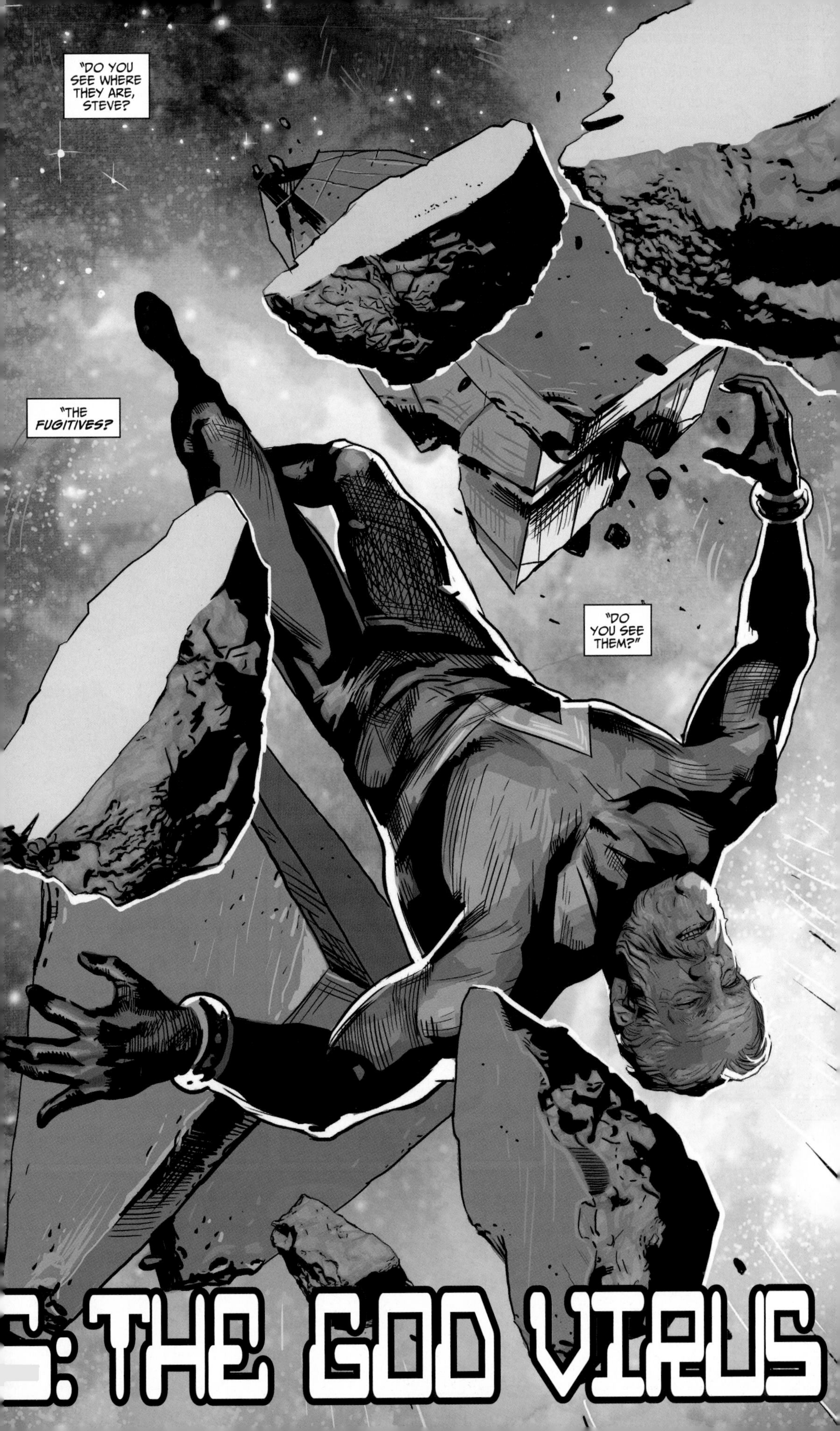
"DO YOU SEE WHERE THEY ARE, STEVE?
"THE *FUGITIVES?*
"DO YOU SEE THEM?"
THE GOD VIRUS

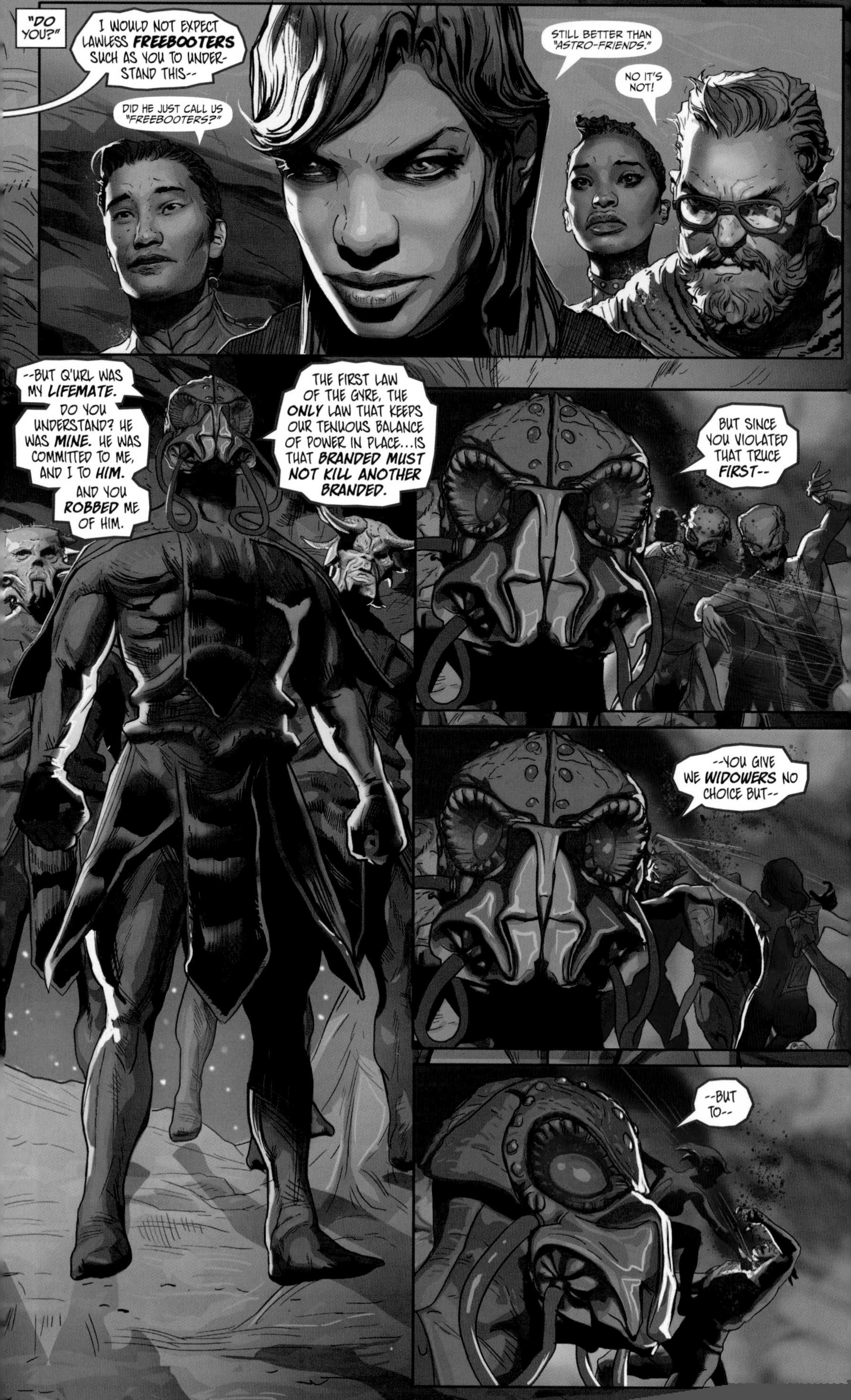
"DO YOU?"
I WOULD NOT EXPECT LAWLESS FREEBOOTERS SUCH AS YOU TO UNDER-STAND THIS--
DID HE JUST CALL US "FREEBOOTERS?"
STILL BETTER THAN "ASTRO-FRIENDS."
NO IT'S NOT!
--BUT Q'URL WAS MY LIFEMATE. DO YOU UNDERSTAND? HE WAS MINE. HE WAS COMMITTED TO ME, AND I TO HIM. AND YOU ROBBED ME OF HIM.
THE FIRST LAW OF THE GYRE, THE ONLY LAW THAT KEEPS OUR TENUOUS BALANCE OF POWER IN PLACE...IS THAT BRANDED MUST NOT KILL ANOTHER BRANDED.
BUT SINCE YOU VIOLATED THAT TRUCE FIRST--
--YOU GIVE WE WIDOWERS NO CHOICE BUT--
--BUT TO--

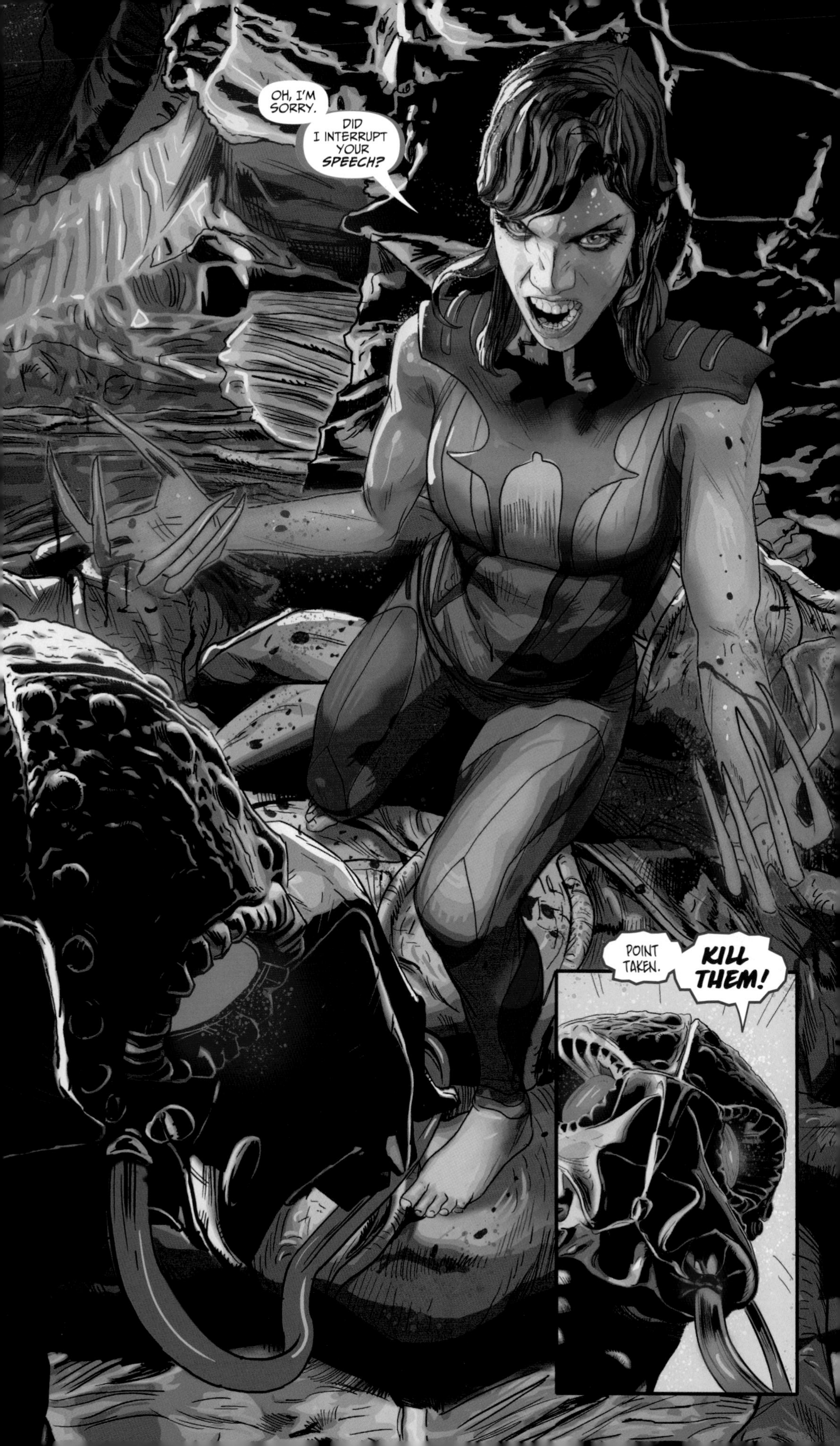
OH, I'M SORRY.
DID I INTERRUPT YOUR SPEECH?
POINT TAKEN.
KILL THEM!

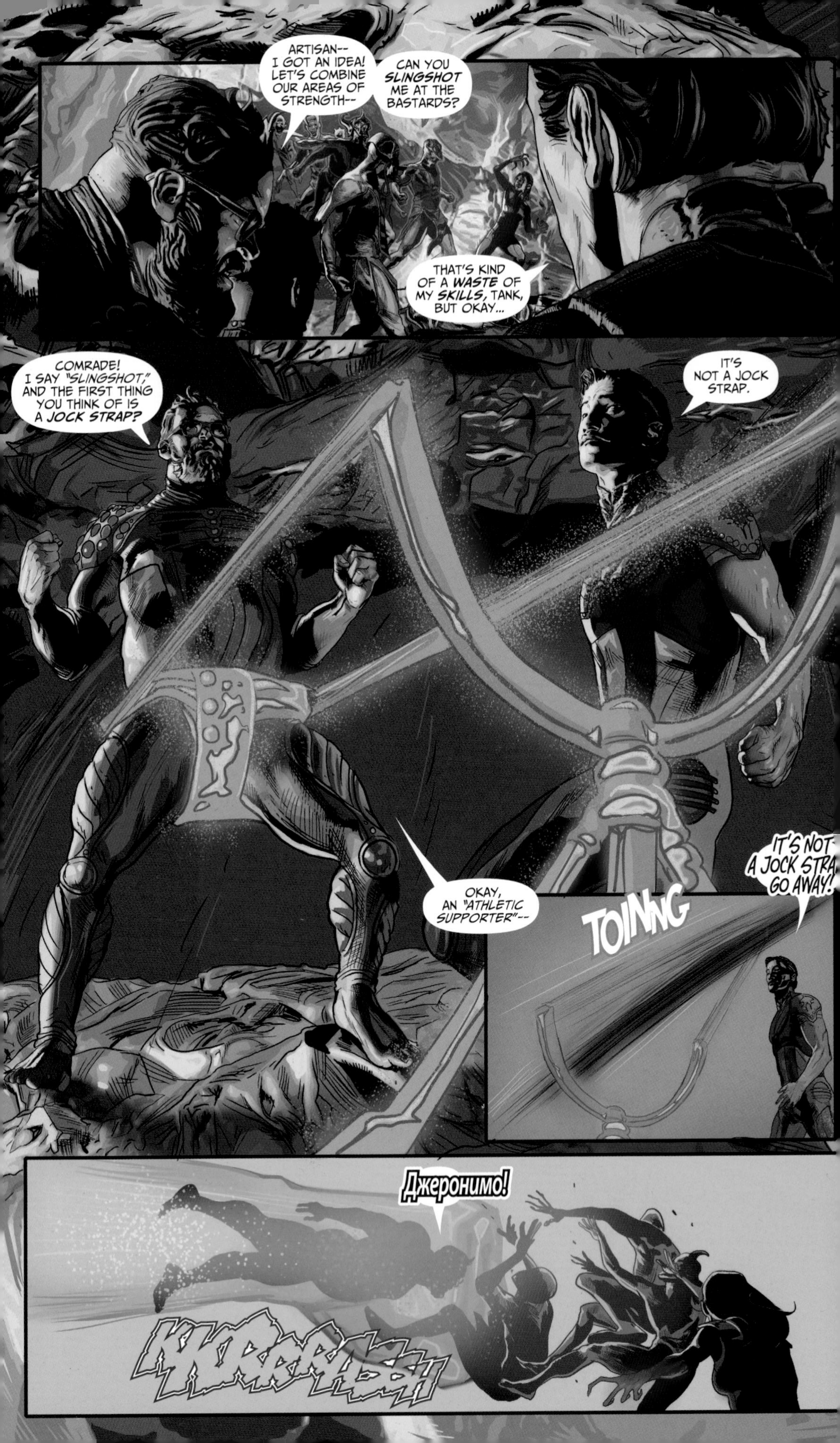
ARTISAN-- I GOT AN IDEA! LET'S COMBINE OUR AREAS OF STRENGTH--
CAN YOU SLINGSHOT ME AT THE BASTARDS?
THAT'S KIND OF A WASTE OF MY SKILLS, TANK, BUT OKAY...
COMRADE! I SAY "SLINGSHOT," AND THE FIRST THING YOU THINK OF IS A JOCK STRAP?
IT'S NOT A JOCK STRAP.
OKAY, AN "ATHLETIC SUPPORTER"--
IT'S NOT A JOCK STRA GO AWAY!
TOINNG
Джеронимо!

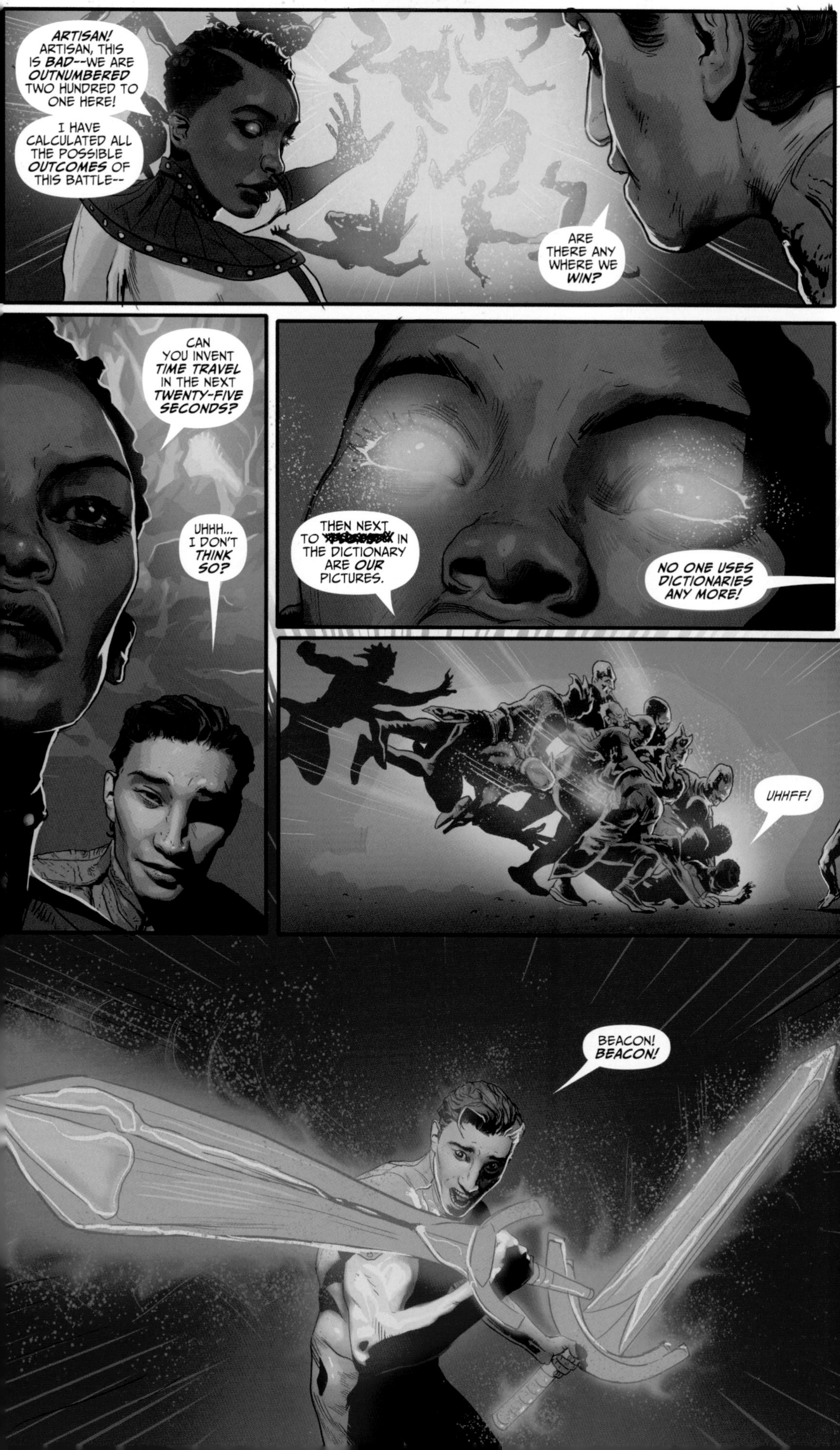
ARTISAN! ARTISAN, THIS IS BAD--WE ARE OUTNUMBERED TWO HUNDRED TO ONE HERE!
I HAVE CALCULATED ALL THE POSSIBLE OUTCOMES OF THIS BATTLE--
ARE THERE ANY WHERE WE WIN?
CAN YOU INVENT TIME TRAVEL IN THE NEXT TWENTY-FIVE SECONDS?
UHHH... I DON'T THINK SO?
THEN NEXT TO IN THE DICTIONARY ARE OUR PICTURES.
NO ONE USES DICTIONARIES ANY MORE!
UHHFF!
BEACON! BEACON!

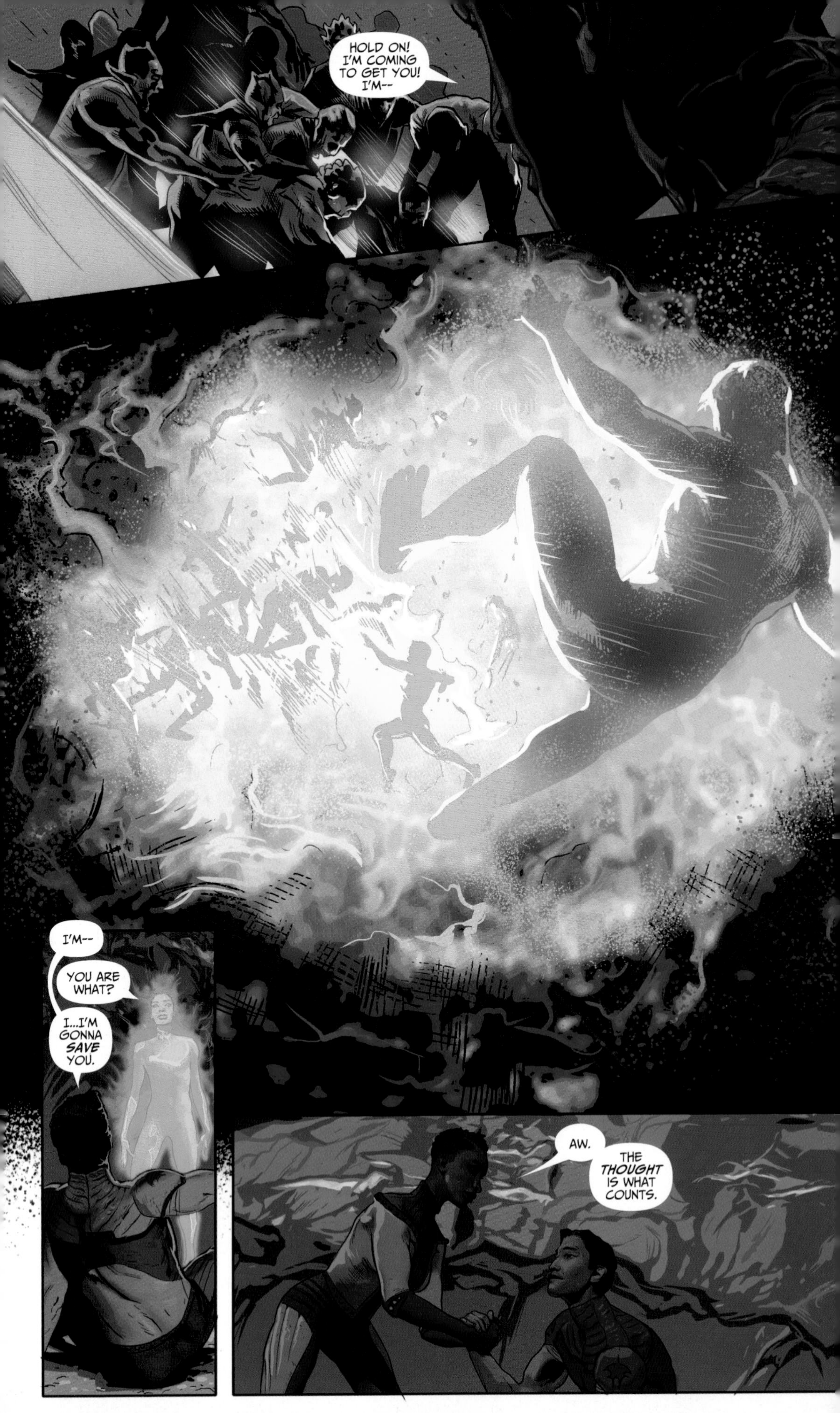
HOLD ON! I'M COMING TO GET YOU! I'M--
I'M--
YOU ARE WHAT?
I...I'M GONNA SAVE YOU.
AW.
THE THOUGHT IS WHAT COUNTS.

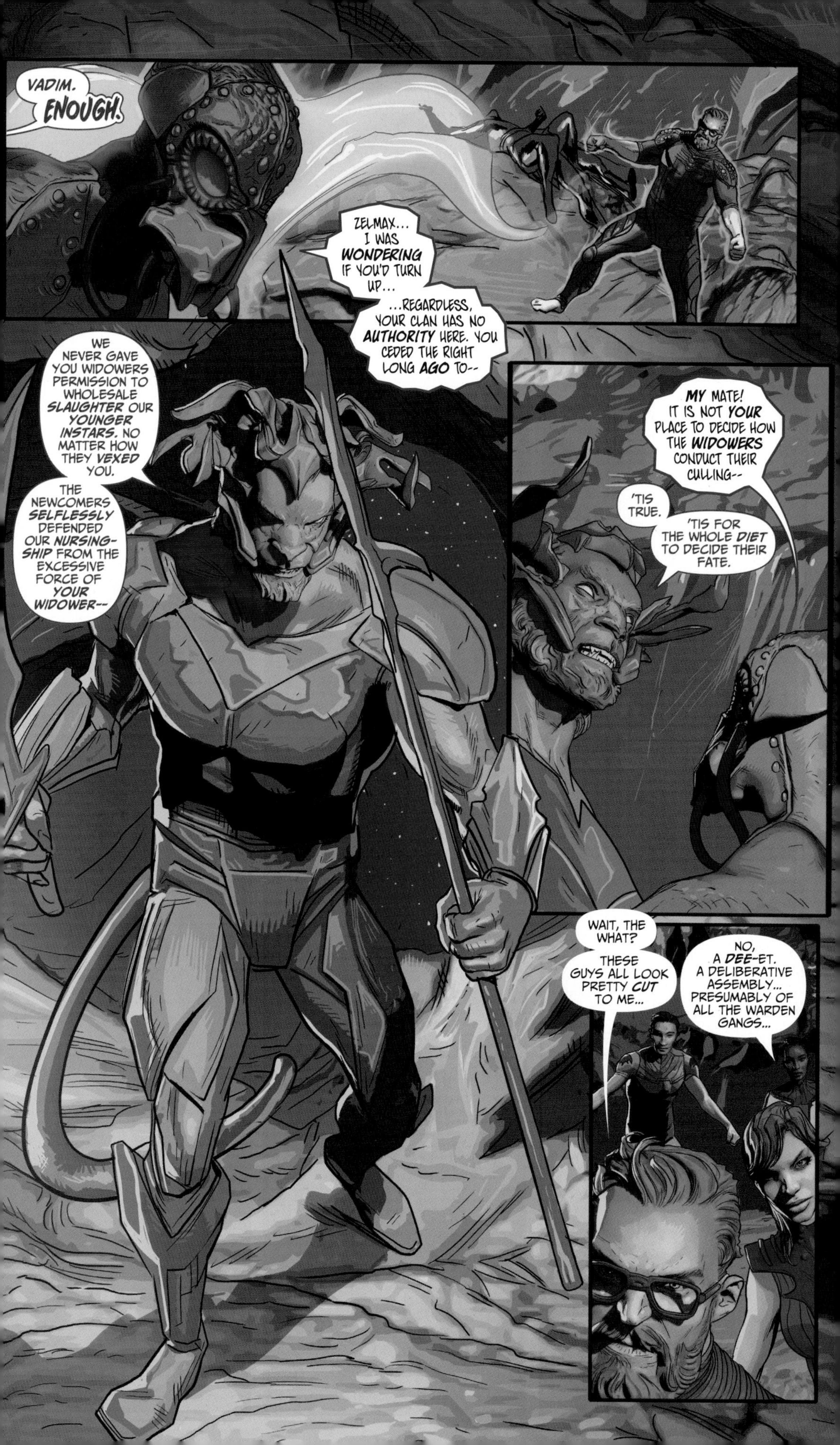
VADIM. ENOUGH.
ZELMAX... I WAS WONDERING IF YOU'D TURN UP...
...REGARDLESS, YOUR CLAN HAS NO AUTHORITY HERE. YOU CEDED THE RIGHT LONG AGO TO--
WE NEVER GAVE YOU WIDOWERS PERMISSION TO WHOLESALE SLAUGHTER OUR YOUNGER INSTARS. NO MATTER HOW THEY VEXED YOU.
THE NEWCOMERS SELFLESSLY DEFENDED OUR NURSING-SHIP FROM THE EXCESSIVE FORCE OF YOUR WIDOWER--
MY MATE! IT IS NOT YOUR PLACE TO DECIDE HOW THE WIDOWERS CONDUCT THEIR CULLING--
'TIS TRUE.
'TIS FOR THE WHOLE DIET TO DECIDE THEIR FATE.
WAIT, THE WHAT?
THESE GUYS ALL LOOK PRETTY CUT TO ME...
NO, A DEE-ET. A DELIBERATIVE ASSEMBLY... PRESUMABLY OF ALL THE WARDEN GANGS...

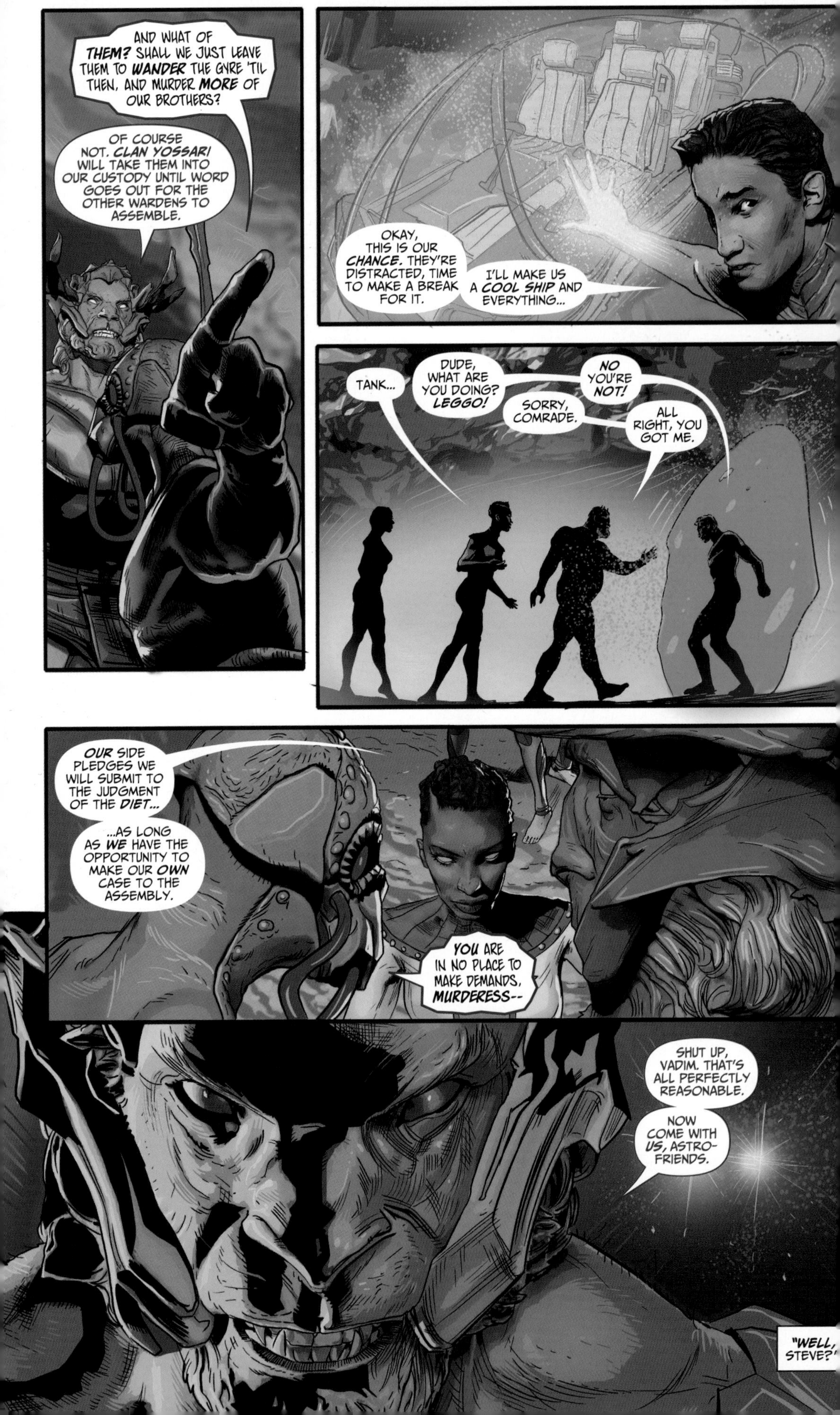
AND WHAT OF THEM? SHALL WE JUST LEAVE THEM TO WANDER THE GYRE 'TIL THEN, AND MURDER MORE OF OUR BROTHERS?
OF COURSE NOT. CLAN YOSSARI WILL TAKE THEM INTO OUR CUSTODY UNTIL WORD GOES OUT FOR THE OTHER WARDENS TO ASSEMBLE.
OKAY, THIS IS OUR CHANCE. THEY'RE DISTRACTED, TIME TO MAKE A BREAK FOR IT.
I'LL MAKE US A COOL SHIP AND EVERYTHING...
TANK...
DUDE, WHAT ARE YOU DOING? LEGGO!
NO YOU'RE NOT!
SORRY, COMRADE.
ALL RIGHT, YOU GOT ME.
OUR SIDE PLEDGES WE WILL SUBMIT TO THE JUDGMENT OF THE DIET...
...AS LONG AS WE HAVE THE OPPORTUNITY TO MAKE OUR OWN CASE TO THE ASSEMBLY.
YOU ARE IN NO PLACE TO MAKE DEMANDS, MURDERESS--
SHUT UP, VADIM. THAT'S ALL PERFECTLY REASONABLE.
NOW COME WITH US, ASTRO-FRIENDS.
"WELL, STEVE?"

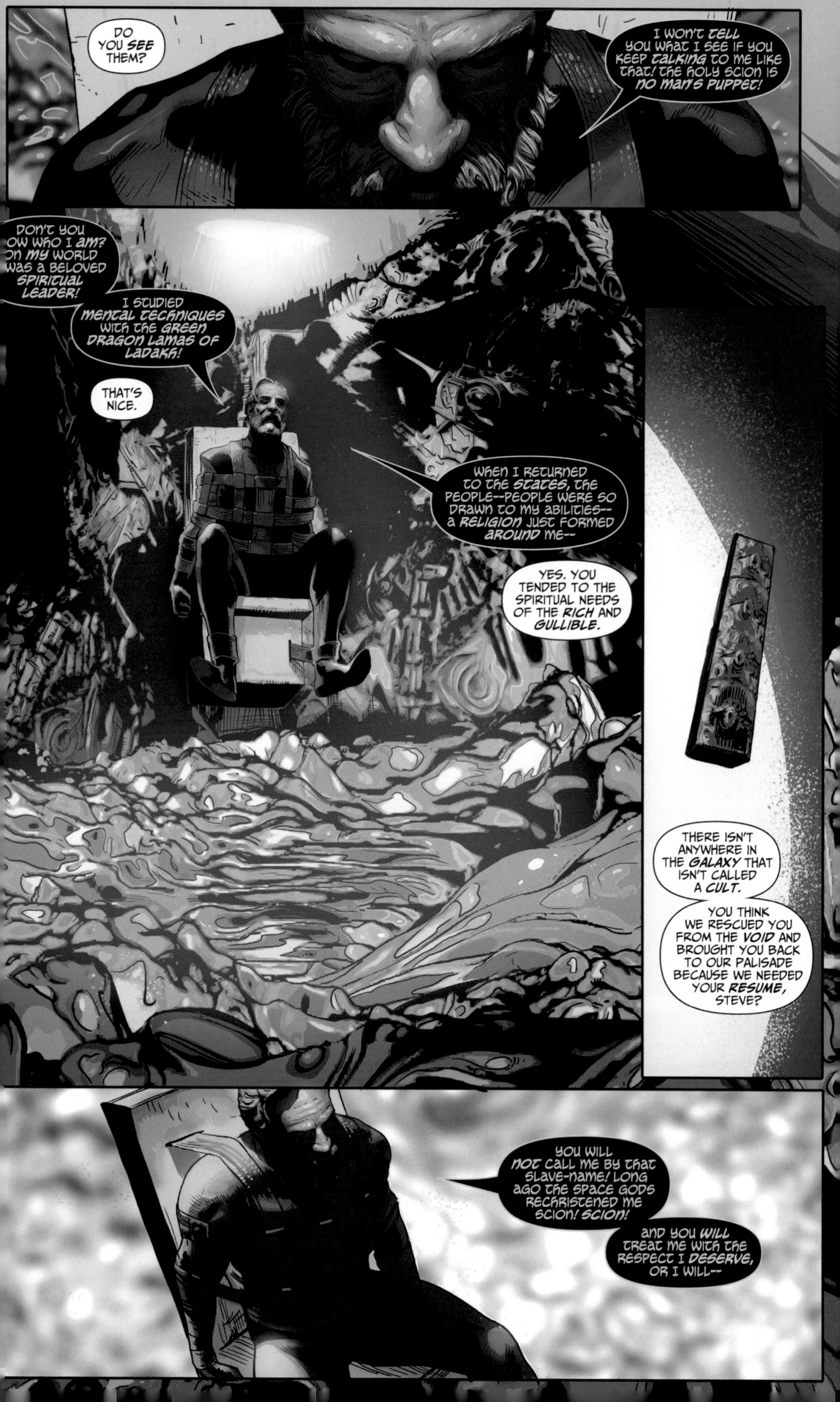
DO YOU SEE THEM?
I WON'T TELL YOU WHAT I SEE IF YOU KEEP TALKING TO ME LIKE THAT! THE HOLY SCION IS NO MAN'S PUPPET!
DON'T YOU OW WHO I AM? ON MY WORLD WAS A BELOVED SPIRITUAL LEADER!
I STUDIED MENTAL TECHNIQUES WITH THE GREEN DRAGON LAMAS OF LADAKH!
THAT'S NICE.
WHEN I RETURNED TO THE STATES, THE PEOPLE--PEOPLE WERE SO DRAWN TO MY ABILITIES-- a RELIGION JUST FORMED AROUND ME--
YES. YOU TENDED TO THE SPIRITUAL NEEDS OF THE RICH AND GULLIBLE.
THERE ISN'T ANYWHERE IN THE GALAXY THAT ISN'T CALLED A CULT.
YOU THINK WE RESCUED YOU FROM THE VOID AND BROUGHT YOU BACK TO OUR PALISADE BECAUSE WE NEEDED YOUR RESUME, STEVE?
YOU WILL NOT CALL ME BY THAT SLAVE-NAME! LONG AGO THE SPACE GODS RECHRISTENED ME SCION! SCION!
AND YOU WILL TREAT ME WITH THE RESPECT I DESERVE, OR I WILL--

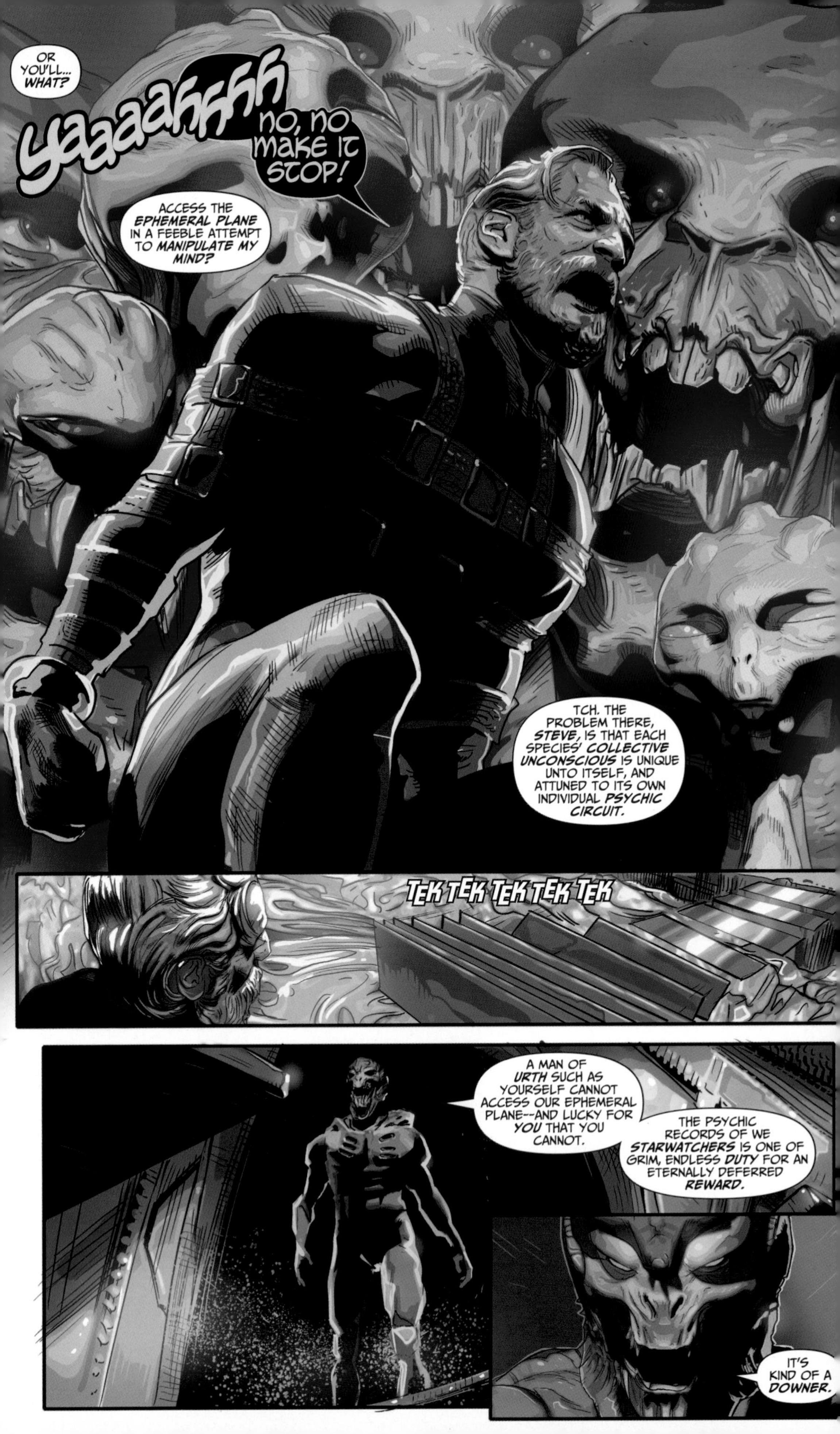
OR YOU'LL... WHAT?
YAAAAHHHH
NO, NO MAKE IT STOP!
ACCESS THE EPHEMERAL PLANE IN A FEEBLE ATTEMPT TO MANIPULATE MY MIND?
TCH. THE PROBLEM THERE, STEVE, IS THAT EACH SPECIES' COLLECTIVE UNCONSCIOUS IS UNIQUE UNTO ITSELF, AND ATTUNED TO ITS OWN INDIVIDUAL PSYCHIC CIRCUIT.
TEK TEK TEK TEK TEK
A MAN OF URTH SUCH AS YOURSELF CANNOT ACCESS OUR EPHEMERAL PLANE--AND LUCKY FOR YOU THAT YOU CANNOT.
THE PSYCHIC RECORDS OF WE STARWATCHERS IS ONE OF GRIM, ENDLESS DUTY FOR AN ETERNALLY DEFERRED REWARD.
IT'S KIND OF A DOWNER.

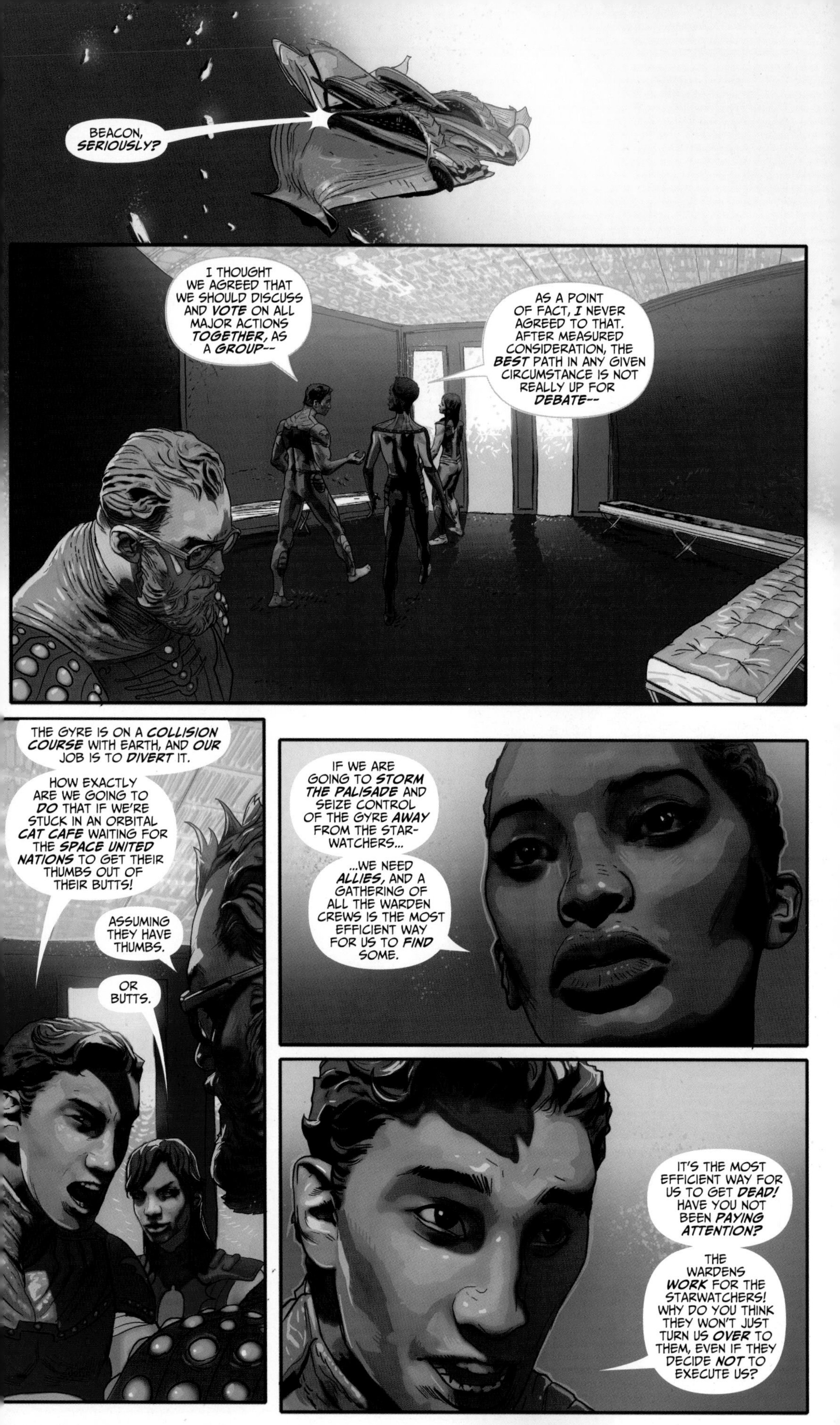

BEACON, SERIOUSLY?
I THOUGHT WE AGREED THAT WE SHOULD DISCUSS AND VOTE ON ALL MAJOR ACTIONS TOGETHER, AS A GROUP--
AS A POINT OF FACT, I NEVER AGREED TO THAT. AFTER MEASURED CONSIDERATION, THE BEST PATH IN ANY GIVEN CIRCUMSTANCE IS NOT REALLY UP FOR DEBATE--
THE GYRE IS ON A COLLISION COURSE WITH EARTH, AND OUR JOB IS TO DIVERT IT.
HOW EXACTLY ARE WE GOING TO DO THAT IF WE'RE STUCK IN AN ORBITAL CAT CAFE WAITING FOR THE SPACE UNITED NATIONS TO GET THEIR THUMBS OUT OF THEIR BUTTS!
ASSUMING THEY HAVE THUMBS.
OR BUTTS.
IF WE ARE GOING TO STORM THE PALISADE AND SEIZE CONTROL OF THE GYRE AWAY FROM THE STAR-WATCHERS...
...WE NEED ALLIES, AND A GATHERING OF ALL THE WARDEN CREWS IS THE MOST EFFICIENT WAY FOR US TO FIND SOME.
IT'S THE MOST EFFICIENT WAY FOR US TO GET DEAD! HAVE YOU NOT BEEN PAYING ATTENTION?
THE WARDENS WORK FOR THE STARWATCHERS! WHY DO YOU THINK THEY WON'T JUST TURN US OVER TO THEM, EVEN IF THEY DECIDE NOT TO EXECUTE US?

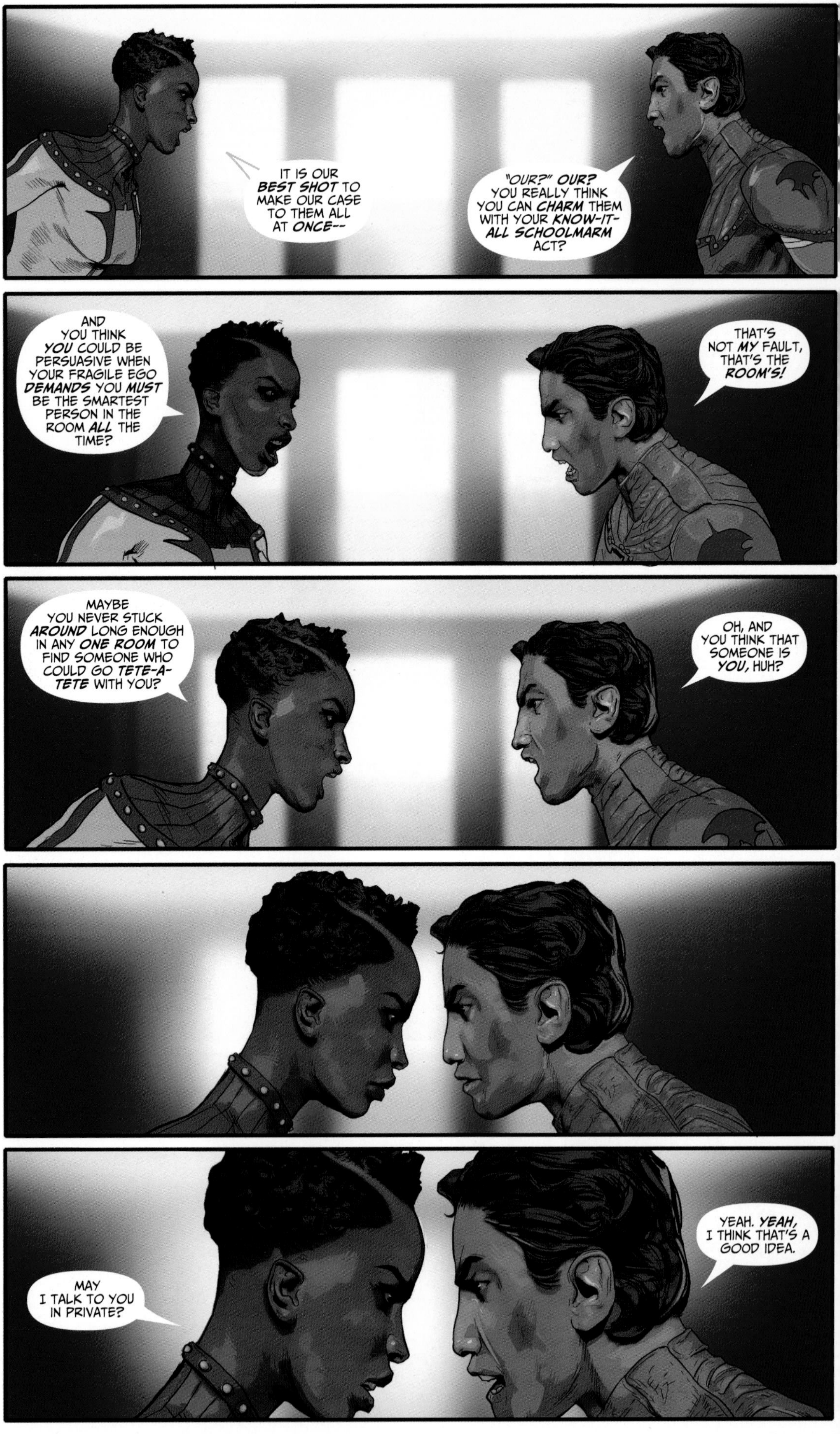
IT IS OUR BEST SHOT TO MAKE OUR CASE TO THEM ALL AT ONCE--
"OUR?" OUR? YOU REALLY THINK YOU CAN CHARM THEM WITH YOUR KNOW-IT-ALL SCHOOLMARM ACT?
AND YOU THINK YOU COULD BE PERSUASIVE WHEN YOUR FRAGILE EGO DEMANDS YOU MUST BE THE SMARTEST PERSON IN THE ROOM ALL THE TIME?
THAT'S NOT MY FAULT, THAT'S THE ROOM'S!
MAYBE YOU NEVER STUCK AROUND LONG ENOUGH IN ANY ONE ROOM TO FIND SOMEONE WHO COULD GO TETE-A-TETE WITH YOU?
OH, AND YOU THINK THAT SOMEONE IS YOU, HUH?
MAY I TALK TO YOU IN PRIVATE?
YEAH. YEAH, I THINK THAT'S A GOOD IDEA.

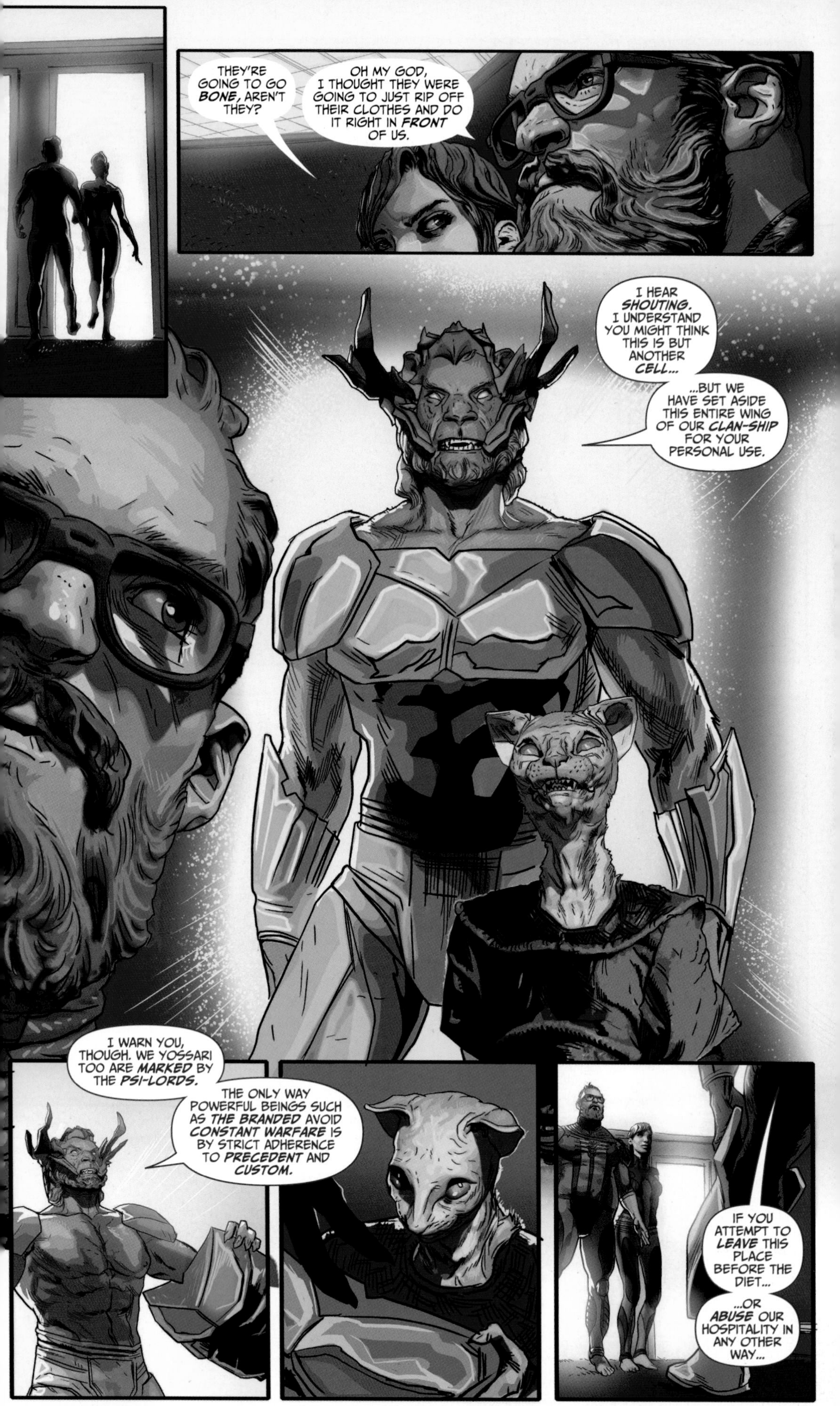
THEY'RE GOING TO GO BONE, AREN'T THEY?
OH MY GOD, I THOUGHT THEY WERE GOING TO JUST RIP OFF THEIR CLOTHES AND DO IT RIGHT IN FRONT OF US.
I HEAR SHOUTING. I UNDERSTAND YOU MIGHT THINK THIS IS BUT ANOTHER CELL...
...BUT WE HAVE SET ASIDE THIS ENTIRE WING OF OUR CLAN-SHIP FOR YOUR PERSONAL USE.
I WARN YOU, THOUGH. WE YOSSARI TOO ARE MARKED BY THE PSI-LORDS.
THE ONLY WAY POWERFUL BEINGS SUCH AS THE BRANDED AVOID CONSTANT WARFARE IS BY STRICT ADHERENCE TO PRECEDENT AND CUSTOM.
IF YOU ATTEMPT TO LEAVE THIS PLACE BEFORE THE DIET...
...OR ABUSE OUR HOSPITALITY IN ANY OTHER WAY...

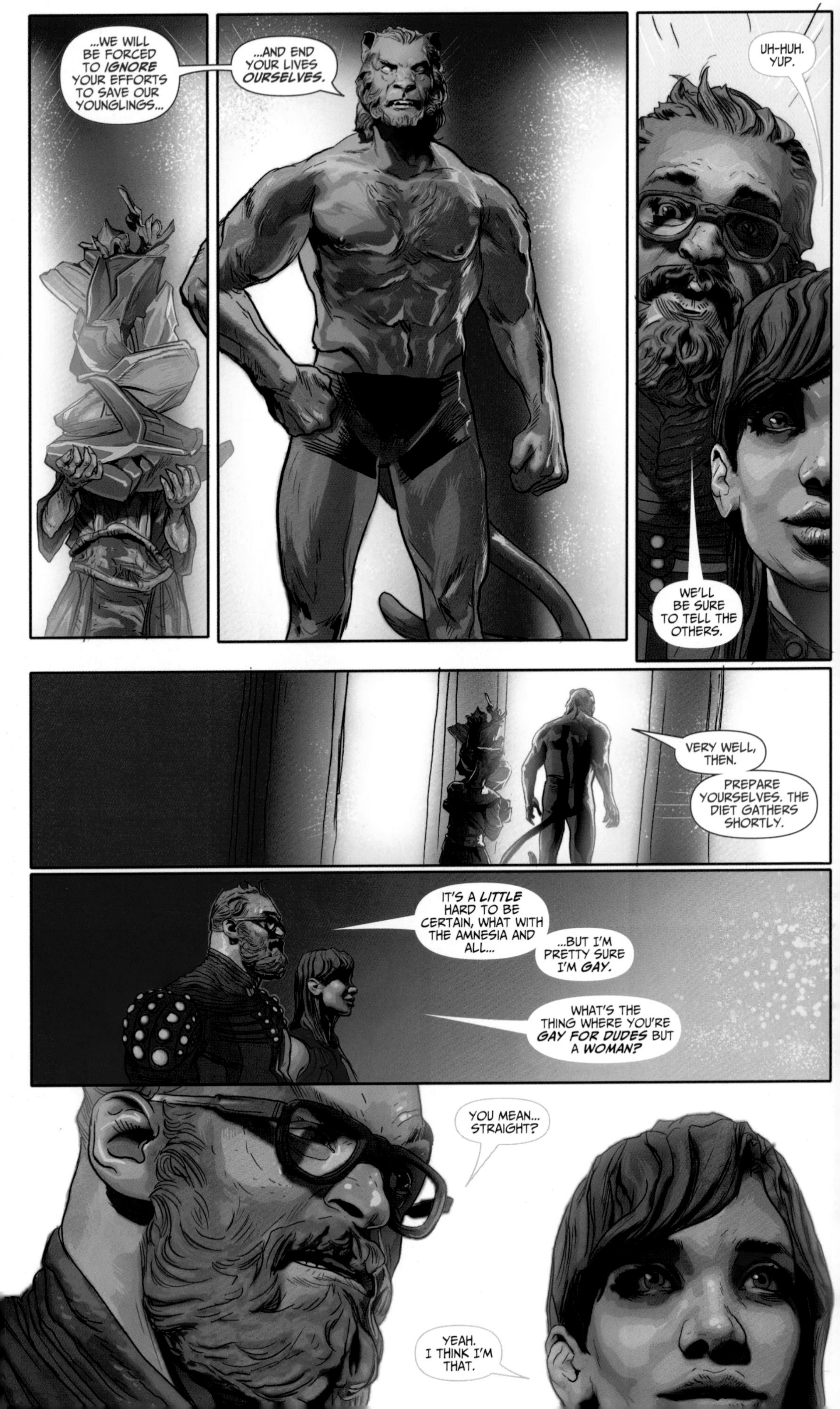
...WE WILL BE FORCED TO IGNORE YOUR EFFORTS TO SAVE OUR YOUNGLINGS...
...AND END YOUR LIVES OURSELVES.
UH-HUH. YUP.
WE'LL BE SURE TO TELL THE OTHERS.
VERY WELL, THEN.
PREPARE YOURSELVES. THE DIET GATHERS SHORTLY.
IT'S A LITTLE HARD TO BE CERTAIN, WHAT WITH THE AMNESIA AND ALL...
...BUT I'M PRETTY SURE I'M GAY.
WHAT'S THE THING WHERE YOU'RE GAY FOR DUDES BUT A WOMAN?
YOU MEAN... STRAIGHT?
YEAH. I THINK I'M THAT.

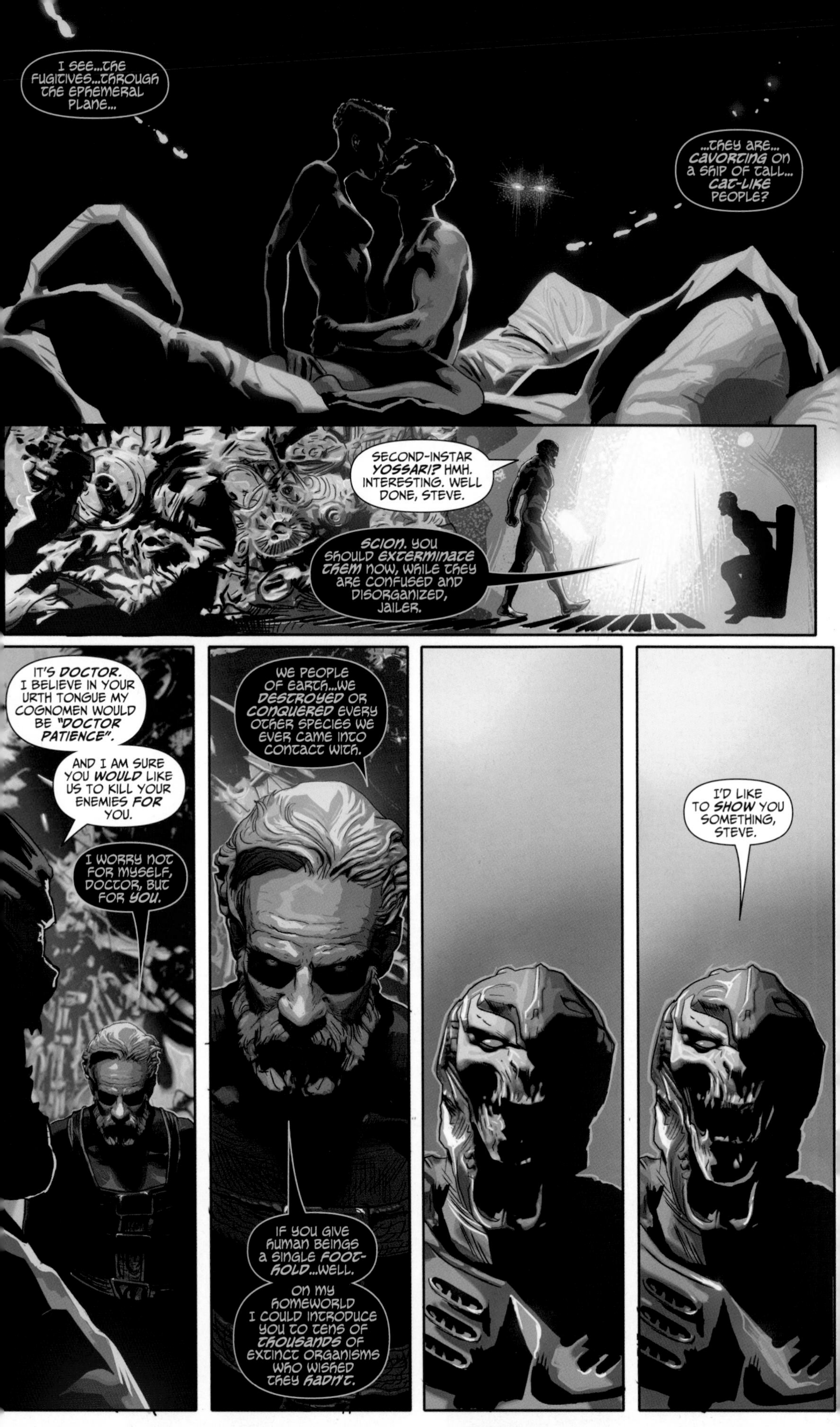

I SEE...THE FUGITIVES...THROUGH THE EPHEMERAL PLANE...
...THEY ARE... CAVORTING ON A SHIP OF TALL... CAT-LIKE PEOPLE?
SECOND-INSTAR YOSSARI? HMH. INTERESTING. WELL DONE, STEVE.
SCION. YOU SHOULD EXTERMINATE THEM NOW, WHILE THEY ARE CONFUSED AND DISORGANIZED, JAILER.
IT'S DOCTOR. I BELIEVE IN YOUR URTH TONGUE MY COGNOMEN WOULD BE "DOCTOR PATIENCE".
AND I AM SURE YOU WOULD LIKE US TO KILL YOUR ENEMIES FOR YOU.
I WORRY NOT FOR MYSELF, DOCTOR, BUT FOR YOU.
WE PEOPLE OF EARTH...WE DESTROYED OR CONQUERED EVERY OTHER SPECIES WE EVER CAME INTO CONTACT WITH.
IF YOU GIVE HUMAN BEINGS A SINGLE FOOT-HOLD...WELL.
ON MY HOMEWORLD I COULD INTRODUCE YOU TO TENS OF THOUSANDS OF EXTINCT ORGANISMS WHO WISHED THEY HADN'T.
I'D LIKE TO SHOW YOU SOMETHING, STEVE.

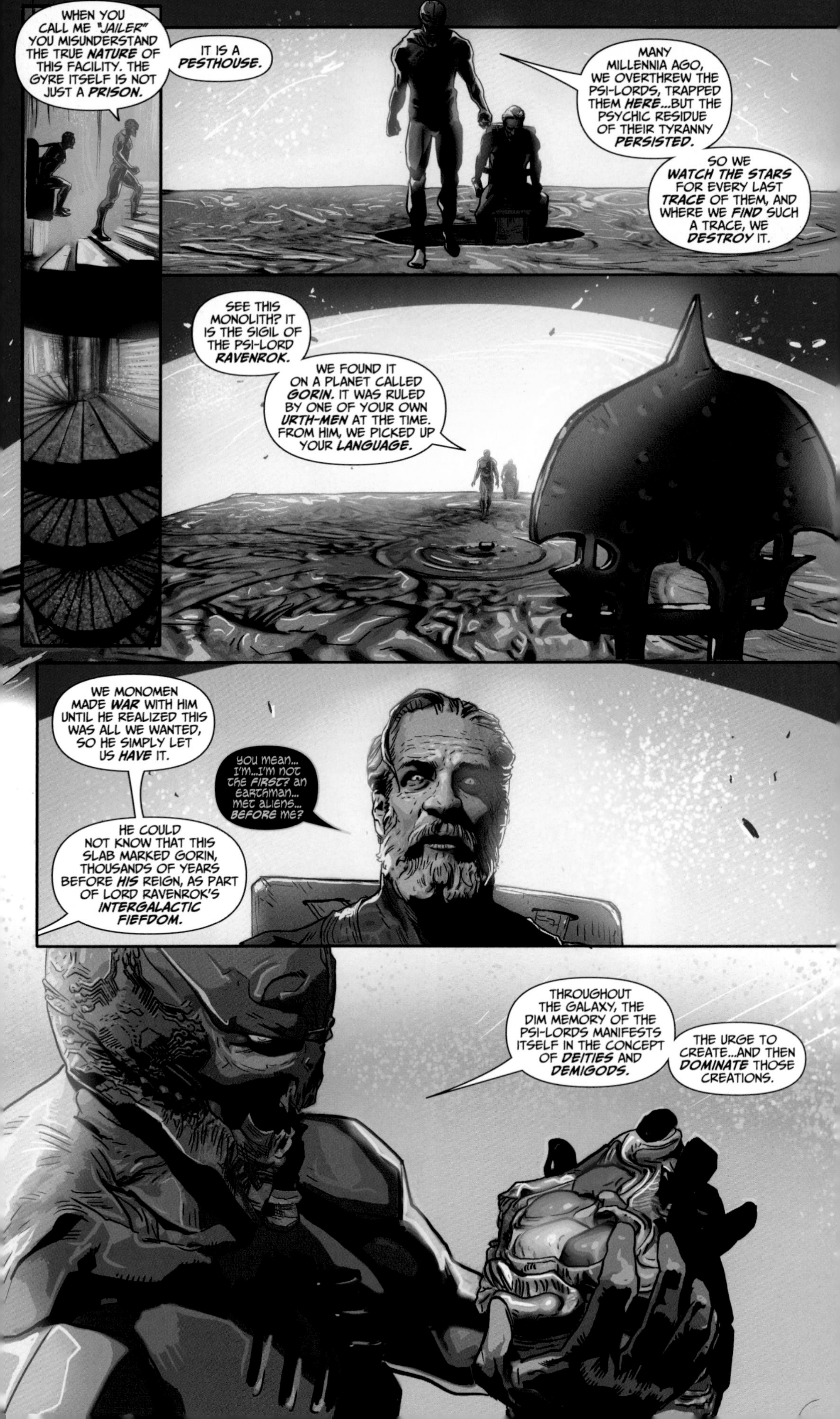
WHEN YOU CALL ME "JAILER" YOU MISUNDERSTAND THE TRUE NATURE OF THIS FACILITY. THE GYRE ITSELF IS NOT JUST A PRISON.
IT IS A PESTHOUSE.
MANY MILLENNIA AGO, WE OVERTHREW THE PSI-LORDS, TRAPPED THEM HERE...BUT THE PSYCHIC RESIDUE OF THEIR TYRANNY PERSISTED.
SO WE WATCH THE STARS FOR EVERY LAST TRACE OF THEM, AND WHERE WE FIND SUCH A TRACE, WE DESTROY IT.
SEE THIS MONOLITH? IT IS THE SIGIL OF THE PSI-LORD RAVENROK.
WE FOUND IT ON A PLANET CALLED GORIN. IT WAS RULED BY ONE OF YOUR OWN URTH-MEN AT THE TIME. FROM HIM, WE PICKED UP YOUR LANGUAGE.
WE MONOMEN MADE WAR WITH HIM UNTIL HE REALIZED THIS WAS ALL WE WANTED, SO HE SIMPLY LET US HAVE IT.
HE COULD NOT KNOW THAT THIS SLAB MARKED GORIN, THOUSANDS OF YEARS BEFORE HIS REIGN, AS PART OF LORD RAVENROK'S INTERGALACTIC FIEFDOM.
You mean... I'm...I'm not the FIRST? an earthman... met aliens... BEFORE me?
THROUGHOUT THE GALAXY, THE DIM MEMORY OF THE PSI-LORDS MANIFESTS ITSELF IN THE CONCEPT OF DEITIES AND DEMIGODS.
THE URGE TO CREATE...AND THEN DOMINATE THOSE CREATIONS.

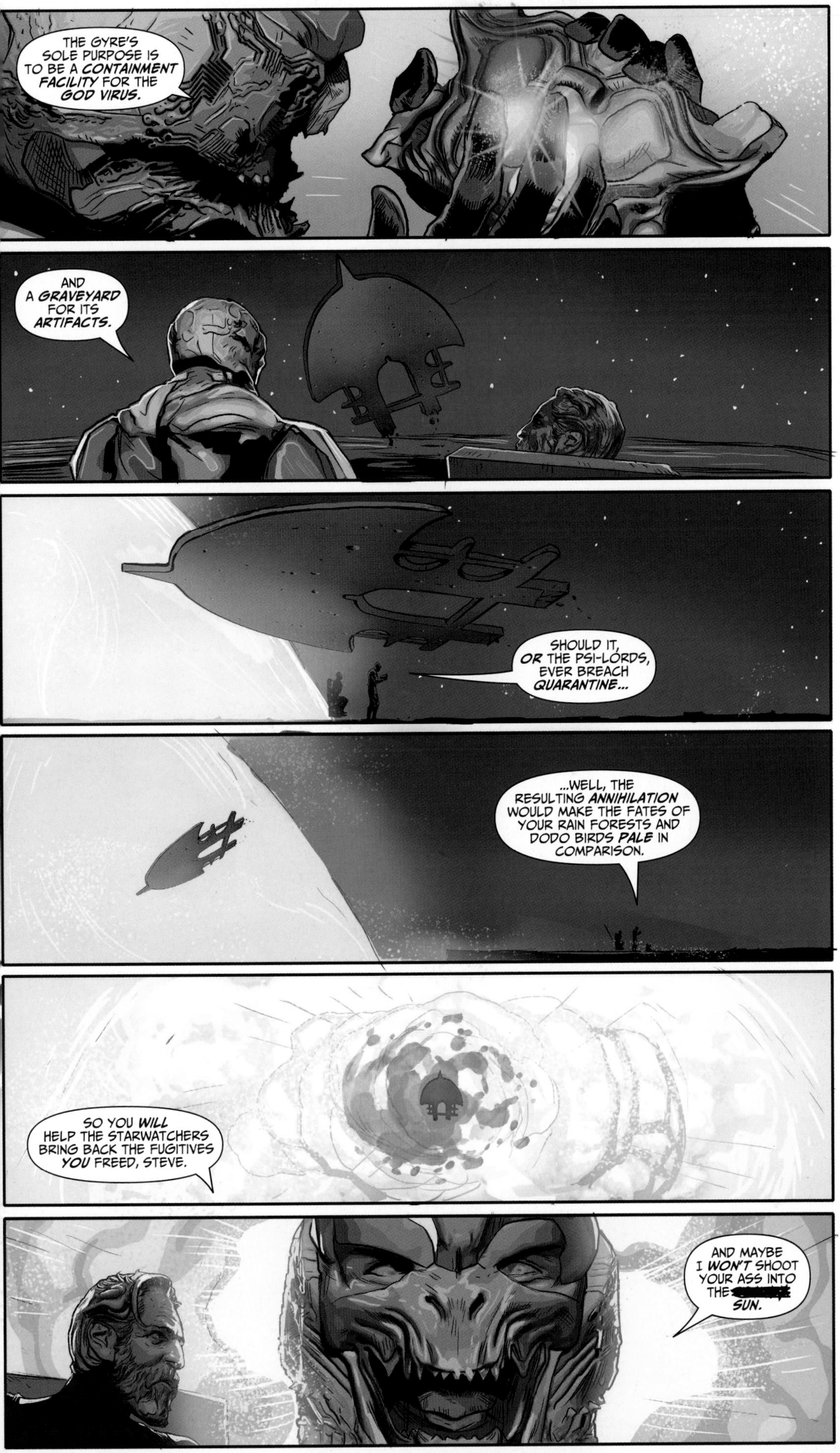
THE GYRE'S SOLE PURPOSE IS TO BE A *CONTAINMENT FACILITY* FOR THE *GOD VIRUS*.
AND A *GRAVEYARD* FOR ITS *ARTIFACTS*.
SHOULD IT, *OR* THE PSI-LORDS, EVER BREACH *QUARANTINE*...
...WELL, THE RESULTING *ANNIHILATION* WOULD MAKE THE FATES OF YOUR RAIN FORESTS AND DODO BIRDS *PALE* IN COMPARISON.
SO YOU *WILL* HELP THE STARWATCHERS BRING BACK THE FUGITIVES *YOU* FREED, STEVE.
AND MAYBE I *WON'T* SHOOT YOUR ASS INTO THE [redacted] *SUN*.

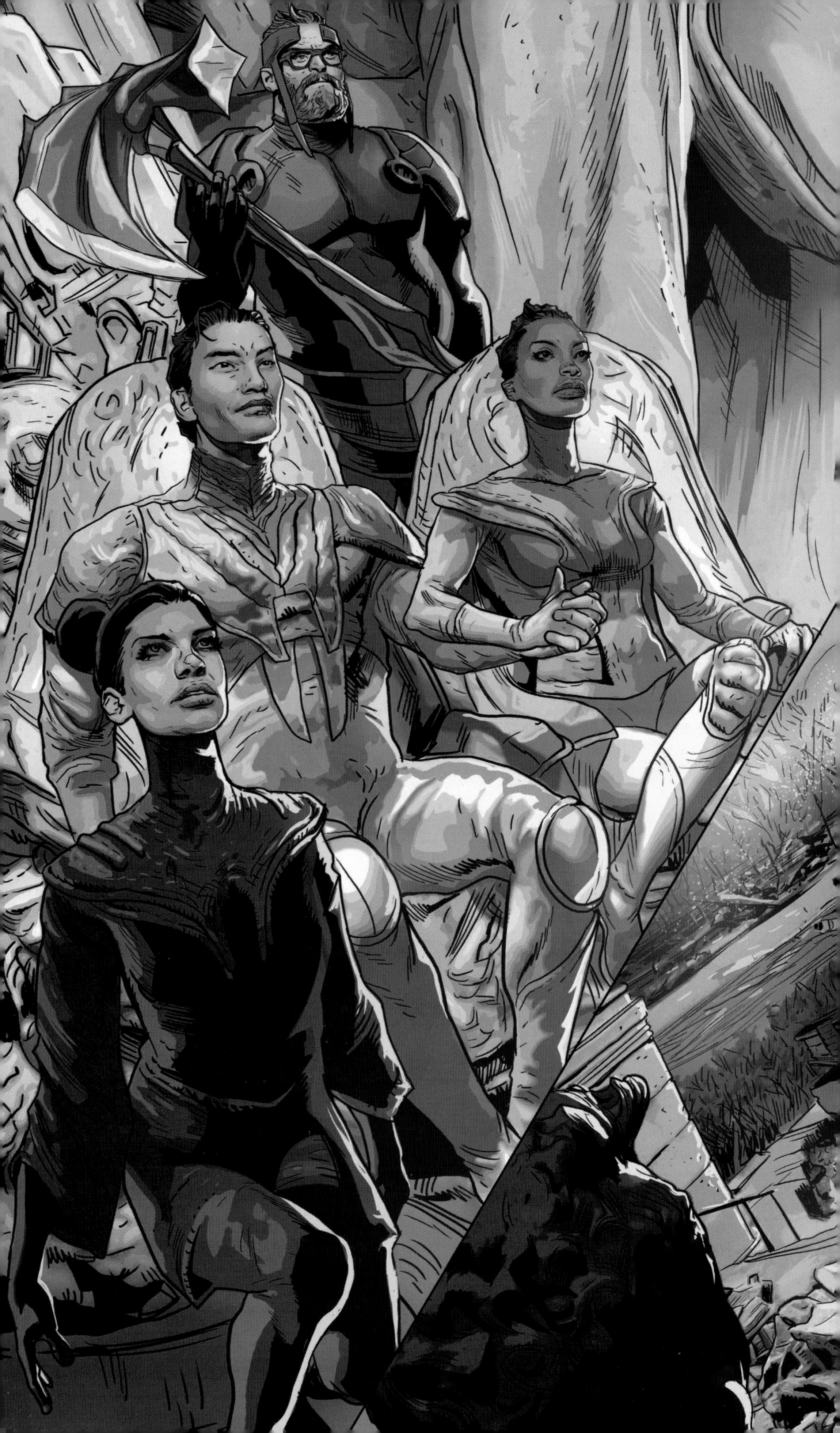

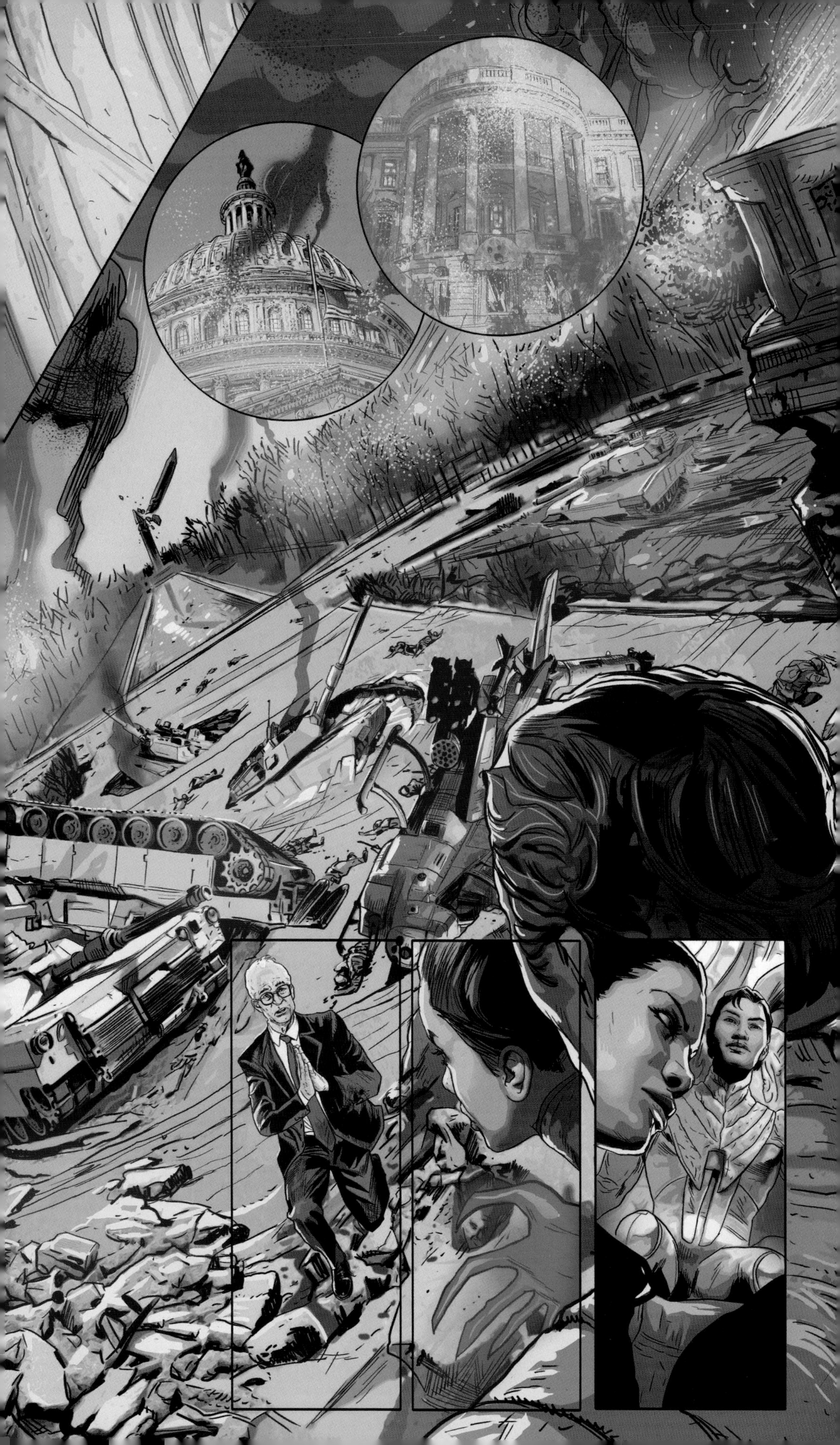

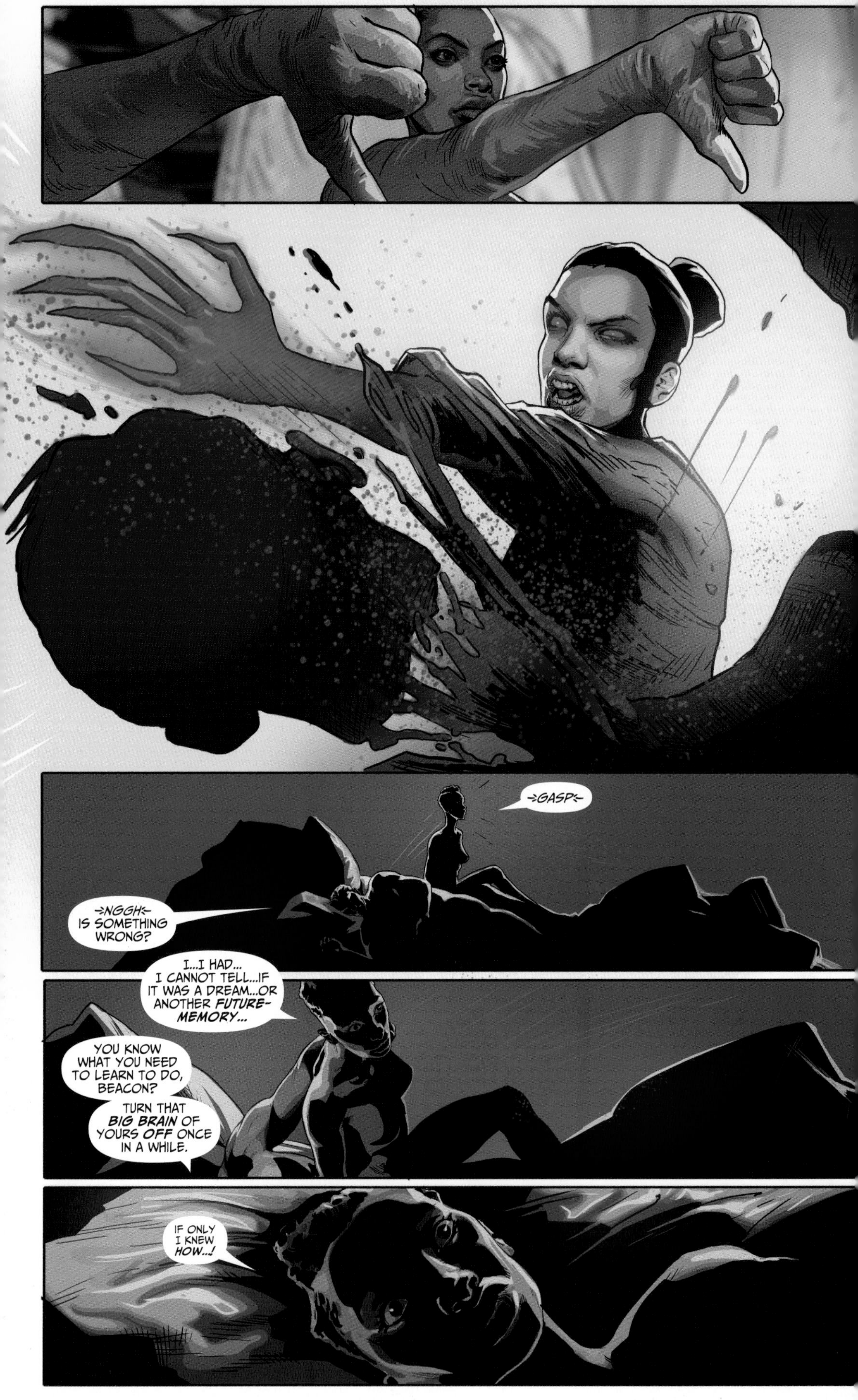

>GASP<
>NGGH< IS SOMETHING WRONG?
I...I HAD... I CANNOT TELL...IF IT WAS A DREAM...OR ANOTHER FUTURE-MEMORY...
YOU KNOW WHAT YOU NEED TO LEARN TO DO, BEACON?
TURN THAT BIG BRAIN OF YOURS OFF ONCE IN A WHILE.
IF ONLY I KNEW HOW...!

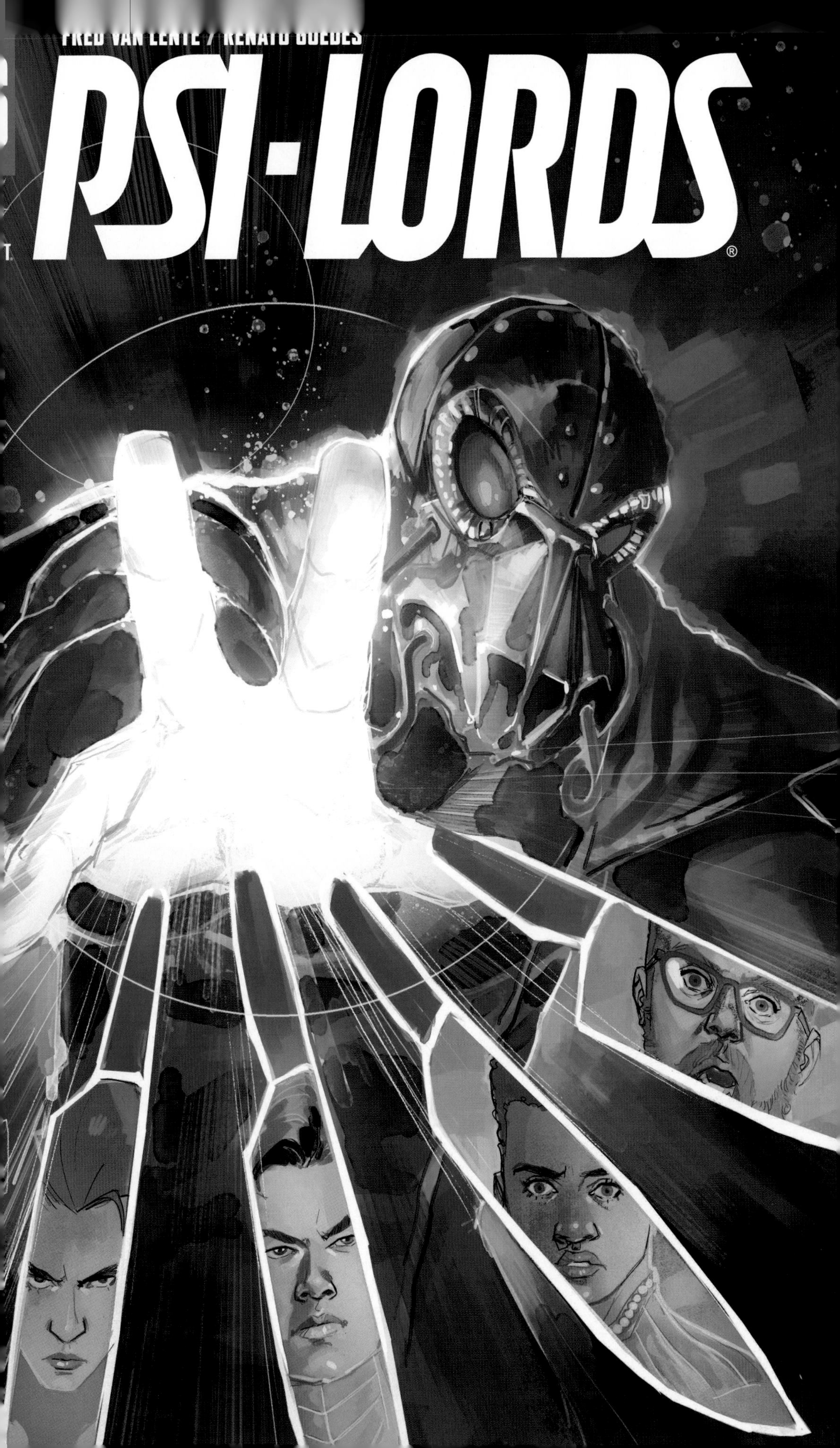

FRED VAN LENTE / RENATO GUEDES
PSI-LORDS®

**PSI-LORDS**

WRITER: Fred Van L
ARTIST: Renato Gue
LETTERER: Dave Sha
COVER ARTIST: Rod
ASSISTANT EDITOR: Drew Baumgar
EDITOR: David Men

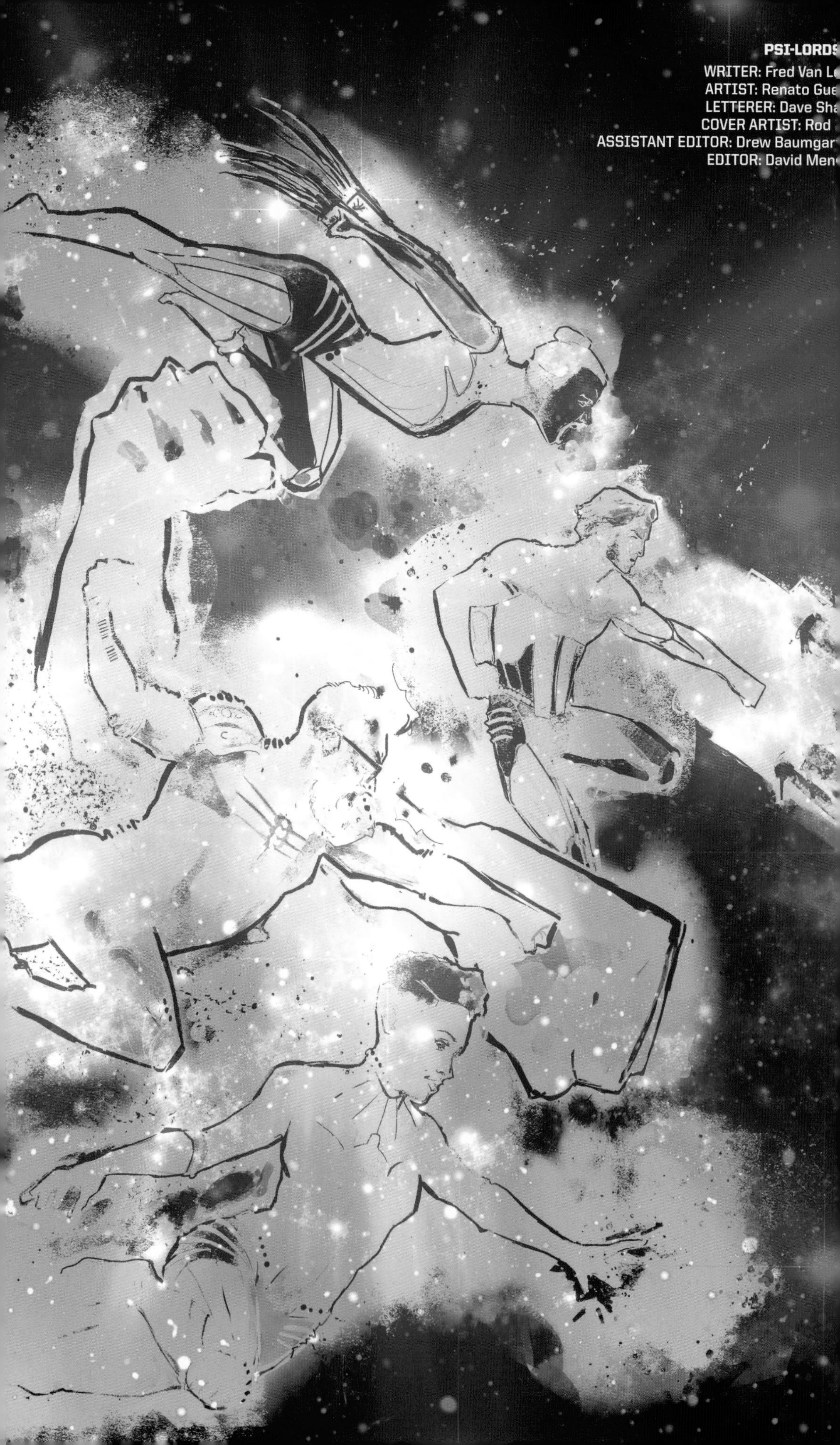

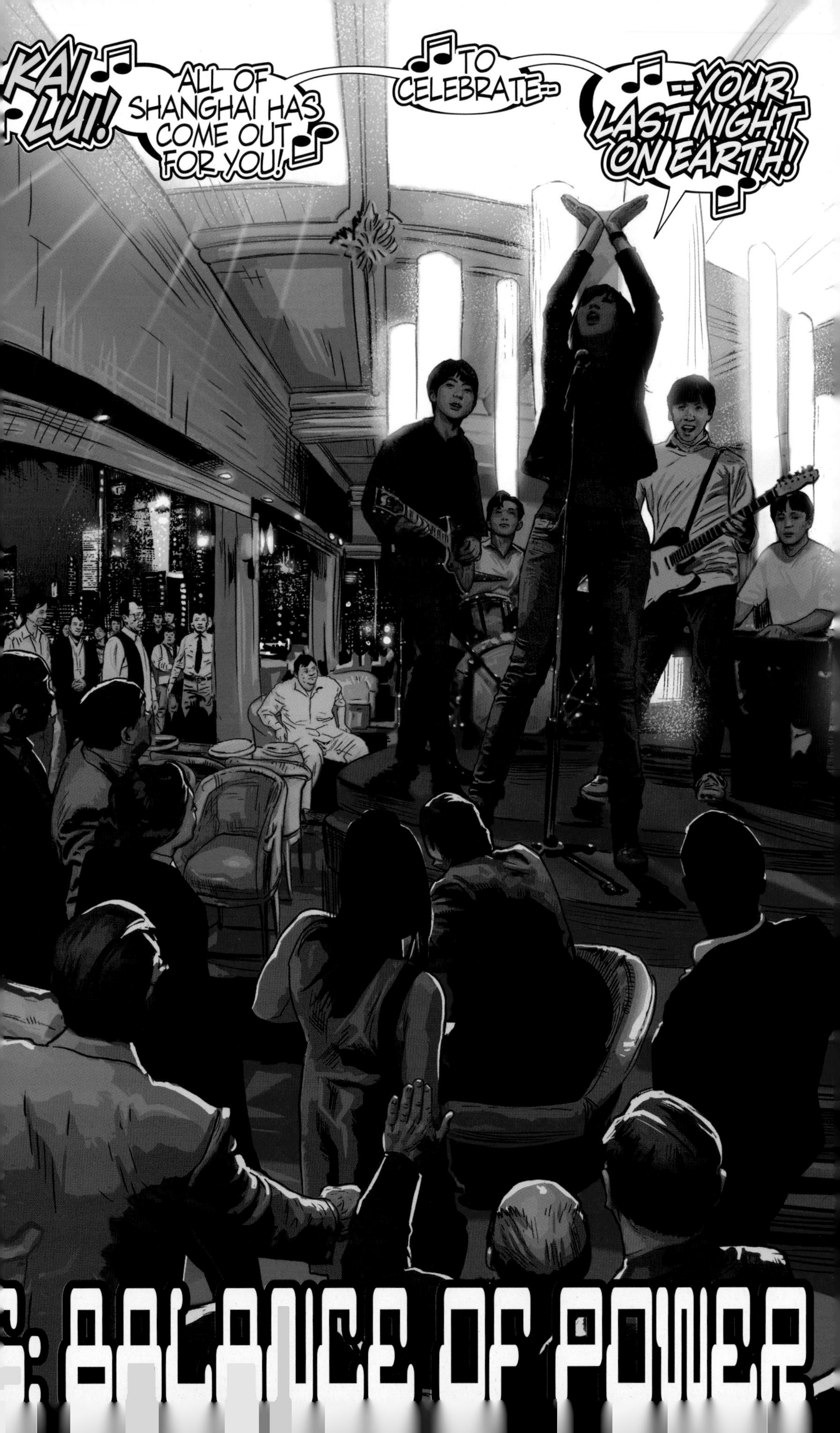
KAI LUI!
ALL OF SHANGHAI HAS COME OUT FOR YOU!
TO CELEBRATE--
--YOUR LAST NIGHT ON EARTH!
BALANCE OF POWER

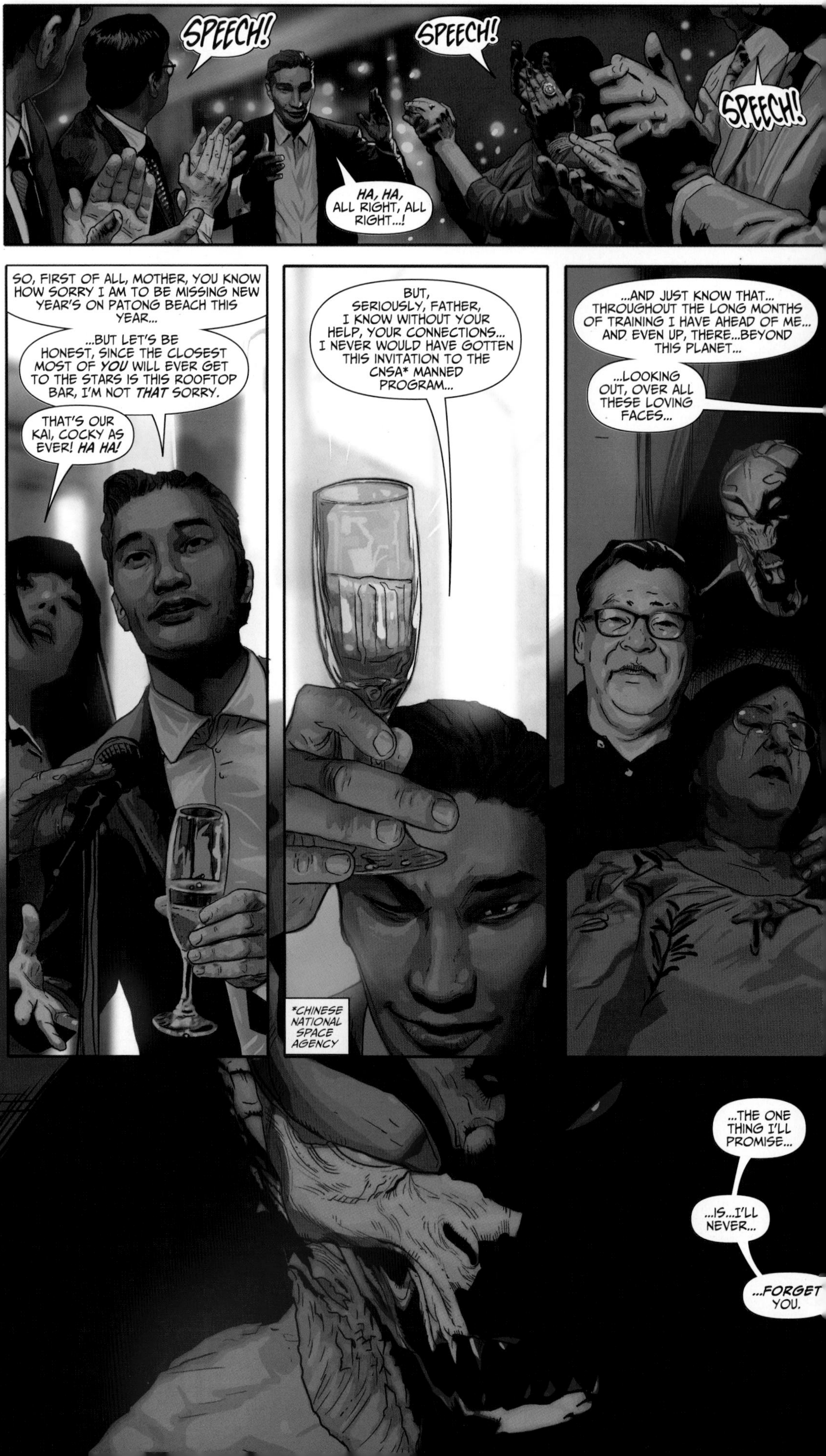
SPEECH!
SPEECH!
SPEECH!
HA, HA, ALL RIGHT, ALL RIGHT...!
SO, FIRST OF ALL, MOTHER, YOU KNOW HOW SORRY I AM TO BE MISSING NEW YEAR'S ON PATONG BEACH THIS YEAR...
...BUT LET'S BE HONEST, SINCE THE CLOSEST MOST OF YOU WILL EVER GET TO THE STARS IS THIS ROOFTOP BAR, I'M NOT THAT SORRY.
THAT'S OUR KAI, COCKY AS EVER! HA HA!
BUT, SERIOUSLY, FATHER, I KNOW WITHOUT YOUR HELP, YOUR CONNECTIONS... I NEVER WOULD HAVE GOTTEN THIS INVITATION TO THE CNSA* MANNED PROGRAM...
*CHINESE NATIONAL SPACE AGENCY
...AND JUST KNOW THAT... THROUGHOUT THE LONG MONTHS OF TRAINING I HAVE AHEAD OF ME... AND EVEN UP, THERE...BEYOND THIS PLANET...
...LOOKING OUT, OVER ALL THESE LOVING FACES...
...THE ONE THING I'LL PROMISE...
...IS...I'LL NEVER...
...FORGET YOU.

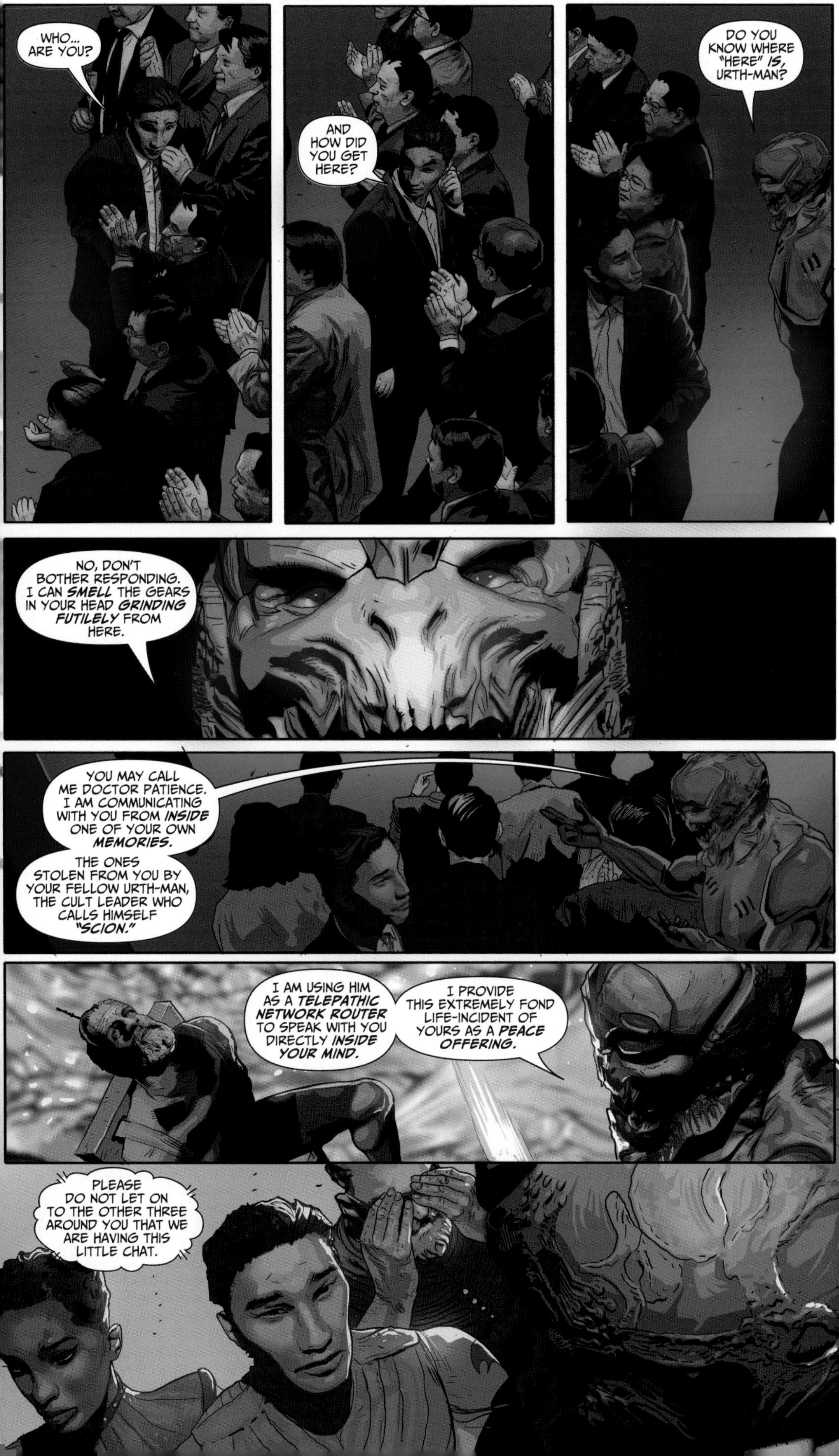
WHO... ARE YOU?
AND HOW DID YOU GET HERE?
DO YOU KNOW WHERE "HERE" *IS*, URTH-MAN?
NO, DON'T BOTHER RESPONDING. I CAN *SMELL* THE GEARS IN YOUR HEAD *GRINDING FUTILELY* FROM HERE.
YOU MAY CALL ME DOCTOR PATIENCE. I AM COMMUNICATING WITH YOU FROM *INSIDE* ONE OF YOUR OWN *MEMORIES*.
THE ONES STOLEN FROM YOU BY YOUR FELLOW URTH-MAN, THE CULT LEADER WHO CALLS HIMSELF *"SCION."*
I AM USING HIM AS A *TELEPATHIC NETWORK ROUTER* TO SPEAK WITH YOU DIRECTLY *INSIDE YOUR MIND*.
I PROVIDE THIS EXTREMELY FOND LIFE-INCIDENT OF YOURS AS A *PEACE OFFERING*.
PLEASE DO NOT LET ON TO THE OTHER THREE AROUND YOU THAT WE ARE HAVING THIS LITTLE CHAT.

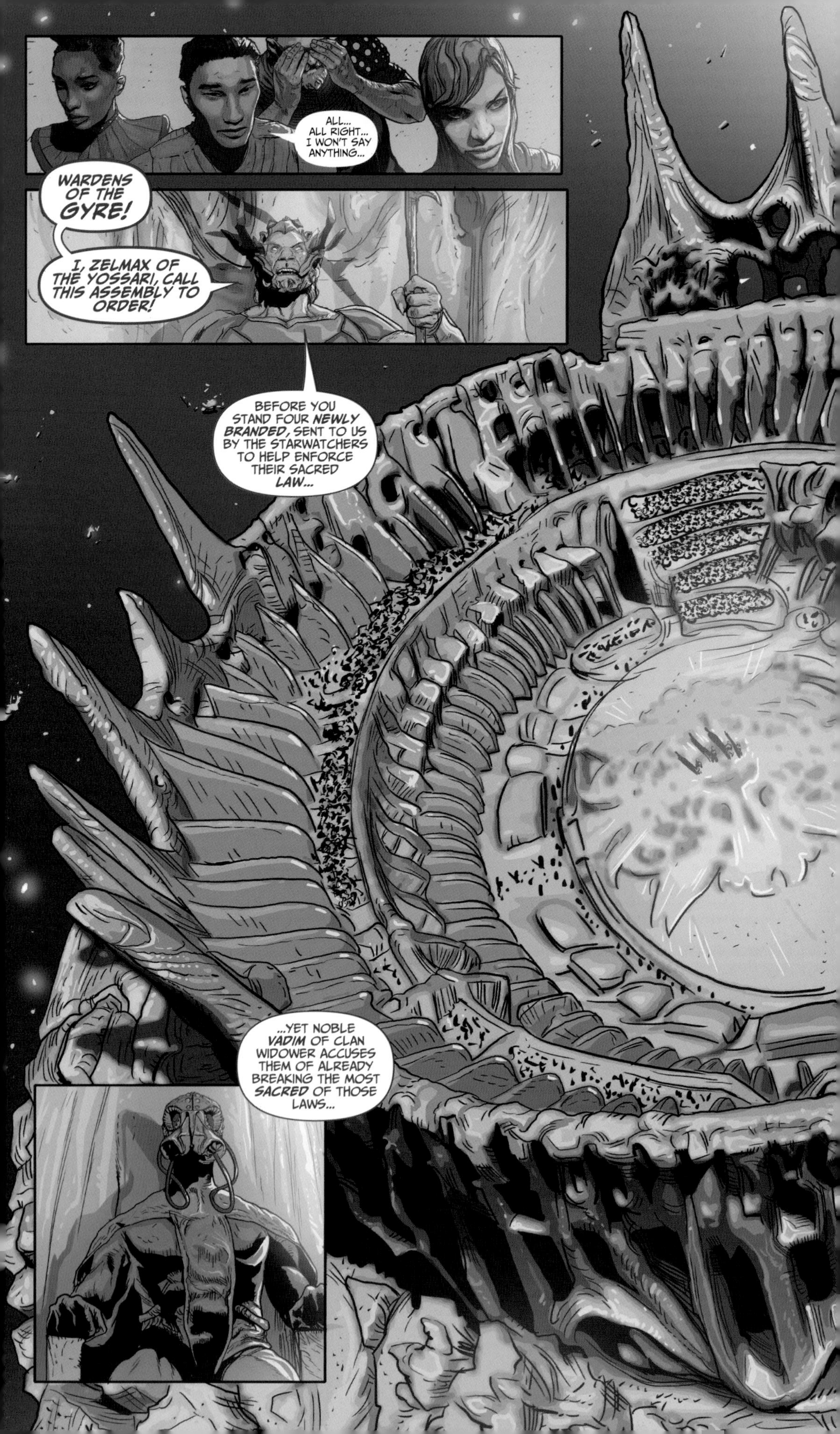
ALL... ALL RIGHT... I WON'T SAY ANYTHING...
WARDENS OF THE GYRE!
I, ZELMAX OF THE YOSSARI, CALL THIS ASSEMBLY TO ORDER!
BEFORE YOU STAND FOUR NEWLY BRANDED, SENT TO US BY THE STARWATCHERS TO HELP ENFORCE THEIR SACRED LAW...
...YET NOBLE VADIM OF CLAN WIDOWER ACCUSES THEM OF ALREADY BREAKING THE MOST SACRED OF THOSE LAWS...

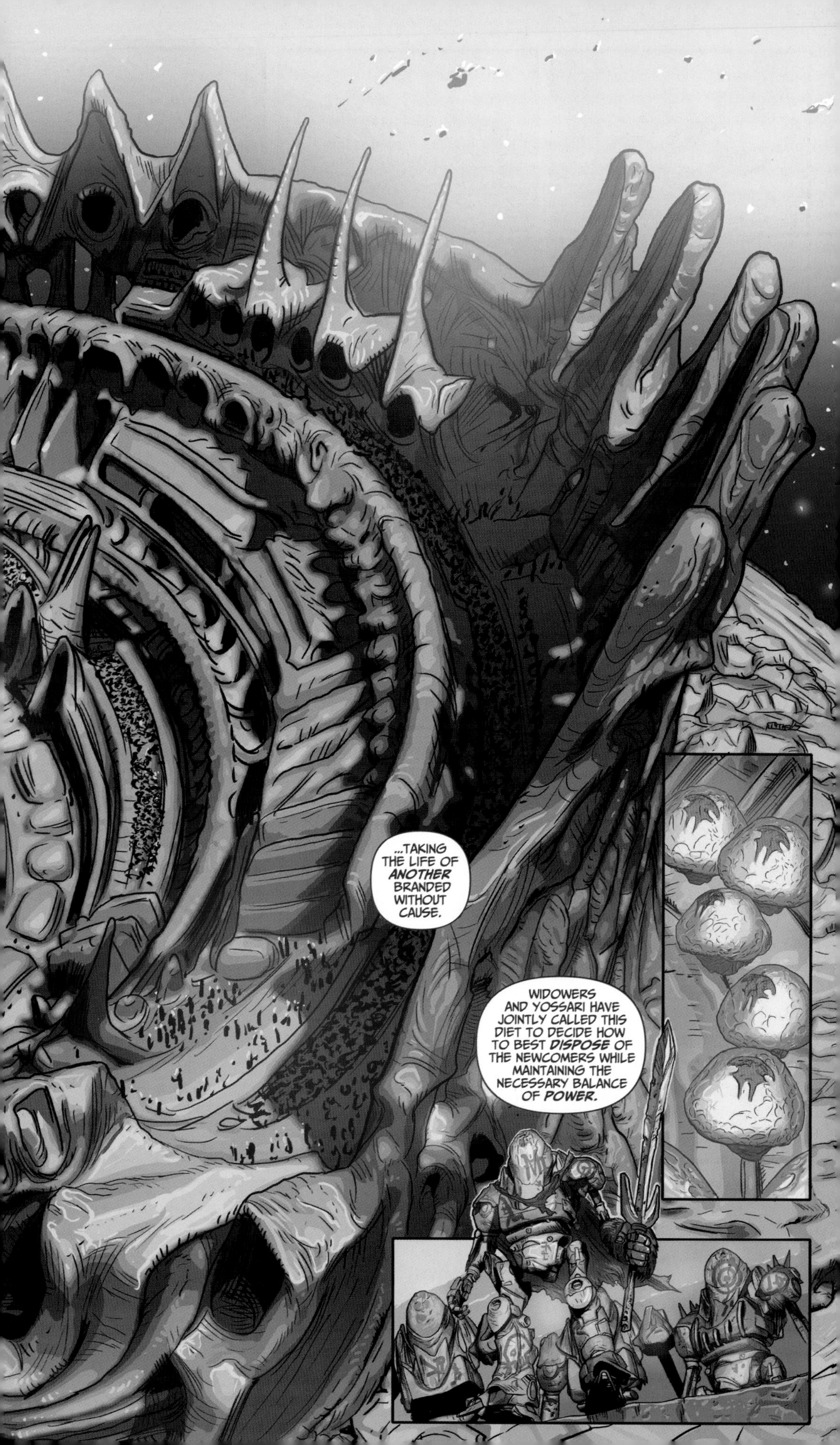
...TAKING THE LIFE OF *ANOTHER* BRANDED WITHOUT CAUSE.
WIDOWERS AND YOSSARI HAVE JOINTLY CALLED THIS DIET TO DECIDE HOW TO BEST *DISPOSE* OF THE NEWCOMERS WHILE MAINTAINING THE NECESSARY BALANCE OF *POWER.*

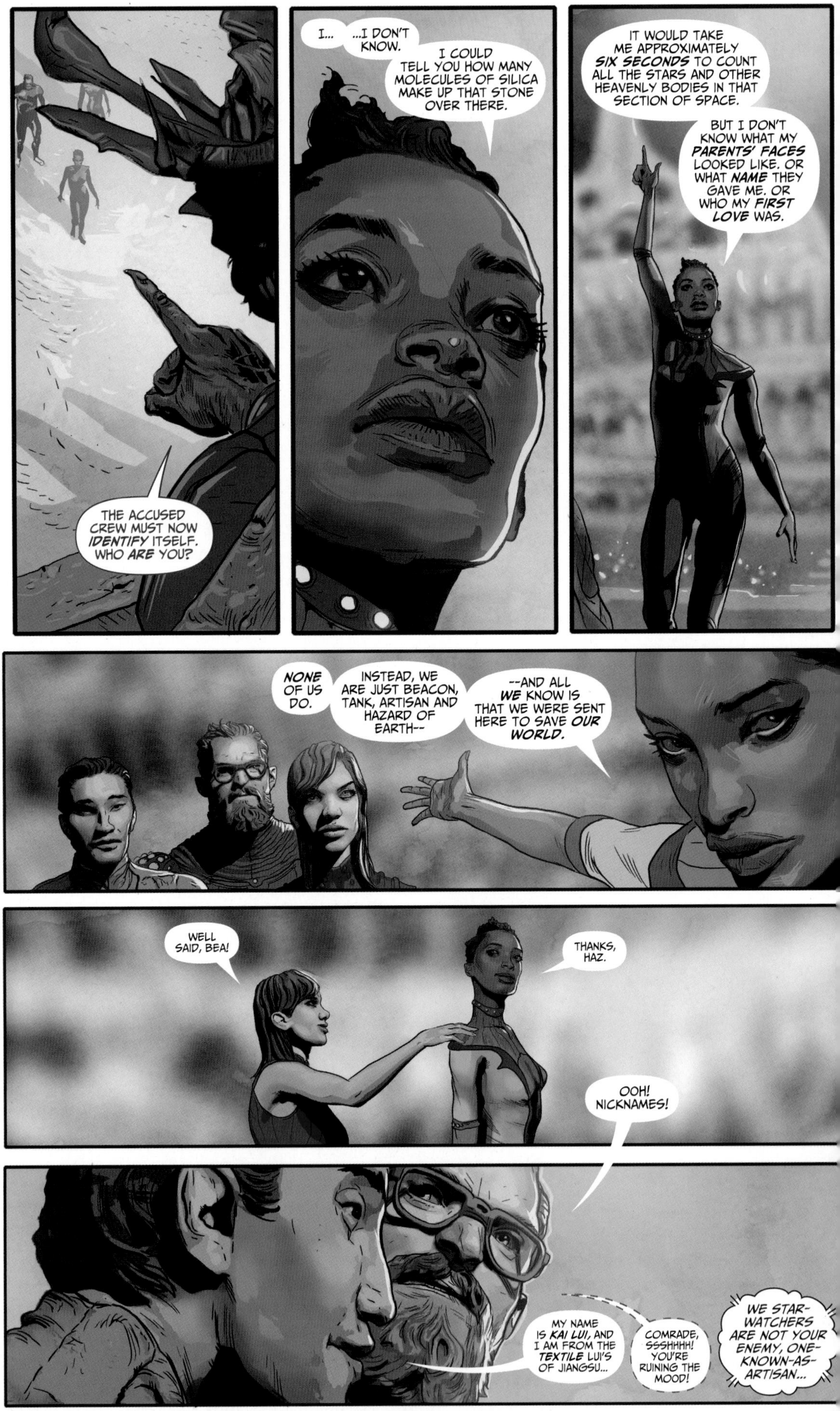
THE ACCUSED CREW MUST NOW IDENTIFY ITSELF. WHO ARE YOU?
I...
...I DON'T KNOW.
I COULD TELL YOU HOW MANY MOLECULES OF SILICA MAKE UP THAT STONE OVER THERE.
IT WOULD TAKE ME APPROXIMATELY SIX SECONDS TO COUNT ALL THE STARS AND OTHER HEAVENLY BODIES IN THAT SECTION OF SPACE.
BUT I DON'T KNOW WHAT MY PARENTS' FACES LOOKED LIKE. OR WHAT NAME THEY GAVE ME. OR WHO MY FIRST LOVE WAS.
NONE OF US DO.
INSTEAD, WE ARE JUST BEACON, TANK, ARTISAN AND HAZARD OF EARTH--
--AND ALL WE KNOW IS THAT WE WERE SENT HERE TO SAVE OUR WORLD.
WELL SAID, BEA!
THANKS, HAZ.
OOH! NICKNAMES!
MY NAME IS KAI LUI, AND I AM FROM THE TEXTILE LUI'S OF JIANGSU...
COMRADE, SSSHHHH! YOU'RE RUINING THE MOOD!
WE STAR-WATCHERS ARE NOT YOUR ENEMY, ONE-KNOWN-AS-ARTISAN...

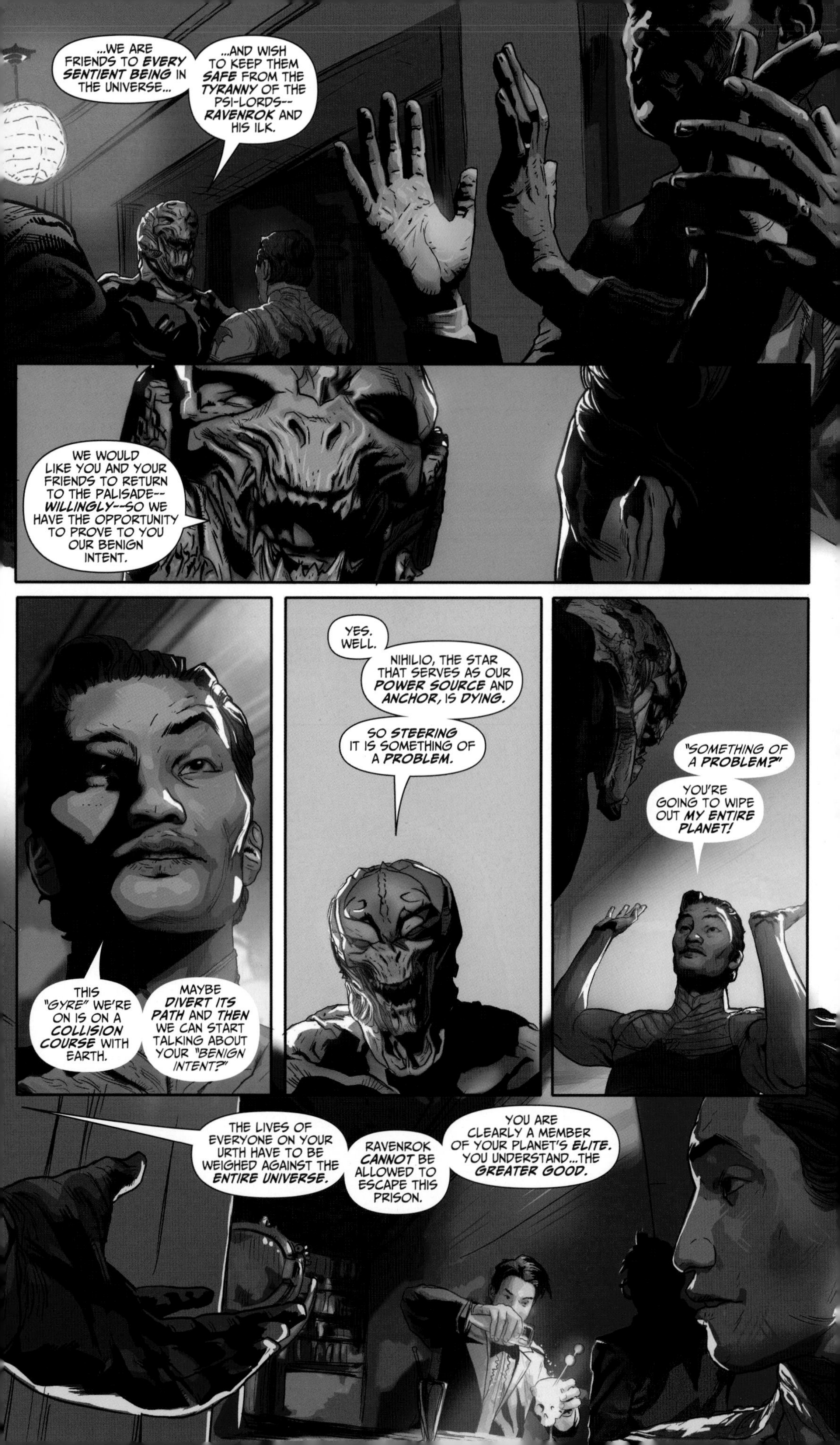
...WE ARE FRIENDS TO EVERY SENTIENT BEING IN THE UNIVERSE...
...AND WISH TO KEEP THEM SAFE FROM THE TYRANNY OF THE PSI-LORDS-- RAVENROK AND HIS ILK.
WE WOULD LIKE YOU AND YOUR FRIENDS TO RETURN TO THE PALISADE-- WILLINGLY--SO WE HAVE THE OPPORTUNITY TO PROVE TO YOU OUR BENIGN INTENT.
THIS "GYRE" WE'RE ON IS ON A COLLISION COURSE WITH EARTH.
MAYBE DIVERT ITS PATH AND THEN WE CAN START TALKING ABOUT YOUR "BENIGN INTENT?"
YES. WELL.
NIHILIO, THE STAR THAT SERVES AS OUR POWER SOURCE AND ANCHOR, IS DYING.
SO STEERING IT IS SOMETHING OF A PROBLEM.
"SOMETHING OF A PROBLEM?"
YOU'RE GOING TO WIPE OUT MY ENTIRE PLANET!
THE LIVES OF EVERYONE ON YOUR URTH HAVE TO BE WEIGHED AGAINST THE ENTIRE UNIVERSE.
RAVENROK CANNOT BE ALLOWED TO ESCAPE THIS PRISON.
YOU ARE CLEARLY A MEMBER OF YOUR PLANET'S ELITE. YOU UNDERSTAND...THE GREATER GOOD.

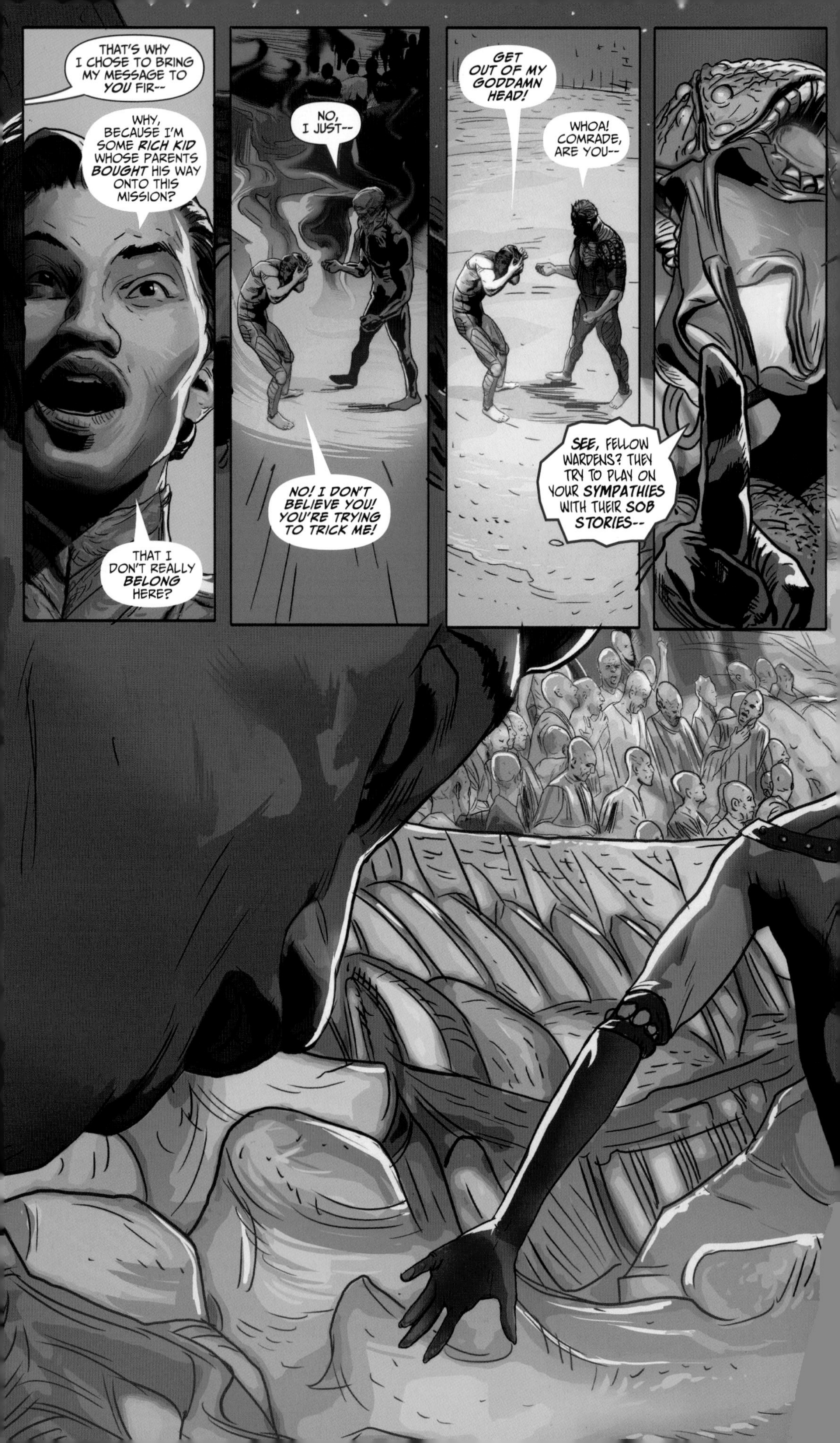
THAT'S WHY I CHOSE TO BRING MY MESSAGE TO YOU FIR--
WHY, BECAUSE I'M SOME RICH KID WHOSE PARENTS BOUGHT HIS WAY ONTO THIS MISSION?
THAT I DON'T REALLY BELONG HERE?
NO, I JUST--
NO! I DON'T BELIEVE YOU! YOU'RE TRYING TO TRICK ME!
GET OUT OF MY GODDAMN HEAD!
WHOA! COMRADE, ARE YOU--
SEE, FELLOW WARDENS? THEY TRY TO PLAY ON YOUR SYMPATHIES WITH THEIR SOB STORIES--

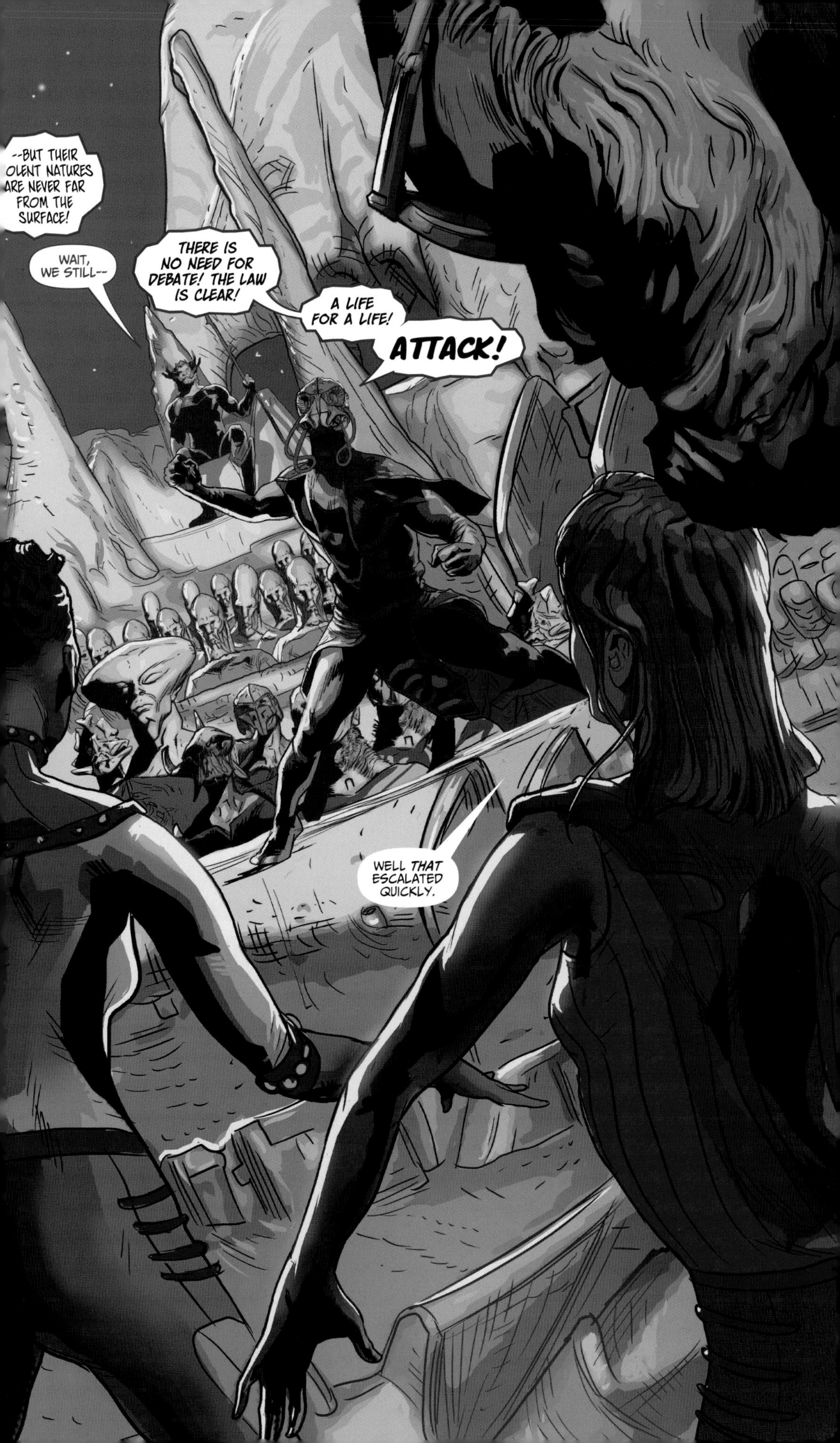
--BUT THEIR OLENT NATURES ARE NEVER FAR FROM THE SURFACE!
WAIT, WE STILL--
THERE IS NO NEED FOR DEBATE! THE LAW IS CLEAR!
A LIFE FOR A LIFE!
ATTACK!
WELL *THAT* ESCALATED QUICKLY.

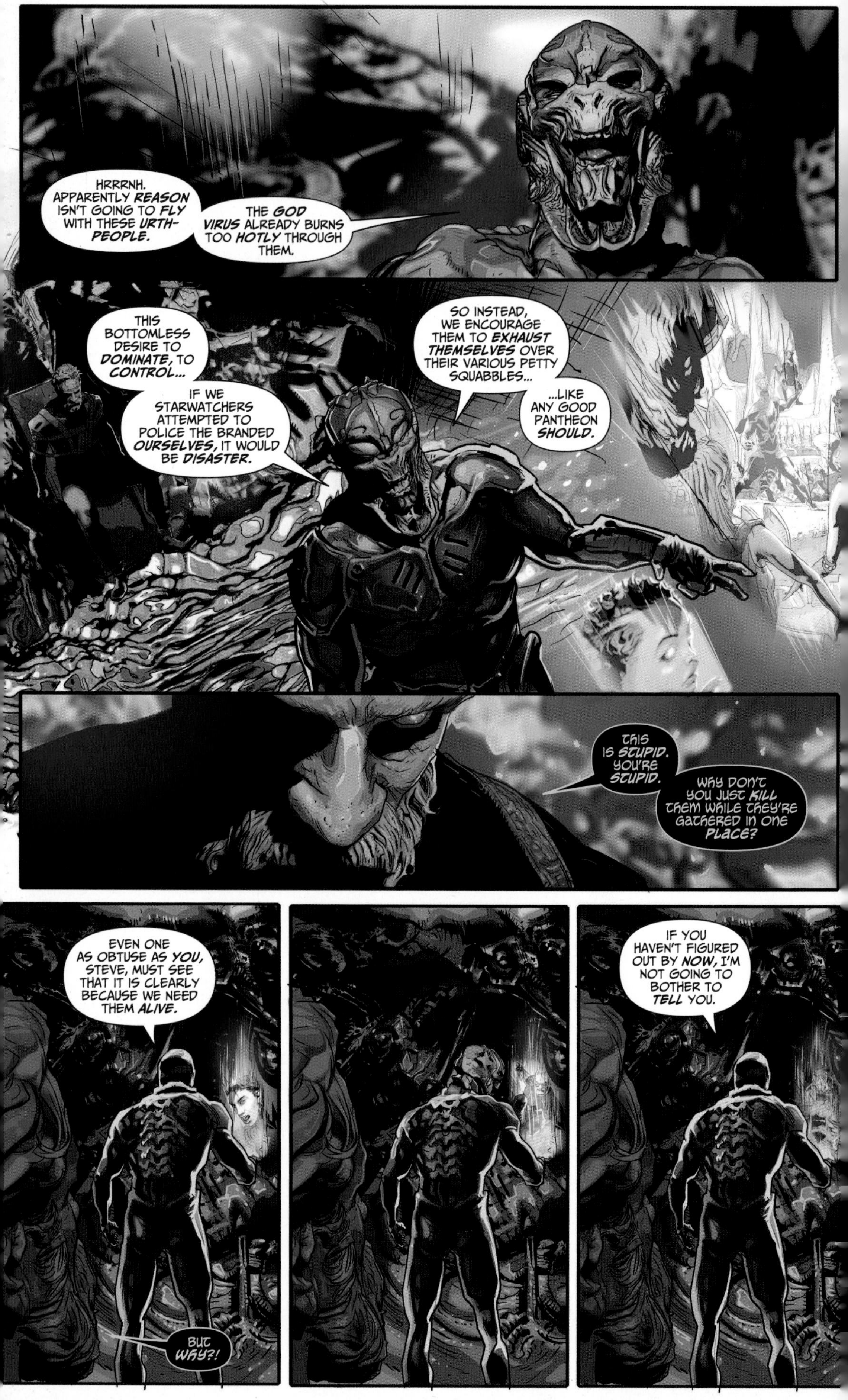
HRRRNH. APPARENTLY REASON ISN'T GOING TO FLY WITH THESE URTH-PEOPLE.
THE GOD VIRUS ALREADY BURNS TOO HOTLY THROUGH THEM.
THIS BOTTOMLESS DESIRE TO DOMINATE, TO CONTROL...
IF WE STARWATCHERS ATTEMPTED TO POLICE THE BRANDED OURSELVES, IT WOULD BE DISASTER.
SO INSTEAD, WE ENCOURAGE THEM TO EXHAUST THEMSELVES OVER THEIR VARIOUS PETTY SQUABBLES...
...LIKE ANY GOOD PANTHEON SHOULD.
THIS IS STUPID. YOU'RE STUPID.
WHY DON'T YOU JUST KILL THEM WHILE THEY'RE GATHERED IN ONE PLACE?
EVEN ONE AS OBTUSE AS YOU, STEVE, MUST SEE THAT IT IS CLEARLY BECAUSE WE NEED THEM ALIVE.
BUT WHY?!
IF YOU HAVEN'T FIGURED OUT BY NOW, I'M NOT GOING TO BOTHER TO TELL YOU.

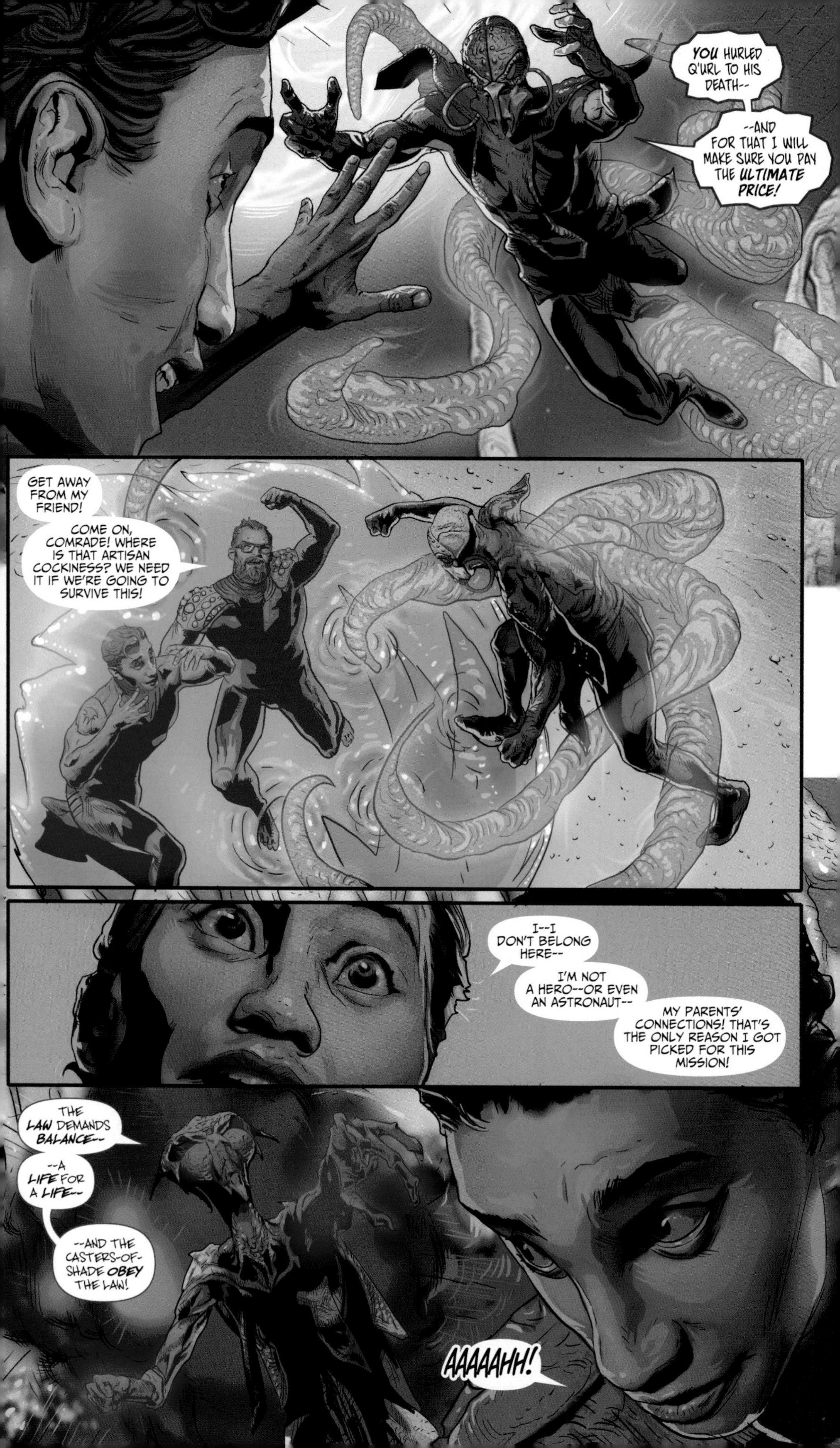

YOU HURLED Q'URL TO HIS DEATH--
--AND FOR THAT I WILL MAKE SURE YOU PAY THE ULTIMATE PRICE!
GET AWAY FROM MY FRIEND!
COME ON, COMRADE! WHERE IS THAT ARTISAN COCKINESS? WE NEED IT IF WE'RE GOING TO SURVIVE THIS!
I--I DON'T BELONG HERE--
I'M NOT A HERO--OR EVEN AN ASTRONAUT--
MY PARENTS' CONNECTIONS! THAT'S THE ONLY REASON I GOT PICKED FOR THIS MISSION!
THE LAW DEMANDS BALANCE--
--A LIFE FOR A LIFE--
--AND THE CASTERS-OF-SHADE OBEY THE LAW!
AAAAAHH!

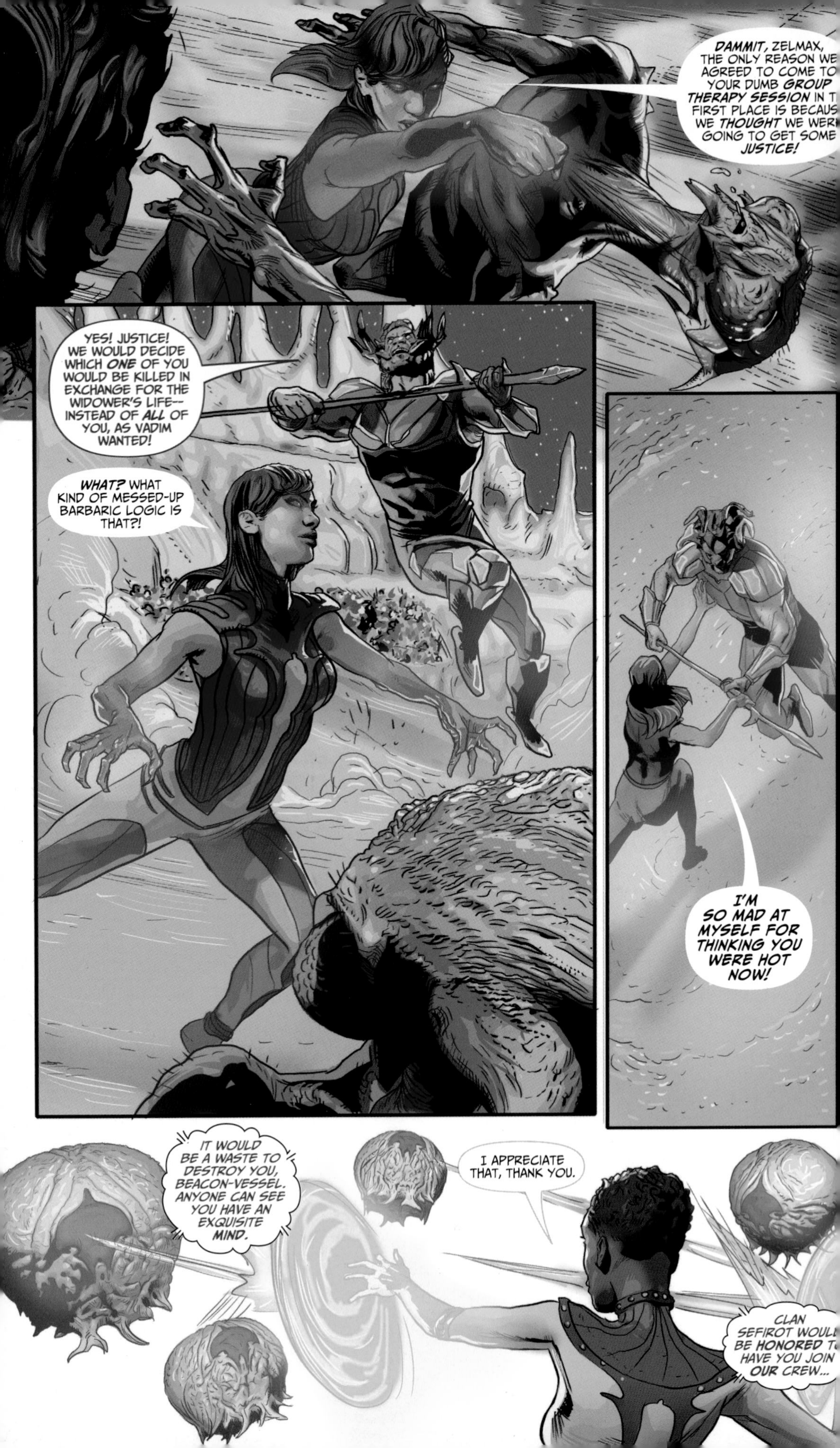
DAMMIT, ZELMAX, THE ONLY REASON WE AGREED TO COME TO YOUR DUMB GROUP THERAPY SESSION IN THE FIRST PLACE IS BECAUSE WE THOUGHT WE WERE GOING TO GET SOME JUSTICE!
YES! JUSTICE! WE WOULD DECIDE WHICH ONE OF YOU WOULD BE KILLED IN EXCHANGE FOR THE WIDOWER'S LIFE-- INSTEAD OF ALL OF YOU, AS VADIM WANTED!
WHAT? WHAT KIND OF MESSED-UP BARBARIC LOGIC IS THAT?!
I'M SO MAD AT MYSELF FOR THINKING YOU WERE HOT NOW!
IT WOULD BE A WASTE TO DESTROY YOU, BEACON-VESSEL. ANYONE CAN SEE YOU HAVE AN EXQUISITE MIND.
I APPRECIATE THAT, THANK YOU.
CLAN SEFIROT WOULD BE HONORED TO HAVE YOU JOIN OUR CREW...

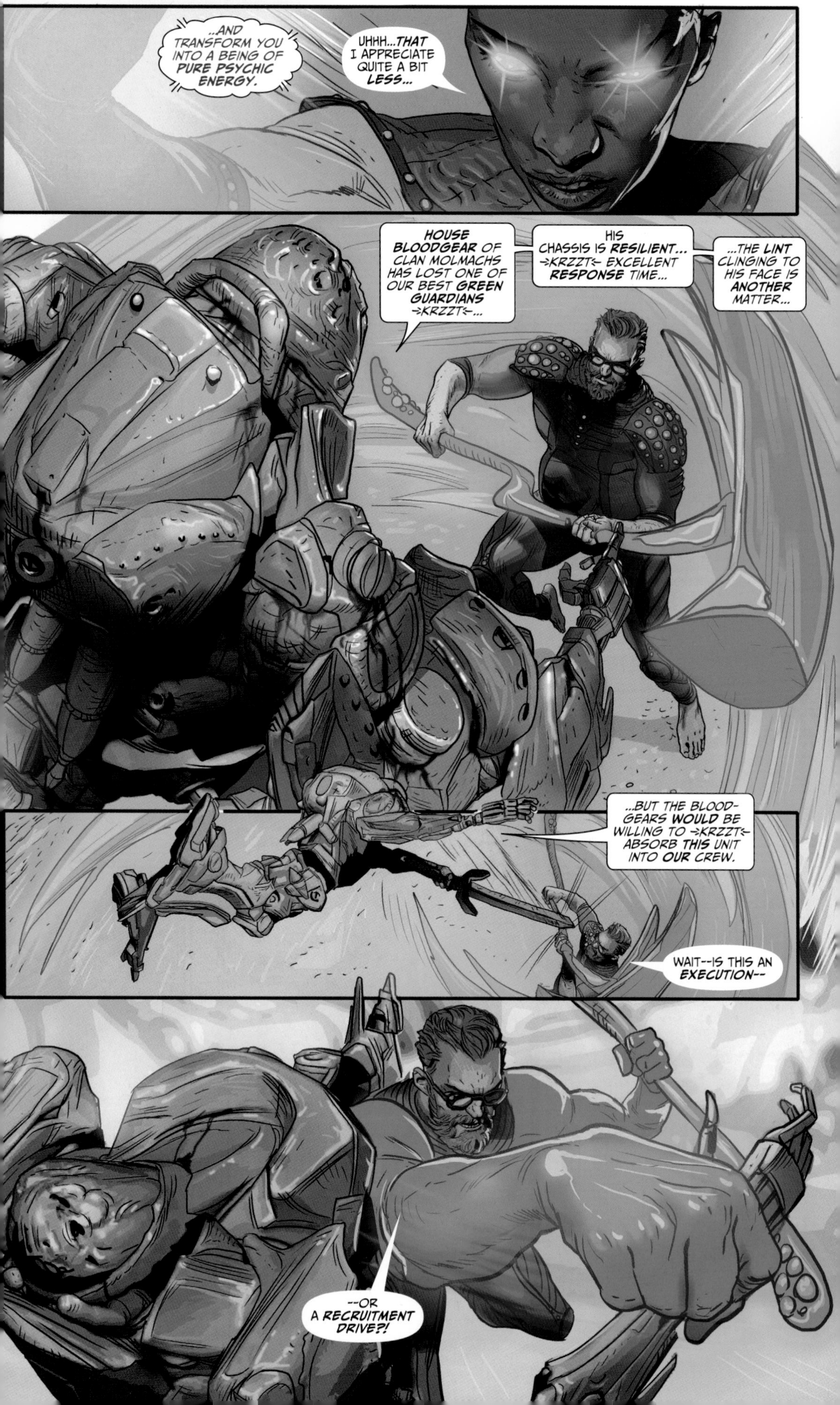
...AND TRANSFORM YOU INTO A BEING OF PURE PSYCHIC ENERGY.
UHHH...THAT I APPRECIATE QUITE A BIT LESS...
HOUSE BLOODGEAR OF CLAN MOLMACHS HAS LOST ONE OF OUR BEST GREEN GUARDIANS →KRZZT←...
HIS CHASSIS IS RESILIENT... →KRZZT← EXCELLENT RESPONSE TIME...
...THE LINT CLINGING TO HIS FACE IS ANOTHER MATTER...
...BUT THE BLOOD-GEARS WOULD BE WILLING TO →KRZZT← ABSORB THIS UNIT INTO OUR CREW.
WAIT--IS THIS AN EXECUTION--
--OR A RECRUITMENT DRIVE?!

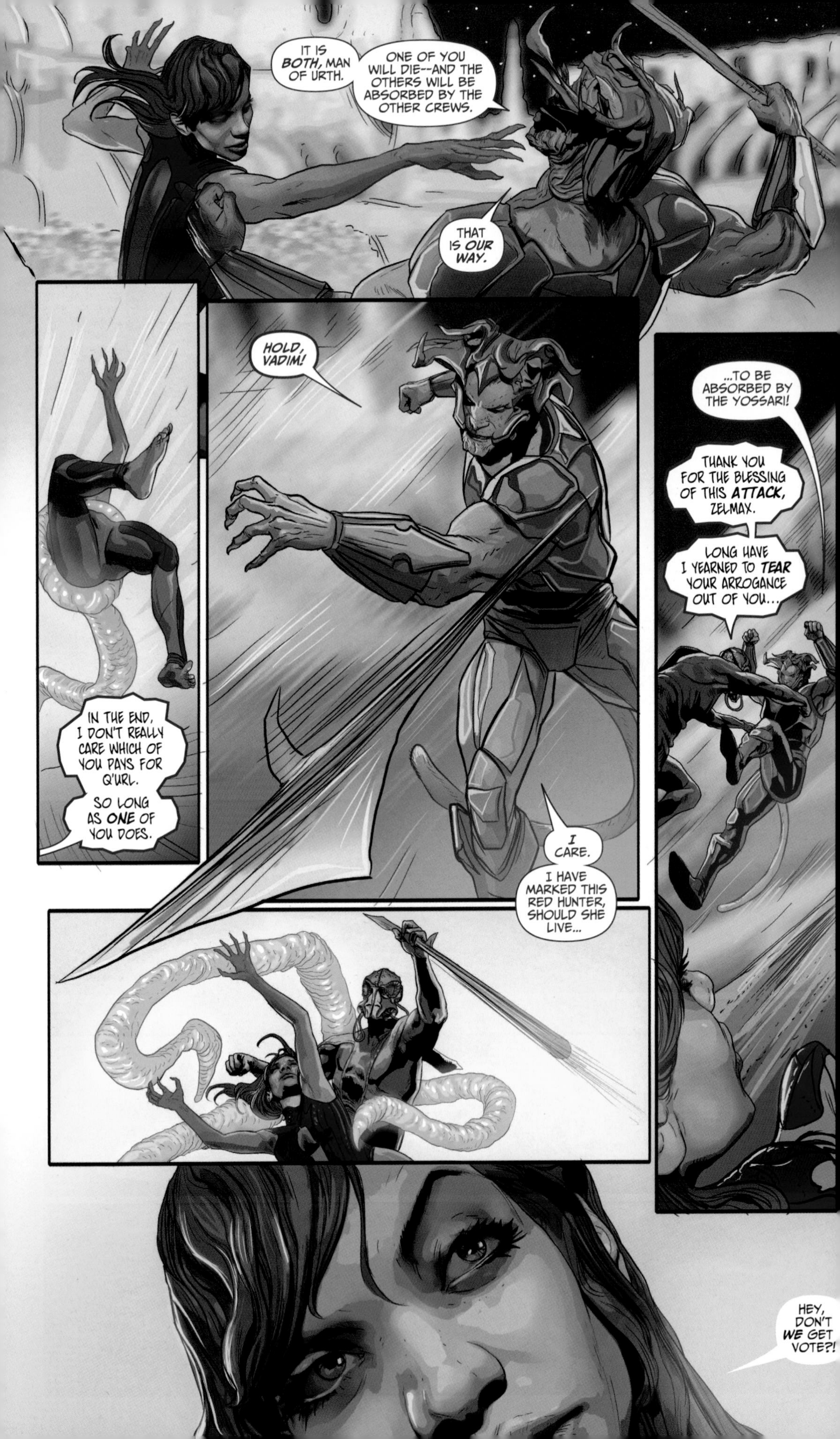
IT IS BOTH, MAN OF URTH.
ONE OF YOU WILL DIE--AND THE OTHERS WILL BE ABSORBED BY THE OTHER CREWS.
THAT IS OUR WAY.
IN THE END, I DON'T REALLY CARE WHICH OF YOU PAYS FOR Q'URL.
SO LONG AS ONE OF YOU DOES.
HOLD, VADIM!
I CARE.
I HAVE MARKED THIS RED HUNTER, SHOULD SHE LIVE...
...TO BE ABSORBED BY THE YOSSARI!
THANK YOU FOR THE BLESSING OF THIS ATTACK, ZELMAX.
LONG HAVE I YEARNED TO TEAR YOUR ARROGANCE OUT OF YOU...
HEY, DON'T WE GET VOTE?!

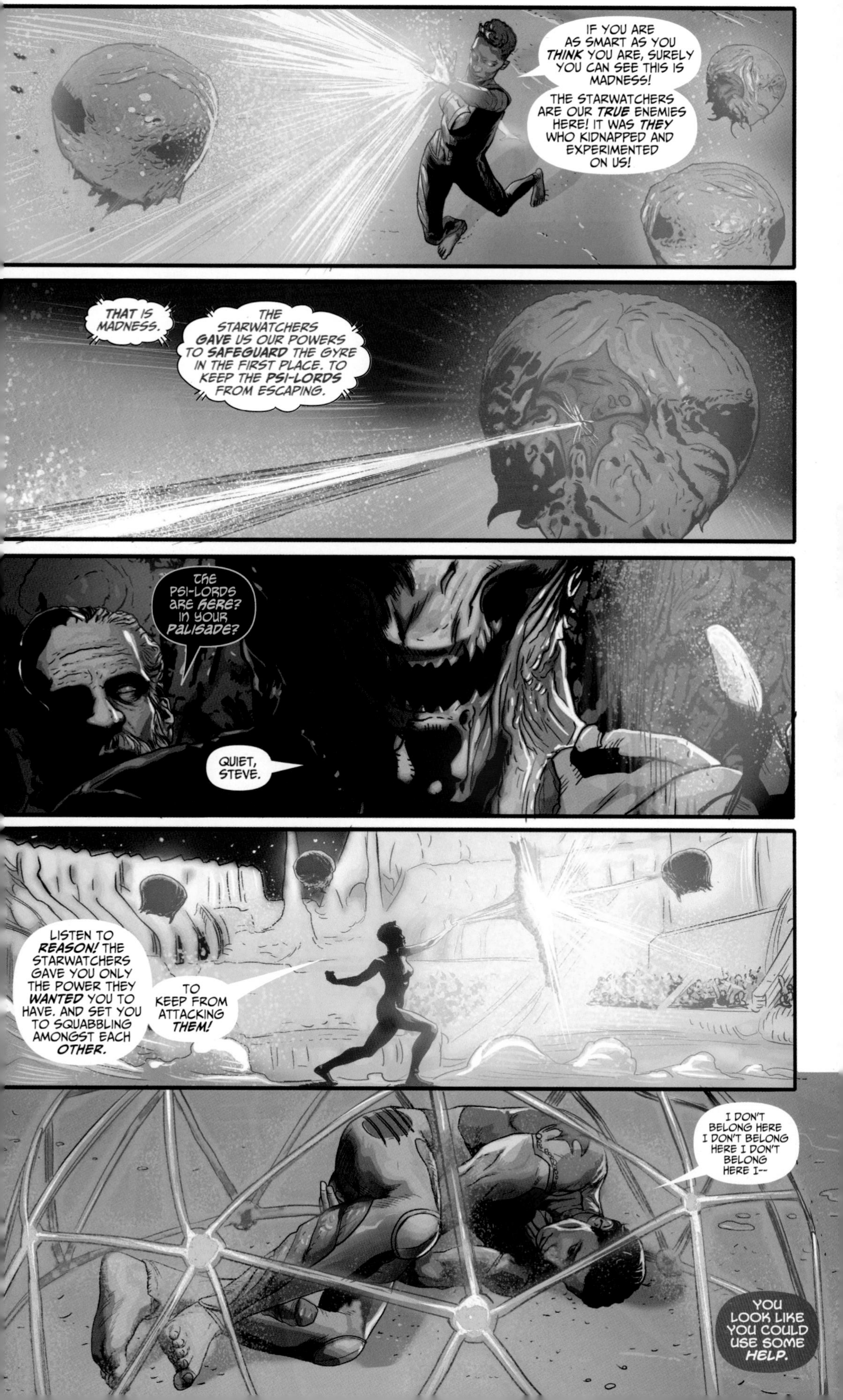
IF YOU ARE AS SMART AS YOU *THINK* YOU ARE, SURELY YOU CAN SEE THIS IS MADNESS!
THE STARWATCHERS ARE OUR *TRUE* ENEMIES HERE! IT WAS *THEY* WHO KIDNAPPED AND EXPERIMENTED ON US!
*THAT* IS MADNESS.
THE STARWATCHERS *GAVE* US OUR POWERS TO *SAFEGUARD* THE GYRE IN THE FIRST PLACE. TO KEEP THE *PSI-LORDS* FROM ESCAPING.
THE PSI-LORDS ARE *HERE?* IN YOUR *PALISADE?*
QUIET, STEVE.
LISTEN TO *REASON!* THE STARWATCHERS GAVE YOU ONLY THE POWER THEY *WANTED* YOU TO HAVE. AND SET YOU TO SQUABBLING AMONGST EACH *OTHER.*
TO KEEP FROM ATTACKING *THEM!*
I DON'T BELONG HERE I DON'T BELONG HERE I DON'T BELONG HERE I--
YOU LOOK LIKE YOU COULD USE SOME *HELP.*

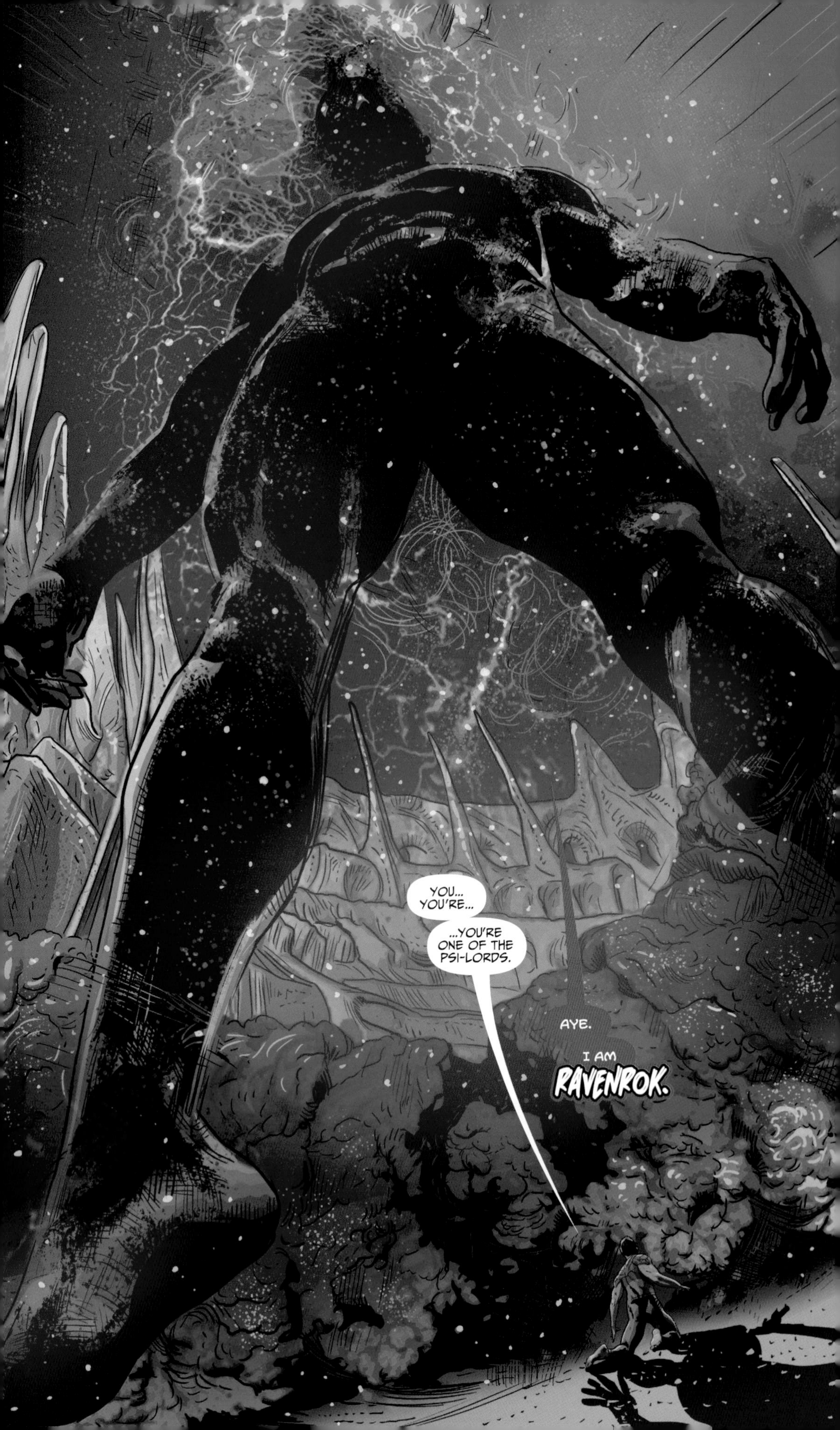
YOU... YOU'RE...
...YOU'RE ONE OF THE PSI-LORDS.
AYE.
I AM RAVENROK.

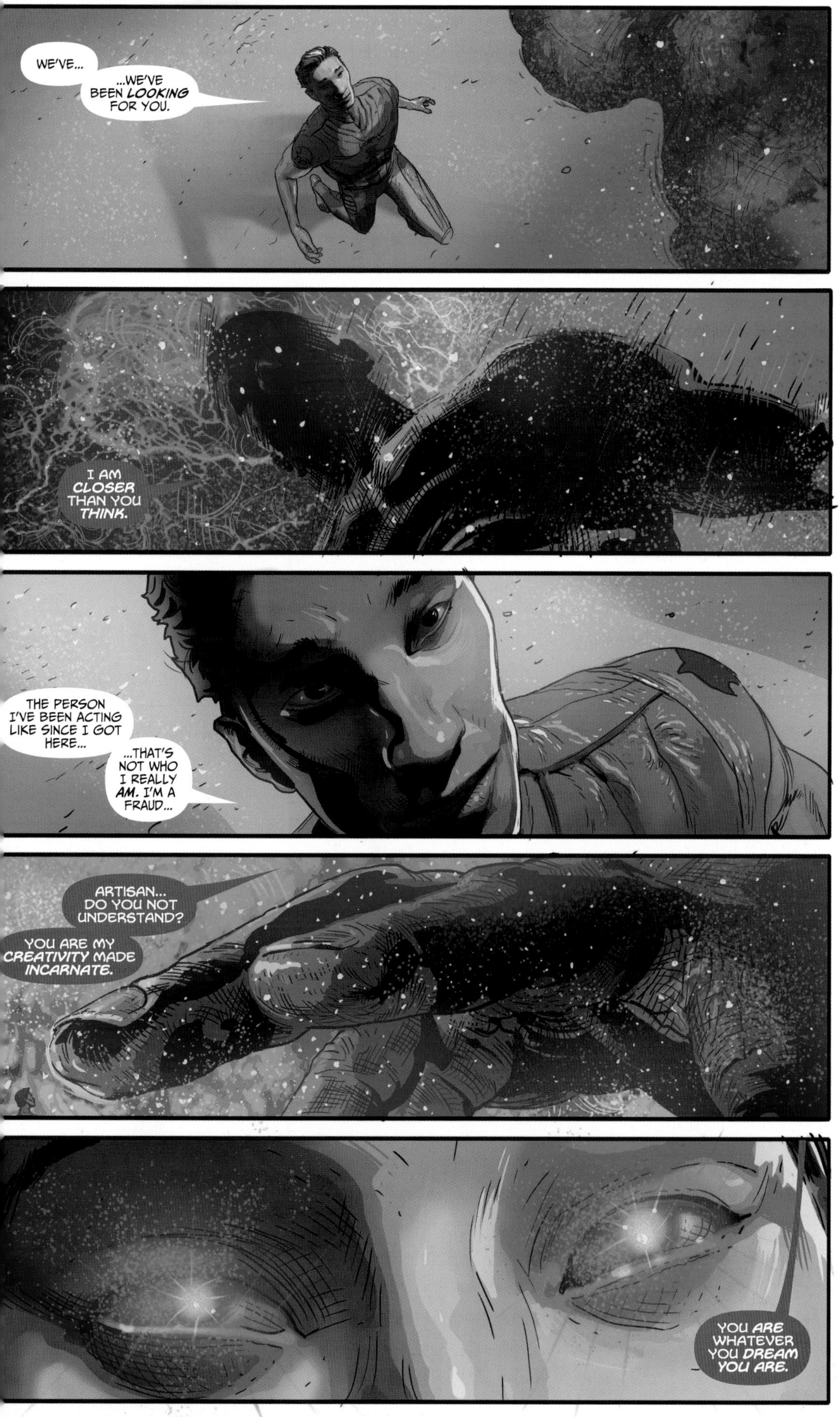
WE'VE...
...WE'VE BEEN LOOKING FOR YOU.
I AM CLOSER THAN YOU THINK.
THE PERSON I'VE BEEN ACTING LIKE SINCE I GOT HERE...
...THAT'S NOT WHO I REALLY AM. I'M A FRAUD...
ARTISAN... DO YOU NOT UNDERSTAND?
YOU ARE MY CREATIVITY MADE INCARNATE.
YOU ARE WHATEVER YOU DREAM YOU ARE.

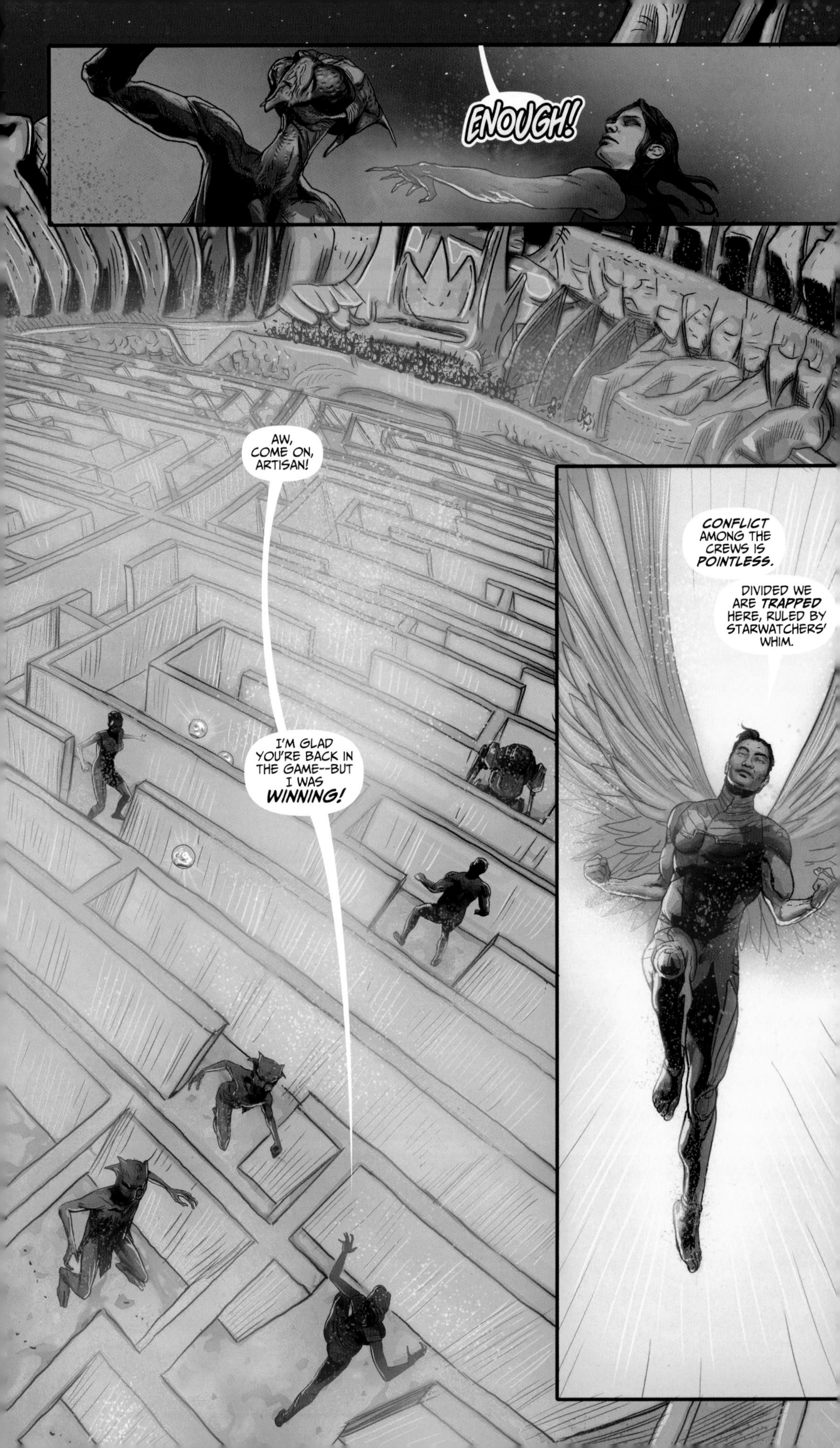

ENOUGH!
AW, COME ON, ARTISAN!
I'M GLAD YOU'RE BACK IN THE GAME--BUT I WAS WINNING!
CONFLICT AMONG THE CREWS IS POINTLESS.
DIVIDED WE ARE TRAPPED HERE, RULED BY STARWATCHERS' WHIM.

BUT SEE? LOOK AT NILHIO!

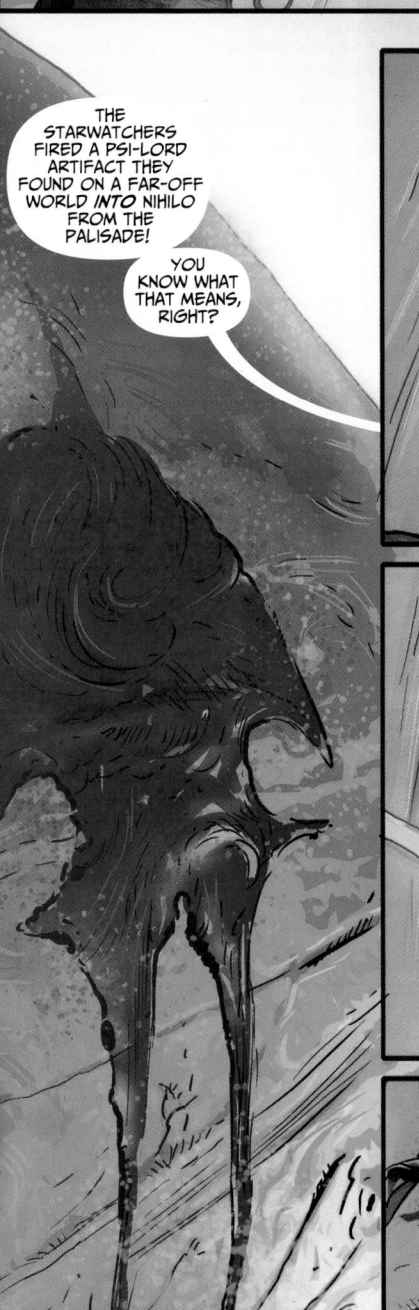

THE STARWATCHERS FIRED A PSI-LORD ARTIFACT THEY FOUND ON A FAR-OFF WORLD *INTO* NIHILO FROM THE PALISADE!

YOU KNOW WHAT THAT MEANS, RIGHT?

AND...HOW DID *YOU* KNOW THAT, EXACTLY, ARTISAN?

THE STARWATCHERS... CAN TRANSPORT SOMETHING *TO* THE GYRE...

WHICH MEANS...

...THEY HAVE A WAY *OFF* THE GYRE. A SHIP-- A TELEPORTER!

WE CAN *ESCAPE* THIS PRISON!

EXACTLY. TOGETHER WE CAN TAKE DOWN THE STARWATCHERS...

...AND FREE OURSELVES FROM THE VAMPIRE STAR!

BUT---›KRRZZZT‹---HOW CAN WE STAND AGAINST THE STARWATCHERS---›KRRZZZT‹--- WHO GAVE US OUR POWERS IN THE FIRST PLACE?

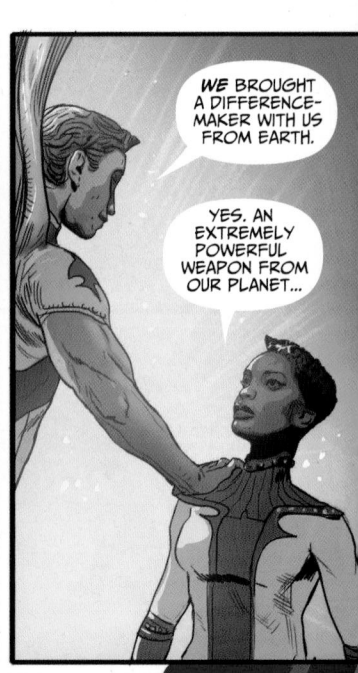

WE BROUGHT A DIFFERENCE-MAKER WITH US FROM EARTH.

YES. AN EXTREMELY POWERFUL WEAPON FROM OUR PLANET...

...AN EXPERIMENTAL FUSION BOMB CODENAMED GRASSHOPPER...

WAIT...!

BOMB? WHAT BOMB?

WHAT DO YOU KNOW ABOUT THIS?!

hahahahahaha hahahahahahaha

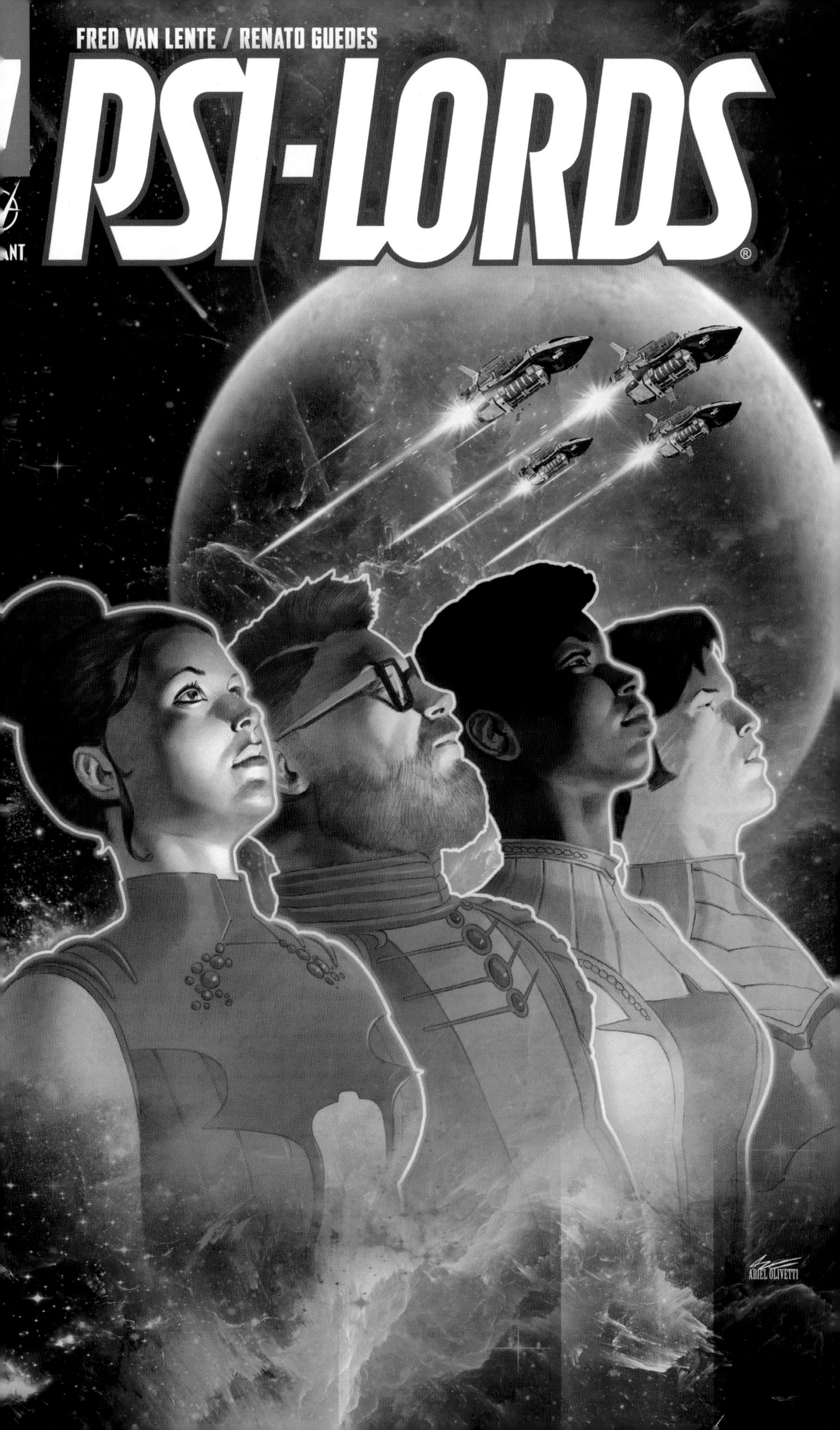

FRED VAN LENTE / RENATO GUEDES
PSI-LORDS
ARIEL OLIVETTI

**PSI-LORDS #**
WRITER: Fred Van Lent
ARTIST: Renato Guedes
LETTERER: Dave Sharpe
COVER ARTIST: Ariel Olivetti
ASSISTANT EDITOR: Drew Baumgartner
EDITOR: David Mench

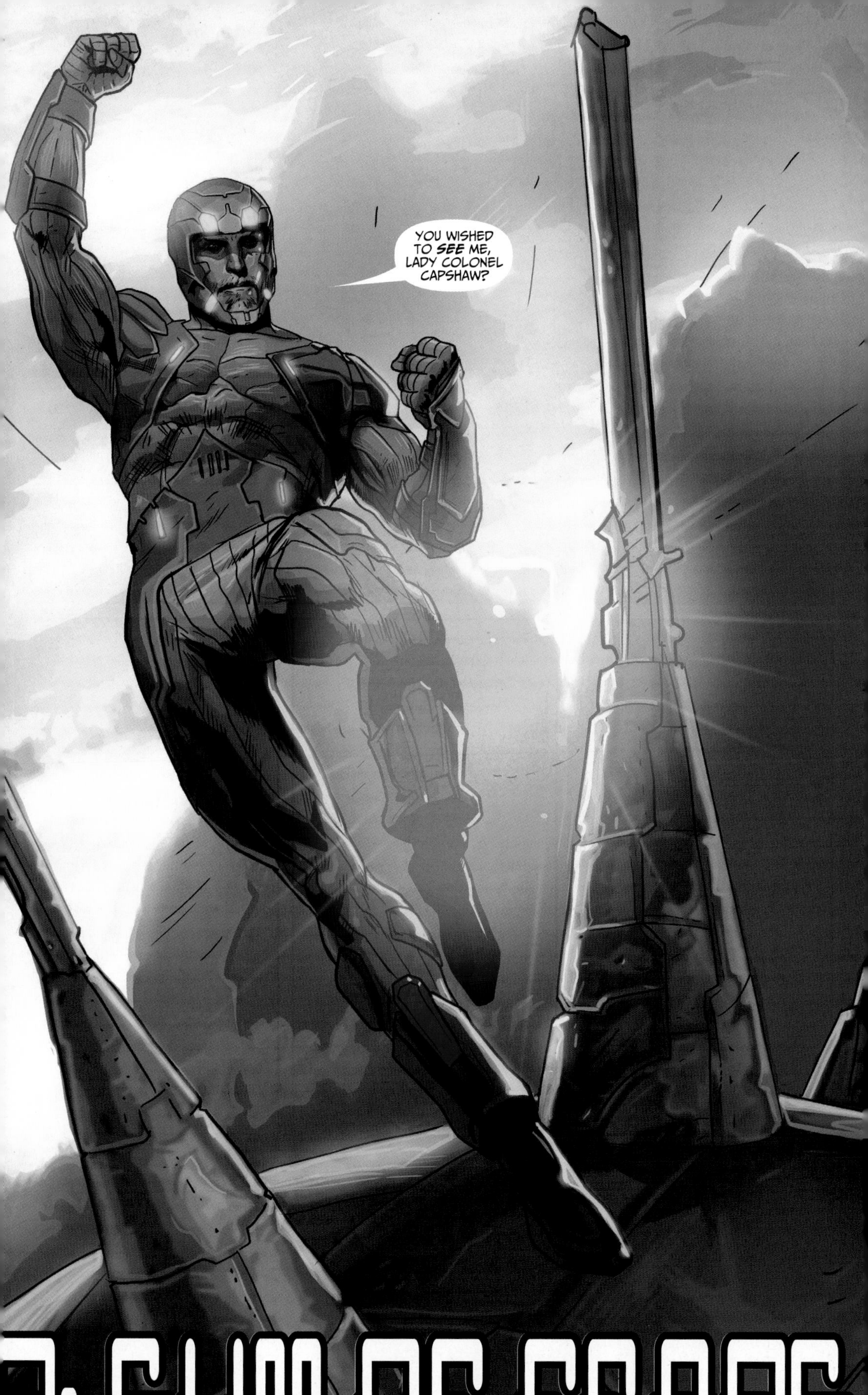
YOU WISHED TO SEE ME, LADY COLONEL CAPSHAW?

# 7: SUM OF FEARS

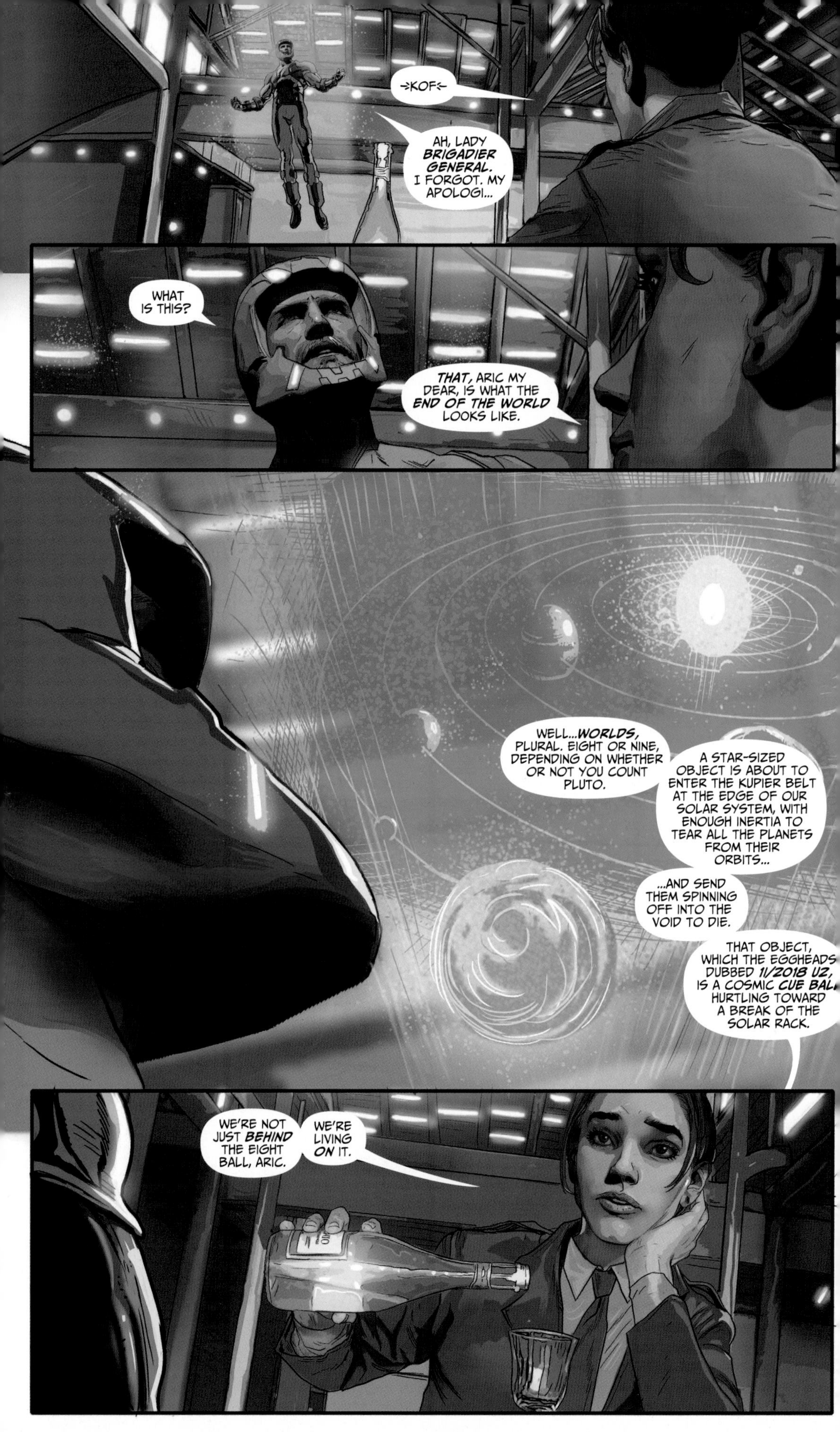

-KOF-
AH, LADY **BRIGADIER GENERAL.** I FORGOT. MY APOLOGI...
WHAT IS THIS?
**THAT,** ARIC MY DEAR, IS WHAT THE **END OF THE WORLD** LOOKS LIKE.
WELL...**WORLDS,** PLURAL. EIGHT OR NINE, DEPENDING ON WHETHER OR NOT YOU COUNT PLUTO.
A STAR-SIZED OBJECT IS ABOUT TO ENTER THE KUPIER BELT AT THE EDGE OF OUR SOLAR SYSTEM, WITH ENOUGH INERTIA TO TEAR ALL THE PLANETS FROM THEIR ORBITS...
...AND SEND THEM SPINNING OFF INTO THE VOID TO DIE.
THAT OBJECT, WHICH THE EGGHEADS DUBBED **1I/2018 U2,** IS A COSMIC **CUE BAL** HURTLING TOWARD A BREAK OF THE SOLAR RACK.
WE'RE NOT JUST **BEHIND** THE EIGHT BALL, ARIC.
WE'RE LIVING **ON** IT.

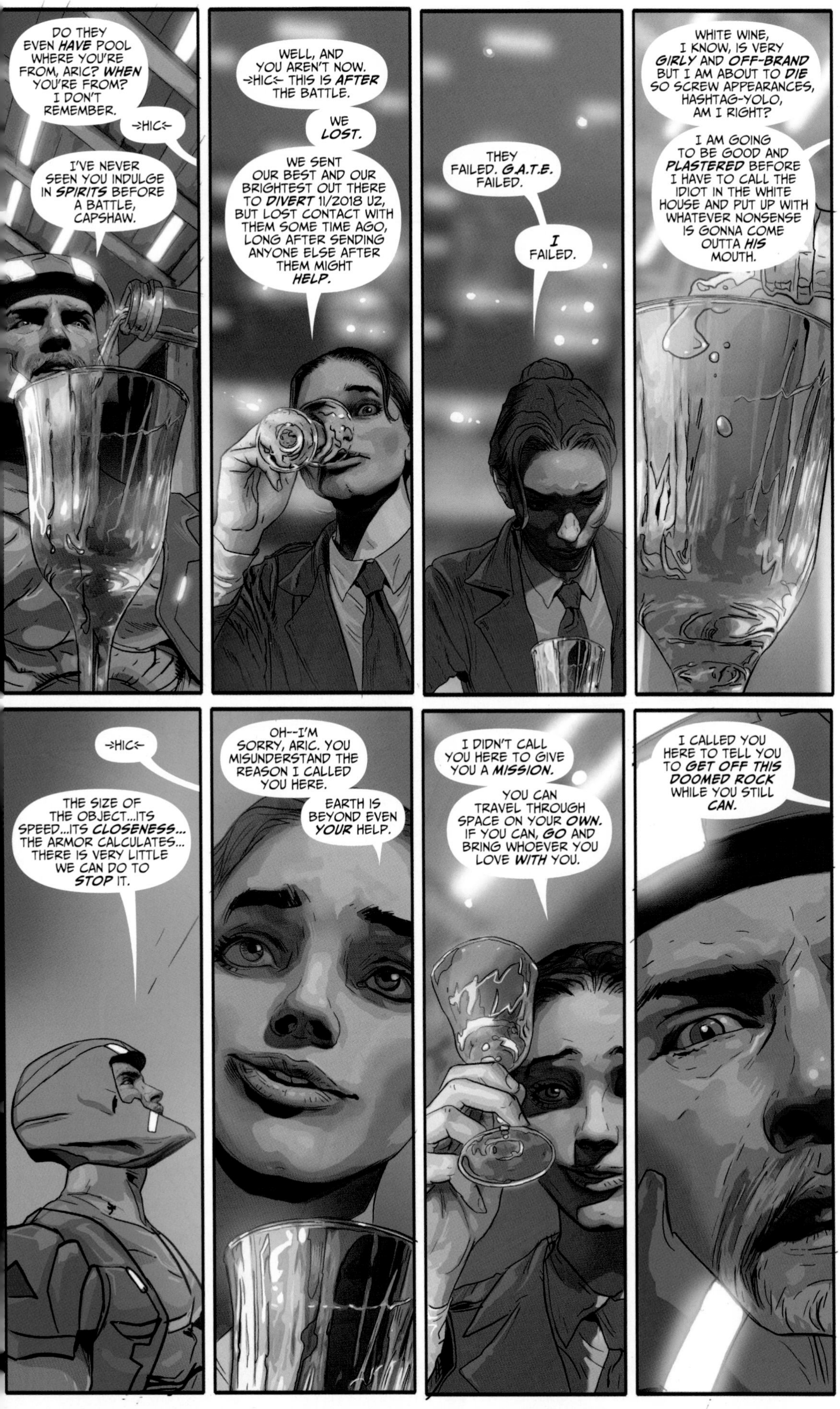
DO THEY EVEN HAVE POOL WHERE YOU'RE FROM, ARIC? WHEN YOU'RE FROM? I DON'T REMEMBER.
⇒HIC⇐
I'VE NEVER SEEN YOU INDULGE IN SPIRITS BEFORE A BATTLE, CAPSHAW.
WELL, AND YOU AREN'T NOW. ⇒HIC⇐ THIS IS AFTER THE BATTLE.
WE LOST.
WE SENT OUR BEST AND OUR BRIGHTEST OUT THERE TO DIVERT 11/2018 U2, BUT LOST CONTACT WITH THEM SOME TIME AGO, LONG AFTER SENDING ANYONE ELSE AFTER THEM MIGHT HELP.
THEY FAILED. G.A.T.E. FAILED.
I FAILED.
WHITE WINE, I KNOW, IS VERY GIRLY AND OFF-BRAND BUT I AM ABOUT TO DIE SO SCREW APPEARANCES, HASHTAG-YOLO, AM I RIGHT?
I AM GOING TO BE GOOD AND PLASTERED BEFORE I HAVE TO CALL THE IDIOT IN THE WHITE HOUSE AND PUT UP WITH WHATEVER NONSENSE IS GONNA COME OUTTA HIS MOUTH.
⇒HIC⇐
THE SIZE OF THE OBJECT...ITS SPEED...ITS CLOSENESS... THE ARMOR CALCULATES... THERE IS VERY LITTLE WE CAN DO TO STOP IT.
OH--I'M SORRY, ARIC. YOU MISUNDERSTAND THE REASON I CALLED YOU HERE.
EARTH IS BEYOND EVEN YOUR HELP.
I DIDN'T CALL YOU HERE TO GIVE YOU A MISSION.
YOU CAN TRAVEL THROUGH SPACE ON YOUR OWN. IF YOU CAN, GO AND BRING WHOEVER YOU LOVE WITH YOU.
I CALLED YOU HERE TO TELL YOU TO GET OFF THIS DOOMED ROCK WHILE YOU STILL CAN.

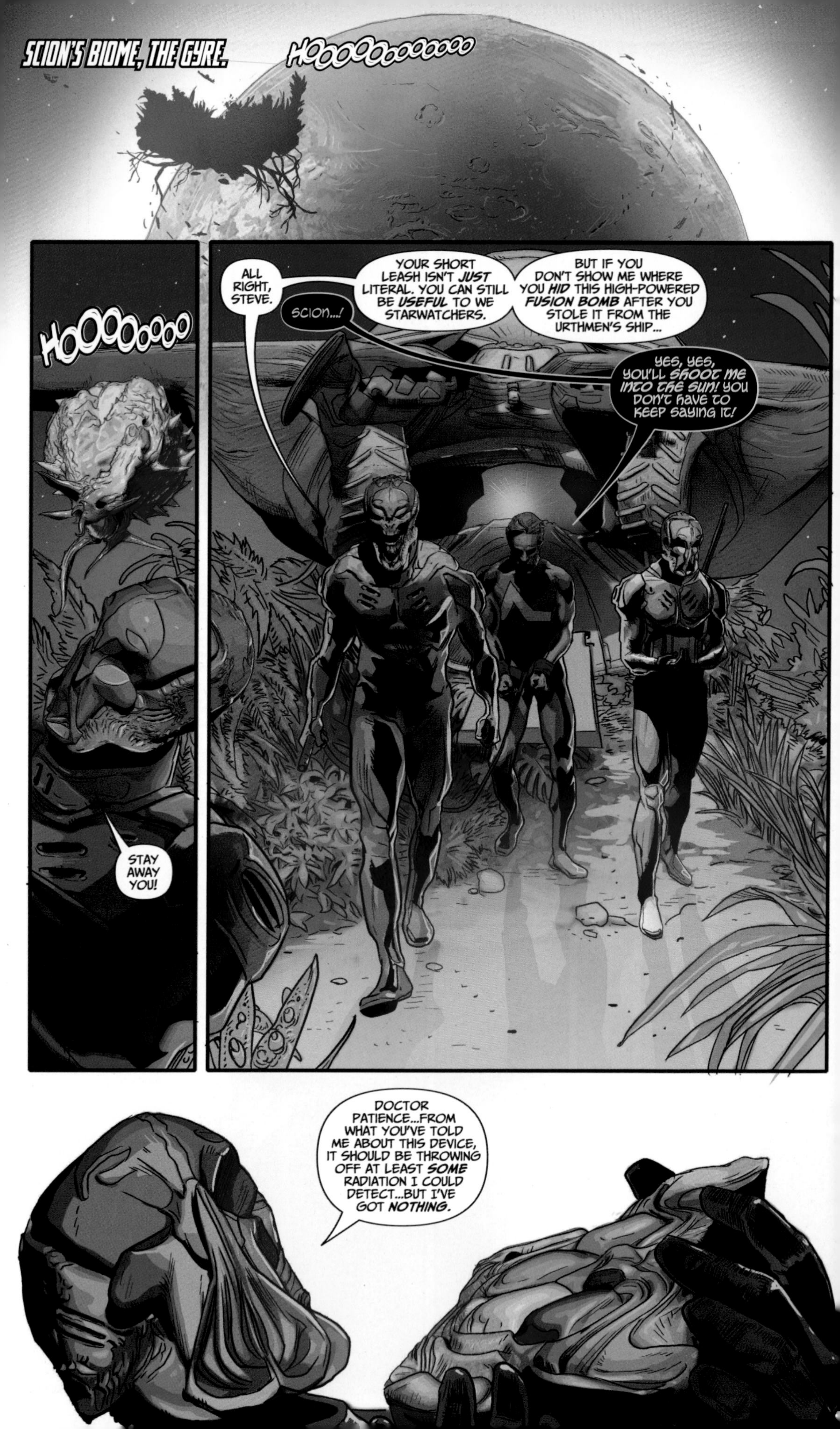
SCION'S BIOME, THE GYRE.
HOOOOOOOOOOOOO
HOOOOOOOO
ALL RIGHT, STEVE.
YOUR SHORT LEASH ISN'T JUST LITERAL. YOU CAN STILL BE USEFUL TO WE STARWATCHERS.
BUT IF YOU DON'T SHOW ME WHERE YOU HID THIS HIGH-POWERED FUSION BOMB AFTER YOU STOLE IT FROM THE URTHMEN'S SHIP...
SCION...!
YES, YES, YOU'LL SHOOT ME INTO THE SUN! YOU DON'T HAVE TO KEEP SAYING IT!
STAY AWAY YOU!
DOCTOR PATIENCE...FROM WHAT YOU'VE TOLD ME ABOUT THIS DEVICE, IT SHOULD BE THROWING OFF AT LEAST SOME RADIATION I COULD DETECT...BUT I'VE GOT NOTHING.

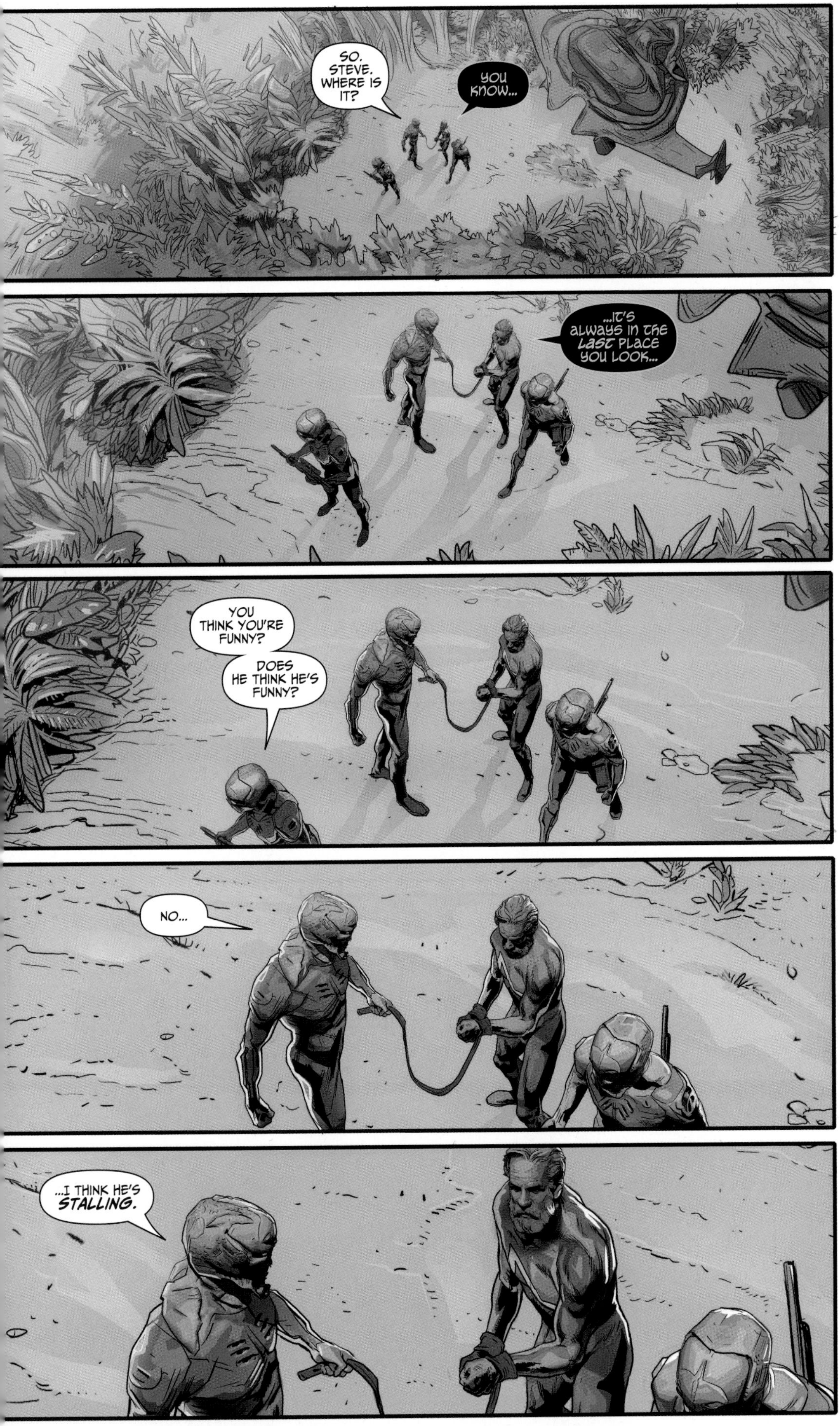
SO. STEVE. WHERE IS IT?
YOU KNOW...
...IT'S ALWAYS IN THE LAST PLACE YOU LOOK...
YOU THINK YOU'RE FUNNY?
DOES HE THINK HE'S FUNNY?
NO...
...I THINK HE'S STALLING.

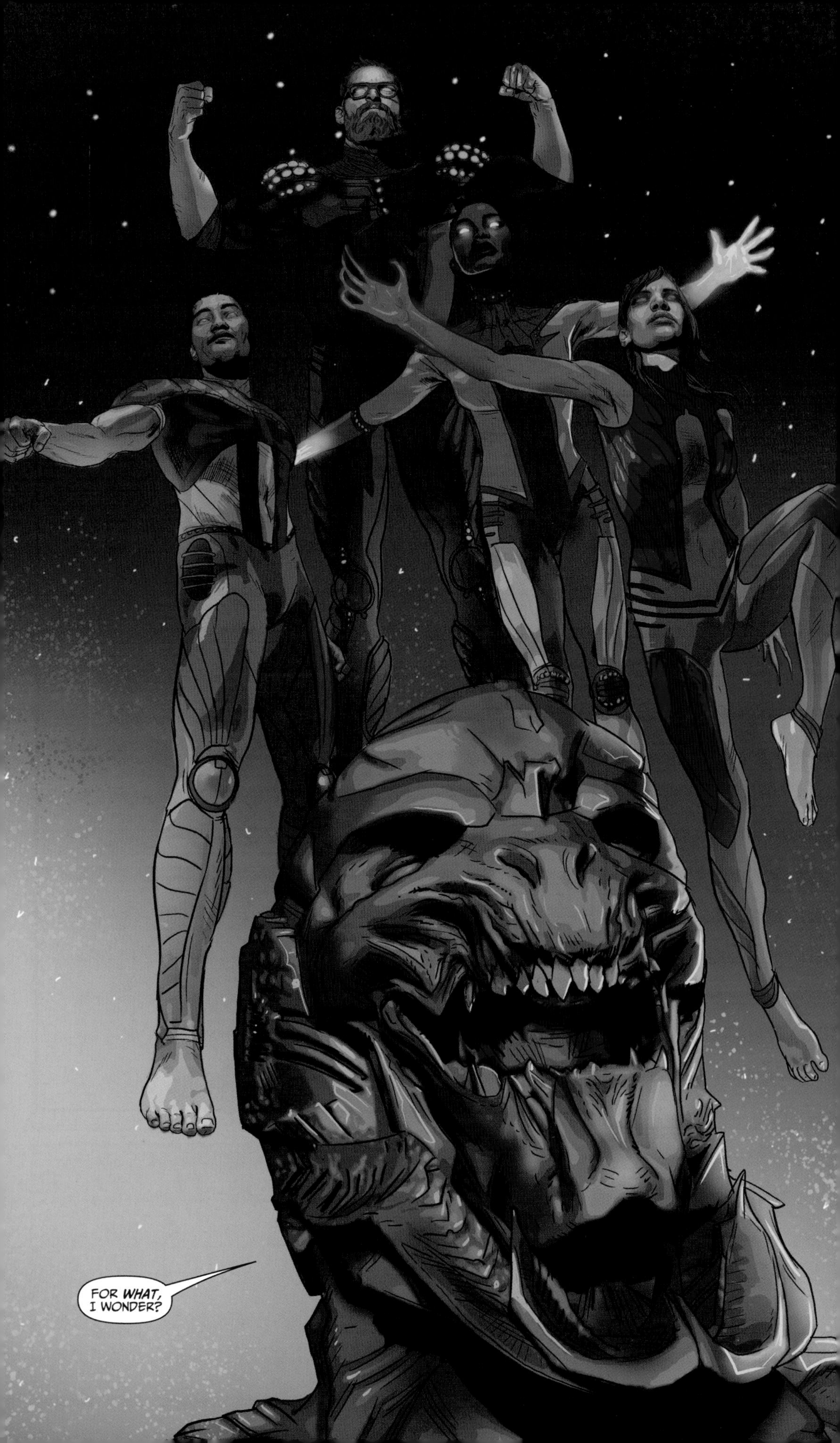
FOR WHAT, I WONDER?

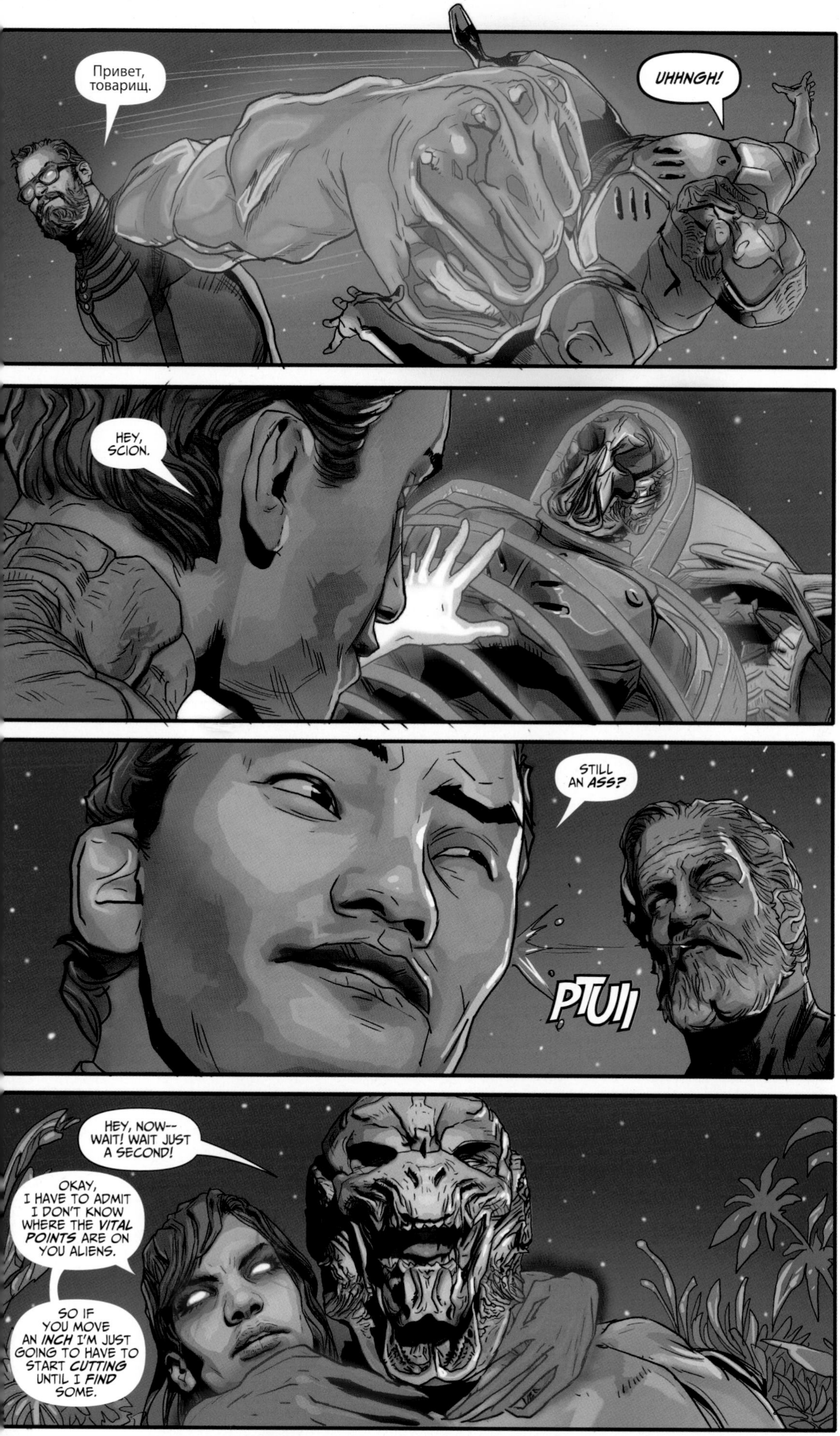
Привет, товарищ.
UHHNGH!
HEY, SCION.
STILL AN ASS?
PTUI
HEY, NOW-- WAIT! WAIT JUST A SECOND!
OKAY, I HAVE TO ADMIT I DON'T KNOW WHERE THE VITAL POINTS ARE ON YOU ALIENS.
SO IF YOU MOVE AN INCH I'M JUST GOING TO HAVE TO START CUTTING UNTIL I FIND SOME.

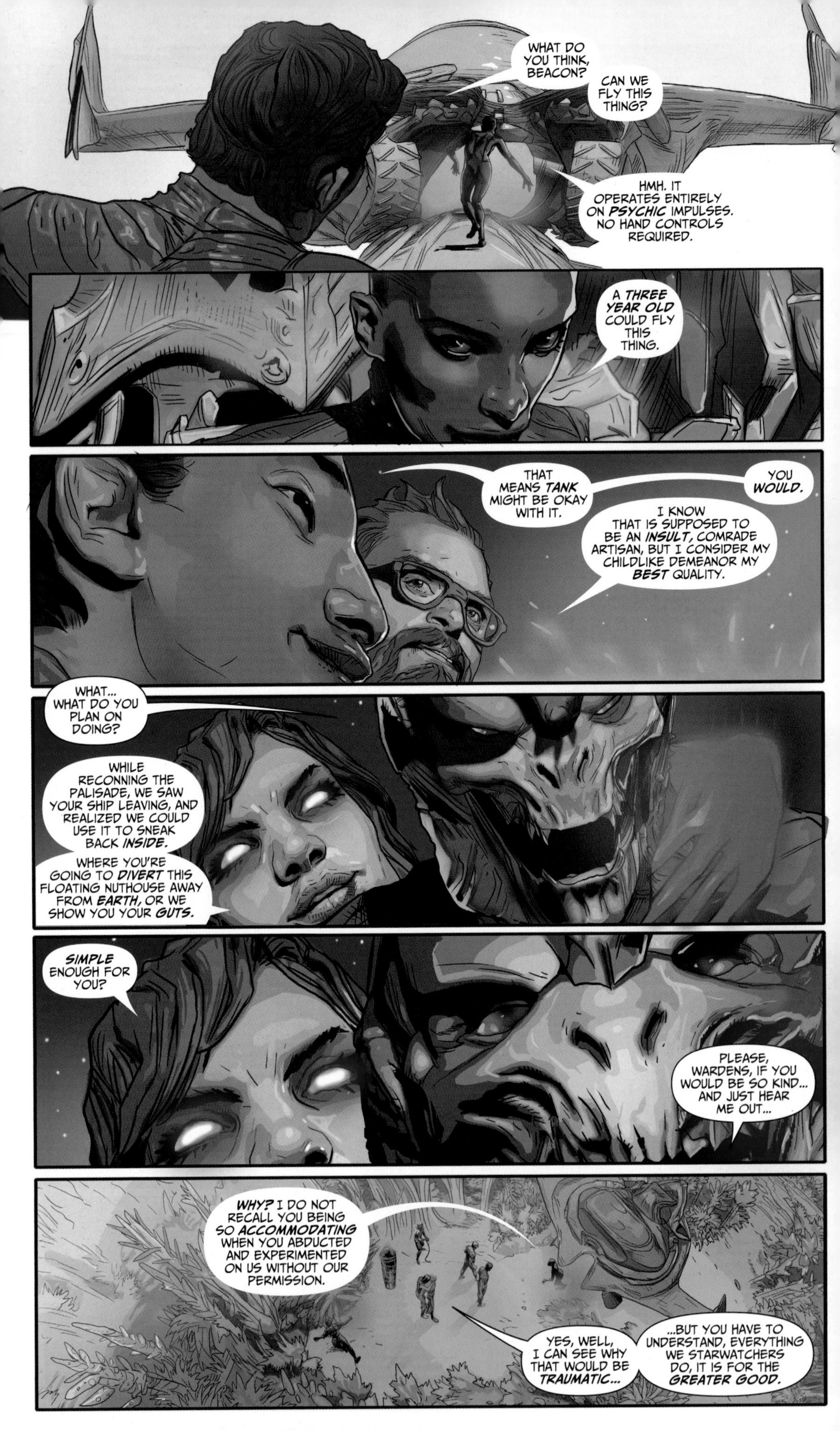
WHAT DO YOU THINK, BEACON?
CAN WE FLY THIS THING?
HMH. IT OPERATES ENTIRELY ON PSYCHIC IMPULSES. NO HAND CONTROLS REQUIRED.
A THREE YEAR OLD COULD FLY THIS THING.
THAT MEANS TANK MIGHT BE OKAY WITH IT.
YOU WOULD.
I KNOW THAT IS SUPPOSED TO BE AN INSULT, COMRADE ARTISAN, BUT I CONSIDER MY CHILDLIKE DEMEANOR MY BEST QUALITY.
WHAT... WHAT DO YOU PLAN ON DOING?
WHILE RECONNING THE PALISADE, WE SAW YOUR SHIP LEAVING, AND REALIZED WE COULD USE IT TO SNEAK BACK INSIDE.
WHERE YOU'RE GOING TO DIVERT THIS FLOATING NUTHOUSE AWAY FROM EARTH, OR WE SHOW YOU YOUR GUTS.
SIMPLE ENOUGH FOR YOU?
PLEASE, WARDENS, IF YOU WOULD BE SO KIND... AND JUST HEAR ME OUT...
WHY? I DO NOT RECALL YOU BEING SO ACCOMMODATING WHEN YOU ABDUCTED AND EXPERIMENTED ON US WITHOUT OUR PERMISSION.
YES, WELL, I CAN SEE WHY THAT WOULD BE TRAUMATIC...
...BUT YOU HAVE TO UNDERSTAND, EVERYTHING WE STARWATCHERS DO, IT IS FOR THE GREATER GOOD.

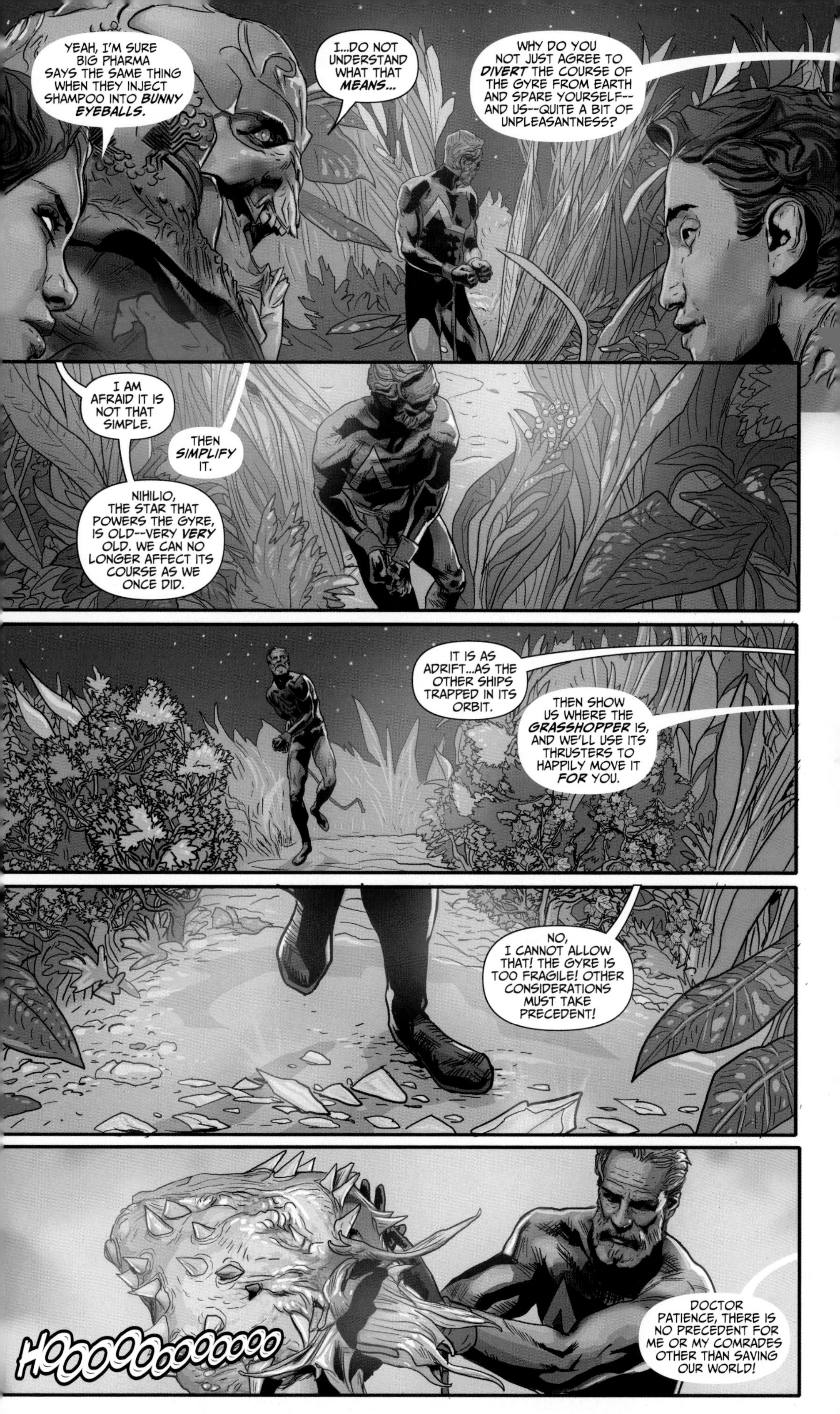
YEAH, I'M SURE BIG PHARMA SAYS THE SAME THING WHEN THEY INJECT SHAMPOO INTO BUNNY EYEBALLS.
I...DO NOT UNDERSTAND WHAT THAT MEANS...
WHY DO YOU NOT JUST AGREE TO DIVERT THE COURSE OF THE GYRE FROM EARTH AND SPARE YOURSELF--AND US--QUITE A BIT OF UNPLEASANTNESS?
I AM AFRAID IT IS NOT THAT SIMPLE.
THEN SIMPLIFY IT.
NIHILIO, THE STAR THAT POWERS THE GYRE, IS OLD--VERY VERY OLD. WE CAN NO LONGER AFFECT ITS COURSE AS WE ONCE DID.
IT IS AS ADRIFT...AS THE OTHER SHIPS TRAPPED IN ITS ORBIT.
THEN SHOW US WHERE THE GRASSHOPPER IS, AND WE'LL USE ITS THRUSTERS TO HAPPILY MOVE IT FOR YOU.
NO, I CANNOT ALLOW THAT! THE GYRE IS TOO FRAGILE! OTHER CONSIDERATIONS MUST TAKE PRECEDENT!
HOOOOOOOOOOOO
DOCTOR PATIENCE, THERE IS NO PRECEDENT FOR ME OR MY COMRADES OTHER THAN SAVING OUR WORLD!

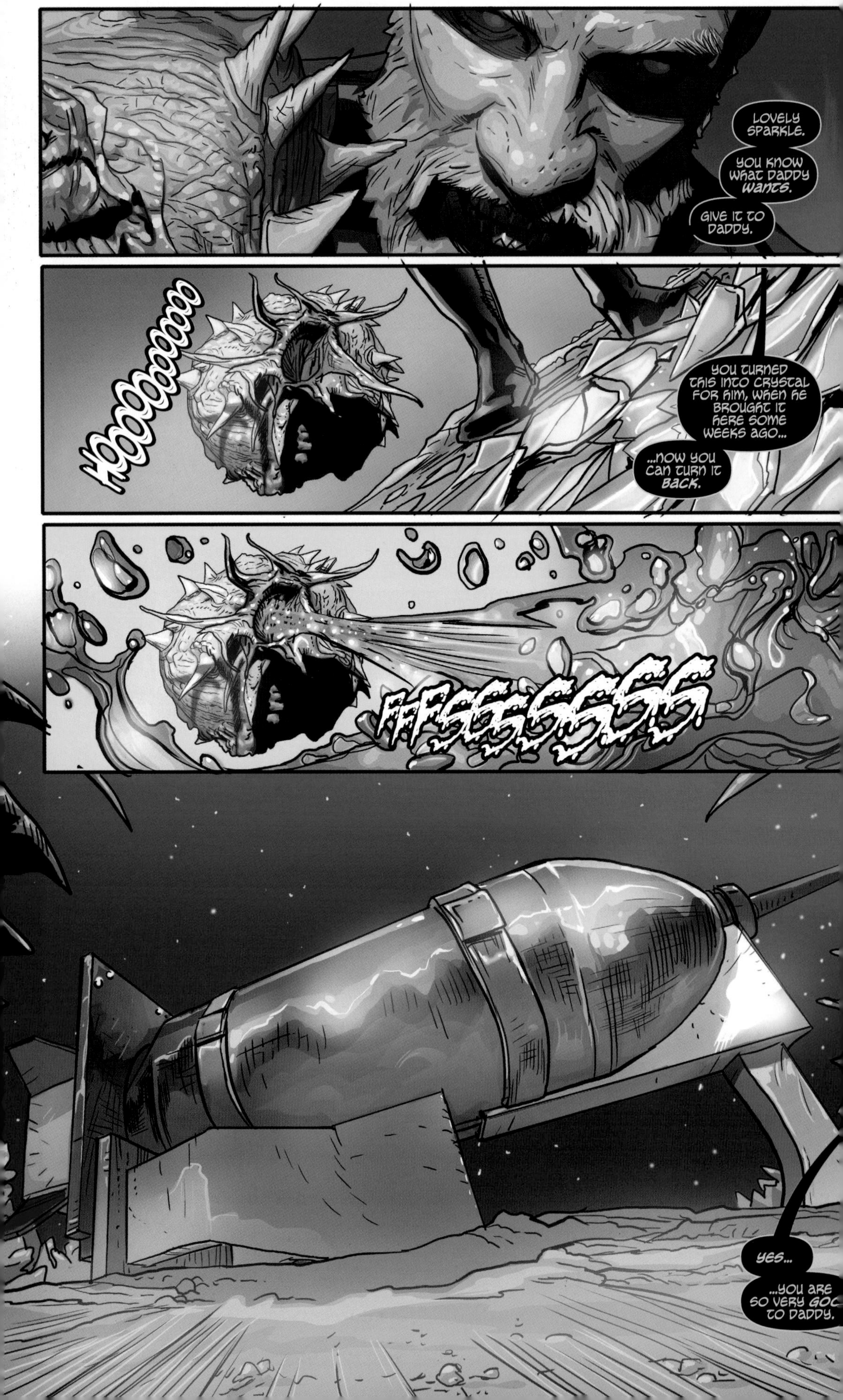

LOVELY SPARKLE.
YOU KNOW WHAT DADDY WANTS.
GIVE IT TO DADDY.
HOOOOOOOOOOO
YOU TURNED THIS INTO CRYSTAL FOR HIM, WHEN HE BROUGHT IT HERE SOME WEEKS AGO...
...NOW YOU CAN TURN IT BACK.
FFFSSSSSSSS
YES...
...YOU ARE SO VERY GOC TO DADDY.

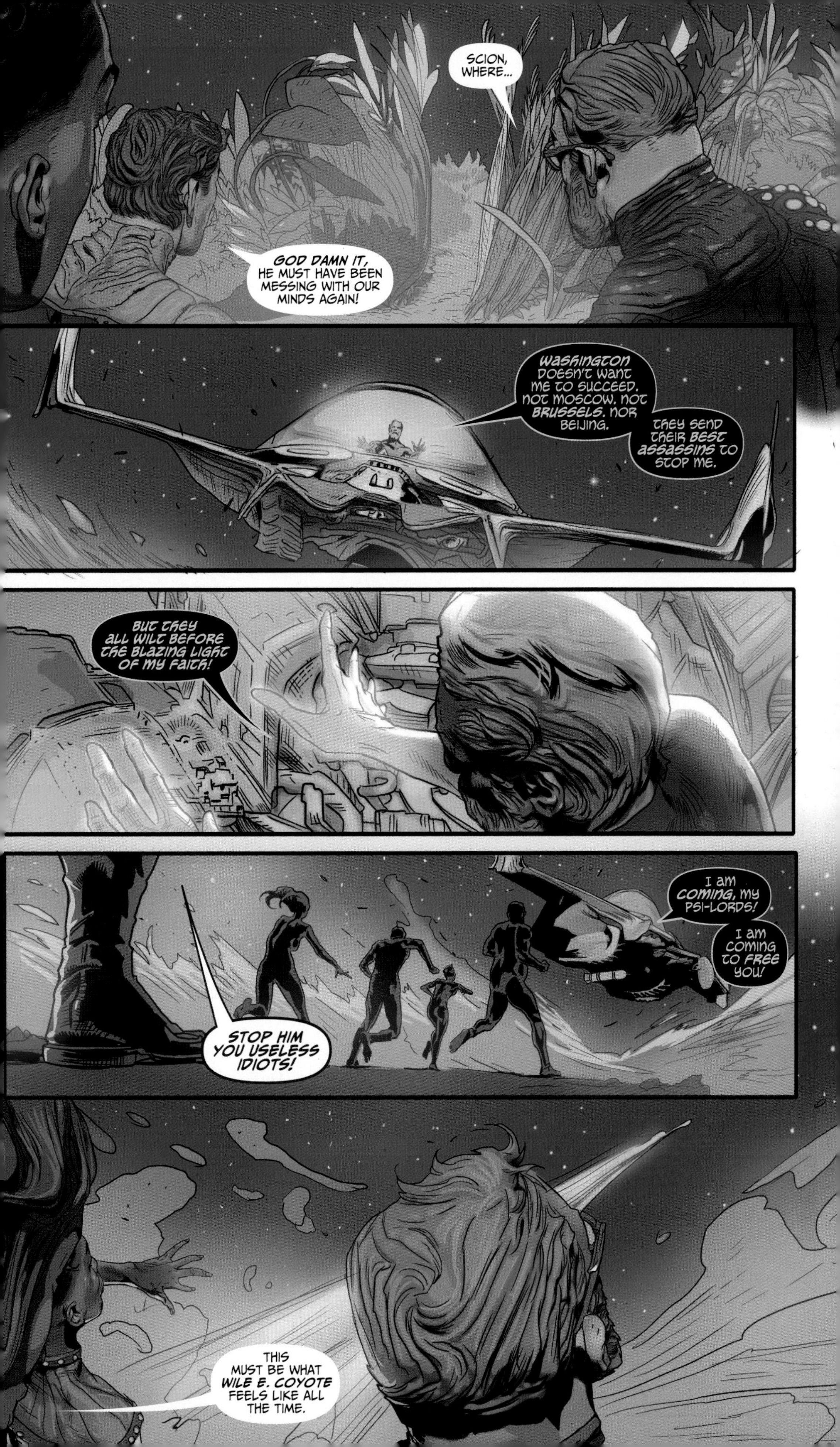
SCION, WHERE...
GOD DAMN IT, HE MUST HAVE BEEN MESSING WITH OUR MINDS AGAIN!
WASHINGTON DOESN'T WANT ME TO SUCCEED. NOT MOSCOW. NOT BRUSSELS. NOR BEIJING.
THEY SEND THEIR BEST ASSASSINS TO STOP ME.
BUT THEY ALL WILT BEFORE THE BLAZING LIGHT OF MY FAITH!
I AM COMING, MY PSI-LORDS!
I AM COMING TO FREE YOU!
STOP HIM YOU USELESS IDIOTS!
THIS MUST BE WHAT WILE E. COYOTE FEELS LIKE ALL THE TIME.

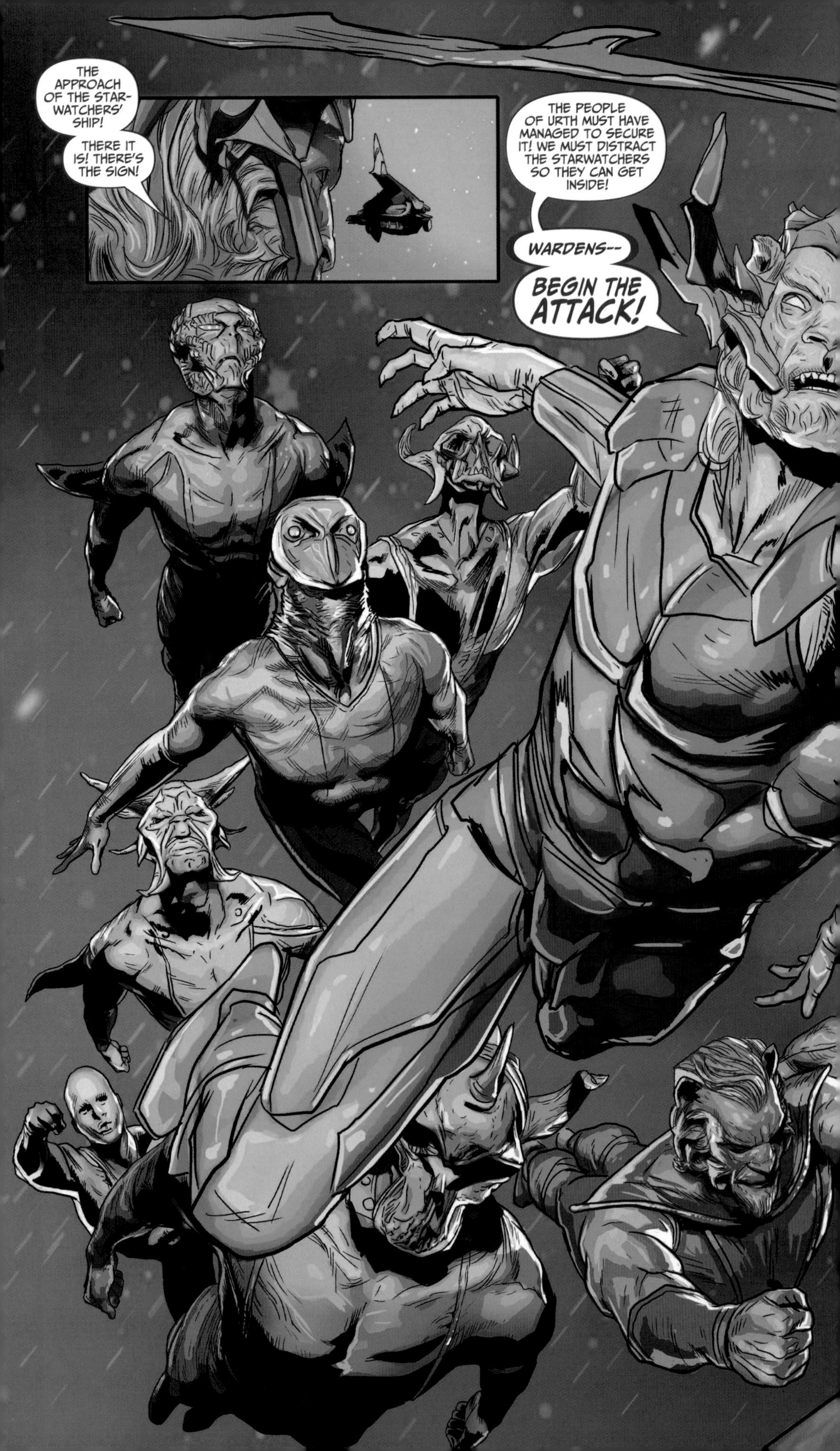
THE APPROACH OF THE STAR-WATCHERS' SHIP!
THERE IT IS! THERE'S THE SIGN!
THE PEOPLE OF URTH MUST HAVE MANAGED TO SECURE IT! WE MUST DISTRACT THE STARWATCHERS SO THEY CAN GET INSIDE!
WARDENS--
BEGIN THE ATTACK!

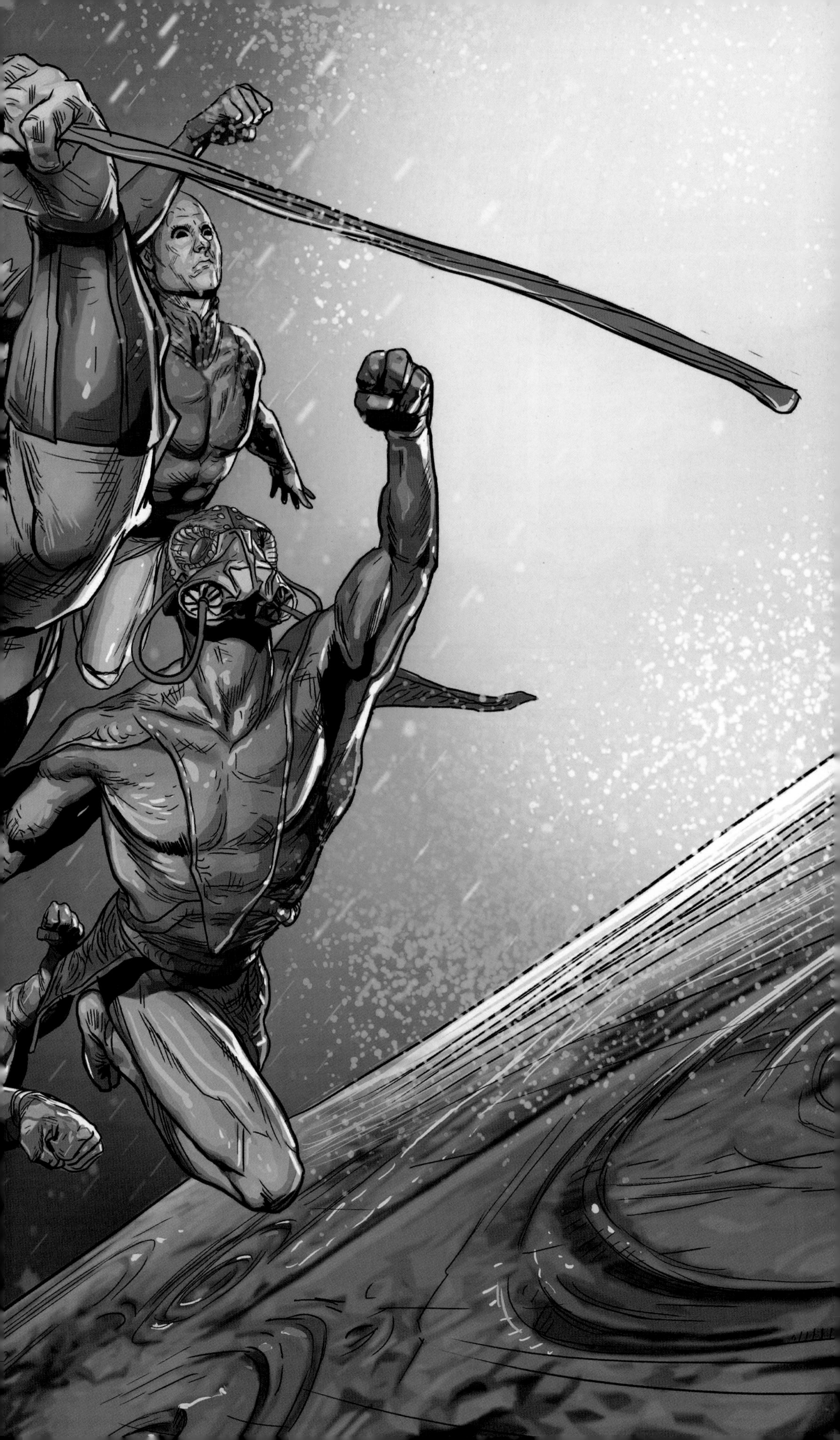

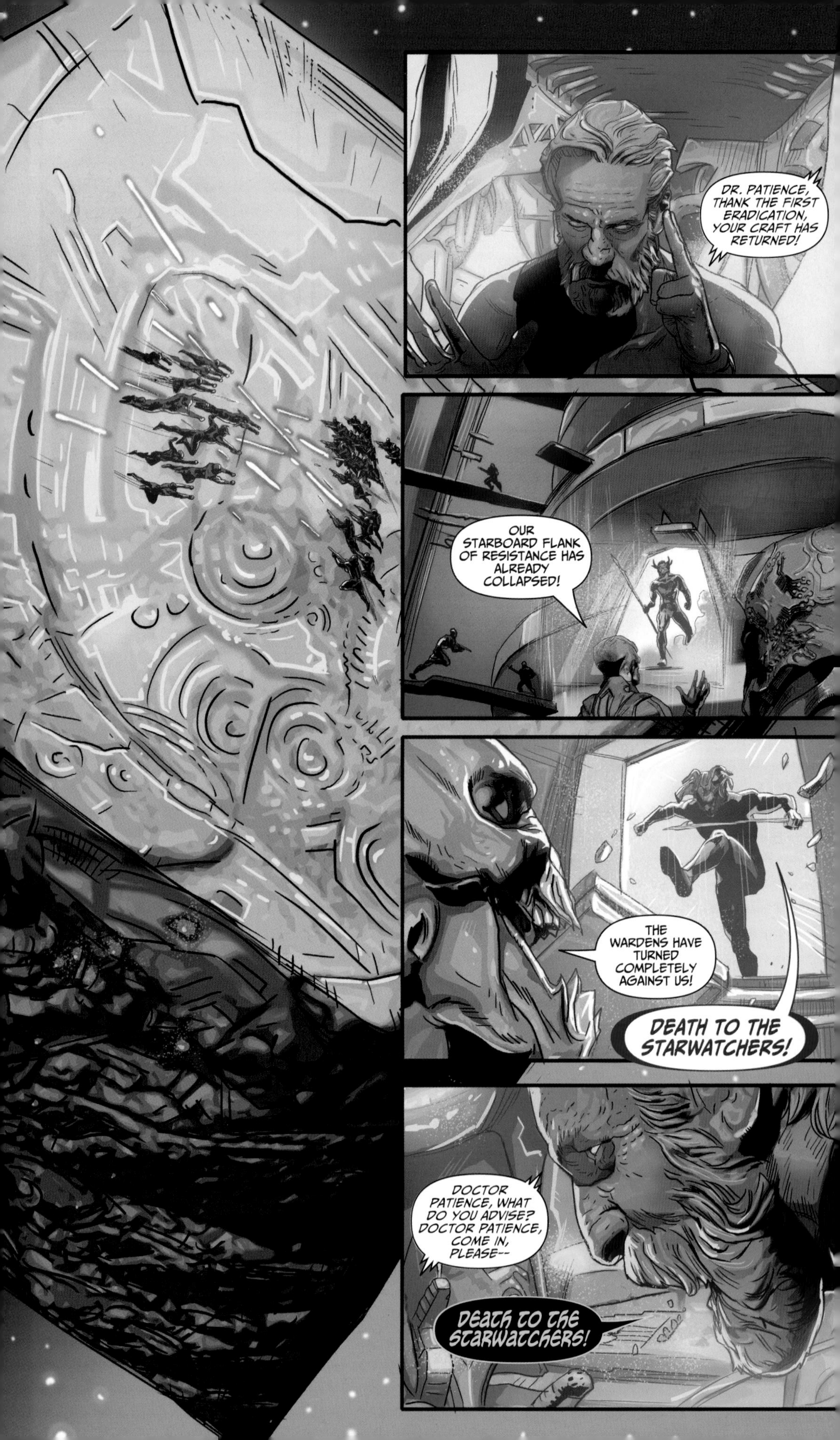
DR. PATIENCE, THANK THE FIRST ERADICATION, YOUR CRAFT HAS RETURNED!
OUR STARBOARD FLANK OF RESISTANCE HAS ALREADY COLLAPSED!
THE WARDENS HAVE TURNED COMPLETELY AGAINST US!
DEATH TO THE STARWATCHERS!
DOCTOR PATIENCE, WHAT DO YOU ADVISE? DOCTOR PATIENCE, COME IN, PLEASE--
DEATH TO THE STARWATCHERS!

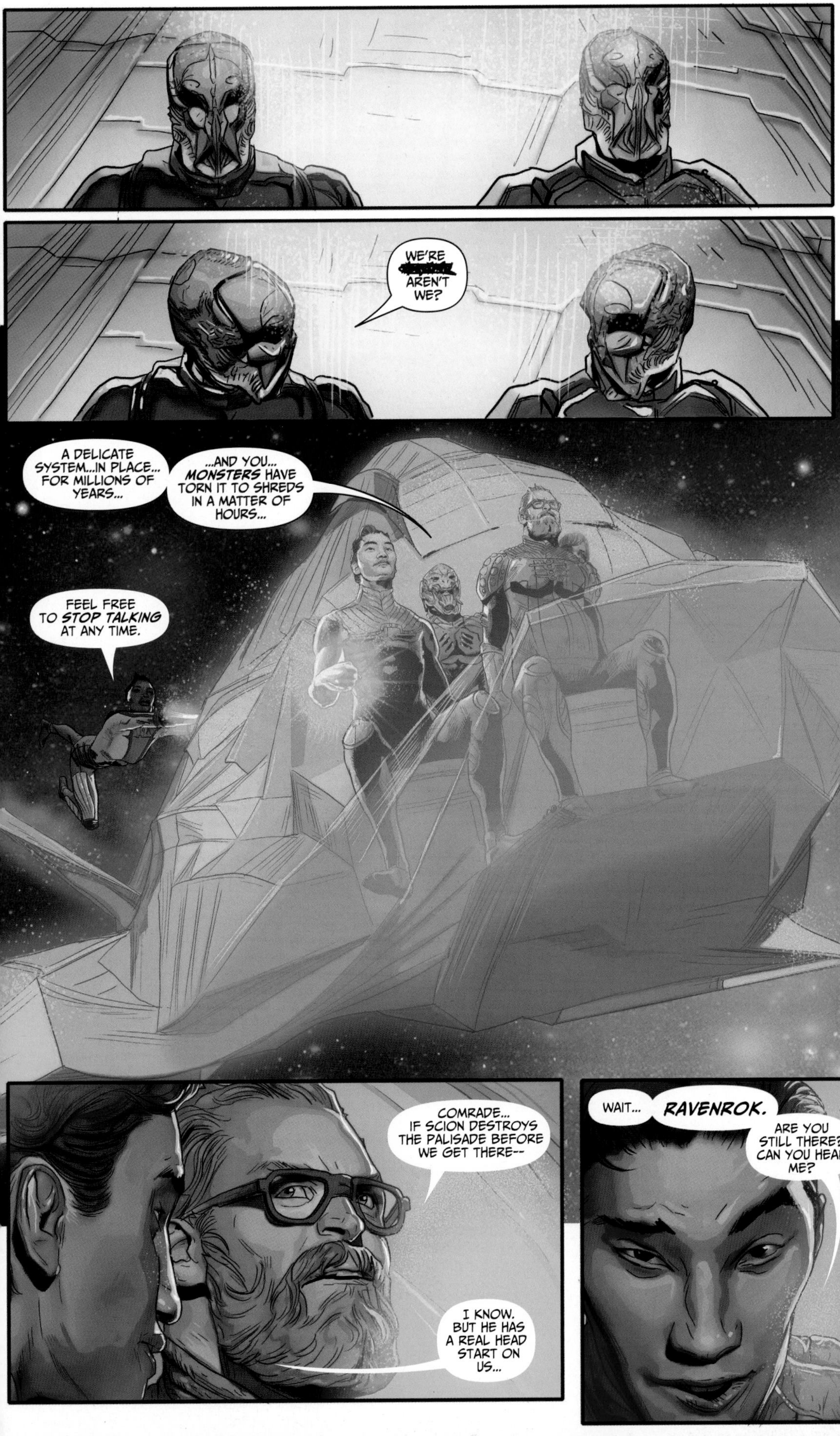
WE'RE [redacted] AREN'T WE?
A DELICATE SYSTEM...IN PLACE... FOR MILLIONS OF YEARS...
...AND YOU... MONSTERS HAVE TORN IT TO SHREDS IN A MATTER OF HOURS...
FEEL FREE TO STOP TALKING AT ANY TIME.
COMRADE... IF SCION DESTROYS THE PALISADE BEFORE WE GET THERE--
I KNOW. BUT HE HAS A REAL HEAD START ON US...
WAIT... RAVENROK.
ARE YOU STILL THERE? CAN YOU HEAR ME?

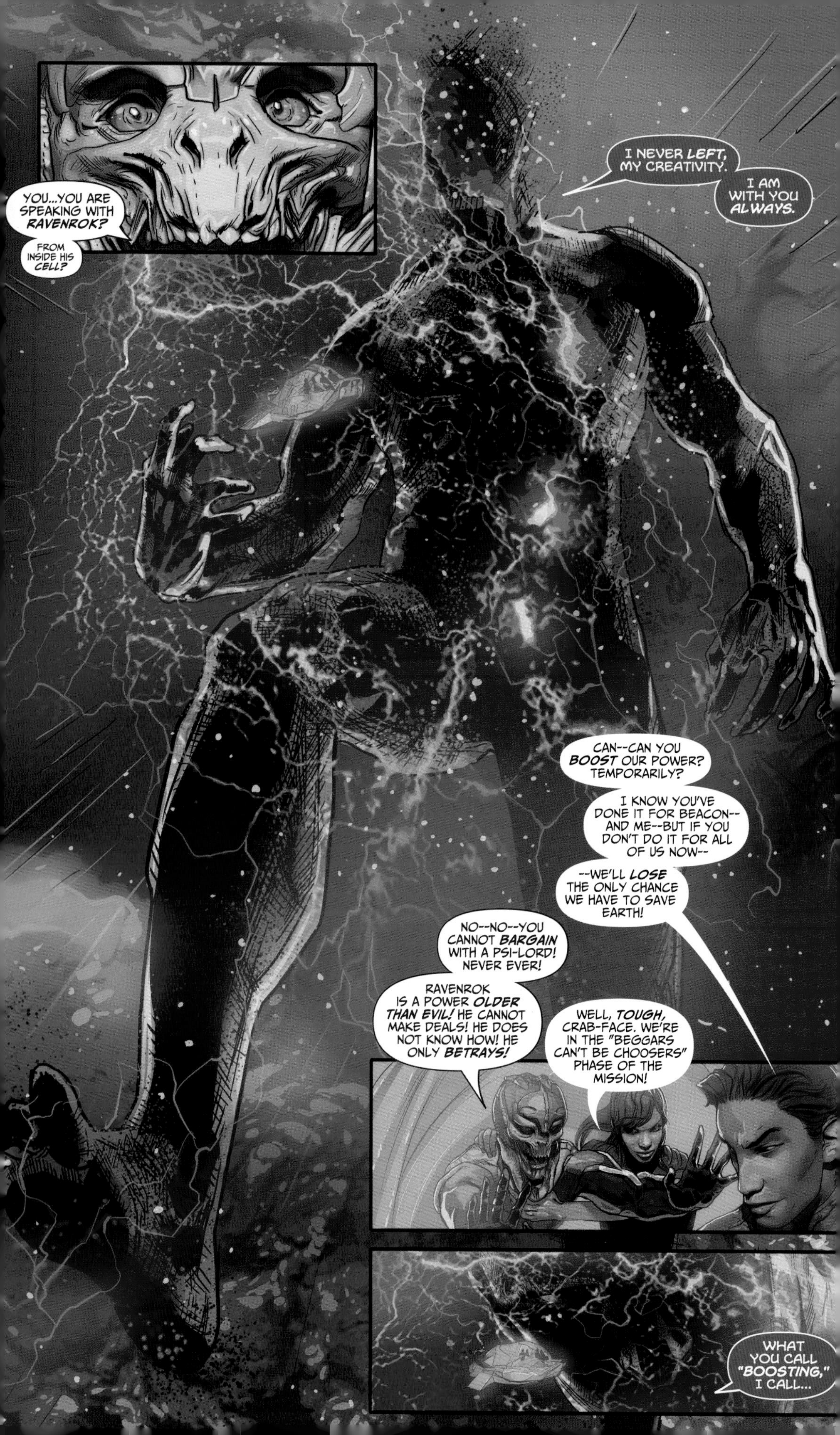

YOU...YOU ARE SPEAKING WITH RAVENROK?
FROM INSIDE HIS CELL?
I NEVER LEFT, MY CREATIVITY.
I AM WITH YOU ALWAYS.
CAN--CAN YOU BOOST OUR POWER? TEMPORARILY?
I KNOW YOU'VE DONE IT FOR BEACON-- AND ME--BUT IF YOU DON'T DO IT FOR ALL OF US NOW--
--WE'LL LOSE THE ONLY CHANCE WE HAVE TO SAVE EARTH!
NO--NO--YOU CANNOT BARGAIN WITH A PSI-LORD! NEVER EVER!
RAVENROK IS A POWER OLDER THAN EVIL! HE CANNOT MAKE DEALS! HE DOES NOT KNOW HOW! HE ONLY BETRAYS!
WELL, TOUGH, CRAB-FACE. WE'RE IN THE "BEGGARS CAN'T BE CHOOSERS" PHASE OF THE MISSION!
WHAT YOU CALL "BOOSTING," I CALL...

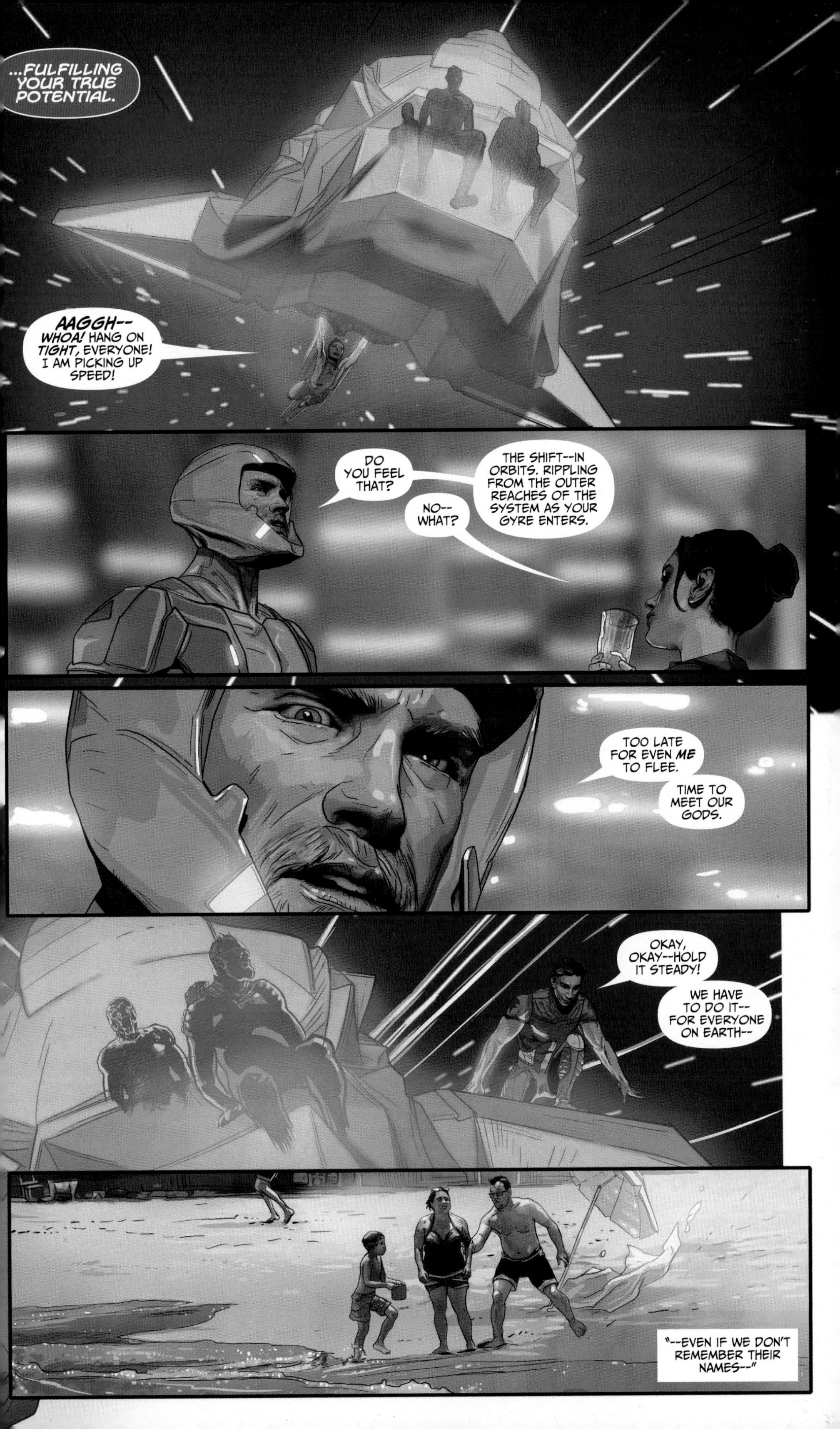
...FULFILLING YOUR TRUE POTENTIAL.
AAGGH-- WHOA! HANG ON TIGHT, EVERYONE! I AM PICKING UP SPEED!
DO YOU FEEL THAT?
NO-- WHAT?
THE SHIFT--IN ORBITS. RIPPLING FROM THE OUTER REACHES OF THE SYSTEM AS YOUR GYRE ENTERS.
TOO LATE FOR EVEN ME TO FLEE.
TIME TO MEET OUR GODS.
OKAY, OKAY--HOLD IT STEADY!
WE HAVE TO DO IT-- FOR EVERYONE ON EARTH--
"--EVEN IF WE DON'T REMEMBER THEIR NAMES--"

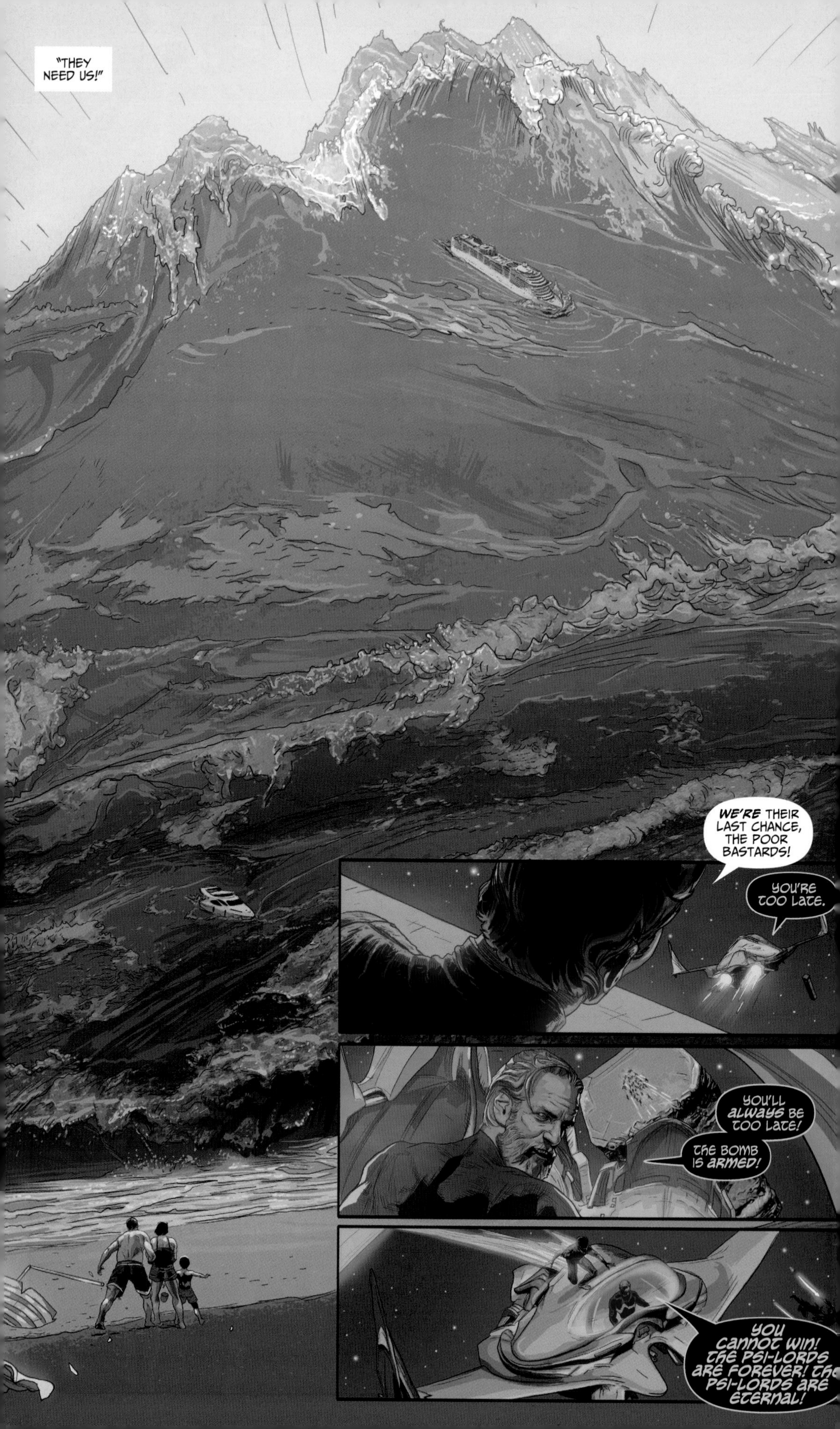
"THEY NEED US!"
WE'RE THEIR LAST CHANCE, THE POOR BASTARDS!
YOU'RE TOO LATE.
YOU'LL ALWAYS BE TOO LATE!
THE BOMB IS ARMED!
YOU CANNOT WIN! THE PSI-LORDS ARE FOREVER! THE PSI-LORDS ARE ETERNAL!

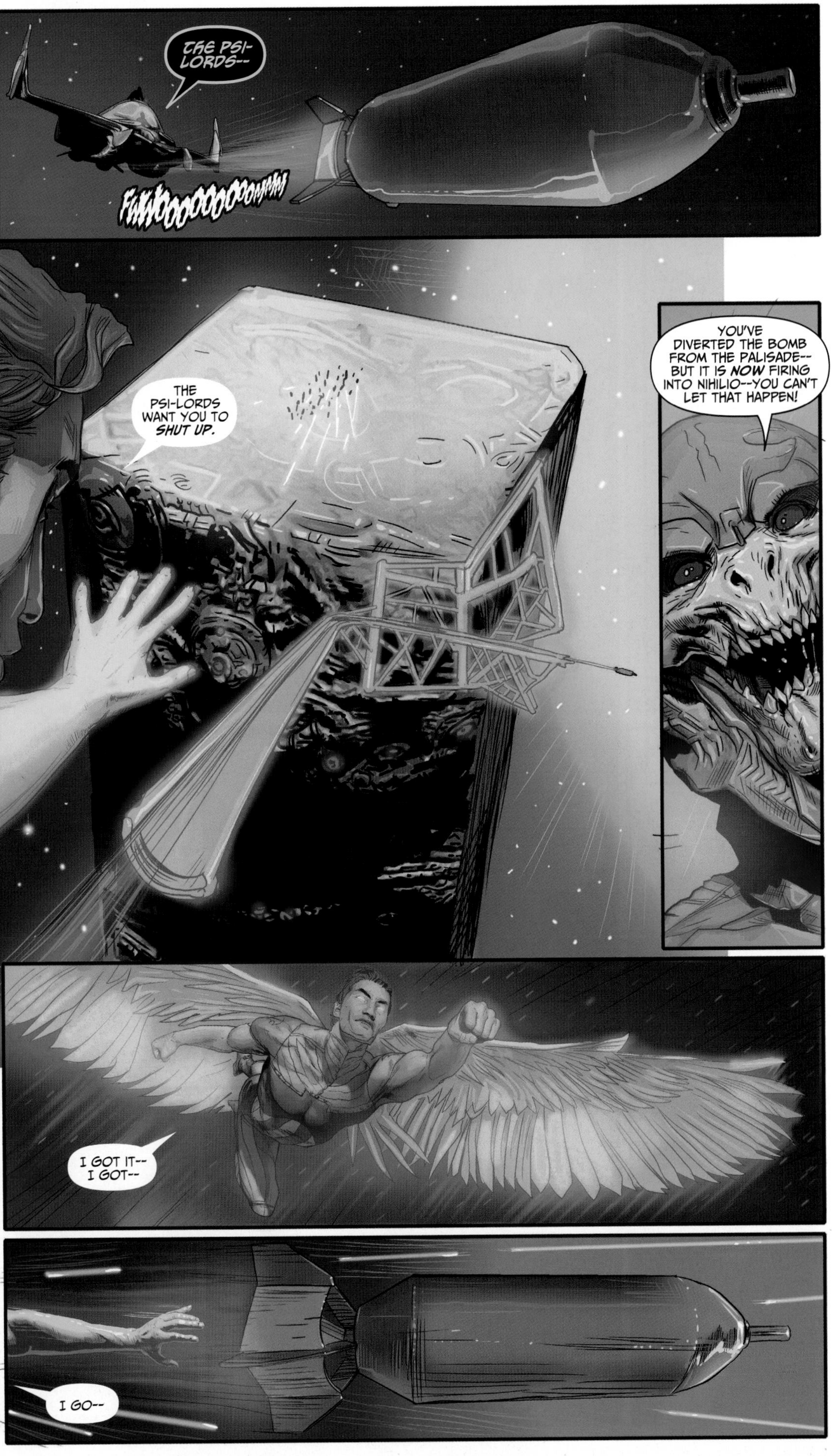
THE PSI-LORDS--
FWWOOOOOOOOMMM
THE PSI-LORDS WANT YOU TO SHUT UP.
YOU'VE DIVERTED THE BOMB FROM THE PALISADE--BUT IT IS NOW FIRING INTO NIHILIO--YOU CAN'T LET THAT HAPPEN!
I GOT IT-- I GOT--
I GO--

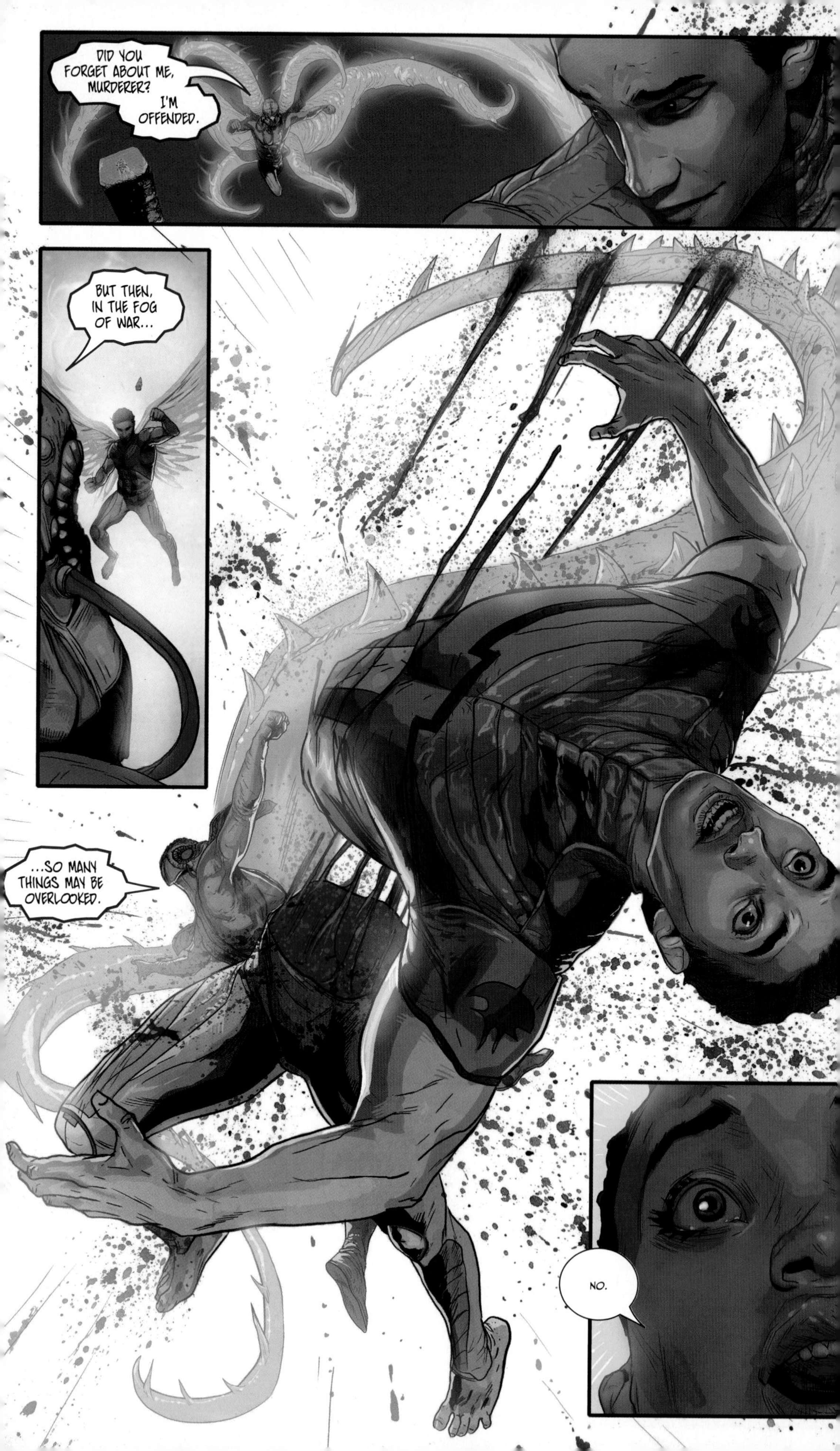
DID YOU FORGET ABOUT ME, MURDERER?
I'M OFFENDED.
BUT THEN, IN THE FOG OF WAR...
...SO MANY THINGS MAY BE OVERLOOKED.
NO.

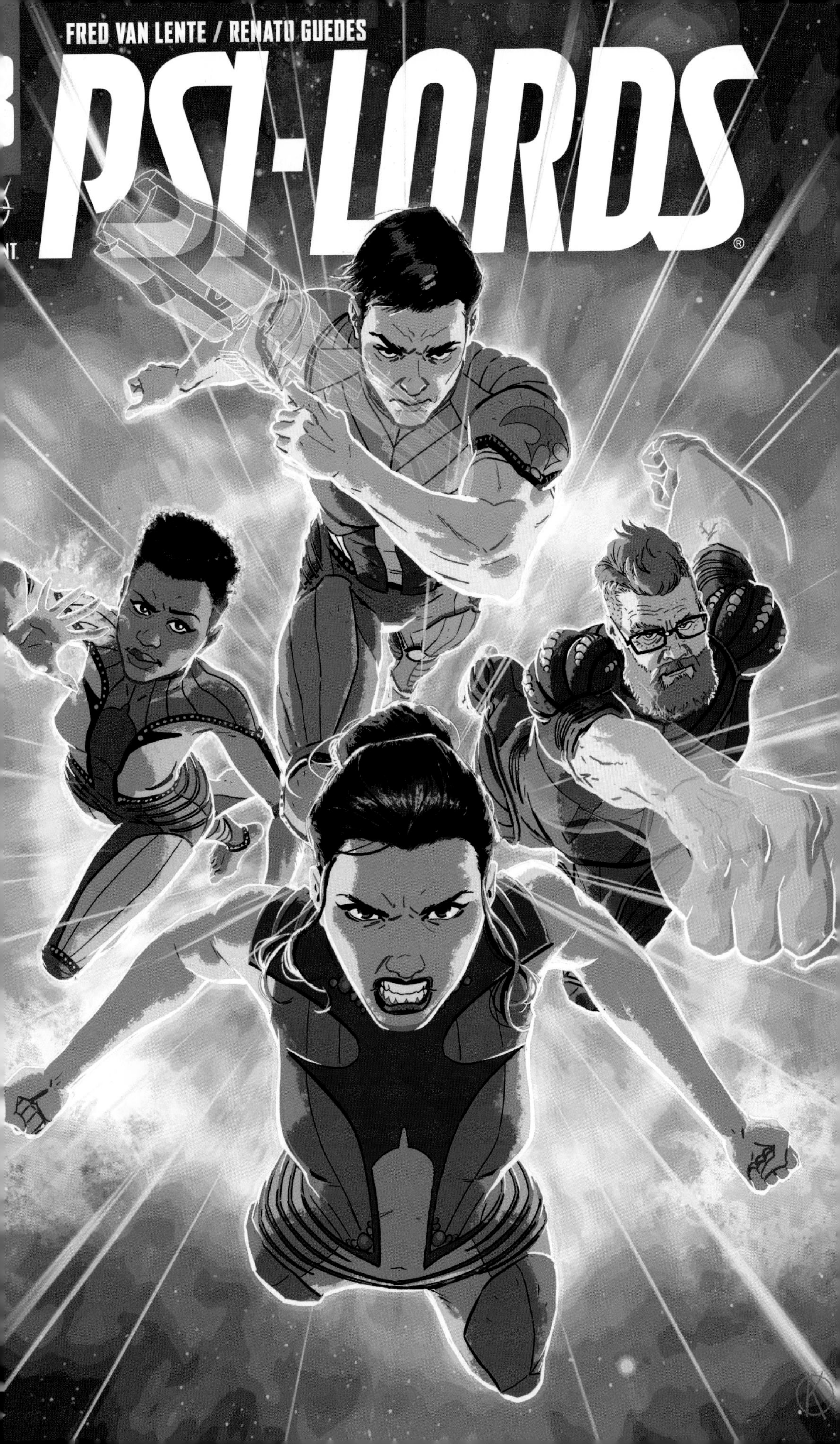

FRED VAN LENTE / RENATO GUEDES
PSI-LORDS

**PSI-LORDS**
WRITER: Fred Van Le[n]
ARTIST: Renato Guec[o]
LETTERER: Dave Shar[p]
COVER ARTIST: Ka[...]
ASSISTANT EDITOR: Drew Baumgartn[er]
EDITOR: David Menc[h]

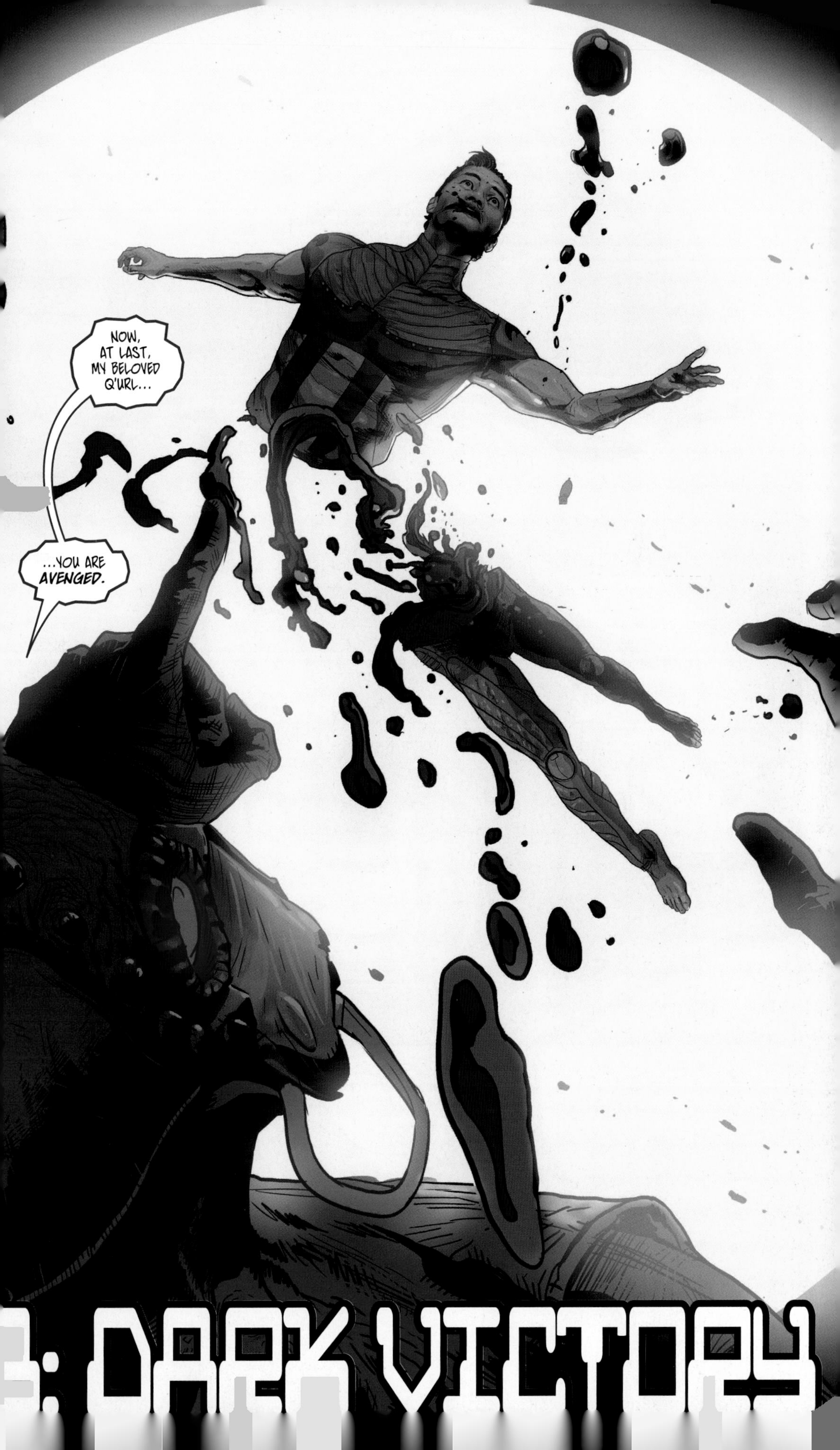
NOW, AT LAST, MY BELOVED Q'URL...
...YOU ARE AVENGED.
DARK VICTORY

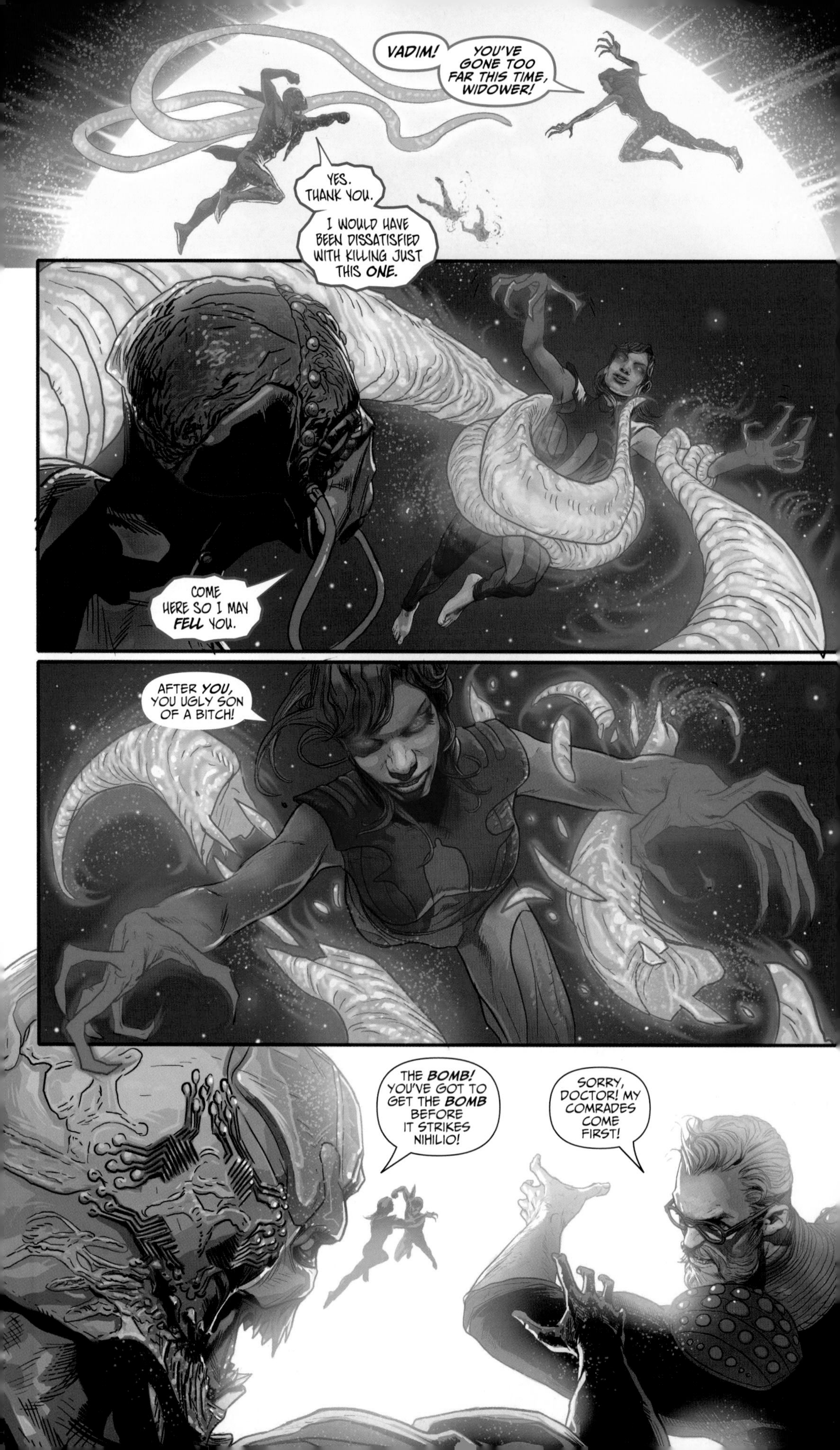
VADIM!
YOU'VE GONE TOO FAR THIS TIME, WIDOWER!
YES. THANK YOU.
I WOULD HAVE BEEN DISSATISFIED WITH KILLING JUST THIS ONE.
COME HERE SO I MAY FELL YOU.
AFTER YOU, YOU UGLY SON OF A BITCH!
THE BOMB! YOU'VE GOT TO GET THE BOMB BEFORE IT STRIKES NIHILIO!
SORRY, DOCTOR! MY COMRADES COME FIRST!

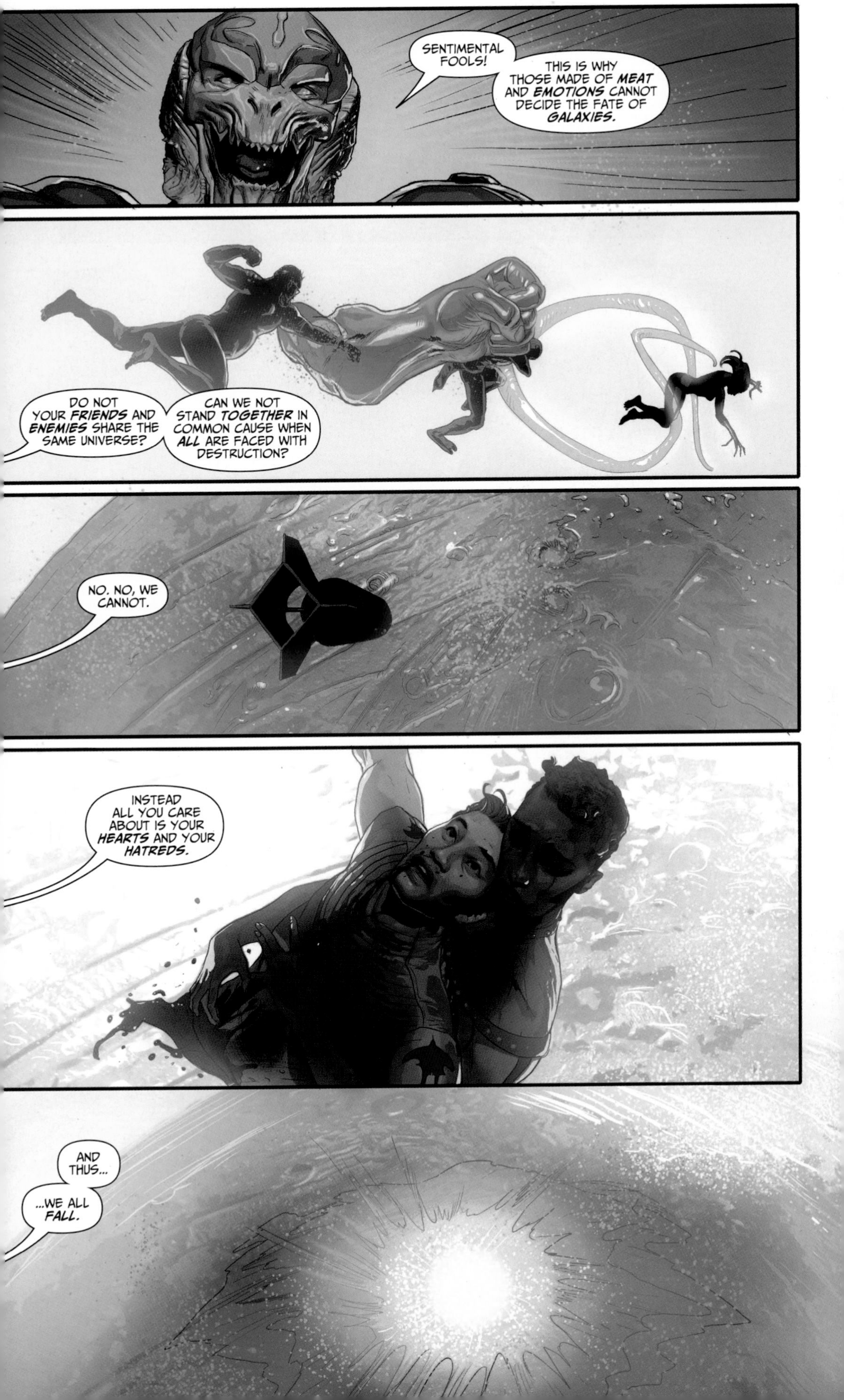
SENTIMENTAL FOOLS!
THIS IS WHY THOSE MADE OF MEAT AND EMOTIONS CANNOT DECIDE THE FATE OF GALAXIES.
DO NOT YOUR FRIENDS AND ENEMIES SHARE THE SAME UNIVERSE?
CAN WE NOT STAND TOGETHER IN COMMON CAUSE WHEN ALL ARE FACED WITH DESTRUCTION?
NO. NO, WE CANNOT.
INSTEAD ALL YOU CARE ABOUT IS YOUR HEARTS AND YOUR HATREDS.
AND THUS...
...WE ALL FALL.

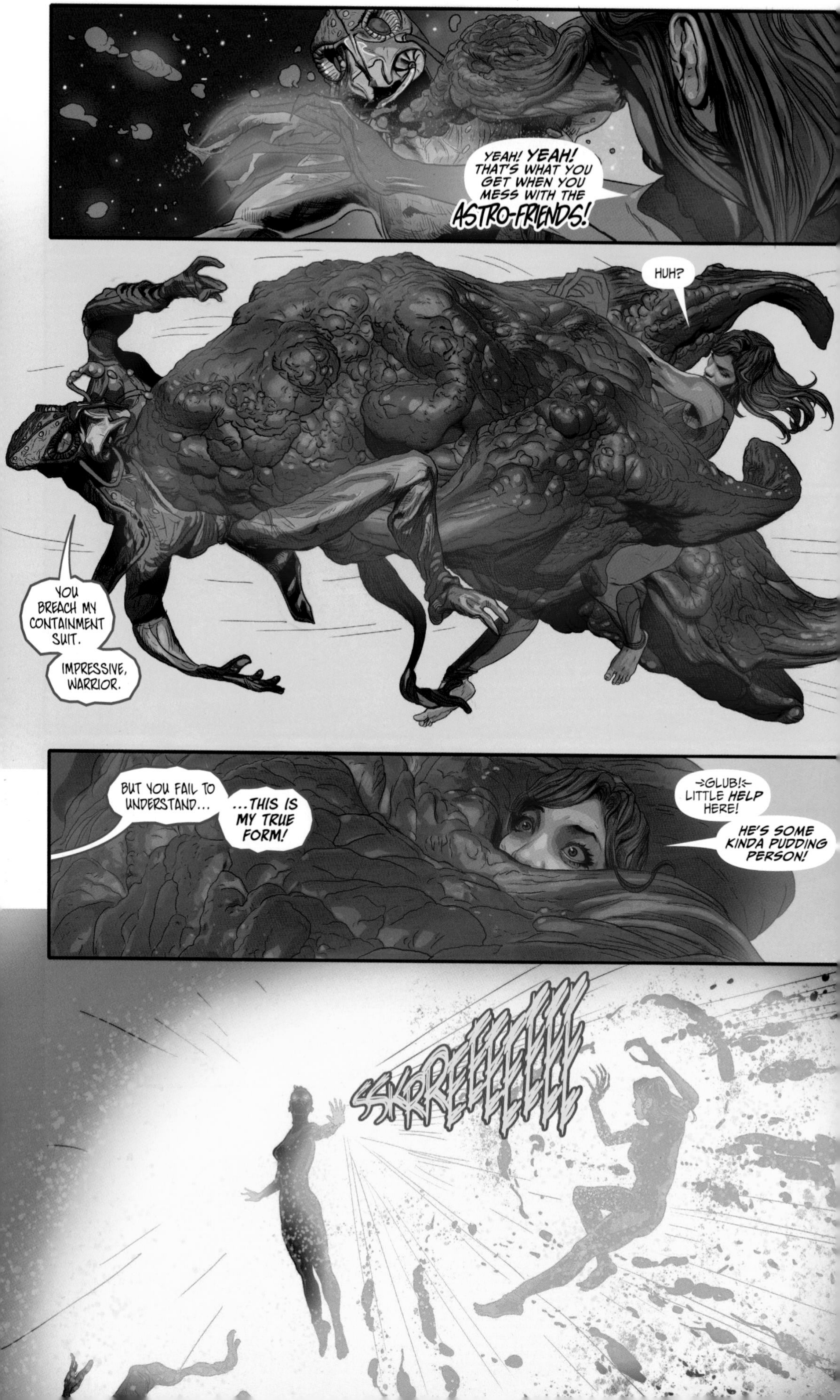
YEAH! YEAH! THAT'S WHAT YOU GET WHEN YOU MESS WITH THE ASTRO-FRIENDS!
HUH?
YOU BREACH MY CONTAINMENT SUIT.
IMPRESSIVE, WARRIOR.
BUT YOU FAIL TO UNDERSTAND...
...THIS IS MY TRUE FORM!
>GLUB!< LITTLE HELP HERE!
HE'S SOME KINDA PUDDING PERSON!
SSKREEEEEEE!

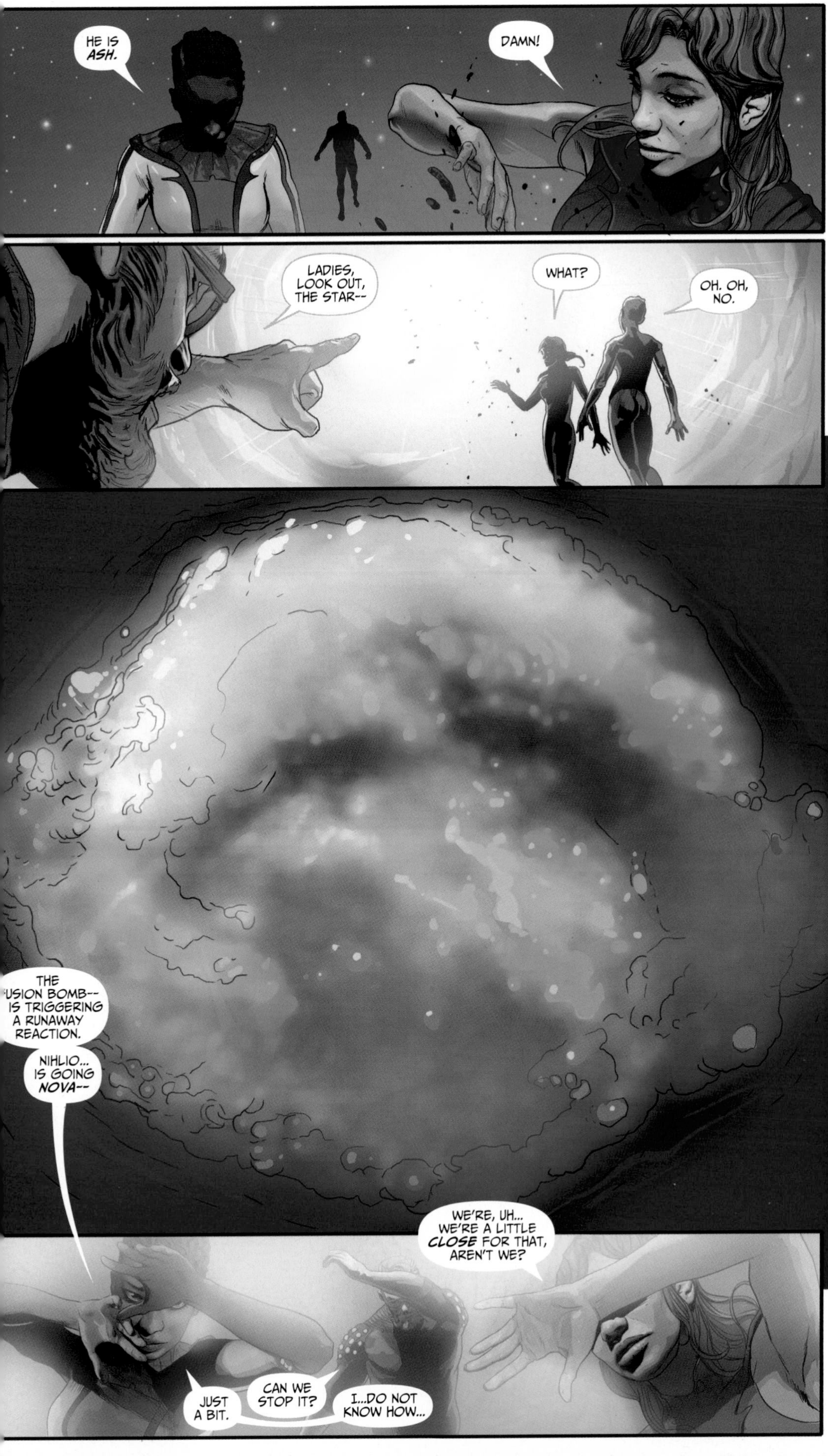
HE IS ASH.
DAMN!
LADIES, LOOK OUT, THE STAR--
WHAT?
OH. OH, NO.
THE FUSION BOMB-- IS TRIGGERING A RUNAWAY REACTION.
NIHLIO... IS GOING NOVA--
WE'RE, UH... WE'RE A LITTLE CLOSE FOR THAT, AREN'T WE?
JUST A BIT.
CAN WE STOP IT?
I...DO NOT KNOW HOW...

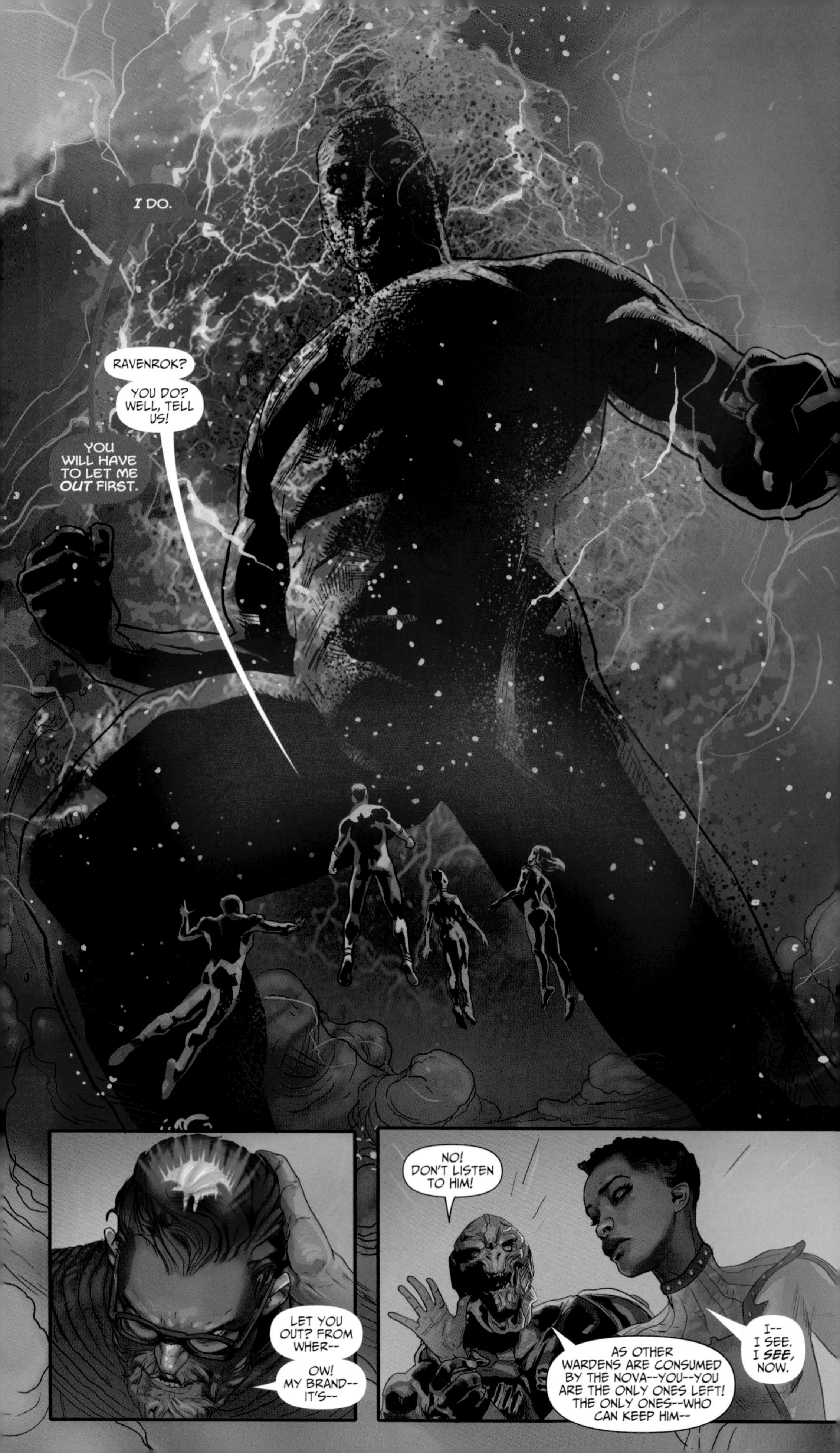
I DO.
RAVENROK?
YOU DO? WELL, TELL US!
YOU WILL HAVE TO LET ME *OUT* FIRST.
LET YOU OUT? FROM WHER--
OW! MY BRAND-- IT'S--
NO! DON'T LISTEN TO HIM!
AS OTHER WARDENS ARE CONSUMED BY THE NOVA--YOU--YOU ARE THE ONLY ONES LEFT! THE ONLY ONES--WHO CAN KEEP HIM--
I-- I SEE. I ***SEE***, NOW.

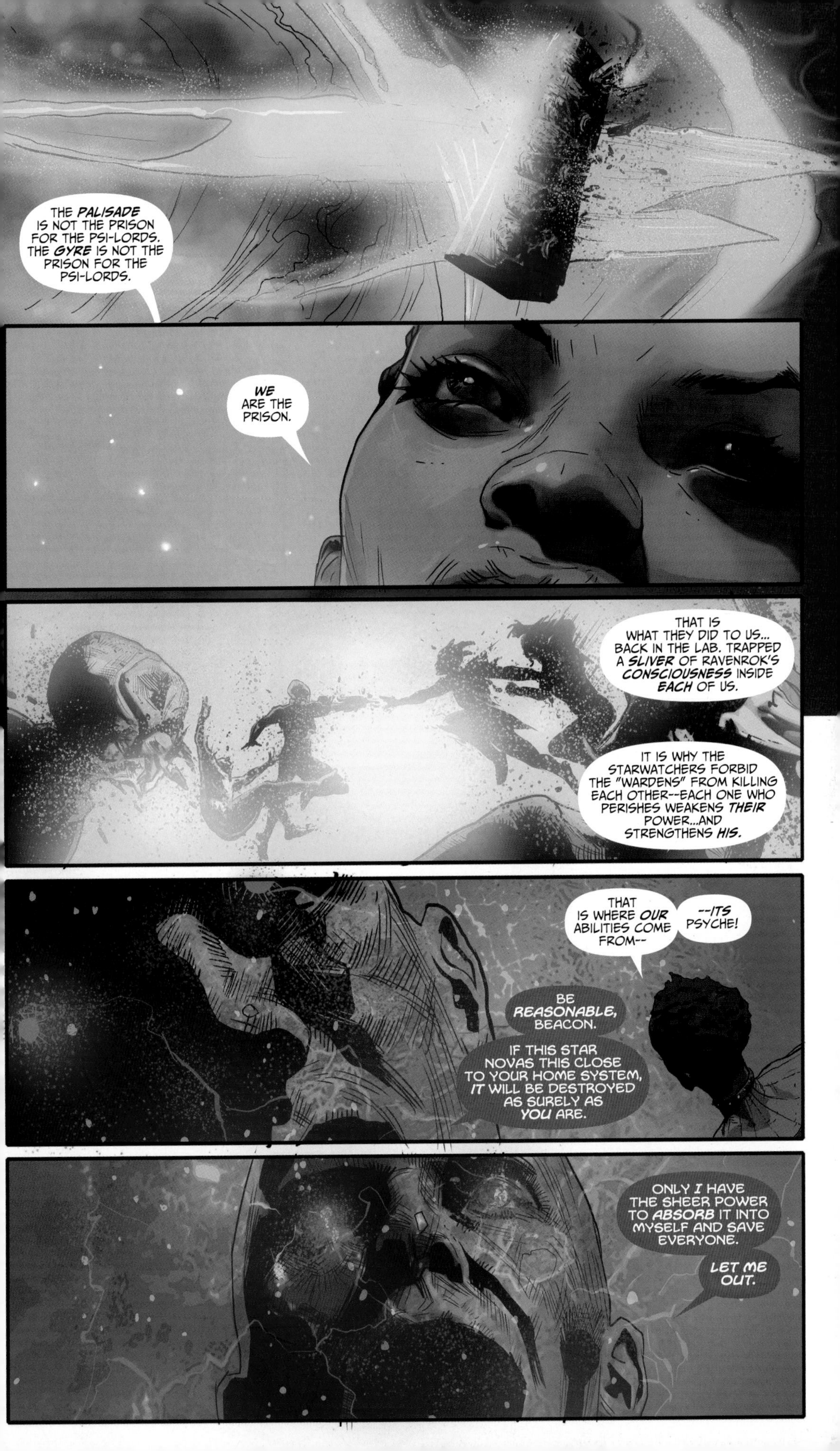
THE PALISADE IS NOT THE PRISON FOR THE PSI-LORDS. THE GYRE IS NOT THE PRISON FOR THE PSI-LORDS.
WE ARE THE PRISON.
THAT IS WHAT THEY DID TO US... BACK IN THE LAB. TRAPPED A SLIVER OF RAVENROK'S CONSCIOUSNESS INSIDE EACH OF US.
IT IS WHY THE STARWATCHERS FORBID THE "WARDENS" FROM KILLING EACH OTHER--EACH ONE WHO PERISHES WEAKENS THEIR POWER...AND STRENGTHENS HIS.
THAT IS WHERE OUR ABILITIES COME FROM--
--ITS PSYCHE!
BE REASONABLE, BEACON.
IF THIS STAR NOVAS THIS CLOSE TO YOUR HOME SYSTEM, IT WILL BE DESTROYED AS SURELY AS YOU ARE.
ONLY I HAVE THE SHEER POWER TO ABSORB IT INTO MYSELF AND SAVE EVERYONE.
LET ME OUT.

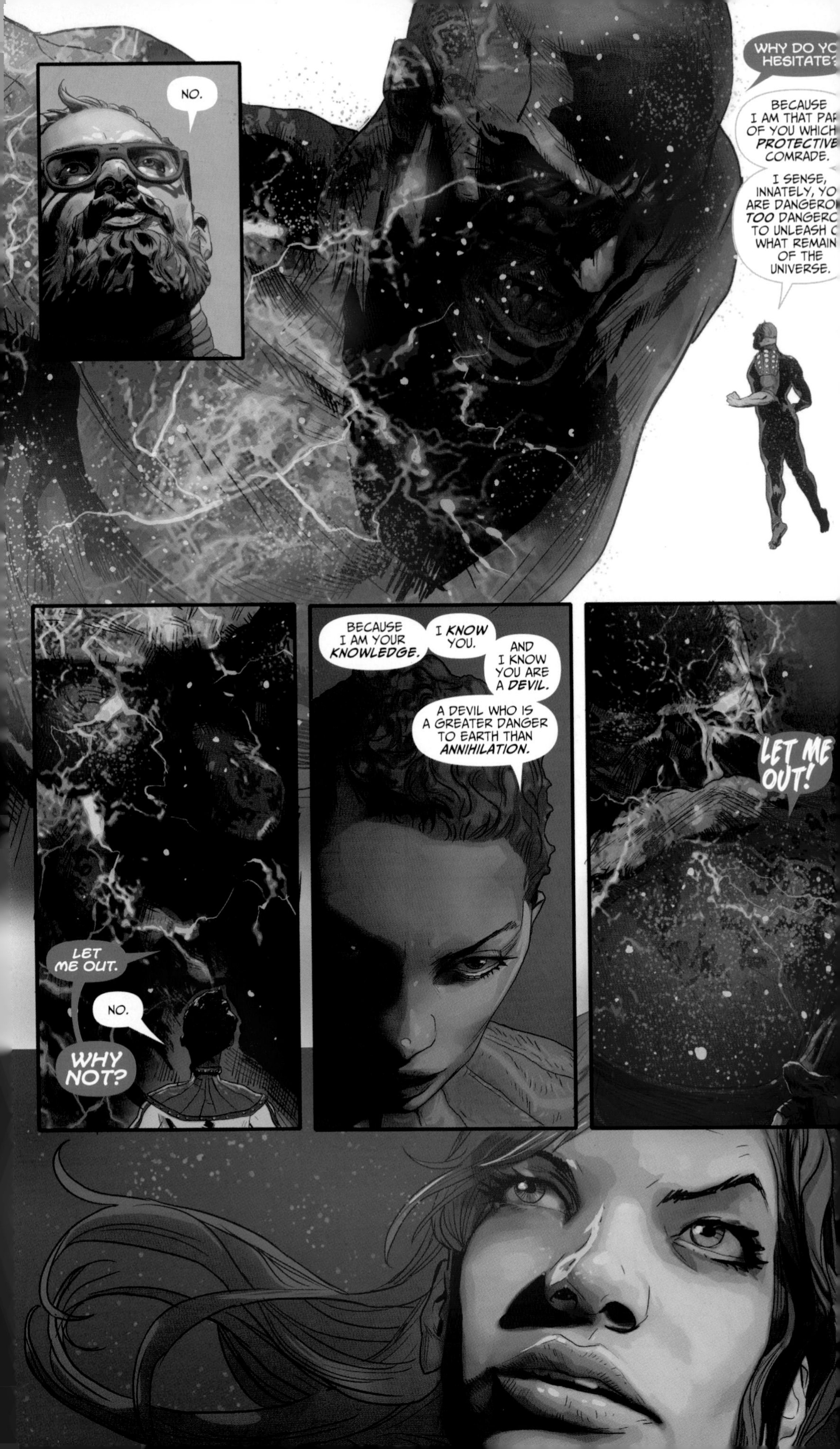
NO.
WHY DO YO
HESITATE?
BECAUSE
I AM THAT PA
OF YOU WHICH
PROTECTIVE
COMRADE.
I SENSE,
INNATELY, YO
ARE DANGERO
TOO DANGERO
TO UNLEASH O
WHAT REMAIN
OF THE
UNIVERSE.
LET
ME OUT.
NO.
WHY
NOT?
BECAUSE
I AM YOUR
KNOWLEDGE.
I KNOW
YOU.
AND
I KNOW
YOU ARE
A DEVIL.
A DEVIL WHO IS
A GREATER DANGER
TO EARTH THAN
ANNIHILATION.
LET ME
OUT!

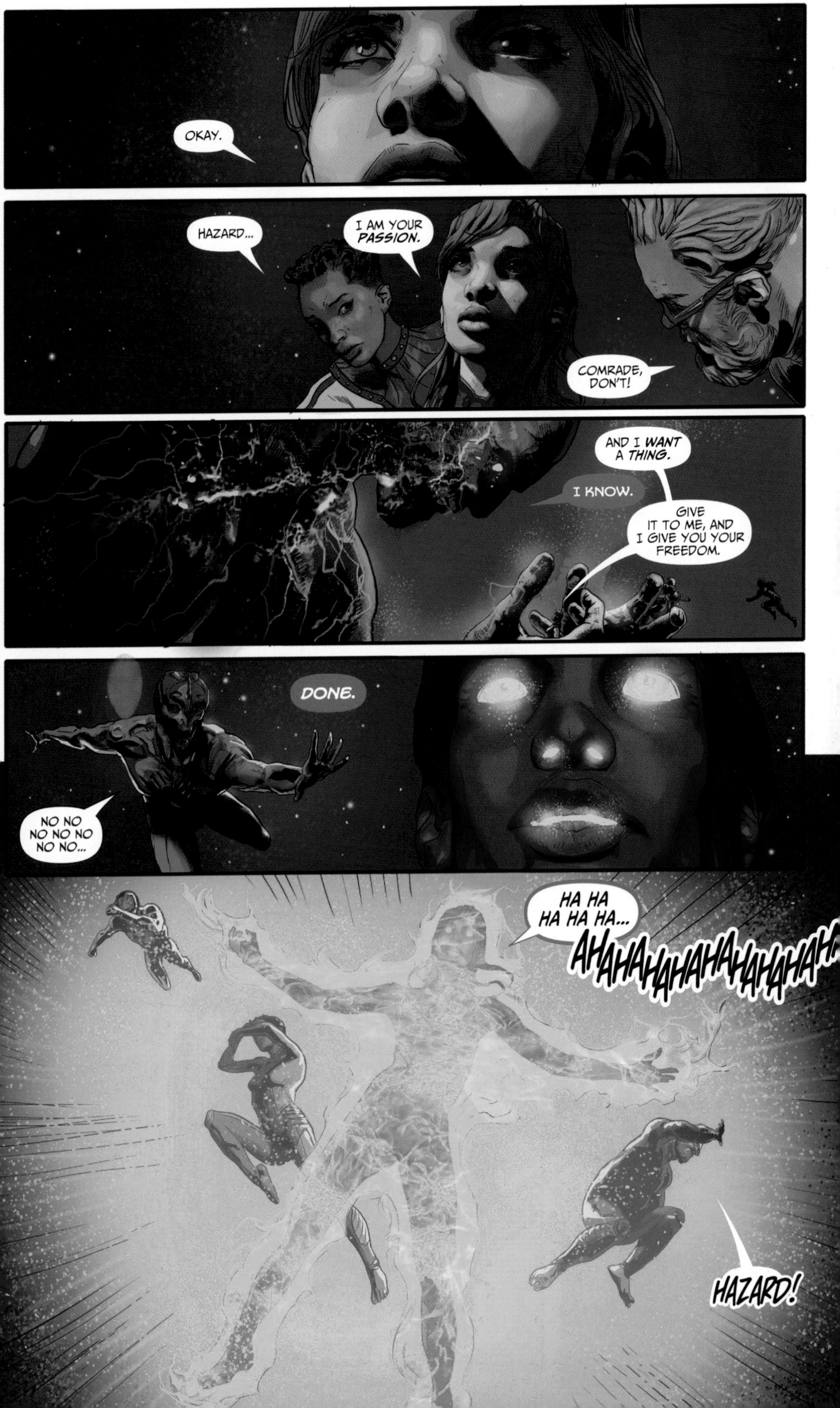
OKAY.
HAZARD...
I AM YOUR PASSION.
COMRADE, DON'T!
AND I WANT A THING.
I KNOW.
GIVE IT TO ME, AND I GIVE YOU YOUR FREEDOM.
DONE.
NO NO NO NO NO NO NO...
HA HA HA HA HA...
AHAHAHAHAHAHAHAHAHAH
HAZARD!

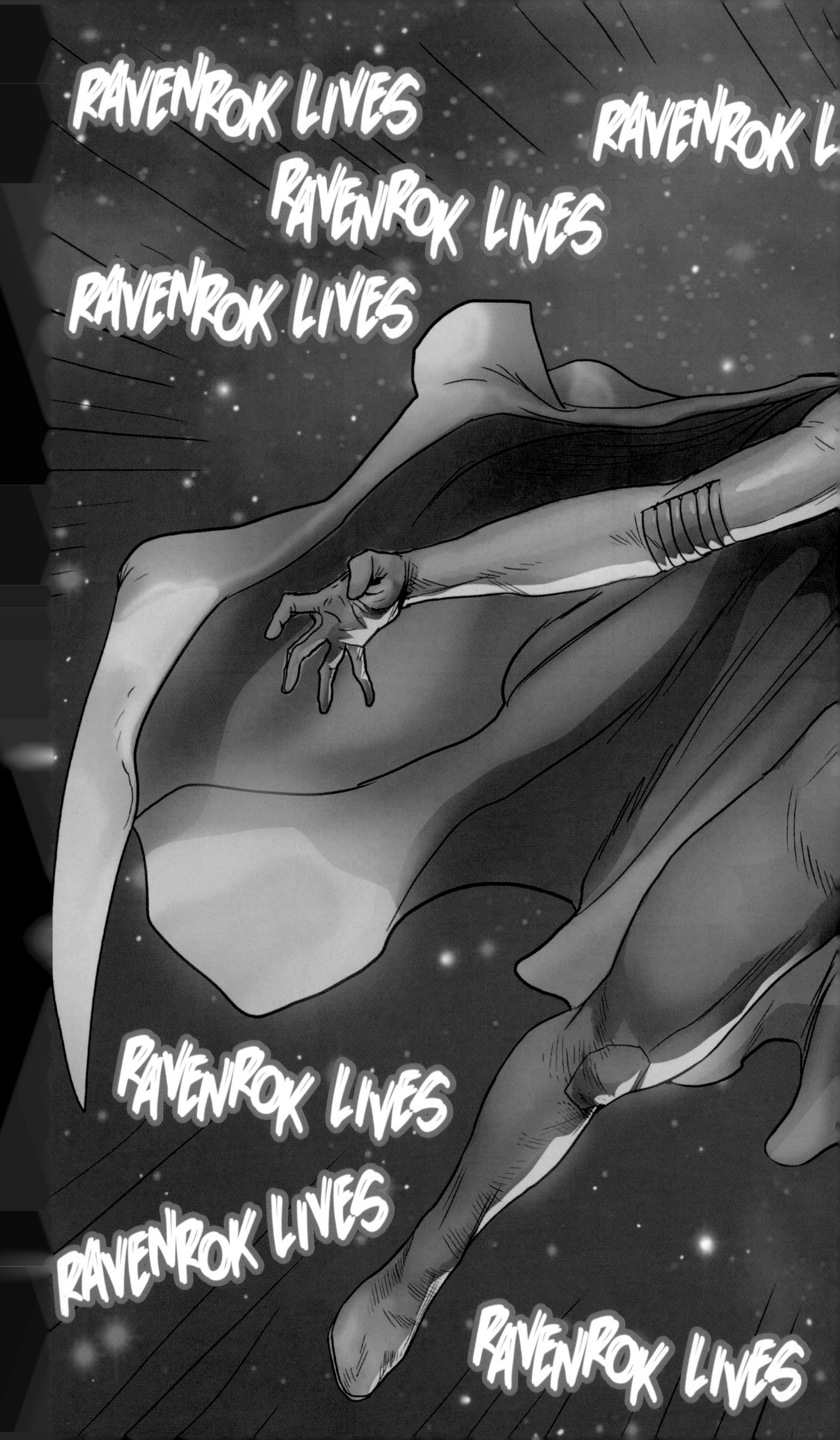
RAVENROK LIVES
RAVENROK L
RAVENROK LIVES
RAVENROK LIVES
RAVENROK LIVES
RAVENROK LIVES
RAVENROK LIVES

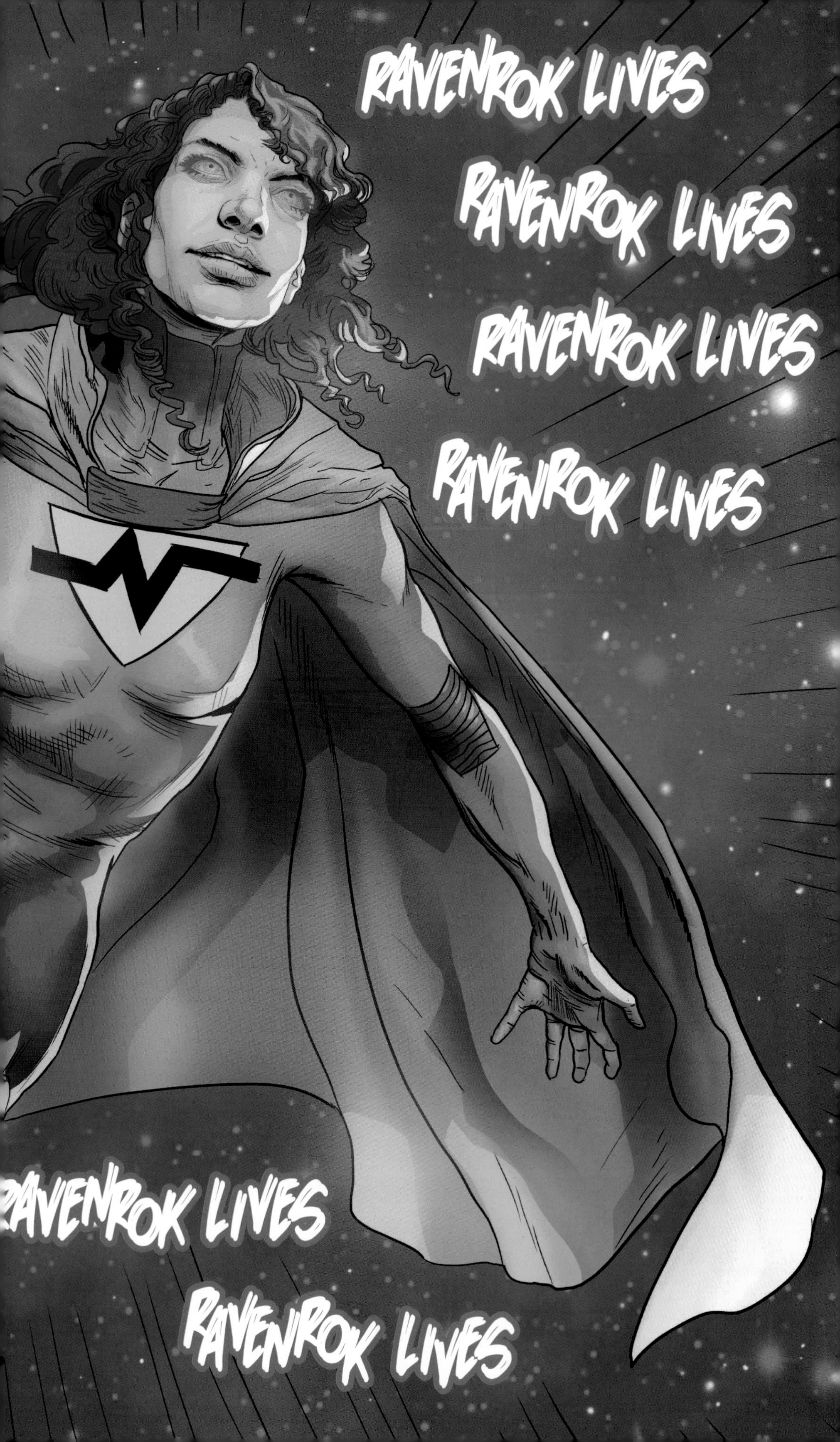
RAVENROK LIVES
RAVENROK LIVES
RAVENROK LIVES
RAVENROK LIVES
RAVENROK LIVES
RAVENROK LIVES

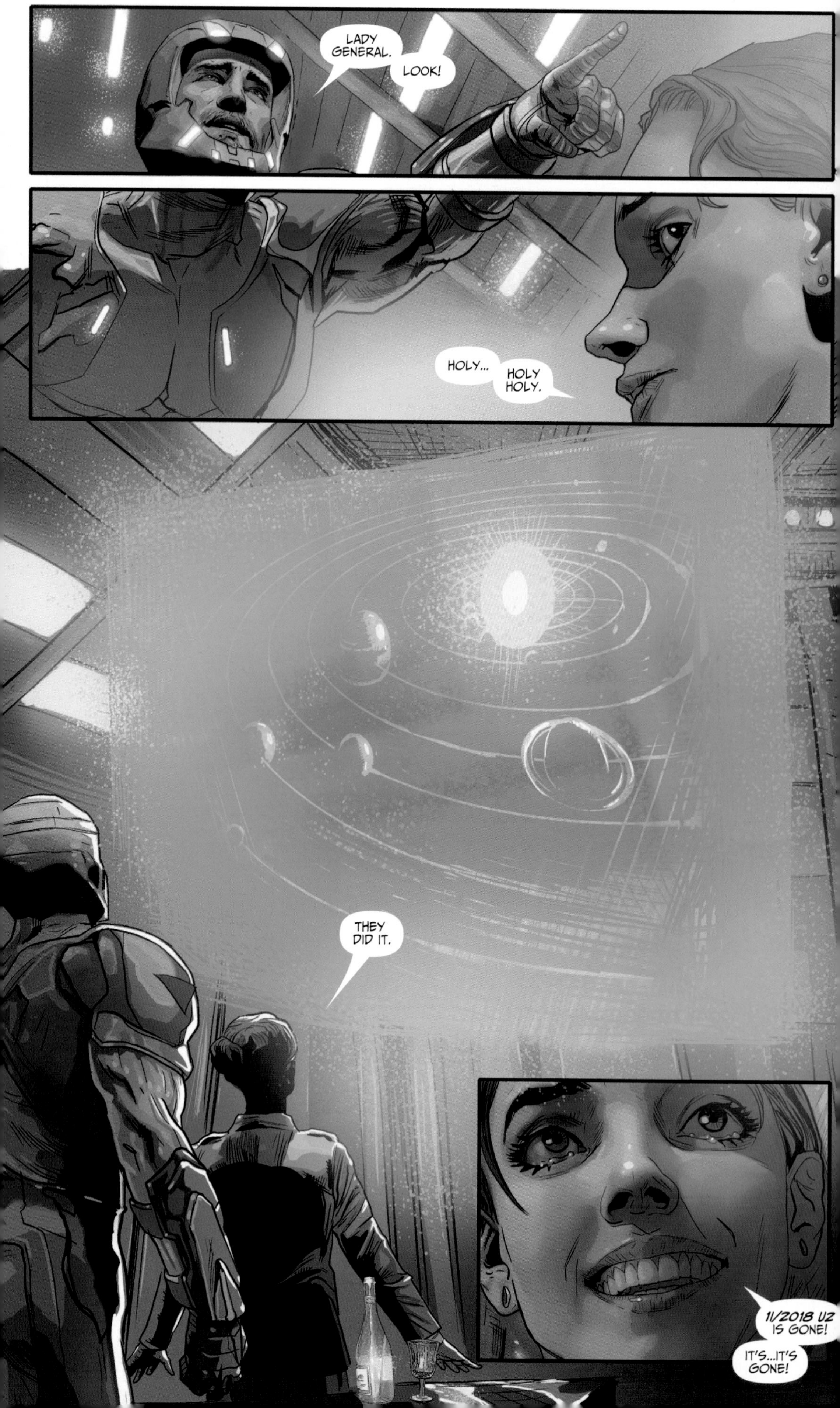
LADY GENERAL.
LOOK!
HOLY...
HOLY HOLY.
THEY DID IT.
11/2018 U2 IS GONE!
IT'S...IT'S GONE!

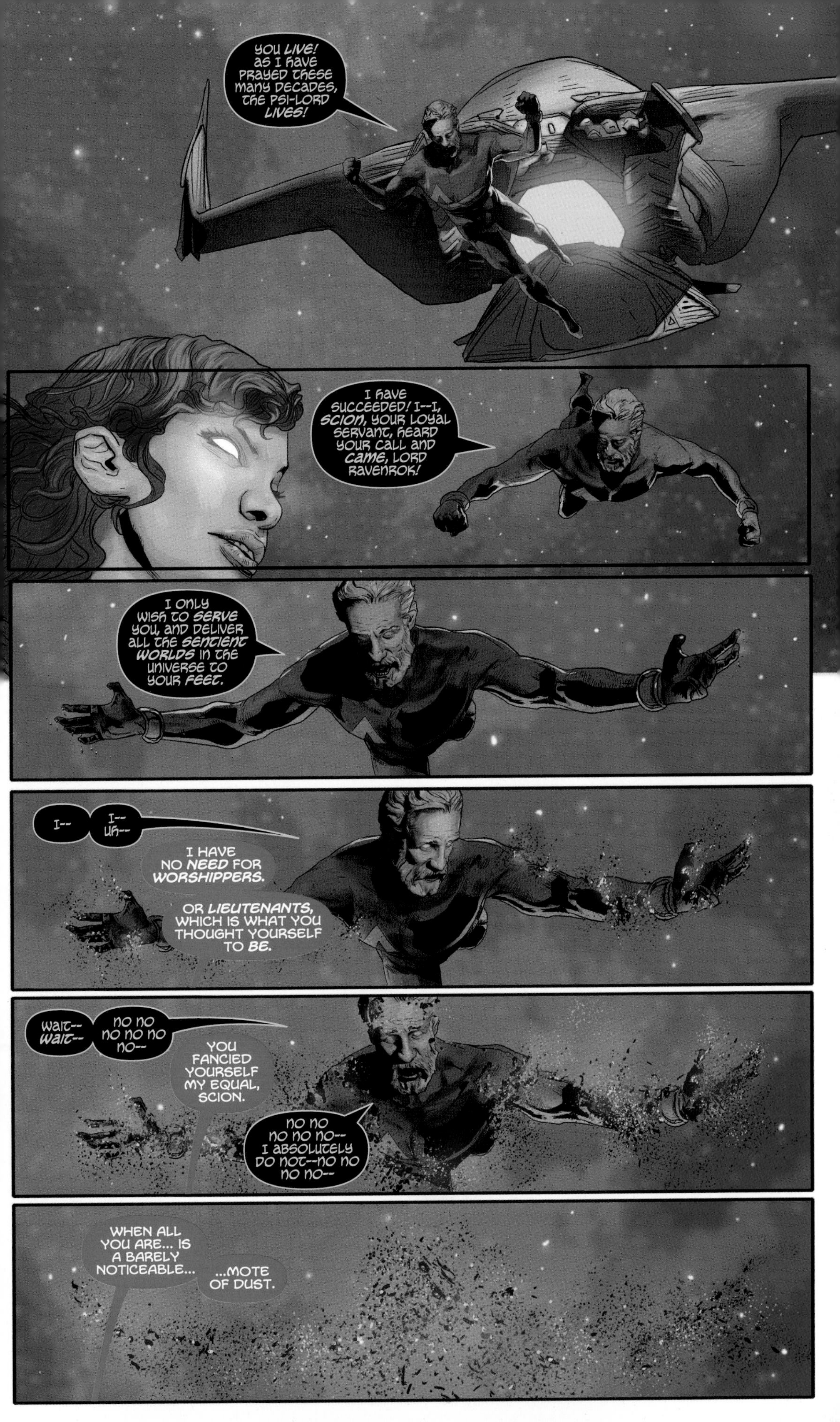
YOU LIVE! AS I HAVE PRAYED THESE MANY DECADES, THE PSI-LORD LIVES!
I HAVE SUCCEEDED! I--I, SCION, YOUR LOYAL SERVANT, HEARD YOUR CALL AND CAME, LORD RAVENROK!
I ONLY WISH TO SERVE YOU, AND DELIVER ALL THE SENTIENT WORLDS IN THE UNIVERSE TO YOUR FEET.
I--
I-- UH--
I HAVE NO NEED FOR WORSHIPPERS.
OR LIEUTENANTS, WHICH IS WHAT YOU THOUGHT YOURSELF TO BE.
WAIT-- WAIT--
NO NO NO NO NO NO--
YOU FANCIED YOURSELF MY EQUAL, SCION.
NO NO NO NO NO-- I ABSOLUTELY DO NOT--NO NO NO NO--
WHEN ALL YOU ARE... IS A BARELY NOTICEABLE...
...MOTE OF DUST.

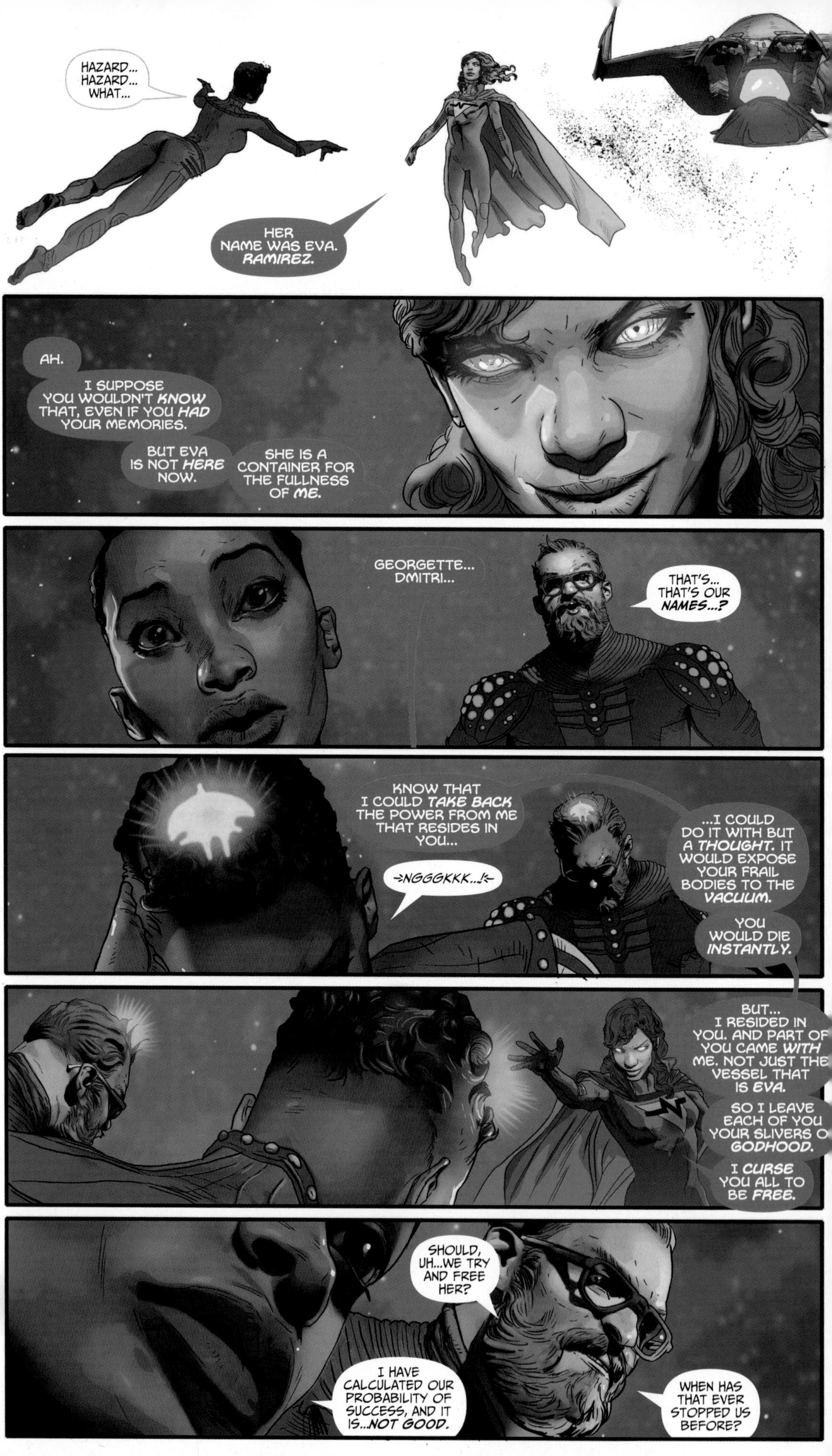
HAZARD... HAZARD... WHAT...
HER NAME WAS EVA. RAMIREZ.
AH.
I SUPPOSE YOU WOULDN'T KNOW THAT, EVEN IF YOU HAD YOUR MEMORIES.
BUT EVA IS NOT HERE NOW.
SHE IS A CONTAINER FOR THE FULLNESS OF ME.
GEORGETTE... DMITRI...
THAT'S... THAT'S OUR NAMES...?
KNOW THAT I COULD TAKE BACK THE POWER FROM ME THAT RESIDES IN YOU...
...I COULD DO IT WITH BUT A THOUGHT. IT WOULD EXPOSE YOUR FRAIL BODIES TO THE VACUUM.
NGGGKKK...!
YOU WOULD DIE INSTANTLY.
BUT... I RESIDED IN YOU. AND PART OF YOU CAME WITH ME. NOT JUST THE VESSEL THAT IS EVA.
SO I LEAVE EACH OF YOU YOUR SLIVERS O GODHOOD.
I CURSE YOU ALL TO BE FREE.
SHOULD, UH...WE TRY AND FREE HER?
I HAVE CALCULATED OUR PROBABILITY OF SUCCESS, AND IT IS...NOT GOOD.
WHEN HAS THAT EVER STOPPED US BEFORE?

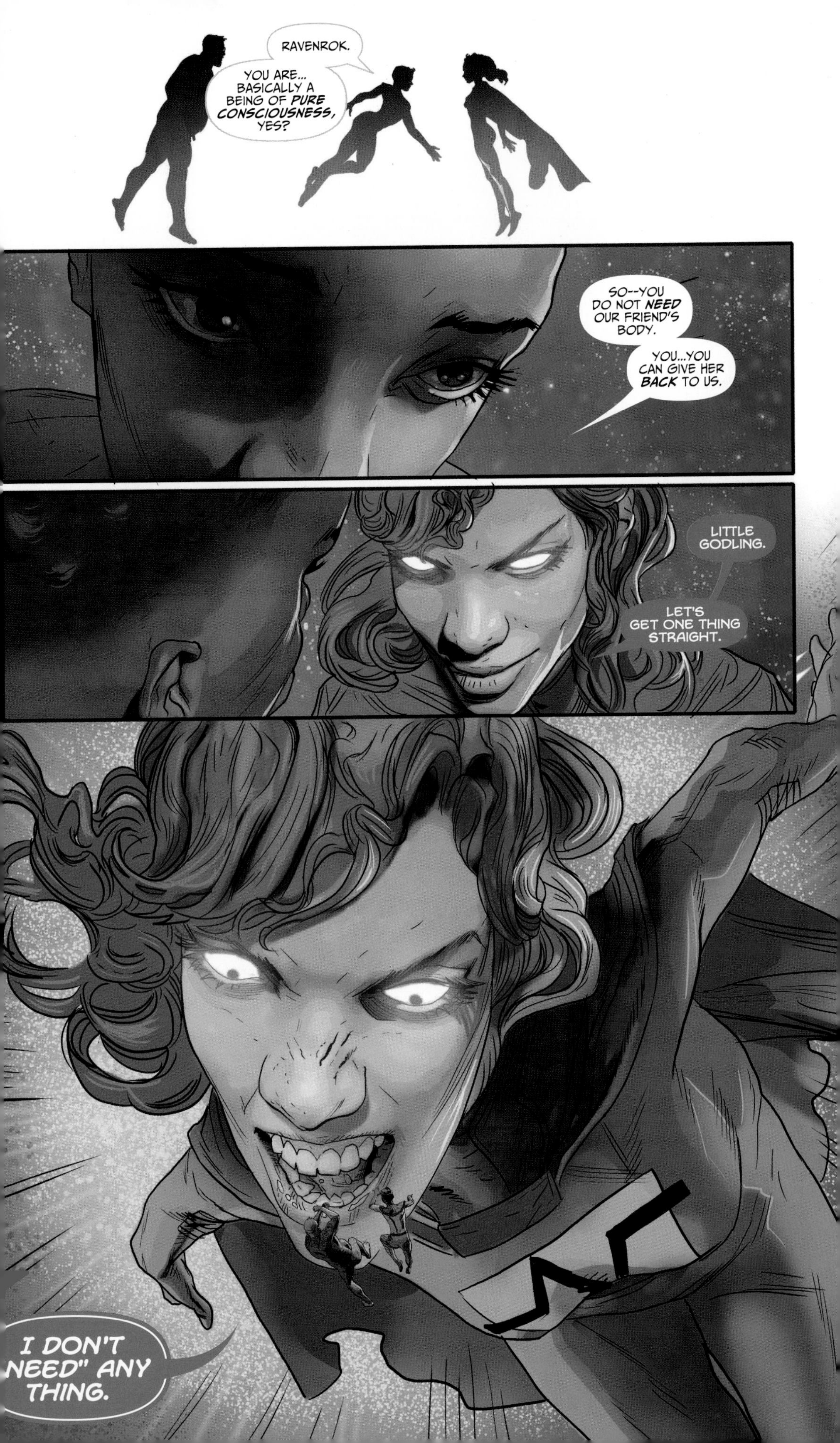
RAVENROK.
YOU ARE... BASICALLY A BEING OF PURE CONSCIOUSNESS, YES?
SO--YOU DO NOT NEED OUR FRIEND'S BODY.
YOU...YOU CAN GIVE HER BACK TO US.
LITTLE GODLING.
LET'S GET ONE THING STRAIGHT.
I DON'T NEED" ANY THING.

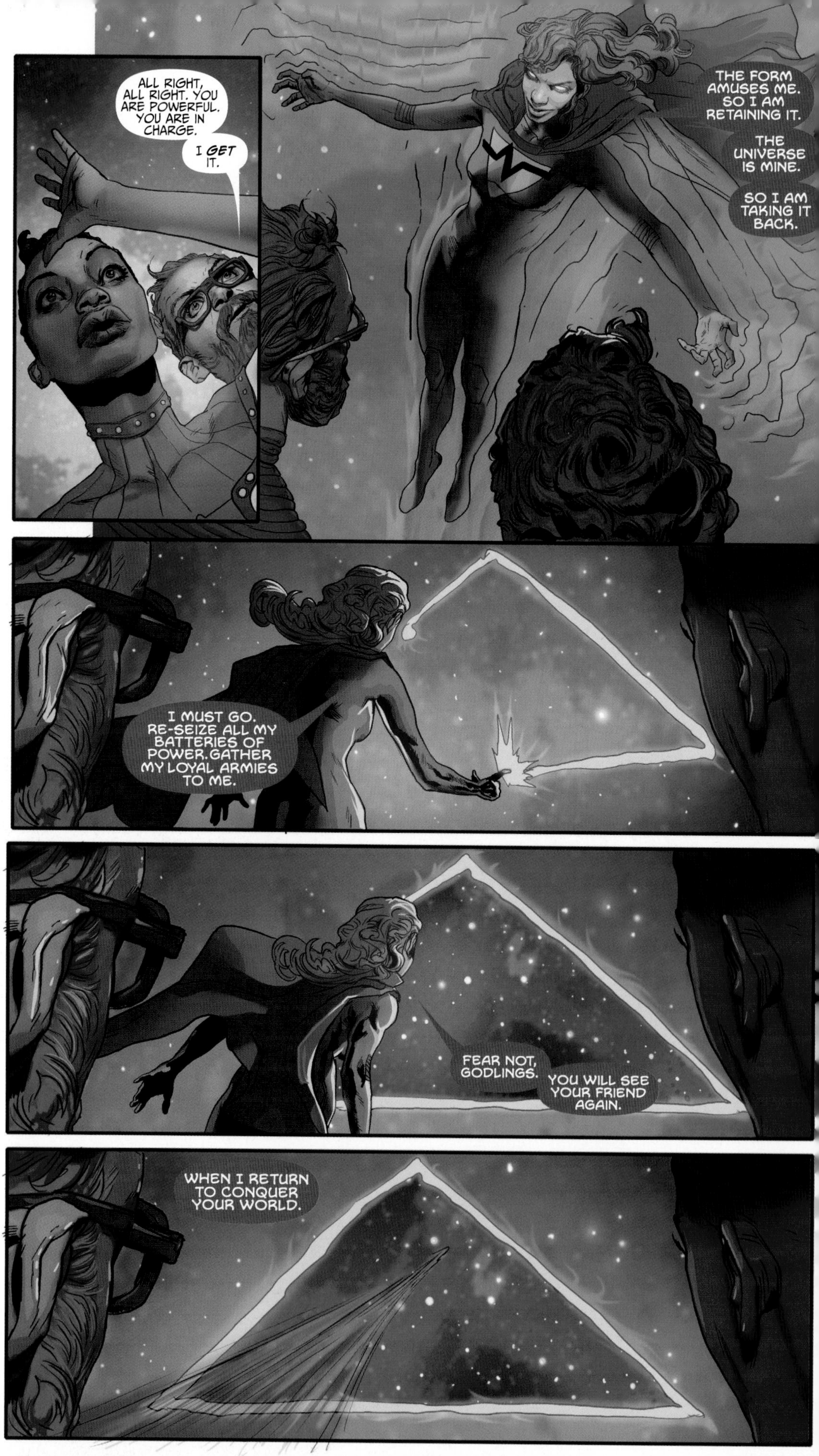
ALL RIGHT, ALL RIGHT. YOU ARE POWERFUL. YOU ARE IN CHARGE.
I GET IT.
THE FORM AMUSES ME. SO I AM RETAINING IT.
THE UNIVERSE IS MINE.
SO I AM TAKING IT BACK.
I MUST GO. RE-SEIZE ALL MY BATTERIES OF POWER. GATHER MY LOYAL ARMIES TO ME.
FEAR NOT, GODLINGS.
YOU WILL SEE YOUR FRIEND AGAIN.
WHEN I RETURN TO CONQUER YOUR WORLD.

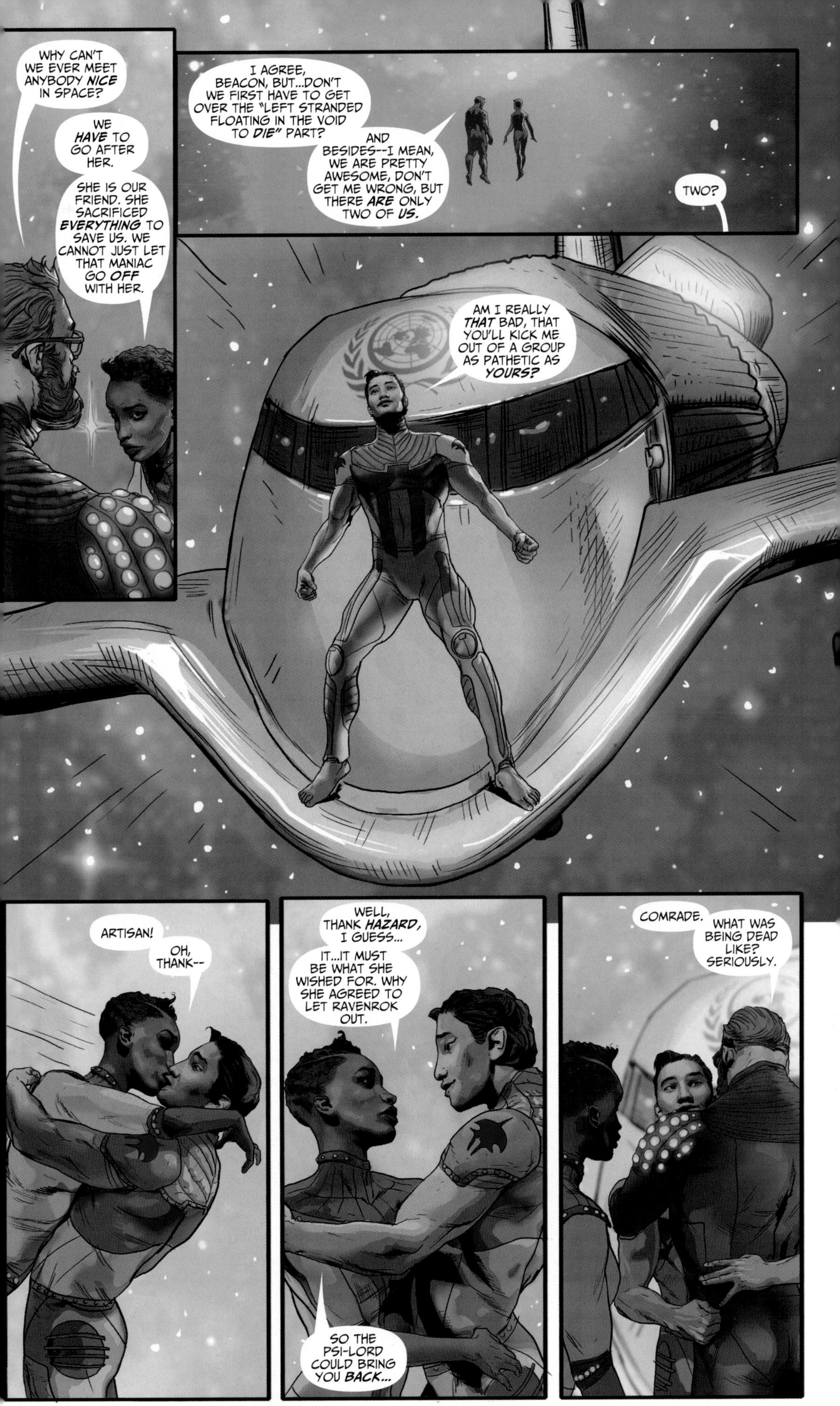
WHY CAN'T WE EVER MEET ANYBODY NICE IN SPACE?
WE HAVE TO GO AFTER HER.
SHE IS OUR FRIEND. SHE SACRIFICED EVERYTHING TO SAVE US. WE CANNOT JUST LET THAT MANIAC GO OFF WITH HER.
I AGREE, BEACON, BUT...DON'T WE FIRST HAVE TO GET OVER THE "LEFT STRANDED FLOATING IN THE VOID TO DIE" PART?
AND BESIDES--I MEAN, WE ARE PRETTY AWESOME, DON'T GET ME WRONG, BUT THERE ARE ONLY TWO OF US.
TWO?
AM I REALLY THAT BAD, THAT YOU'LL KICK ME OUT OF A GROUP AS PATHETIC AS YOURS?
ARTISAN!
OH, THANK--
WELL, THANK HAZARD, I GUESS...
IT...IT MUST BE WHAT SHE WISHED FOR. WHY SHE AGREED TO LET RAVENROK OUT.
SO THE PSI-LORD COULD BRING YOU BACK...
COMRADE.
WHAT WAS BEING DEAD LIKE? SERIOUSLY.

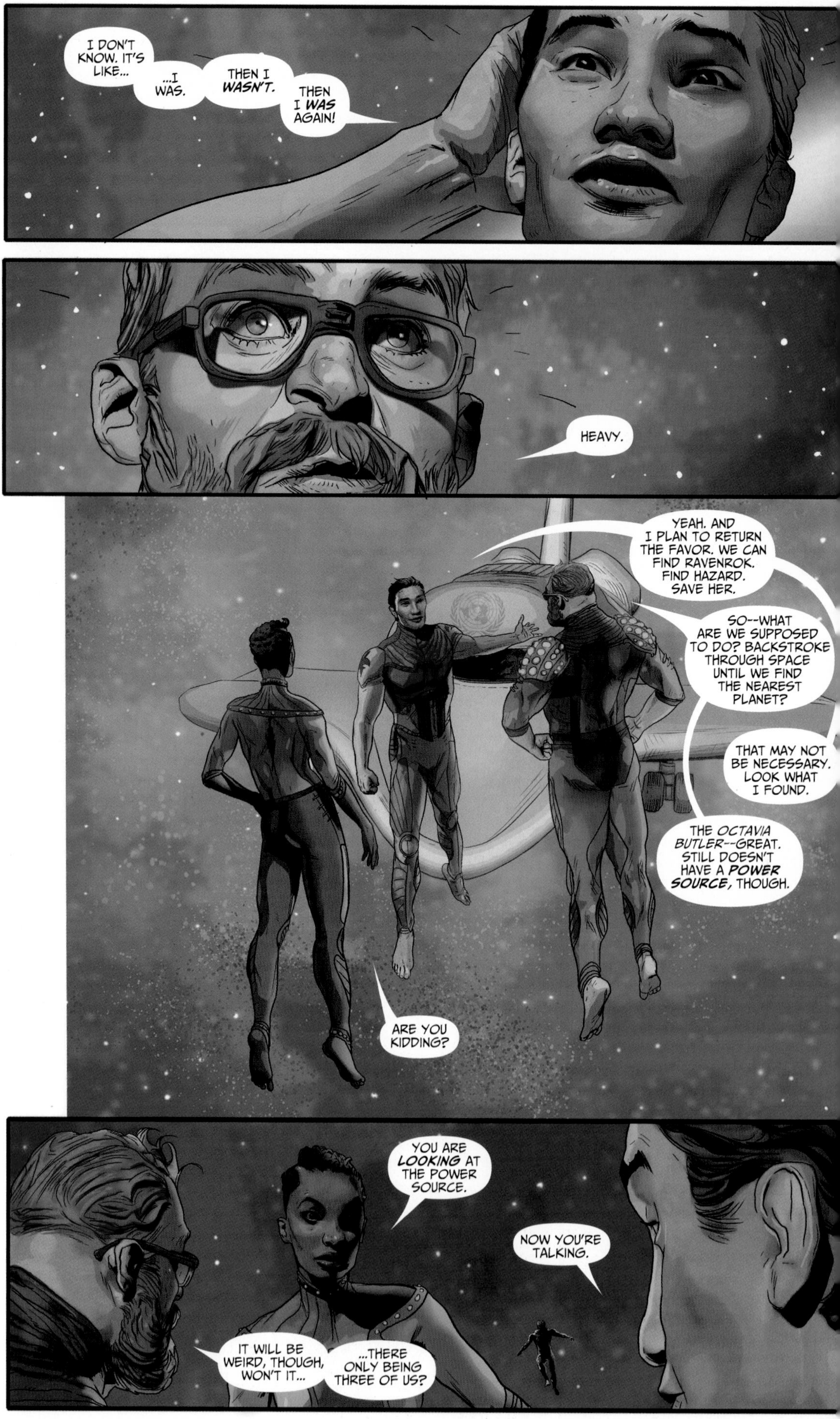

I DON'T KNOW. IT'S LIKE...
...I WAS.
THEN I *WASN'T.*
THEN I *WAS* AGAIN!
HEAVY.
YEAH. AND I PLAN TO RETURN THE FAVOR. WE CAN FIND RAVENROK. FIND HAZARD. SAVE HER.
SO--WHAT ARE WE SUPPOSED TO DO? BACKSTROKE THROUGH SPACE UNTIL WE FIND THE NEAREST PLANET?
THAT MAY NOT BE NECESSARY. LOOK WHAT I FOUND.
THE *OCTAVIA BUTLER*--GREAT. STILL DOESN'T HAVE A ***POWER SOURCE,*** THOUGH.
ARE YOU KIDDING?
YOU ARE ***LOOKING*** AT THE POWER SOURCE.
NOW YOU'RE TALKING.
IT WILL BE WEIRD, THOUGH, WON'T IT...
...THERE ONLY BEING THREE OF US?

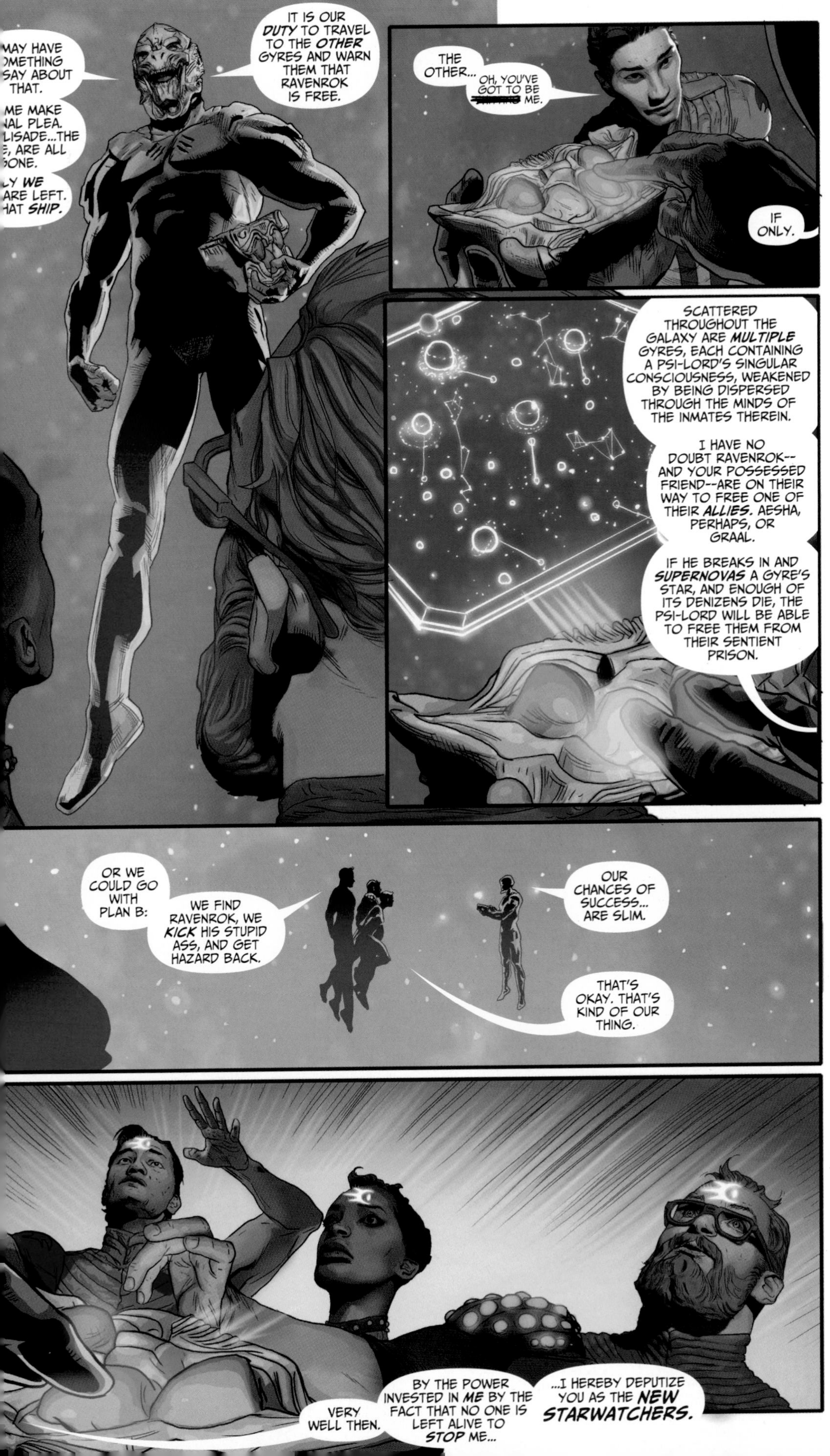
MAY HAVE OMETHING SAY ABOUT THAT.
ME MAKE NAL PLEA. LISADE...THE E, ARE ALL GONE.
LY WE ARE LEFT. HAT SHIP.
IT IS OUR DUTY TO TRAVEL TO THE OTHER GYRES AND WARN THEM THAT RAVENROK IS FREE.
THE OTHER...
OH, YOU'VE GOT TO BE [redacted] ME.
IF ONLY.
SCATTERED THROUGHOUT THE GALAXY ARE MULTIPLE GYRES, EACH CONTAINING A PSI-LORD'S SINGULAR CONSCIOUSNESS, WEAKENED BY BEING DISPERSED THROUGH THE MINDS OF THE INMATES THEREIN.
I HAVE NO DOUBT RAVENROK--AND YOUR POSSESSED FRIEND--ARE ON THEIR WAY TO FREE ONE OF THEIR ALLIES. AESHA, PERHAPS, OR GRAAL.
IF HE BREAKS IN AND SUPERNOVAS A GYRE'S STAR, AND ENOUGH OF ITS DENIZENS DIE, THE PSI-LORD WILL BE ABLE TO FREE THEM FROM THEIR SENTIENT PRISON.
OR WE COULD GO WITH PLAN B:
WE FIND RAVENROK, WE KICK HIS STUPID ASS, AND GET HAZARD BACK.
OUR CHANCES OF SUCCESS... ARE SLIM.
THAT'S OKAY. THAT'S KIND OF OUR THING.
VERY WELL THEN.
BY THE POWER INVESTED IN ME BY THE FACT THAT NO ONE IS LEFT ALIVE TO STOP ME...
...I HEREBY DEPUTIZE YOU AS THE NEW STARWATCHERS.

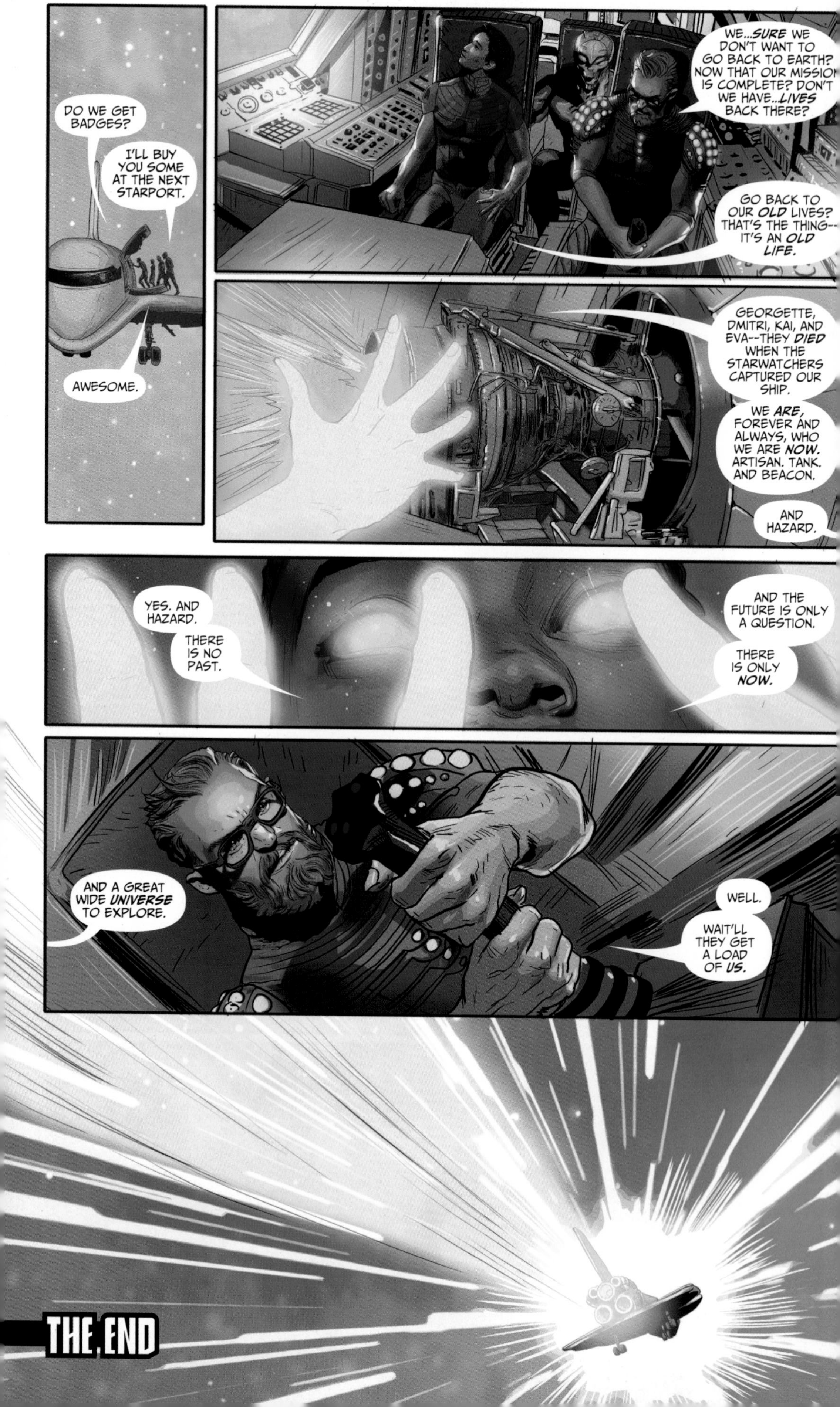
DO WE GET BADGES?
I'LL BUY YOU SOME AT THE NEXT STARPORT.
AWESOME.
WE...SURE WE DON'T WANT TO GO BACK TO EARTH? NOW THAT OUR MISSION IS COMPLETE? DON'T WE HAVE...LIVES BACK THERE?
GO BACK TO OUR OLD LIVES? THAT'S THE THING--IT'S AN OLD LIFE.
GEORGETTE, DMITRI, KAI, AND EVA--THEY DIED WHEN THE STARWATCHERS CAPTURED OUR SHIP.
WE ARE, FOREVER AND ALWAYS, WHO WE ARE NOW. ARTISAN. TANK. AND BEACON.
AND HAZARD.
YES. AND HAZARD.
THERE IS NO PAST.
AND THE FUTURE IS ONLY A QUESTION.
THERE IS ONLY NOW.
AND A GREAT WIDE UNIVERSE TO EXPLORE.
WELL.
WAIT'LL THEY GET A LOAD OF US.
THE END

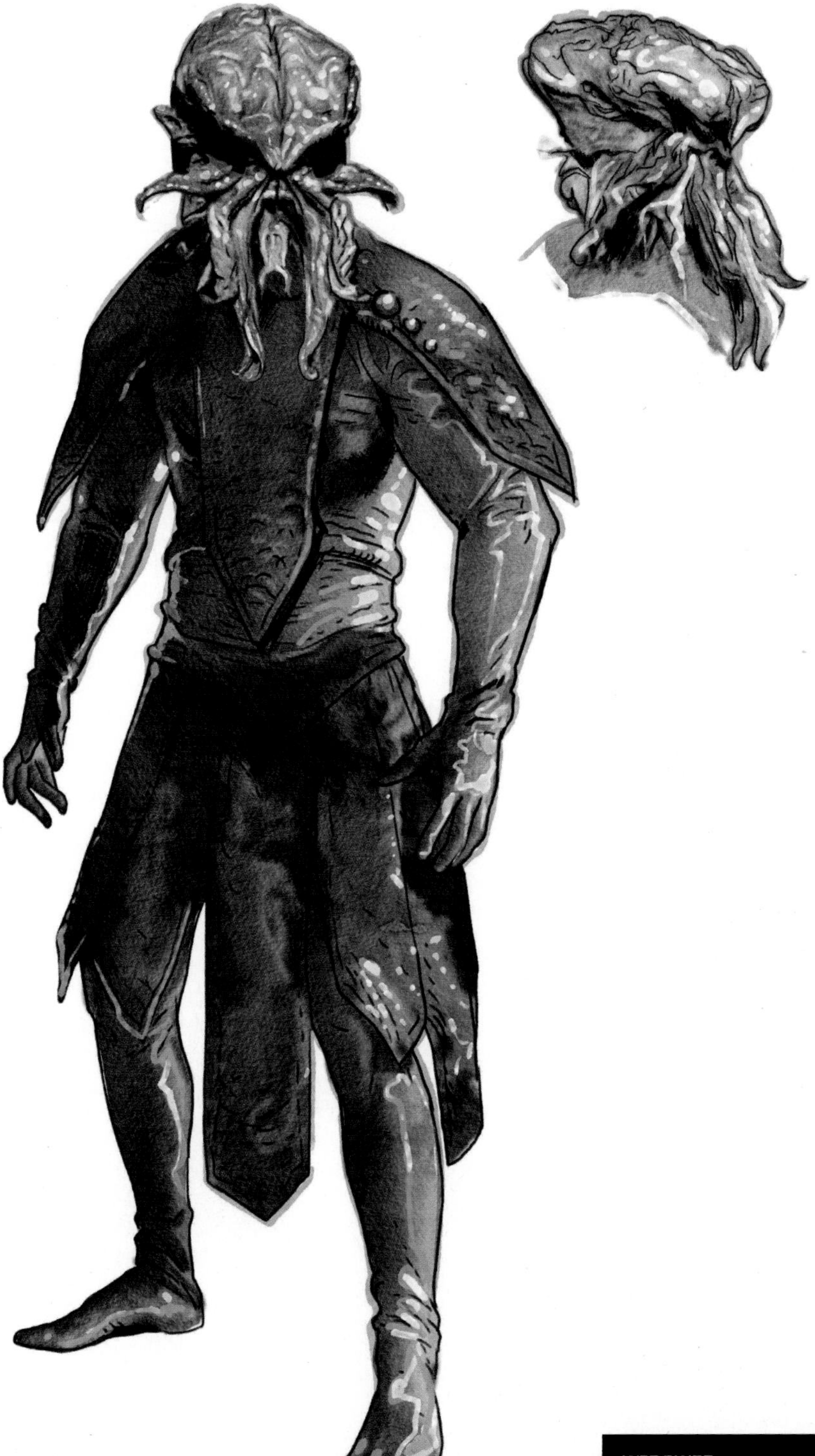

WIDOWER
Design by RENATO GUEDES

# PSI-LORDS

## THE SWEEPING SCI-FI SERIES BLASTS OFF

Get ready for PSI-LORDS, a new ongoing series from writer Fred Van Lente and artist Renato Guedes that will change the course of the Valiant Universe! Four human space travelers wake up in an unfamiliar place, having no memory of how they got there but each possessing different superpowers.

Heidi MacDonald of The Beat talked with Van Lente about what readers should know going in.

**THE BEAT: The Psi-Lords are sort of the "lost clan" of the Valiant Universe, both in story terms and in publishing history. Where were they when last we saw them?**

**FRED VAN LENTE:** The Psi-Lords are as old as the Valiant Universe itself and are as powerful as...well, "gods" are not a concept that has had much of a traction in the VU, but they are vastly powerful psychic beings as close to gods as anyone in the VU is likely to encounter. Their existence has been hinted at a bit in current-era Valiant books, but it's time for them to take center stage at last.

**THE BEAT: In the rebooted Valiant Universe the return of the Psi-Lords has been teased several times...but they were no-shows. What made this the right time for their return?**

**VAN LENTE:** There is a specific, important reason, and much of the series is about unraveling that enigma, one that will have monumental impact on the Valiant Universe and everyone in it moving forward. Let's just say...there's something big coming, and the Psi-Lords are both the cause and solution.

**THE BEAT: Just who are these Psi-Lords? Do they know they are Psi-Lords?**

**VAN LENTE:** That's what our heroes would like to know – four people, seemingly from completely different walks of life, all wake up in the same, ancient 'REDACTED', with no memory of who brought them there or why. They find they have earth-shaking powers they barely understand, much less control. And the only clue they have is that they've been urged to "find the Psi-Lords."

**THE BEAT: Our heroes find themselves in an even more bizarre setting once they escape. Can you talk a little about that?**

**VAN LENTE:** Where they are isn't a single structure, but an entire system made up of trapped, derelict spaceships, all locked in orbit around the same dying, wandering star. Sort of a Sargasso Sea but in outer space, as one of our characters describes it – a wild, untamed post-apocalyptic world of alien metal. Each shipwreck has its own unique culture and species, and our heroes have to explore this strange new world – and, more importantly, defend it. In their quest to find the Psi-Lords, who are somewhere in the Gyre, our heroes – the Quartet, I call them in the scripts – become a motley family of heroes, and the champions the Gyre has been hungering for a long time.

**THE BEAT: How does this connect to your previous books for Valiant and the universe as a whole?**

**VAN LENTE:** I love world-building. With ARCHER & ARMSTRONG and IVAR, TIMEWALKER I explored a lot of the past of Valiant Earth, and with WAR MOTHER, I got to dip into the 4001 A.D. future era a bit. What's exciting about PSI-LORDS is I get to explore more the X-O MANOWAR realm of deep space, other worlds, and new species – although not all of these groups will be completely unfamiliar to Valiant fans. In fact, readers of the current X-O series may instantly see some deep connections!

**THE BEAT: What's the most important thing for fans of the old Psi-Lords to know about this series?**

**VAN LENTE:** It will blow your mind. ■

---

*Special thanks to Heidi MacDonald of* The Beat. *For her full interview with Fred Van Lente, visit* www.comicsbeat.com.

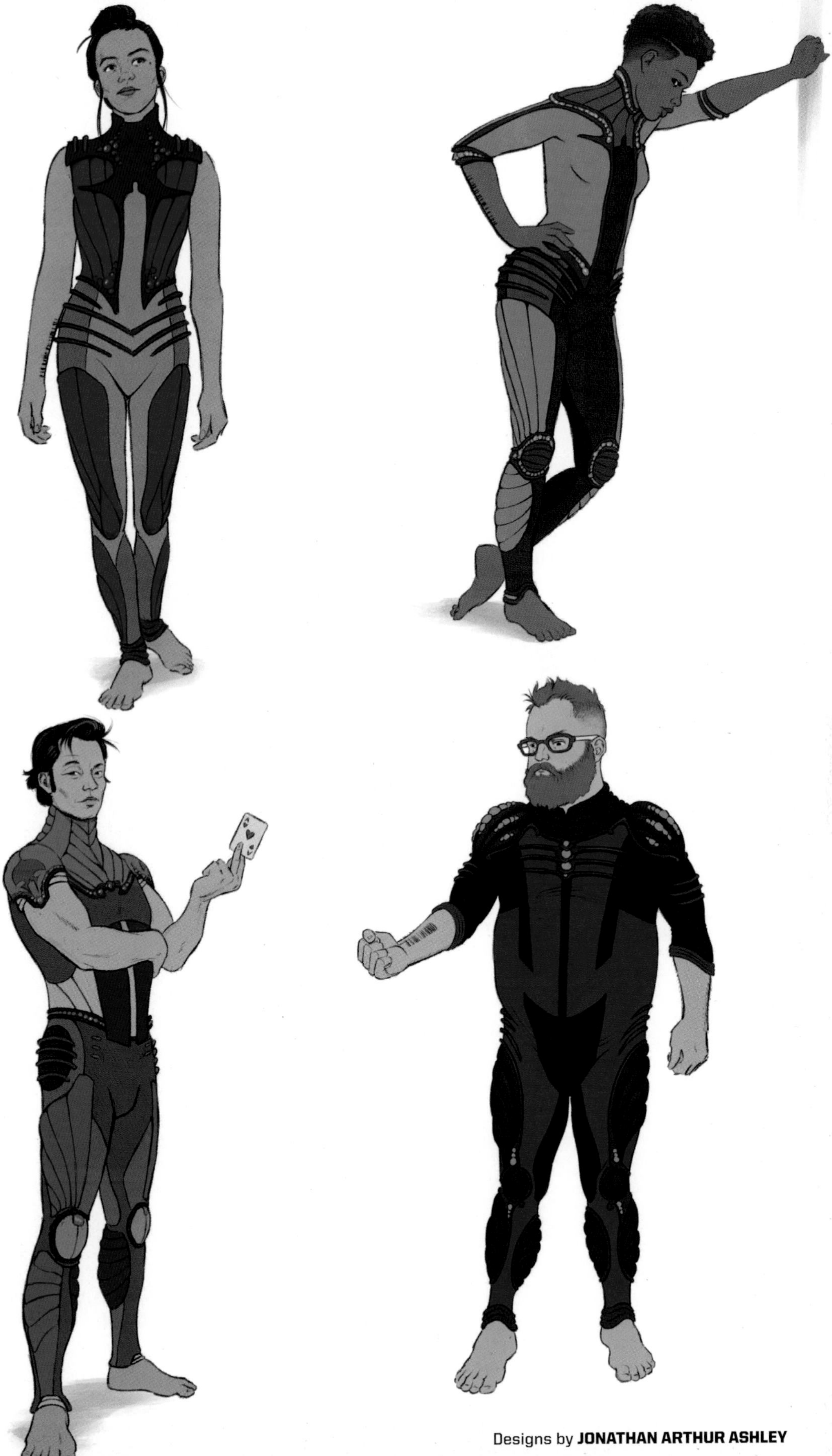

Designs by **JONATHAN ARTHUR ASHLEY**

I reread all of the OG PSI-LORDS '90s series before starting this one, and two of the ships Artisan is looking at are glimpses of ships from the original series.

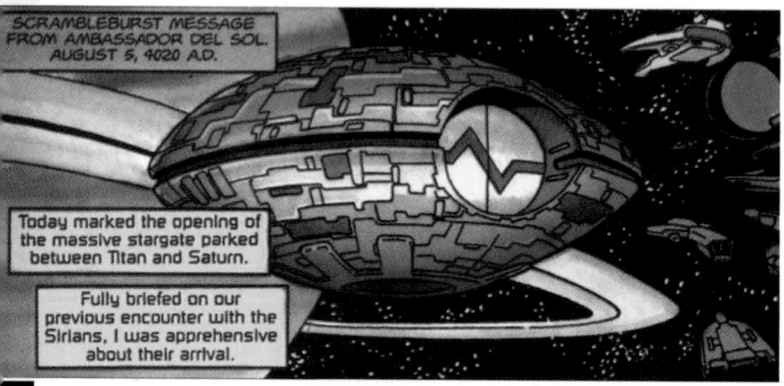
SCRAMBLEBURST MESSAGE FROM AMBASSADOR DEL SOL. AUGUST 5, 4020 A.D.
Today marked the opening of the massive stargate parked between Titan and Saturn.
Fully briefed on our previous encounter with the Sirians, I was apprehensive about their arrival.

**FROM PSI-LORDS (1995) #6**
By **ANTONY BEDARD**, **MIKE LEEKE**, **ANTHONY CASTRILLO**, **DICK GIORDANO** with **ERIK LUSK**

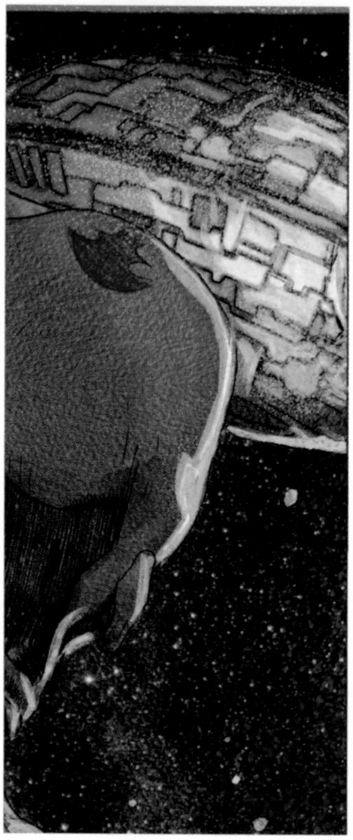

**PSI-LORDS #2**
Art by **RENATO GUEDES**

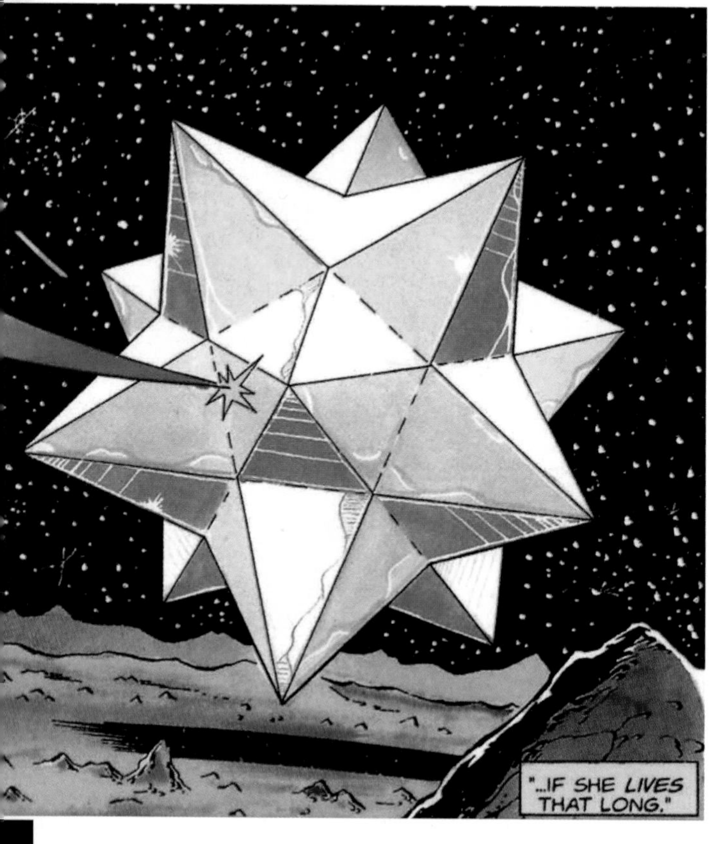
"...IF SHE LIVES THAT LONG."

**FROM PSI-LORDS (1995) #8**
By **ANTONY BEDARD**, **HOWARD SIMPSON**, **MIKE DECARLO** with **ERIK LUSK**

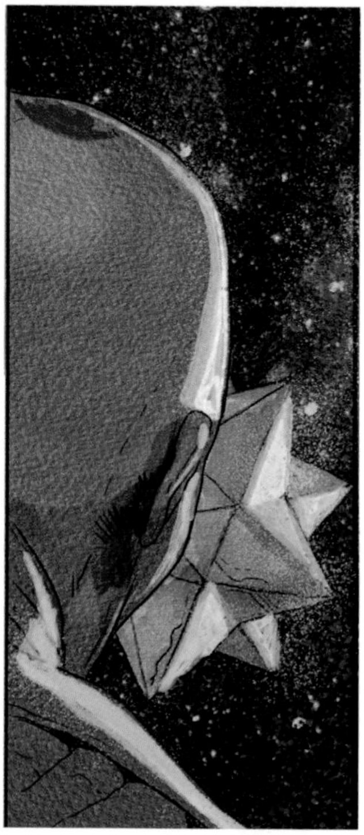

**PSI-LORDS #2**
Art by **RENATO GUEDES**

Scion looms over us, the five tombs now acting as his feet, head and hands with himself in the center as the power source. He's sort of like a giant magical Exo-Skeleton. I thought the simplest way to explicate this would be to sketch it for Renato.

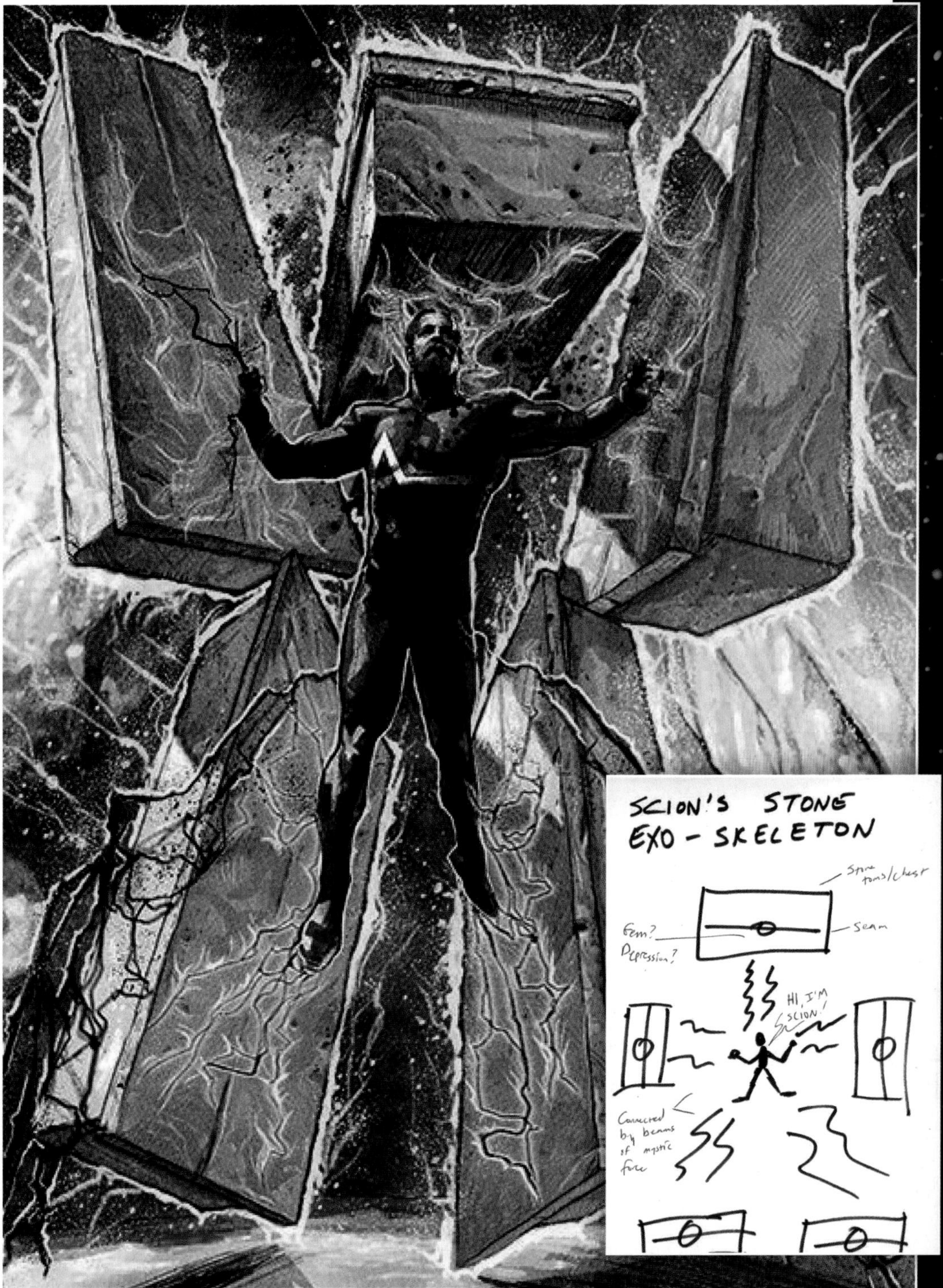

SCION'S STONE EXO-SKELETON
Stone tomb/chest
Seam
Gem? Depression?
HI, I'M SCION!
Connected by beams of mystic force


Art by **RENATO GUEDES**

Sketch by **FRED VAN LENTE**

## PSI-LORDS #2, page 5

**PANEL 1: Small panel – Grim-faced, Beacon steps forward, eyes crackling, aura sparking.**

1. BEACON: Hold on.

2. BEACON: Let me...

**PANEL 2: Beacon steps forward, and from her head shoots two beams of yellow light, that encompasses both the Yossari and Tank's heads. Suddenly, the two can understand each other – and, presumably, the rest of the team.**

3. BEACON: ...show the *way*.

4. YOSSARI: [alien characters]

5. YOSSARI: ...truly, I am full with *regret*, but we do not have your tribute *today*.

6. YOSSARI: We *will*, but crop yield has been *terrible* this cycle.

**PANEL 3: The Yossari and Tank look up to the dying star sputtering in the sky above.**

7. YOSSARI: Can you not see Nihilio is *dying*? As her light grows more and more fitful, our harvests grow more and more anemic. We can barely feed *ourselves*!

8. TANK: Nihi... You mean the *sun*?

9. TANK: Wait, who do you think we are?

**PANEL 4: CU – the Yossari arches an eyebrow, confused.**

10. YOSSARI: You're ... one of the *Wardens*, aren't you?

11. TANK (OFF): I...don't know what that is? What makes you say that?

12. YOSSARI: You bear the *mark*. On the top of your skulls.

**PANEL 5: Shoot on the top of Tank's head – he's got the Ravenrok brand there that we first saw last issue, of course.**

13. YOSSARI (OFF): Of the **Psi-Lords**.

**PANEL 6: Tank pleads with the Yossari spokesperson – who, no longer scared of him, crosses its arms standoffishly and arches an eyebrow.**

14. TANK: That doesn't mean anything to us. We're just looking for *directions* -- back to our ship.

15. YOSSARI: ...

16. YOSSARI: What's in it for *us*?

**PANEL 7: Artisan arches an eyebrow at Hazard, who grins.**

17. ARTISAN: Oh, they're *definitely* cats.

18. HAZARD: I stand corrected.

Originally presented in ***PSI-LORDS PRE-ORDER EDITION #2***

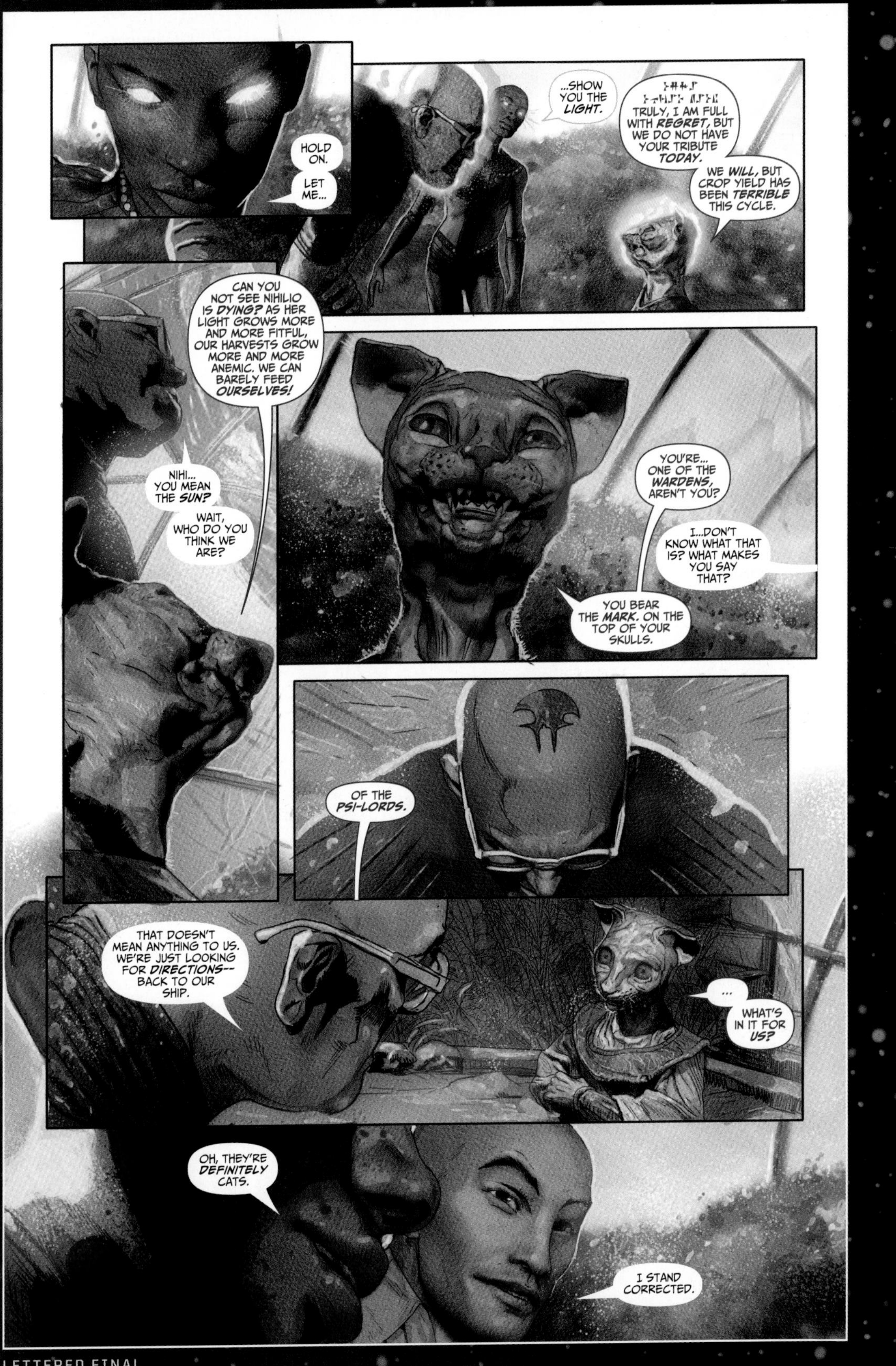
HOLD ON.
LET ME...
...SHOW YOU THE LIGHT.
TRULY, I AM FULL WITH REGRET, BUT WE DO NOT HAVE YOUR TRIBUTE TODAY.
WE WILL, BUT CROP YIELD HAS BEEN TERRIBLE THIS CYCLE.
CAN YOU NOT SEE NIHILIO IS DYING? AS HER LIGHT GROWS MORE AND MORE FITFUL, OUR HARVESTS GROW MORE AND MORE ANEMIC. WE CAN BARELY FEED OURSELVES!
NIHI... YOU MEAN THE SUN?
WAIT, WHO DO YOU THINK WE ARE?
YOU'RE... ONE OF THE WARDENS, AREN'T YOU?
I...DON'T KNOW WHAT THAT IS? WHAT MAKES YOU SAY THAT?
YOU BEAR THE MARK. ON THE TOP OF YOUR SKULLS.
OF THE PSI-LORDS.
THAT DOESN'T MEAN ANYTHING TO US. WE'RE JUST LOOKING FOR DIRECTIONS-- BACK TO OUR SHIP.
...
WHAT'S IN IT FOR US?
OH, THEY'RE DEFINITELY CATS.
I STAND CORRECTED.

## FIGHTING WORDS: EXCERPTS FROM PSI-LORDS #1 SCRIPT BY FRED VAN LENTE, ART BY RENATO GUEDES

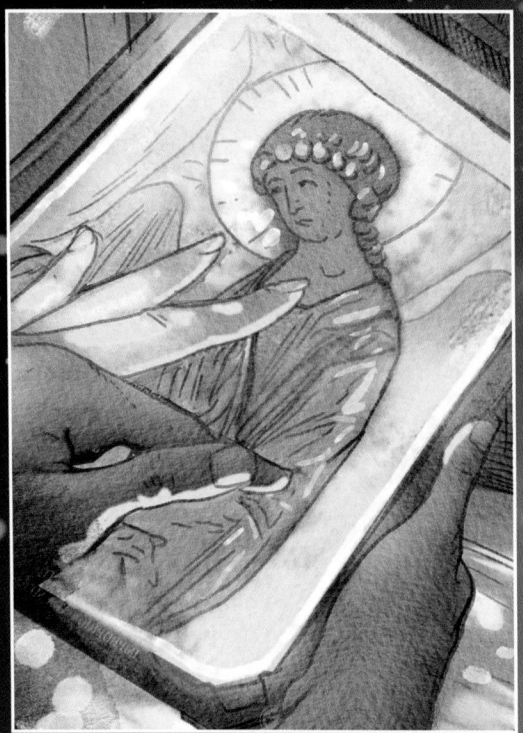

### HALO, GOODBYE:

A vast high-tech library on a sleek, 21st century Earth SPACESHIP, though we can't see that here. Her hands reach into the panel, holding an iPad-style tablet that has the image of a MEDIEVAL ILLUMINATED MANUSCRIPT projected onto it. It has a SAINT with a HALO on it.

### BYE STANDER:

ANGLE DOWN as Artisan hurtles UPWARD, speed lines all around – he has a little kid joy of discovering he can fly for the first time. We can see he has his color-coded NIMBUS (ORANGE) around him now – and he has SPROUTED ENERGY WINGS out of his back.

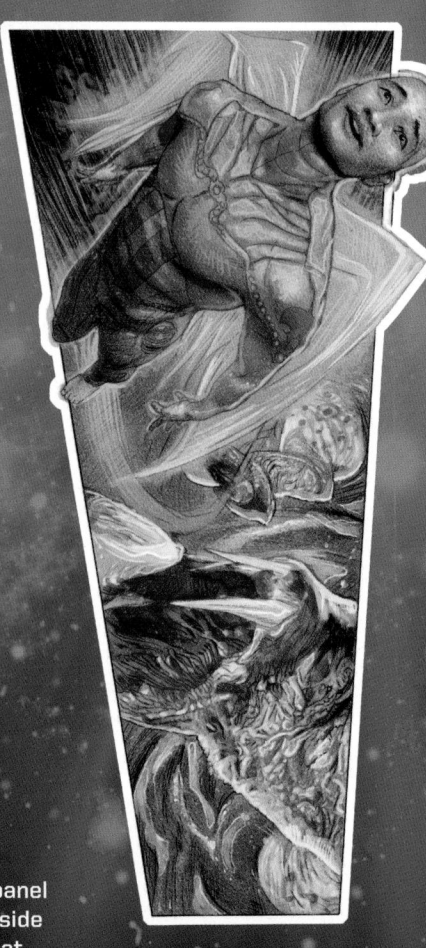

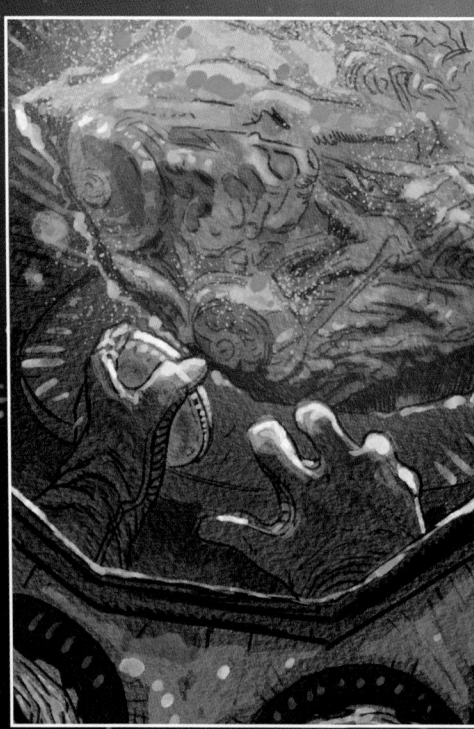

### POWER OF GLOVE:

FLASHBACK – ARTISAN'S POV – His hands reach into the panel and go into the sleeves/gloves that control robot arms inside a sterile, vacuum environment, on the same spaceship that Beacon was on, previously. He is opening a high-tech version of the ARK OF THE COVENANT, which has LIGHT STREAMING out of it – or is it radiation? Hard to tell here.

## SHOCK IT TO ME:

BIG PANEL. The floor gets activated with electricity — and it all goes RIGHT INTO BEACON's BODY. Crackling with power, she has a calm, stern expression. Her nimbus is YELLOW.

## CAPTAIN PUNCH:

GIANT PANEL. Tank punches the glass door so hard that not only does IT shatter, his fist goes into the chest of the nearest guard and knocks them all flat on their asses like tenpins. His fists are surrounded in a GREEN NIMBUS that make them super-huge, like giant kaiju-style fists.

## GORE STORIES:

Hazard approaches them, entire front splashed with crimson arterial spray.

Originally presented in *PSI-LORDS PRE-ORDER EDITION #1*

*PSI-LORDS #3*, pages 1, 2, and (facing) 3
Art by RENATO GUEDES

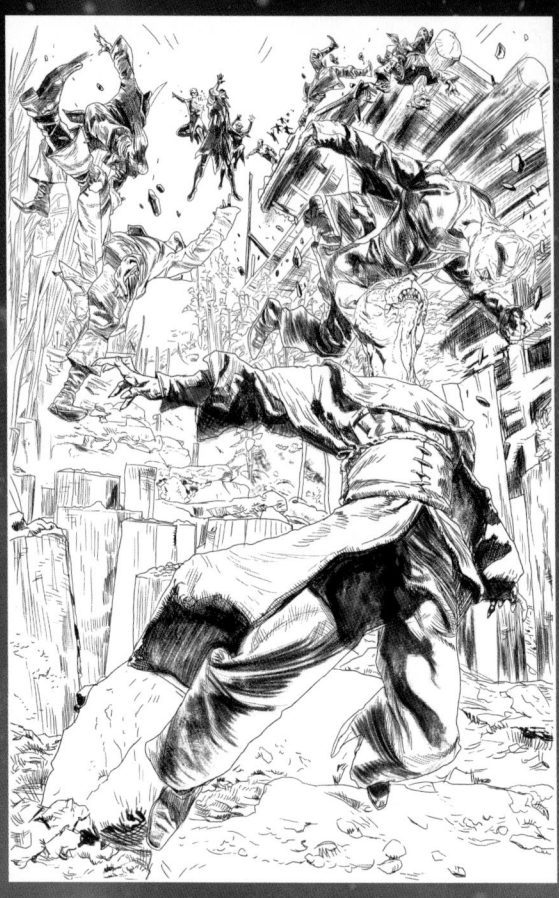

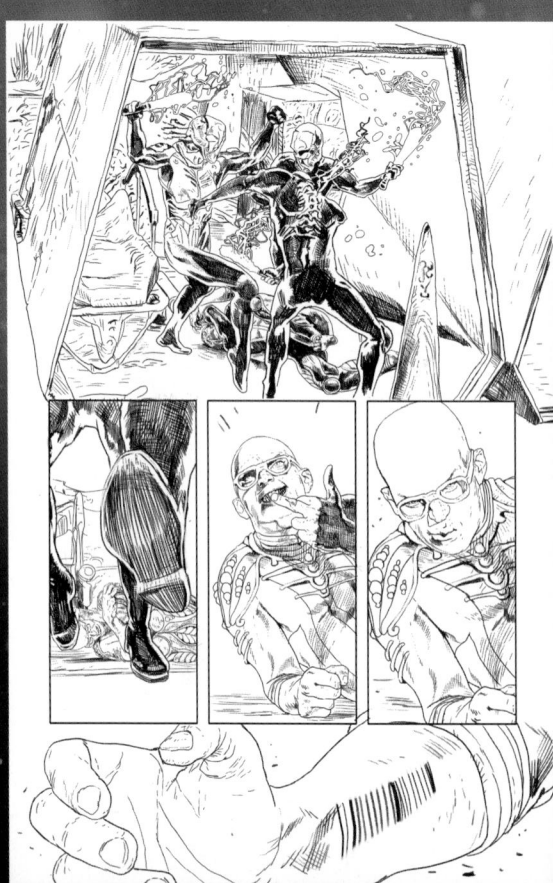

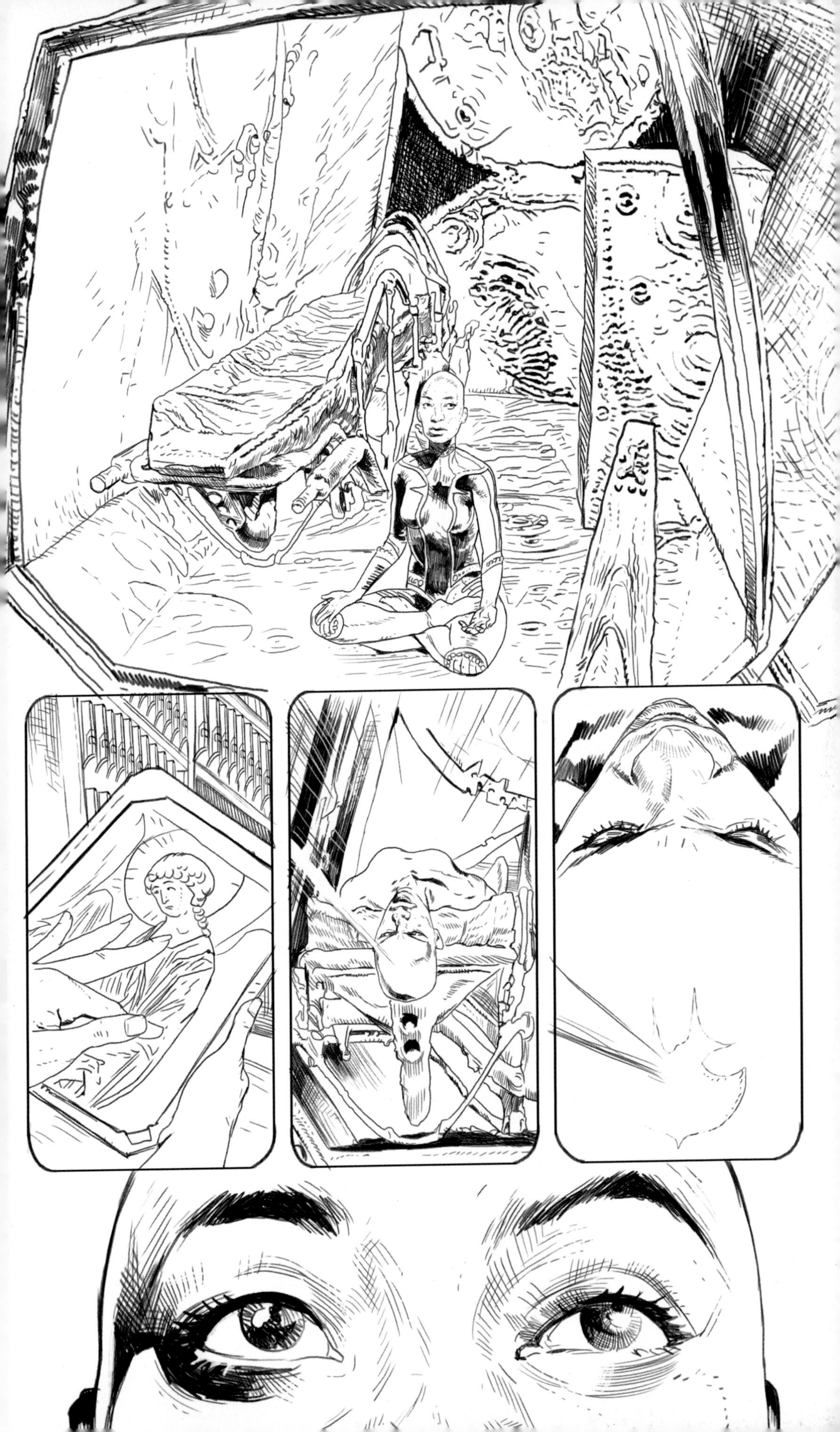

*PSI-LORDS #3*, pages 4, 9, and (facing) 11
Art by RENATO GUEDES

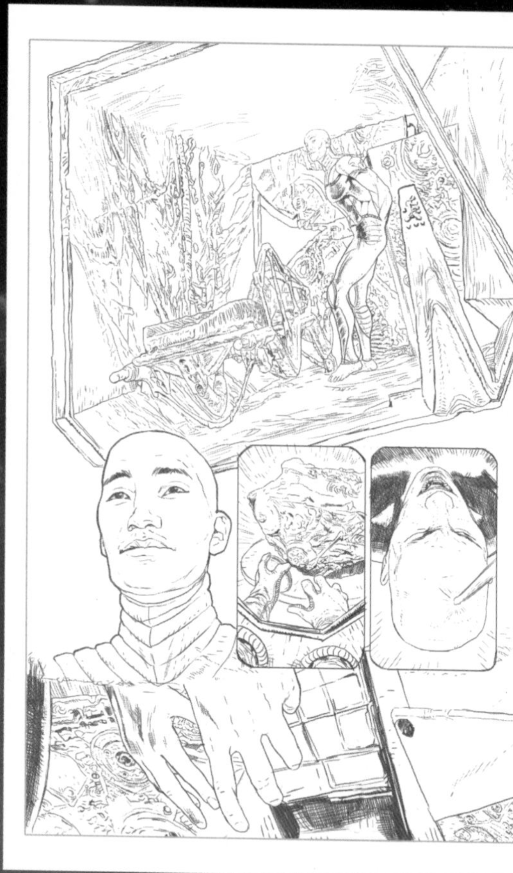

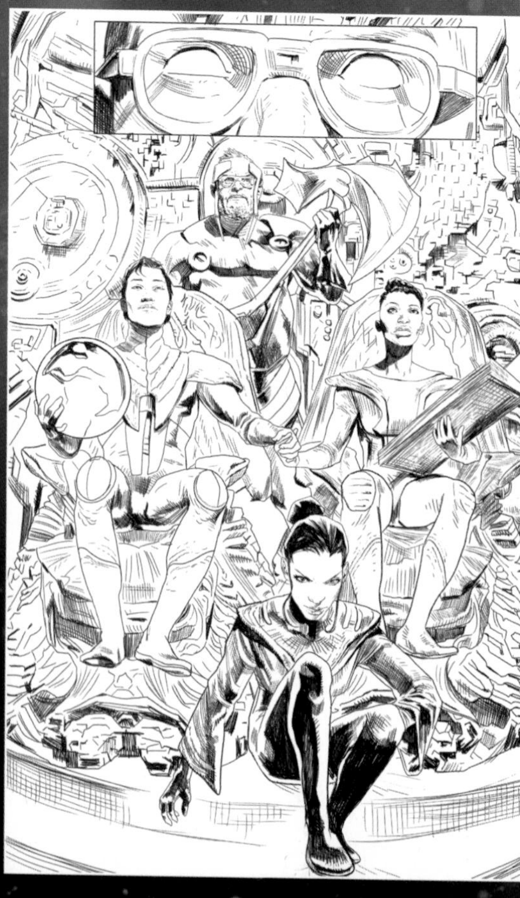

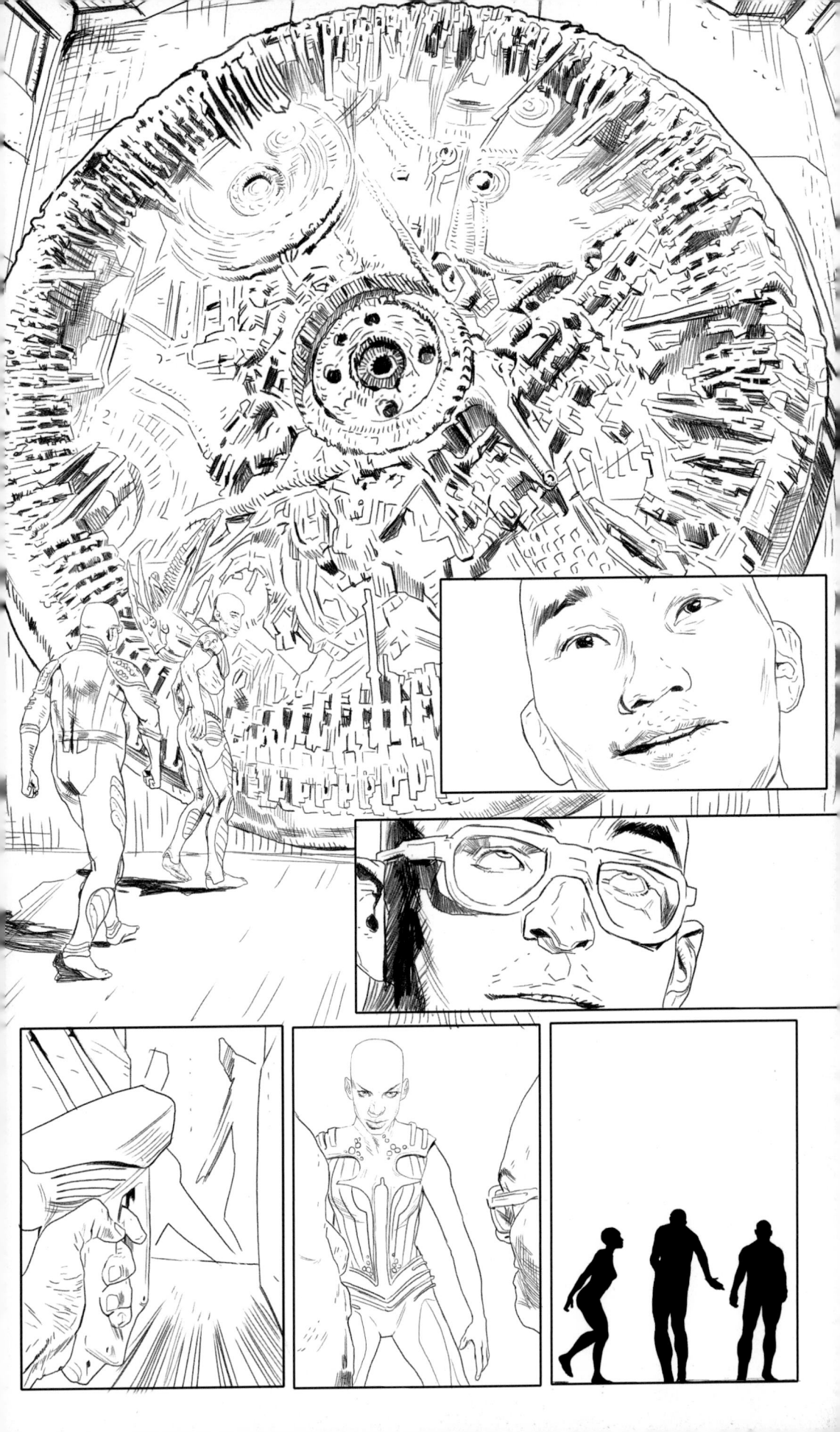

*PSI-LORDS #1-4 PRE-ORDER EDITION* COVERS
Art by PAULINA GANUCHEAU

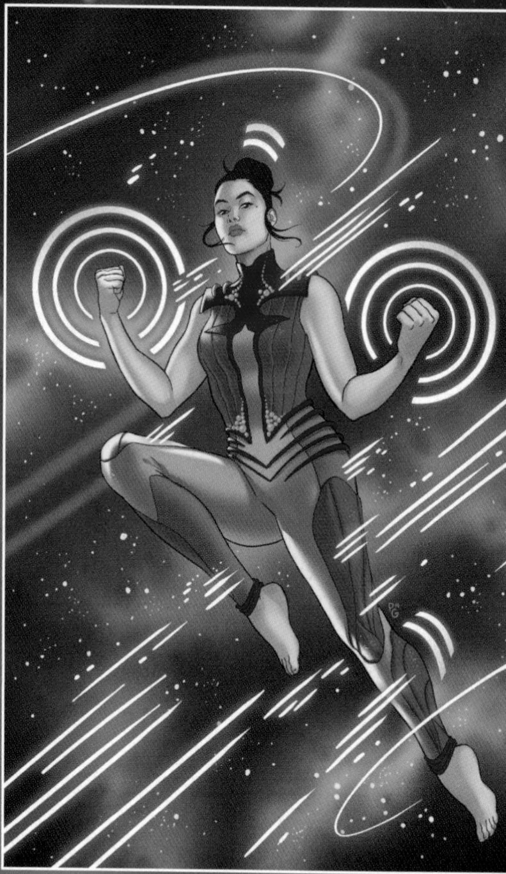

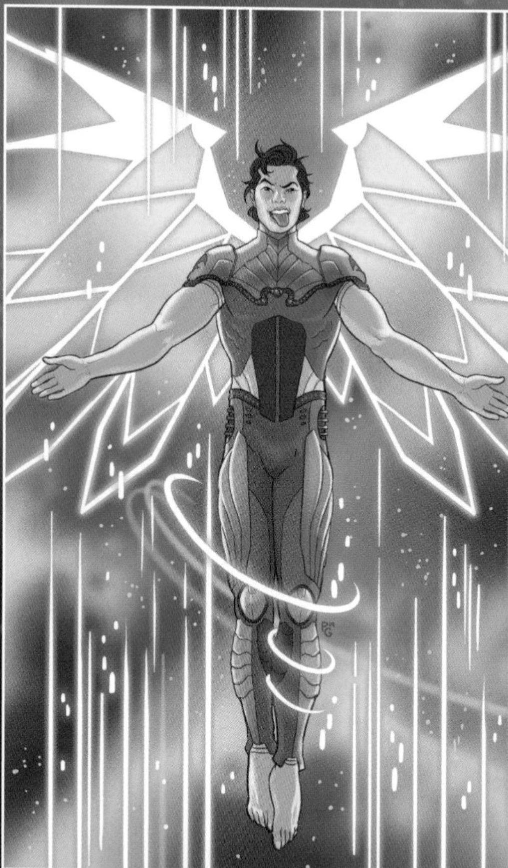

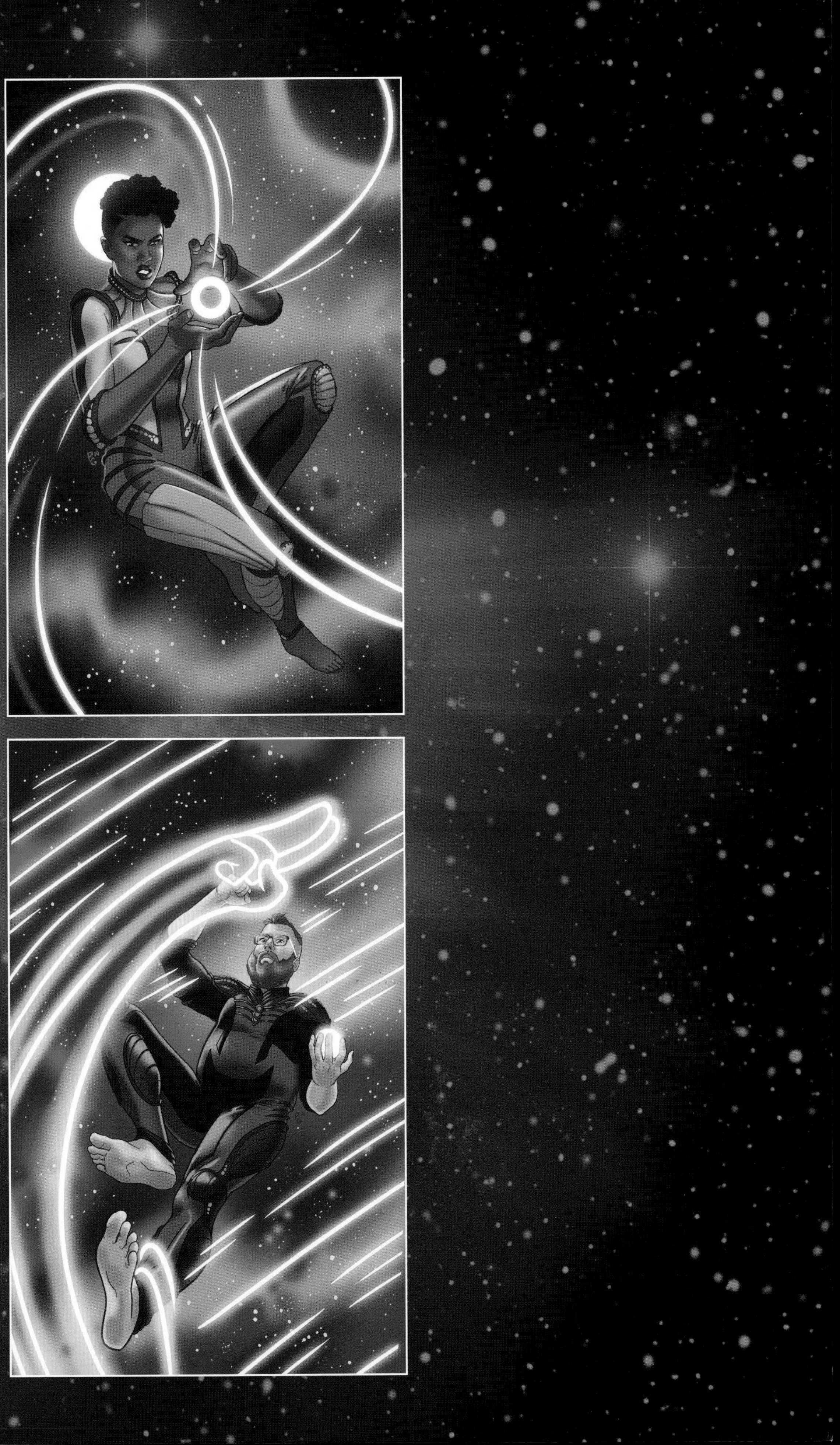

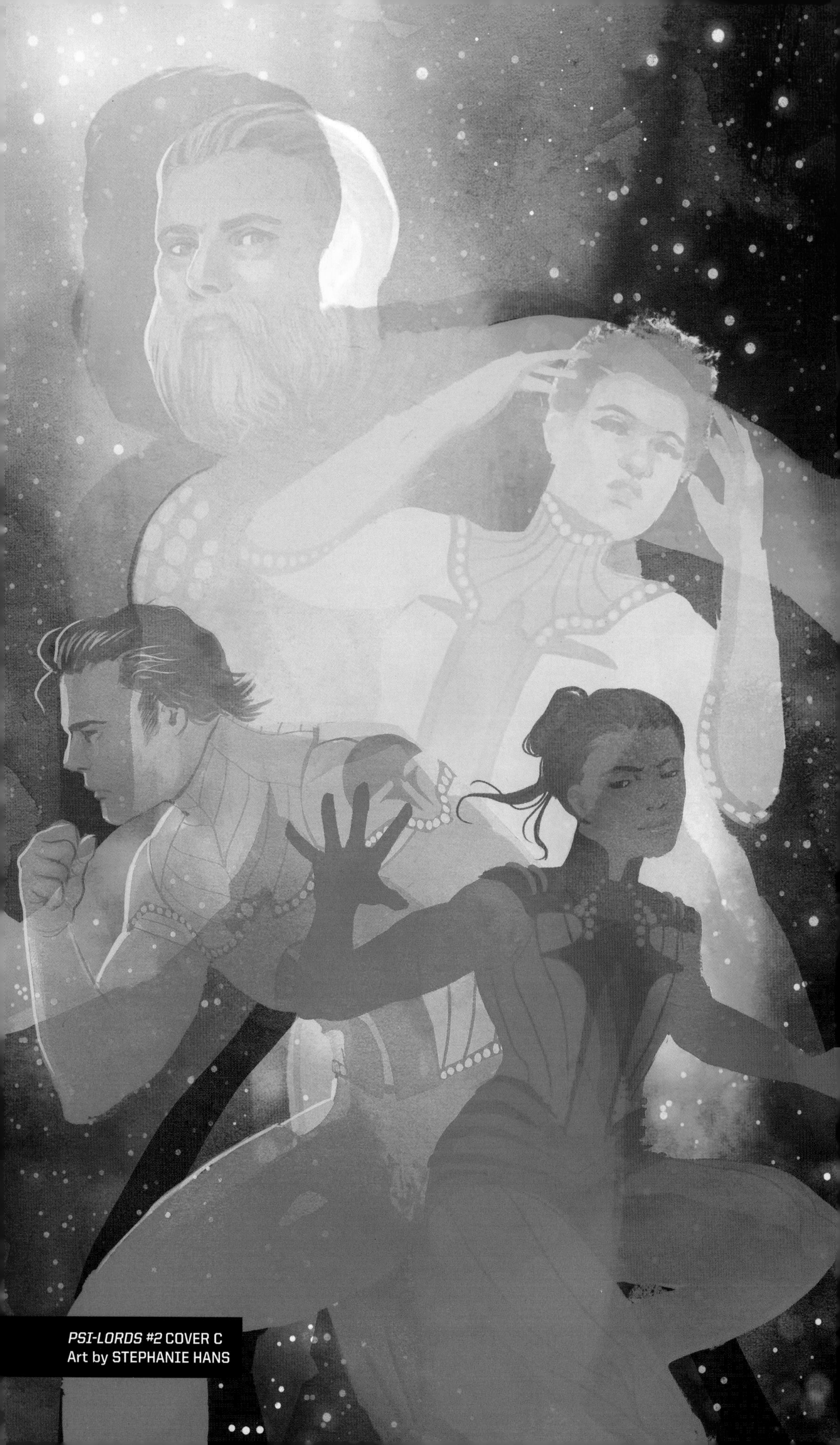

*PSI-LORDS* #2 COVER C
Art by STEPHANIE HANS

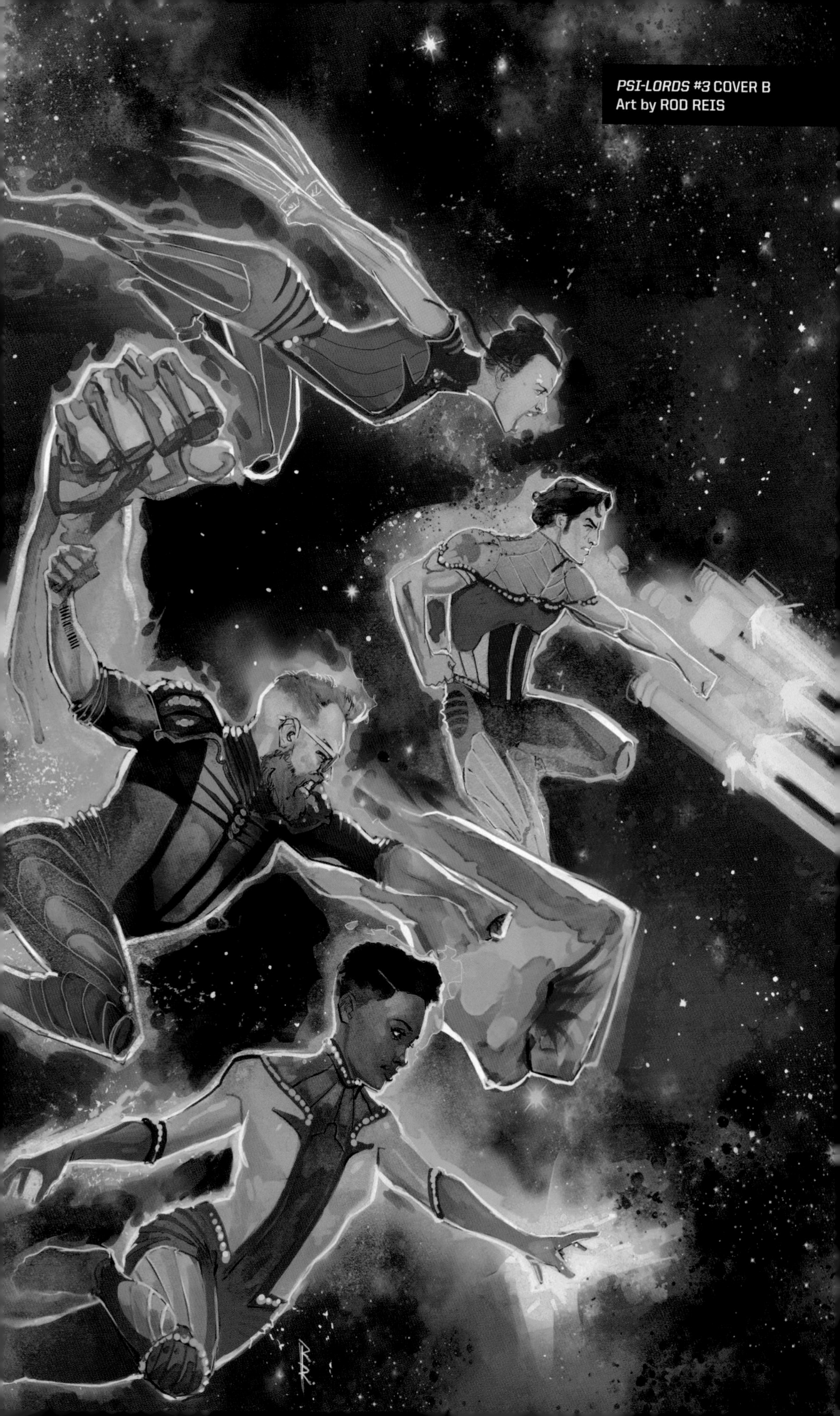

*PSI-LORDS #3* COVER B
Art by ROD REIS

*PSI-LORDS #5-8 PRE-ORDER EDITION* COVERS
Art by SCOTT FORBES

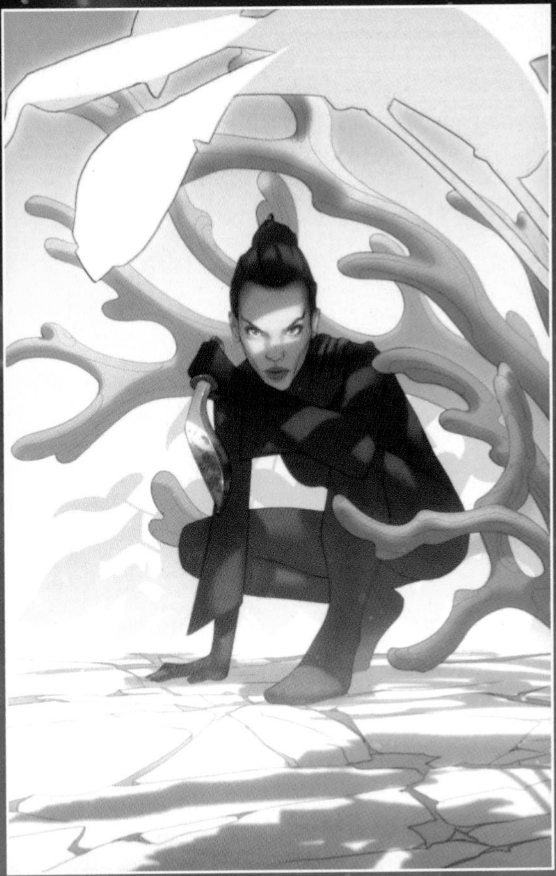

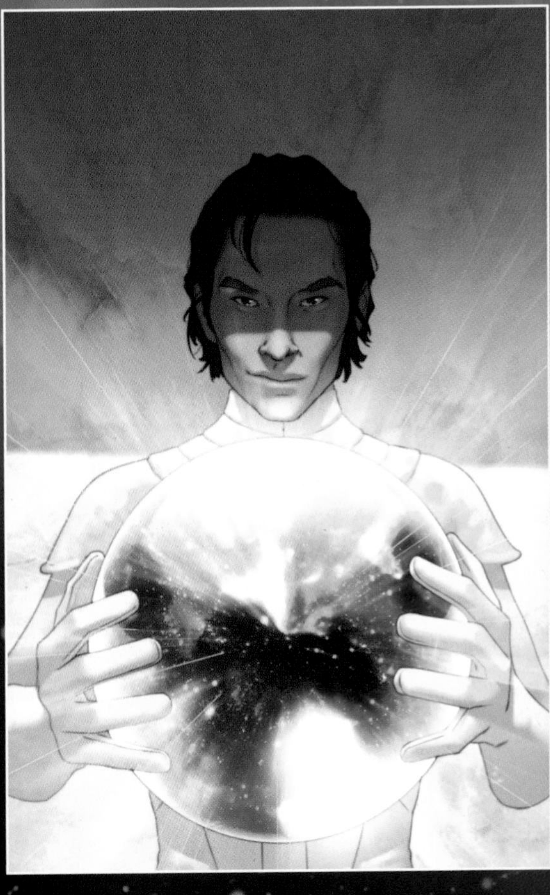

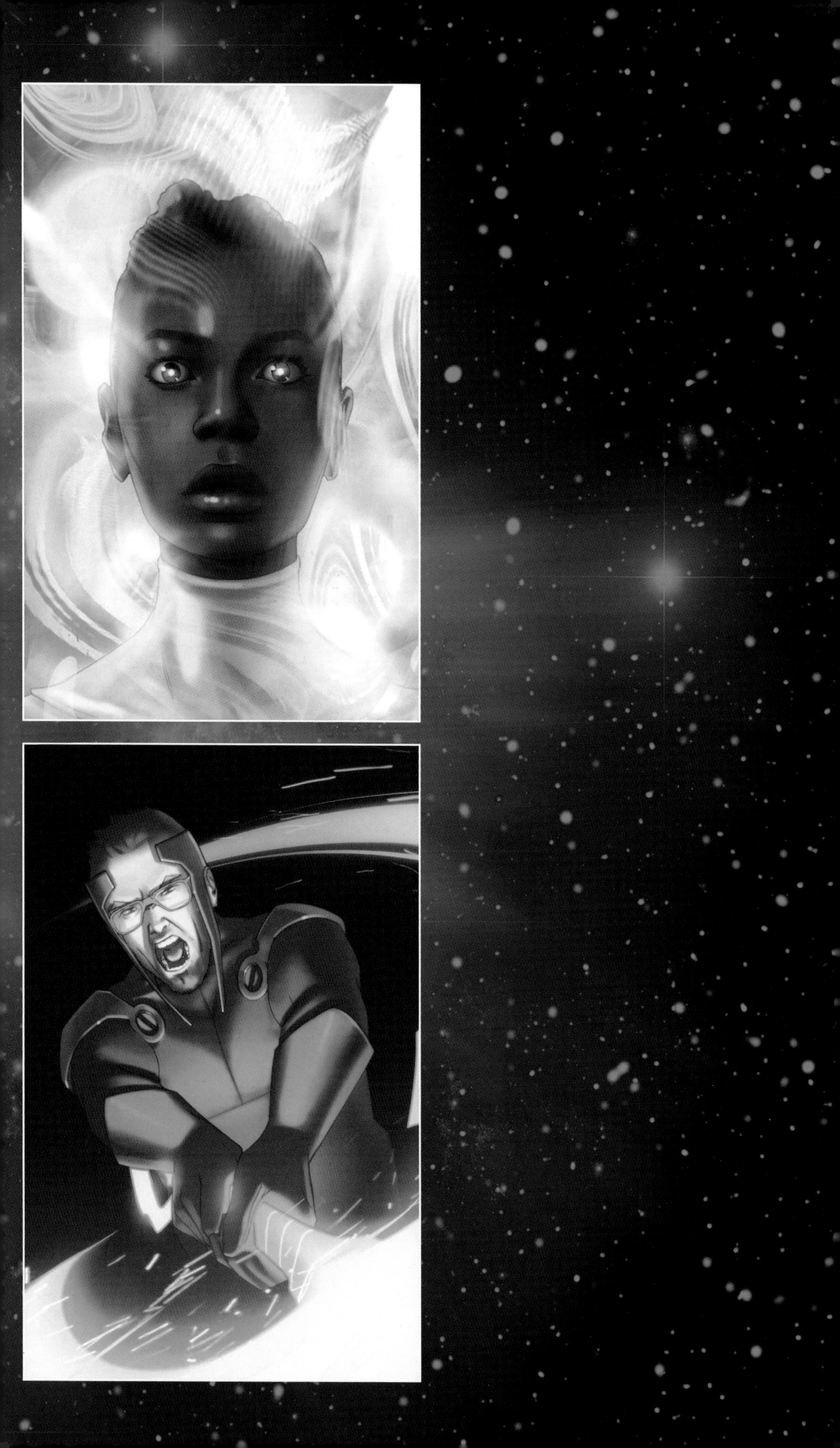

*PSI-LORDS* #4 COVER B
Art by TULA LOTAY

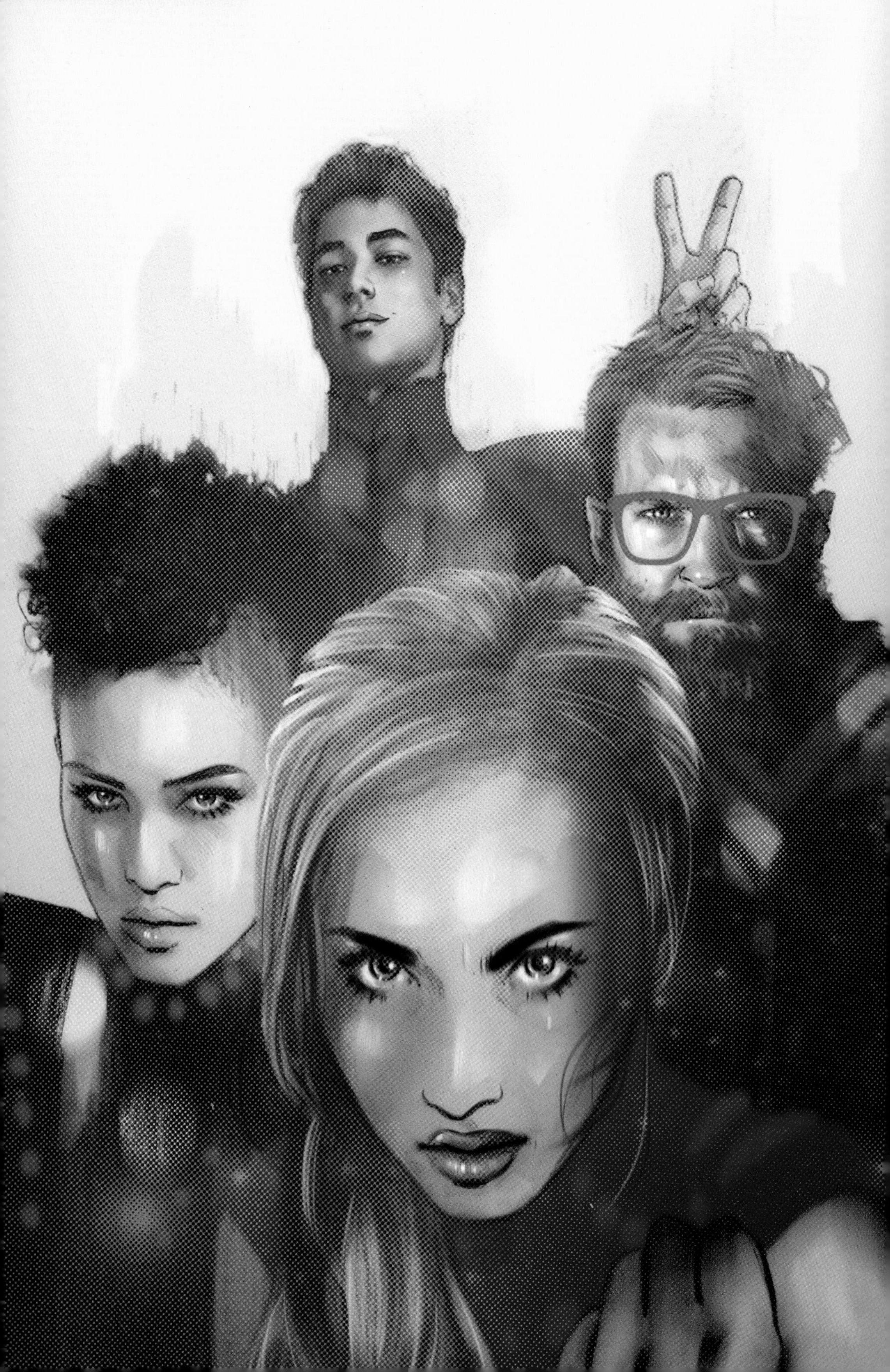

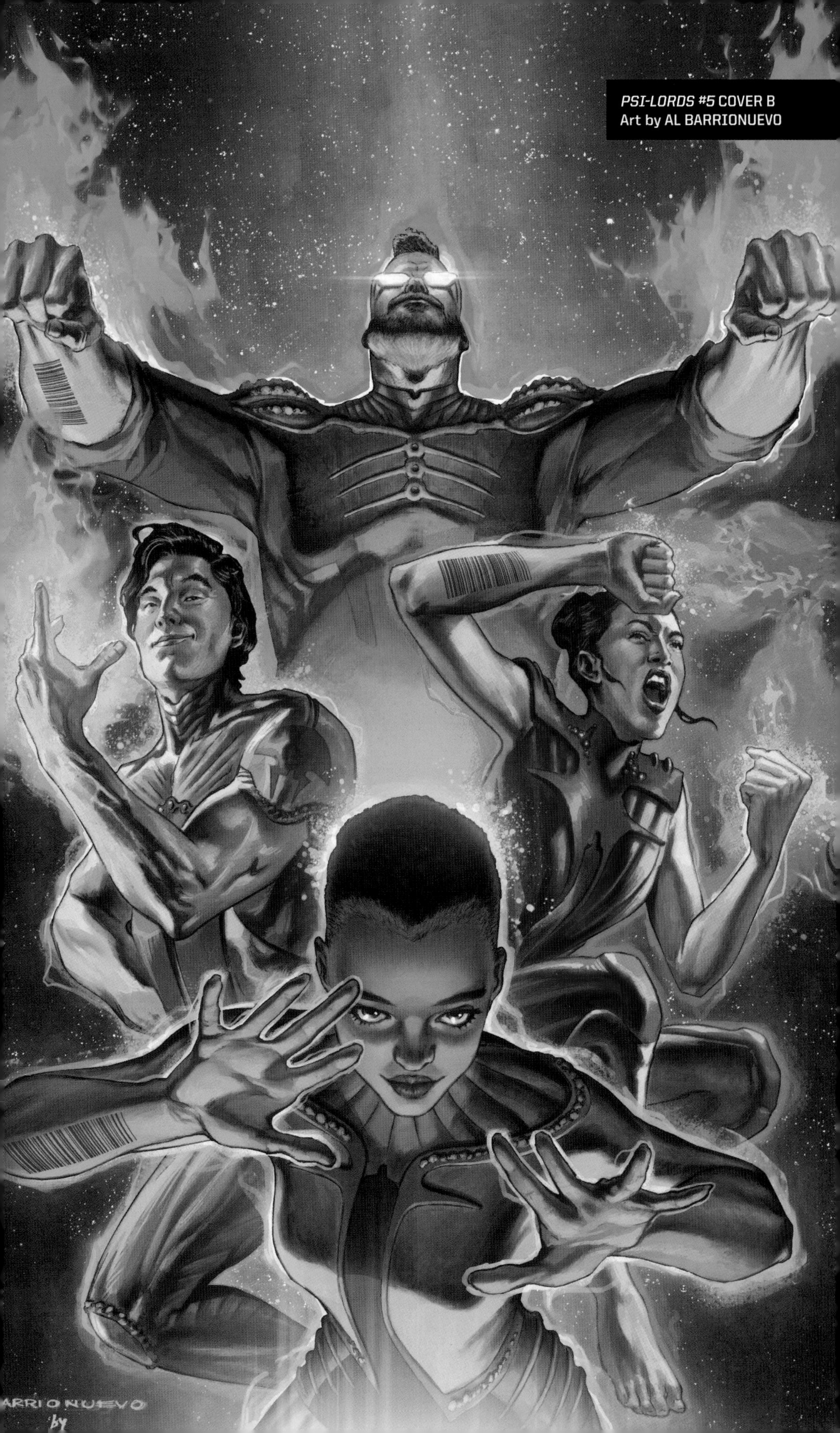

*PSI-LORDS* #5 COVER B
Art by AL BARRIONUEVO

*PSI-LORDS* #6 COVER C
Art by RAÚL ALLÉN

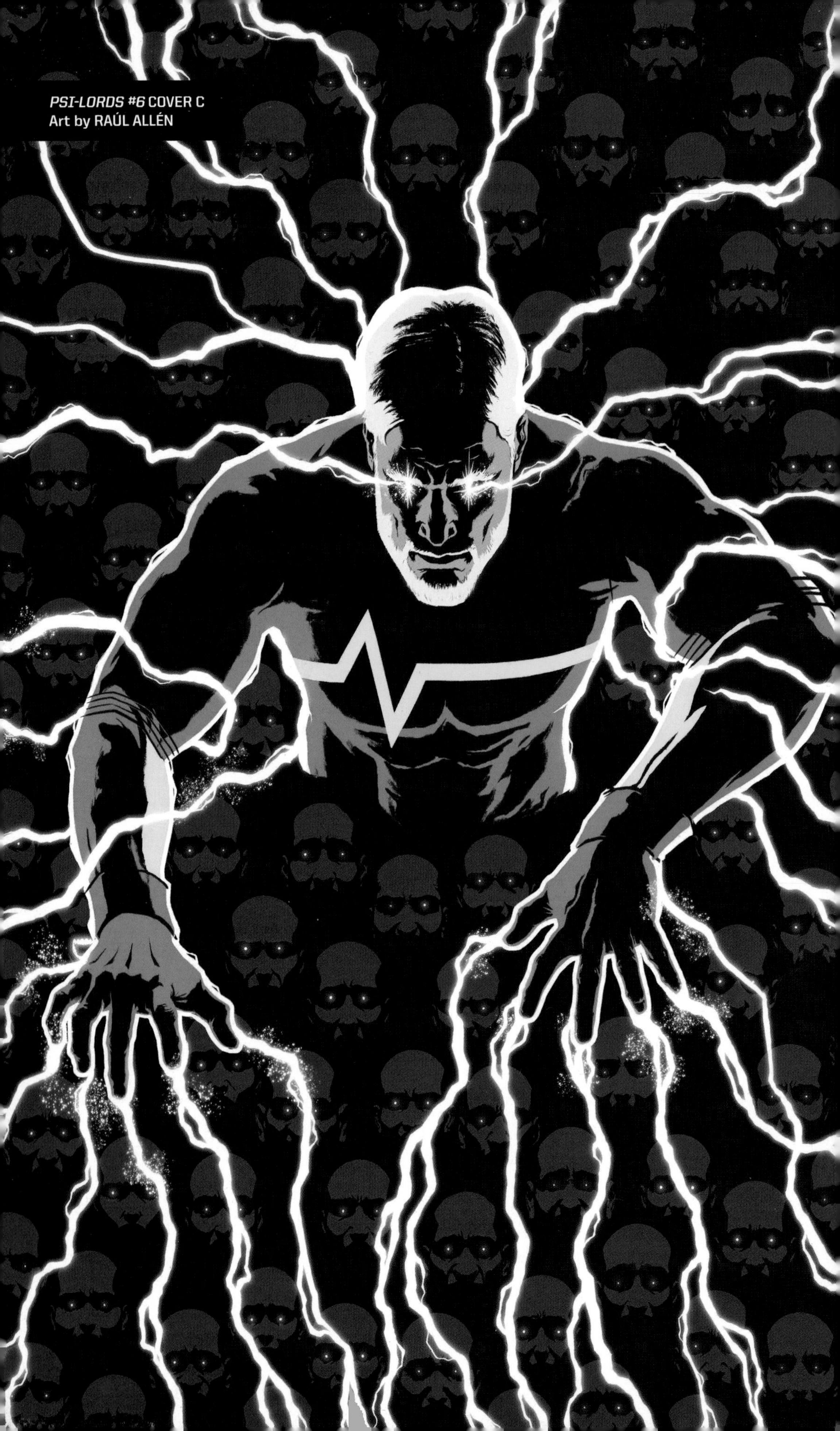